Please return or renew this item by the last date shown.
You may renew items (unless they have been requested
by another customer) by telephoning, writing to or calling
in at any library.   100% recycled paper   *BKS 1 (5/95)*

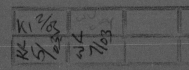

Nicaragua

The travel guide

Footprint Handbook

Richard Leonardi

*Green plumes of the palm trees. Far off,
rough with antiquity, solemn with myth,
stands the stone tribe of old volcanoes
which, like all else, await their instant
of infinity.*

Rubén Darío, *Noon*

Nicaragua Handbook
First edition
© Footprint Handbooks Ltd 2001

Published by Footprint Handbooks
6 Riverside Court
Lower Bristol Road
Bath BA2 3DZ. England
T +44 (0)1225 469141
F +44 (0)1225 469461
Email discover@footprintbooks.com
Web www.footprintbooks.com

ISBN 1 903471 14 1
CIP DATA: A catalogue record for this
book is available from the British Library

Distributed in the USA by
Publishers Group West

Credits

Series editors
Patrick Dawson and Rachel Fielding

Editorial
Editor: Felicity Laughton
Maps: Sarah Sorensen

Production
Typesetting: Mark Thomas, Emma Bryers
and Jo Morgan
Maps: Robert Lunn, Claire Benison and
Maxine Foster
Colour maps: Kevin Feeney
Proofreading: Jane Franklin and
Carol Franklin
Cover: Camilla Ford

Design
Mytton Williams

Photography
Front cover: Impact Photo Library
Back cover: Panos Pictures
Inside colour section: Edward Aves,
South American Pictures, Impact Photo
Library, Panos Pictures, Robert Harding
Picture Library, Hutchison Picture Libary

Print
Manufactured in Italy by LEGOPRINT

Nicaragua

Caribbean Sea

HONDURAS

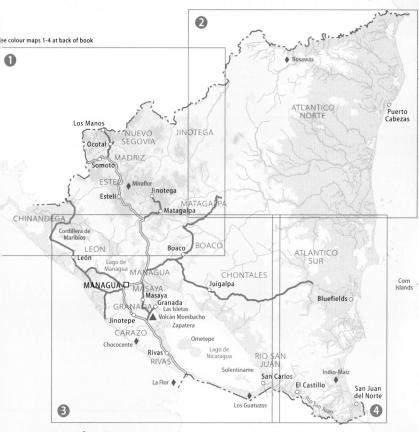

ee colour maps 1-4 at back of book

1

2

◆ Bosawás

ATLÁNTICO
NORTE

○ Puerto
Cabezas

Los Manos

NUEVO
SEGOVIA

JINOTEGA

Ocotal ○

MADRIZ

Somoto ○

ESTELÍ   ◆ Miraflor

Estelí ○   Jinotega ○

MATAGALPA

CHINANDEGA

Matagalpa ○

Cordillera de
Maribios

LEÓN

Boaco ○   BOACO

León ○

Lago de
Managua   MANAGUA

ATLÁNTICO
SUR

Corn
Islands

MANAGUA □   MASAYA

CHONTALES

Masaya ○

Juigalpa ○

Bluefields ○

GRANADA   Granada ○
            Las Isletas

Jinotepe ○   ▲ Volcán Mombacho

CARAZO   Zapatera

◆ Chococente

Ometepe

RÍO SAN
JUAN

Rivas ○   Lago de
Nicaragua   Solentiname

Indio-Maíz ◆

RIVAS

San Carlos ○   El Castillo ○

San Juan
del Norte

La Flor ◆

◆ Los Guatuzos

Río San Juan

3

4

Pacific Ocean

COSTA RICA

	Altitude in metres		Pan-American Highway
	1000		Main road
	600		Secondary road
	150		Seasonal unpaved road, track
	75		Rail
	0		International border
	Neighbouring Country		

Zapatera Natural feature

Lake Nicaragua Water feature

N

0 km   50

0 miles   50

Contents

Right: Colourful sails on the Atlantic Coast.

n the door

4

Left: The perfect cone of Volcán Concepción on Isla de Ometepe, the two-mountain island.
Below: Herding the cattle and bringing in the kindling during the dry season; traditions die hard in Nicaragua.

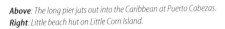

Above: The long pier juts out into the Caribbean at Puerto Cabezas.
Right: Little beach hut on Little Corn Island.

Nature first

Nicaragua is a friendly and peaceful country which has received some negative press over the years. But maybe that's not such a bad thing for, while other countries in the region have been flooded by tourists, Nicaragua has managed to preserve its authenticity and character. In addition, after more than a decade of political stability, Nicaragua, with some irony, has become one of the safest places to visit on the continent.

Giving peace a chance

As the last land mass to rise from the sea and connect North and South America, Nicaragua is really an emerging land bridge between the Atlantic and Pacific oceans. Water is everywhere and travel means crossing, navigating, surfing and swimming in lakes, rivers, lagoons or seas. Central America's biggest lakes and longest rivers are here, along with 15 volcanic crater lakes, vast coastal lagoons, and hundreds of kilometres of seacoast. Unique fish species and lake shark inhabit the warm waters of massive Lago de Nicaragua, which alone has over 425 volcanic islands, sandy beaches and numerous pre-Columbian sites.

Water, water everywhere

Running from the northwestern shores of the Golfo de Fonseca down into the great Lago de Nicaragua is a chain of 58 Pacific volcanoes, one of which is always in sight. And what a sight they are, rising off the flat Pacific Basin floor, to form a rugged, burning spine of earthen monuments. Many Nicaraguans believe that their eruptions are punishment for the environmental injustices perpetuated by modern man against Mother Earth. Perhaps they are, but what is certain is that the two continental plates colliding beneath the surface of Nicaragua are doing so more energetically than anywhere in the hemisphere, creating a landscape that is animated, growing and changing. In the middle of Lake Nicaragua, two volcanoes make up the world's largest lake island. Approaching Ometepe from the mainland is a surreal experience. The active Volcán Concepción looms on the horizon like an angry green giant, while its alter ego, the extinct Volcán Maderas, dozes in the soft haze of its dense cloud forest. This extraordinary and beautiful island is steeped in legend and rich in ancient pre-Columbian relics.

Smoke on the water

Nicaragua is also a land of forest. It is home to the biggest expanse of uncut rainforest north of the Amazon Basin. Much of this forest, and its spectacular flora and fauna (with hundreds of species of bird, mammal and insect), is protected in 75 nature reserves, the largest of which are Bosawás in the north of the country and Indio-Maíz in the south. Despite deforestation in the Pacific Basin, this region is home to several pristine cloud forest reserves as well as coastal tropical dry forest reserves.

Plenty in reserve

The Miskito (no, not 'mosquito') Coast is named after its indigenous people, the Miskitos, who still number more than 150,000 along the eastern seaboard of Nicaragua. Their world is a world apart from the Nicaraguan Pacific; their customs and language are different and they have only limited contact with the rest of the country. The Miskitos share their coast and river basins with the descendants of other pre-Hispanic groups who, centuries ago, arrived from the Andes and Upper Amazon Basin: the Rama and Sumu people, as well as two Afro-Caribbean cultures. A trip to Miskito country means new architecture, food, music and dance, and a paradise of coastal lagoons, deserted cays, clear turquoise waters and white-sand beaches; and well, yes, plenty of mosquitoes.

The coast with the most

People and places

Capital gains Arriving in Managua is a bit puzzling. It is like no other capital in the world. The original city centre was destroyed by the horrific earthquake of 1972 when half the population was left homeless. Since then, Managua has grown outwards, not up, sprawling over hills and across the flat southern shores of Lake Managua. In reality, there is no downtown Managua, only a very busy, seemingly endless suburbia. There are no less than four volcanic crater lakes within the city boundaries and two more on the western outskirts; and along the northern edge of the city is Central America's second biggest body of water. Managua is certainly one of a kind, if you can only figure out when you are actually in it.

The land that time forgot Nicaragua is rustic. It's impossible not to notice. Many of the rural villages look like sets for films staged in the 19th century. Cowboys are still rugged characters who have been riding since they were knee-high to the proverbial grasshopper, and ox and horse carts are still used to haul supplies off the farms. With León and Granada, Nicaragua has two of the oldest Spanish colonial cities in the Americas. Villages, towns and cities all have their traditional *parque central* with adobe church and a busy, buzzing street life you can't help but become part of.

Beyond the Revolution Latin America's post-colonial history has been marked by persistent social unrest in attempts to shed unjust governments. Mostly these uprisings have been painful and costly failures. Nicaragua is one of the few countries that can boast to have actually succeeded in a post-colonial revolution. The cost was great and what once was a strong little export economy has become one of the poorest in the world, thanks in part to foreign opposition to its post-Revolution government. But today Nicaragua is a democratic country and its turbulent past has created a more hopeful future.

Poetry devotion It has been said that all Nicaraguans are poets until proven otherwise. But few outsiders are aware that they are a nation of poets and poetry lovers. Since the late 19th century Nicaragua has been at the forefront of poetry in the Spanish language. Nicaragua's greatest national hero, Rubén Darío, takes much of the credit for this passion, but he has been followed by a long line of poets. Every week new poems appear in the Nicaraguan newspapers and even people who can barely read are able to recite beautiful verses. Poetry is an art form open to all Nicaraguans and an important part of its national psyche.

Irony in the soul If poetry is the essence of Nicaraguan culture, the national pastime is the joke. The Nicaraguan sense of humour is ironic and direct, and everyone is a potential subject; the ability to laugh at yourself is essential. Raucous laughter can be heard in every social situation, whether it be the country's president breaking up in chuckles during an important government meeting or opposing players during the tense final moments of a national sports championship. A good grasp of Spanish is necessary to appreciate the subtleties of Nicaraguan humour, but the relentless and unrestrained laughter and smiles can be enjoyed by all.

Left: Larger than life: giant figure in a Granada Carnival parade.
Below: Colourful straw crafts on a street stall.

Above: Rattan furniture for sale in León.
Right: Harvesting the pitaya fruit.
Next page: The memory of Augusto César Sandino lives on in a León mural.

Essentials

2

Essentials

Planning your trip

Where to go

Practically the whole of Nicaragua is well off the beaten track with large nature reserves and small villages entirely void of travellers and commercialization. However, there are many sights of interest within easy reach of the capital Managua and a great deal of ground can be covered in a matter of days using express public bus services, local tour operators or private vehicles. Road communication in the Pacific Basin is good and most areas of interest are less than 200 km from the capital. Travel between the two coasts and to the rainforest areas on the east side of the great lakes is more difficult and involves marathon bus rides, or journeys by boat and/or small aircraft.

Managua

Since it is the nation's capital and the main point of arrival in Nicaragua, most people will want to visit the sites of Managua before moving on to dramatically more attractive countryside, colonial cities and villages. A couple of days in Managua is enough for most pleasure travellers. Beyond its importance as the country's business centre, the best part of the city is its nightlife and access to international services. The original centre of Managua is worth visiting to see the **Museo de las Huellas**, the **lakefront**, **Palacio Nacional de la Cultura**, **Museo Nacional**, **Teatro Nacional**, new **Casa Presidencial** and the adjacent ruins of the **old Cathedral**. The newer city centre at Metrocentro, next to the controversial **new Cathedral**, is a good place to enjoy the area's many restaurants and clubs or to do some last-minute shopping before heading out of town. Even those short on time can make it to **Masaya**'s famous craft market and to the **national volcano park** (where you can see inside an active crater), both less than 30 km south of the capital. Other day trips are to the nearby Pacific beaches of **Montelimar** and **Pochomil**, or east of the great lakes to the cowboy towns of **Boaco** and **Juigalpa**. Managua is also the jumping-off point for trips to the **Río San Juan** rainforest reserves, **Corn Island**, **Puerto Cabezas**, **Bluefields** and other destinations best reached via light aircraft from the capital.

Colonial cities & villages

A seven- to 10-day stay on the Pacific Coast allows most travellers to get a good taste of the twin colonial cities of Granada and León and some of the easy-access ecological sites in the western region of the country. As colonial capital and intellectual and artistic centre, **León** is a must. A couple of days will be enough to visit the surrounding attractions such as **Poneloya** beach and the **Maribios volcanic range**. Around Masaya (see above) are the charming and hard-working villages called **Los Pueblos**, which are famous throughout the region for their festivals and handmade products. **Granada**, just south of Masaya, offers a relaxed air and a good variety of lodging in one of the continent's oldest European settlements. Near by are the **Mombacho Volcano** cloud forest reserve and the island archipelago of Las Isletas in Lake Nicaragua (see below).

Lake Nicaragua

Arrival in Granada marks the beginning of the great Lake Nicaragua. It would be easy to spend several weeks exploring this tropical body of water and its islands. One week on the lake will provide a chance to visit **Ometepe**, a dual volcano island that is a hikers' paradise with two forest reserves as well as many attractions of cultural interest. That week visit to Ometepe will combine well with a trip to the southern Nicaraguan **Pacific Coast**, its wildlife reserves, like the **La Flor turtle nesting site**, and the bay of **San Juan del Sur**. In the archipelago **Las Isletas**, near Granada, it is possible to sleep on one of the 354 tiny islands of a water-bound community. From there or its mainland docks you can travel one hour south by fast boat to the country's most important archaeological sites on the **Zapatera Archipelago**.

Essentials

Río San Juan — Lovers of rainforest flora and fauna will find the southeastern part of Lake Nicaragua and its Caribbean drainage, the Río San Juan, Nicaragua's principal attraction. One week travelling in this region will reveal the country's two finest wildlife reserves in the wetlands and gallery forest of the **Los Guatuzos Wildlife Refuge** and the primary rainforest of the **Indio-Maíz Biological Reserve** which houses Central America's best-preserved rainforest. The pristine **Archipelago Solentiname** in Lake Nicaragua is also home to rich bird life and a very interesting school of rural artists and artisans. Travel to the river, lake, reserves and islands uses the jungle capital of **San Carlos** as a jumping off point, after which boat travel is the only option.

Northern mountains — An interesting four- to six-day extension will take you back in time to the relatively cool highlands north of Managua. This region is different from the rest of Nicaragua for its rugged mountains and pine forests. **Matagalpa** and **Jinotega** are key coffee-growing regions, full of political history and some precious cloud forest reserves. Across the northern range is **Estelí**, the home of Nicaraguan cigars and starting point for visits to many quaint **northern villages** in the region with historic churches, unusual traditions and crafts.

Caribbean Coast — One or two weeks can be spent experiencing the 'other Nicaragua', its eastern seaboard. Most people opt for a three- to four-day stay on **Corn Island** to enjoy the white sand beaches and coral reefs. But with an additional three or four days, you can also visit **Bluefields** and the majestic **Pearl Lagoon**, or head north deep into **Miskito** country and **Puerto Cabezas**, cultural odysseys that include a good dose of tropical nature. Both Bluefields and Puerto Cabezas have remote forests, lagoons and villages; most are a challenge to reach, but worth the effort for those who want to really explore.

When to go

Climate — Most people prefer to visit **Western Nicaragua** during the **rainy season** – mid-May to late November – or shortly after the rains have ended. For the rest of the year the Pacific Basin receives practically no rain at all and from mid-February until the rains arrive in May the region is very hot and dry. During the rainy season the Pacific Basin is bright green and freshened daily by the rains, which normally last for less than two hours in the afternoon before clearing and then falling again during the night. December is an extraordinarily beautiful time to visit the Nicaraguan Pacific, with all the landscape in bloom, the air still fresh and visibility excellent across the volcanic ranges.

Nicaraguans consider the dry season (Dec-May) summer and the rainy season (mid-May-Nov) winter, which can lead to confusion considering the country lies well north (11-16°) of the Equator

The dry season becomes shorter the further east you travel, and in the **Caribbean Basin** it can rain at any time of year. For snorkelling in the Caribbean the end of the dry season offers the best chance of finding calm waters with great visibility. For bird-watching in the rainforest areas of the Río San Juan the dry season is best as you'll have the chance to see the many migratory species and nesting birds. However, during the rainy season, other species of fauna venture into more accessible areas and are therefore more visible.

During Easter Week and between Christmas and New Year all of Nicaragua rushes to the beach, lake and river front areas to swim, drink and dance; avoid these dates if you don't want to encounter massive crowds.

Tours and tour operators

For tour operators in Managua, see page 74 — Many tour operators specializing in Latin American travel will arrange trips to Nicaragua if requested although few of them actually know the country well. The companies listed below have specific knowledge of Nicaragua and will offer private, small group and/or special interest programmes:

UK *Condor Journeys*, 1 Valley Rise, Mill Bank, Sowerby Bridge, Yorks HX6 3EG, **Europe**
T01422-822068, F01422-825276, www.condorjourneys-adventures.com Private, varied special interest programmes. *Exodus Travels*, T020-87723822, www.exodus.
co.uk Small group adventure travel. *Expedition Company*, PO Box 17, Wiveliscombe,
Taunton TA4 2YL, T01984-624780, F01984-629045, www.expedition.co.uk Trekking
and jungle programmes, small groups and private. *Journey Latin America*, 12 Heathfield Terrace, Chiswick, London W4 4JE, T020-87478555, F020-87421312,
www.journeylatinamerica.co.uk Group and private programmes. *Pura Aventura*, 18
Bond Street, Brighton BN1 1RD, T01273-676774, F01273-676774,
www.pura-aventura.com Small group nature programmes. *South American Experience*, 47 Causton Street, Pimlico, London, SW1P 4AT, T020-79765511, F020-79766908,
www.sax.mcmail.com Private programmes.

Essentials

France *Images du Monde*, 14 rue Lahire, 75013 Paris, T01-44248788, F01-45862773, images.du.monde@wanadoo.fr Private programmes with cultural emphasis. **Germany** *Centro Calypso Tours*, Am Burghof 11, 66625 Nohfelden, T0685-2900511, F0685-2900555, CentroLA@aol.com Private programmes. *AMIK*, Severinstrabe 10-12, 50678 Köln, T221-3101841, F221-3101843, amik@tkc.de Private programmes, hotel booking, car rental. **Italy** *Evasioni*, Via Ressi, 12–20125 Milan, T02-6705518, F02-6705674, www.evasioni.it Small group travel with beach empha-sis. **Netherlands** *ARA Tours*, Rijnstraat 77, NL–3441, BR Woerden, T034-8434560, F034-8433868, www.aratours.nl Private programmes, hotel bookings. *Sawadee Reizen*, Rokin 105, 1012 KM Amsterdam, T020-4202220, F020-6250038, www.sawadee.nl Group travel in combination with Costa Rica. *Rese Konsulterna*, Vallgatan 15, SE-411, 16 Goteborg, Sweden, T463-1101275, F463-1139751, www.resek.se Group programmes. **Switzerland** *Nicaragua Tours*, Via F Pelli 24-6900 Lugano, T91-9212812, dsemandeni@tinet.ch Private ecotours.

United States *Destination by Design, Inc*, 1303 North Pine Avenue, Arlington Heights, Illinois 60004, T186-63927865, F847-3926934, www.destinationbydesign.com Custom-designed programmes and group departures. *Eco-Spirit-Adventures*, 50 Antilla Avenue, Suite 4, Coral Gables, Florida 33134, T305-4412795, amalia@bellsouth.net Yoga and spiritual small groups. *Latin American Escapes*, T1800-5105999, F925-9450154, www.latinamericanescapes.com Private and group departures, trekking, cultural and ecological special interest programmes. *MILA Tours*, 100 S Greenleaf Av, Gurnee, Il 60031, T1-800-367-7378, F847-249-2772, www.MILAtours.com Group and private programmes.

Finding out more

Good reliable sources on Nicaragua are generally hard to come by. The best bet is the internet although many sites are poorly researched and the information is often inaccurate.

Useful websites **www.intur.gob.ni** Official government tourist office site, a good starting place.
www.guideofnicaragua.com This is the magazine you might find inside a good hotel room in Nicaragua; light fluff for the traveller, but it is in English.
www.laprensa.com The country's best newspaper. If you read Spanish this is a good way to check up on what's happening before you arrive and after you return home. The most responsible of the daily periodicals, though they are prone to hyperventilate over the day's big story. Still the best way to follow the always-controversial political scene. Others to check include: **www.nicaraguaenimagenes.com**, **www.nicaweb.com**, **www.virtualtourist.com/Central_America** and **www.nicaragua.com**

Language

English is widely spoken on the Caribbean coast Spanish is the official language although understanding Nicaraguan dialect is difficult for most non-fluent Spanish speakers. But if you look lost people are usually helpful and happy to repeat themselves. English is spoken in the more upmarket hotels in Managua, Granada and León, as well as at tour operators and car rental agencies. It is of little use elsewhere except on the Caribbean coast where Spanish, Creole English, Sumo, Rama and Miskito are all spoken – many locals are able to converse in three lan-guages. Nicaraguan Creole is similar to the English spoken in Jamaica and other Carib-bean states and most native English speakers will find it decipherable. Efforts to communicate are appreciated on both coasts.

Hablando Nica – Nicaraguan Spanish

Great, you've done your Spanish course and you're ready to talk to the Nicaraguan people. But wait, what's that? ¿Cómo, um, perdón? ¿Qué dice? It seems all that hard work has yet to pay off. Nicaraguans (Nicas) are famous for their creativity and humour; nothing is sacred. Some words are invented, others just twisted and played with. Here are some essentials that will give you a head start:

Nica	Literal translation	Nicaraguan meaning
boludo	drunk (from 'bolo')	lazy
chele	from 'leche' (milk)	white person
chochada	from 'chocho' (senile)	stupid thing
chocho		Wow!
fachento	from 'fachada' (façade)	arrogant or conceited
jaña		girlfriend
palmado		broke, penniless
tapudo	from 'tapón' (plug)	gossip or big-mouth
tuanis		cool
turcazo	From 'turco' (Turkish)	a hard punch

Disabled travellers

Nicaragua is not an ideal place for disabled travellers, though many Nicaraguans were left disabled by the war of the late 1970s and 80s and people are often willing to lend a hand. Emotional solidarity may not compensate, however, for lack of wheelchair ramps, user-friendly bathrooms, etc. There are elevators in the more expensive hotels and one hotel in Managua, *Legends* (see page 67), has special disabled rooms on its first floor for a slightly higher cost.

Gay and lesbian travellers

Nicaragua is as macho as any Latin American country, although the Sandinista regime of the 80s did result in a more liberal attitude in terms of accepting gay and lesbian life-styles and there are several gay nightclubs in Managua. That said, public displays of gay affection are likely draw a loud (and often mocking) response in Managua and an even less sympathetic reaction in rural Nicaragua.

Student travellers

If you are in full-time education you will be entitled to an International Student Identity Card, which is distributed by student travel offices and travel agencies in 77 countries. The **ISIC** gives you discounted prices on all forms of public transport and access to a variety of other concessions and services. If you need to find the location of your nearest ISIC office contact: The ISIC Association, Box 9048, 1000 Copenhagen, Denmark T+45-3393-9303.

Travelling with children

Nicaragua is not a difficult country for travelling with children and the Nicaraguan peo-ple, renowned for their kindness and openness, are even friendlier when you are with children. However, the lack of sophisticated medical services in rural Nicaragua can make travelling with babies less attractive - in fact travel outside Managua, León and Granada is not recommended for people with children under two.

Older children (ie over the age of five) will find much of interest and, with some effort, communication with Nicaraguan children of their own age will be a very rewarding and enlightening experience. Many of the luxuries taken for granted in the modern world will be unavailable and children should be prepared mentally for this change. Snack bars and the like can be invaluable for keeping a food link with the home country, which is usually the major sore point for children travelling in Nicaragua.

Most hotels do not charge for children under two and offer a discount rate for 2-12 year olds; those aged 13 and above are charged as adults. Very small children sitting on their parent's lap should travel free on public buses and boats. On internal flights children under the age of two pay 10% the normal fare; 2-12 year olds pay 50% and anyone aged 13 or older pays the adult fares.

Women travellers

A woman walking alone in Nicaragua is a sight to behold for almost all Nicaraguan men: horns will sound, words of romance (and, in Managua, some less than romantic phrases) will be proffered and in general you may well feel as if you are on stage. Attitudes to foreign women are much more reserved, though, and actually touching a woman they don't know, Nicaraguan or otherwise, is not at all socially acceptable and rarely occurs. The best advice is to dress for the amount of attention you desire; it is not necessary to travel clothed as a nun, but any suggestive clothing will bring double its weight in suggestions. In Managua there may be some danger in walking alone at night, but this is related to risk of robbery and is equally inadvisable for men. Two women walking together are less likely to be targeted by thieves.

Working in Nicaragua

Finding work in Nicaragua is a challenge for Nicaraguans and even more so for visitors who hope to get by in the country by working for a short period of time. It is a good idea to research your own country's aid programmes to Nicaragua and to make contact well in advance of arrival. The sister-city programmes that most countries have with Nicaragua are examples; the Dutch-sister city programme is probably the strongest of these, but other countries like England and the United States support the concept with visiting work projects. Finding English teaching work may be possible although rents are high and survival on a teaching salary will be difficult.

Before you travel

Getting in

Visitors to Nicaragua must have a passport with a minimum validity of six months. In rare cases you may be asked to show proof of an onward ticket or some cash, but this has not been reported for years and a credit card will suffice if no onward ticket has been purchased. Most visitors who do not require visas (see below) will simply pay the tourist card fee (US$5 at the airport and between US$5-8 at land and river immigration check points; see individual chapters for details).

An entrance visa is required only by citizens of the following 20 countries: Afghanistan, Albania, Bosnia-Herzegovina, China, Colombia, Cuba, Haiti, India, Iran, Iraq, Jordan, Lebanon, Libya, Nepal, North Korea, Pakistan, Somalia, Sri Lanka, Vietnam and Yugoslavia. The requirements for visa application can be found on the website of the Nicaraguan foreign ministry **www.cancilleria.gob.ni/consular/visas.html** It is advisable to make your application before travelling; visa application at the border is

Visas & immigration

Essentials

Nicaraguan embassies abroad

In America

Costa Rica *Avenida Central 2440, Barrio La California, San José, T222-2373, F221-5481.*

El Salvador *71 Avenida Norte y Primera Calle Poniente 164, Col Escalón, San Salvador, T298-6549, F223-7201.*

Guatemala *10 Avenida, 14-72, Zona 10, T268-0785, F337-4264.*

Honduras *Col Tepeyac, Bloque M-1, No 1130, Tegucigalpa, T232-7224, F239-5225.*

Mexico *Prado Norte No 470, Col Lomas de Chapultepec, CP11000, México DF, T5540-5625 , F5520-6960.*

Panama *Intersección de Avenida Federico Boyd y Calle 50, Apartado 772 - Zona 1, Corregimiento Bella Vista, Panamá, T223-0981, F211-2080.*

United States and Canada *1627 New Hampshire Avenue NW, Washington, DC 20009, USA, T202-939-6531, F202-939-6532.*

In Europe

Germany *Konstantinstrasse 41, D-53159 Bonn/2, T362-505, F354-001.*

Spain *Paseo La Castellana 127, 10-B, 28046 Madrid, T555-5510 , F555-5737.*

France *34 Avenue Bugeaud, 75116 Paris, T01-45004102, F01-45009681.*

Great Britain *Vicarage House, Suite 12, 58-60 Kensington Church Street, London W8 4DB, T020-79382373, F020-79370952.*

Italy *Via Brescia 16, Scala 1, Int. 7-700198, Rome, T841-4693, F884-1695.*

not recommended as approval could be very slow. Visitors from any country not listed above do not need a visa.

Immigration hours are 0700-1400, Mon-Fri If you need an **extension** beyond the standard 30 days you receive upon entering the country, you will have to visit the *Dirección de Migración y Extranjería* in Managua, Semáforo Tenderí, 1½ c al norte, T244-3989, ext 3. Direct questions (in Spanish) to dgm@migracion.gob.ni Go to information, preferably in the early morning (they close at 1400), with your passport and ask for an extension form, which you will buy from the corresponding window (usually three córdobas). You can fill out the form while waiting in line at the bank (to the left as you exit the immigration building). The bank has the up-to-date information on the cost of the extension, will charge you accordingly and provide a receipt. The current rate for a 30- or 60-day extension is US$18. Bring the proof of payment and completed form with your passport to the appropriate window and wait. The whole procedure should not take more than two hours, unless queues are unusually long. Another option would be to leave the country for three days or more before returning, though this practice done more than once will not be appreciated by the authorities. **NB** Citizens of Colombia, Cuba, Ecuador, Bangladesh, China and India may have difficulties acquiring an extension.

Customs Duty-free import of ½ kg of tobacco products, three litres of alcoholic drinks and one large bottle (or three small bottles) of perfume is permitted. If you are bringing in large quantities of film or other items that could, in theory, be resold, it is wise to take them out of their original packages. Nicaraguan customs agents are reasonable and you only need convince them that what you have brought is for personal use.

Avoid buying products made from snakeskin, crocodile skin, black coral or other protected species on sale in some Nicaraguan markets. Apart from the fact that they may be derived from endangered species, there may be laws in your home country outlawing their import. **NB** Taking pre-Columbian or early colonial pieces out of Nicaragua is illegal and will be rewarded with two years in a Nicaraguan prison.

Vaccinations No vaccinations are required to enter Nicaragua (see Health, page 42 for specific recommendations).

Travelling light is recommended. Your specific list will depend greatly on what kind of travelling you plan to do. Cotton clothes are versatile and suitable for most situations. A hat, sun lotion and sunglasses will protect you from any instant grilling that the Nicaragua sun could cause. A light sweater or very light jacket is useful for those heading into the highlands or rainforest. English-language books are very rare in Nicaragua, so bring all reading material with you. Contact lens wearers and people with special medical needs must bring all prescription medicines, lens-cleaning products, etc. If you intend to hike in the volcanoes you will need very sturdy, hard-soled trekking shoes, which should also ideally be lightweight and very breathable. A lightweight pack filled with energy bars and a flask is useful (snack bars are still unknown in Nicaragua).Take mosquito netting if travelling to the jungle or Caribbean coastal regions. Rubber (Wellington) boots, worn by the locals in the countryside, will let you tackle any rainforest trail with comfort and protection. Insect repellent is a must in these areas. Rain poncho, zip-lock bags (for documents, film, money, etc) and heavy-duty bin liners/trash bags (for backpacks) are needed for rainforest travel. A fairly powerful torch flashlight is of use all over Nicaragua's countryside as electric power is either irregular or non-existent. A selection of photographs of your family at home will help make conversation and friends. Anyone shooting slide film in their cameras should bring along a good supply, as it is very expensive in Nicaragua; note that 400 ASA or faster is needed for forest wildlife shots. A Swiss Army knife and a roll of duck tape are the traveller's indispensable, all-purpose items; they could probably have saved the Titanic and are useful for less serious travel emergencies as well.

What to take

Essentials

Money

The unit of currency is the **córdoba** (C), divided into 100 **centavos**. The exchange rate as of October 2001 was 13.62 C to US$1. Notes are used for 10, 20, 50 and 100 córdobas and coins for one and five córdoba, with both coins and special small notes used for 25 and 50 centavos. There are also small notes for one and five centavos, which no one wants or accepts apart from banks and supermarkets. 100 córdoba notes can be a problem to change for small purchases, buses and taxis, so use them at super and mini-markets as well as in restaurants and hotels and hang on to the smaller notes for other purchases. For money exchange in all banks US dollars are the currency of choice and no identification is required. You can pay for almost anything in US dollars as well, but the exchange rate will be unfavourable and change will be given in córdobas. Costa Rican and Honduran currencies can only be changed at the respective borders. Travellers entering the country with more than US$10,000.00 will need to report the amount to customs upon arrival in Nicaragua.

Currency
Nicaraguans often use the generic term 'pesos' to describe the córdoba. 'Cinco reales' means 50 centavos

Travellers' cheques are a problem in Nicaragua, with only two banks and *one casa de cambio* willing to cash them. Multicambios' one location, in Managua's Plaza España, is the first place to try for low commissions, but they are at times inexplicably without dollars and offer very bad rates for changing travellers' cheques into córdobas. The two Nicaraguan banks that change travellers' cheques are Banco de América Central (BAC) also home to Credomatic, which are one and the same, and Banco de Finanzas (BDF). Both banks will change travellers' cheques at any one of their branches for a commission of 3%, but BDF only deals with American Express while BAC will change any type. However, BAC has fewer branches outside Managua than BDF. Check the chapters of your desired destinations to see which cities have local branches of BAC and BDF. With some pleading and/or luck you may be able to change cheques at some outlying hotels, but do not rely on this option.

Travellers' cheques

Million dollar Coke – hyperinflation in the 1980s

At the end of the 1980s and beginning of the 1990s, Nicaraguans would say in an ironic tone that they were a country of millionaires. Everyone had millions and millions of córdobas, but it was barely enough for a taxi ride or to buy a Coke.

This phenomenon known as hyperinflation began in 1989, when agricultural exports dropped at the same time as the country was suffering the effects of a prolonged rebel war and an economic embargo imposed by the United States. To make things worse, the Socialist Bloc, the country's biggest supporter, went into crisis in this same year. These factors contributed to a rise in the official exchange rate from 2,000 córdobas to US$1 in January 1989, to 38,150 córdobas to the dollar in December 1989. The following year, the exchange rate shot up to 3,000,000 córdobas for US$1: a 12-ounce bottle of Coke cost more than 1,000,000 córdobas.

To keep up with the hyperinflation, the government had to re-stamp the paper money with higher denominations. The 100 córdoba note was rubber stamped to a value of 100,000 córdobas and the 1,000 córdoba note became 1,000,000 córdobas, the highest denomination. At the beginning of the 1990s, the re-stamped bills of the Sandinista government were recalled and new paper money was issued. The highest denomination was 10,000,000 córdobas. Today, they are sold as souvenirs to tourists and collectors.

Credit & debit cards Credit cards are a far wiser alternative to travellers' cheques in Nicaragua. You will avoid paying commission and they are accepted all over the country (provided there are telephones available) in hotels, restaurants and most shops. VISA, Mastercard and American Express are widely accepted with VISA being the most prevalent. ATM machines are found in shopping malls, banks and petrol station convenience stores in Managua. Outside Managua ATMs are rare to non-existent. Still, debit cards using the Cirrus and Mastercard credit systems work with the 'Red Total' or Credomatic system which can be found in shopping malls, Banco de América Central (BAC) and Texaco, Shell and Esso station stores. However, outside of Managua there is only one 'Red Total' machine (in an Esso station store at the entrance to Masaya). It would be unwise to rely too heavily on debit/credit cards: always have some cash at hand on arrival, and when leaving Managua take all that you will spend in cash. **NB** If there are communication problems with the outside world, which is not uncommon, Nicaraguan ATMs cannot approve the card transactions and you will have to try again later.

It is important to brief yourself on lost card procedures before leaving your home country and, if you have more than one card, to spread them around different parts of your body. Credit card fraud is almost unheard of in Nicaragua, but normal precautions should be taken. Make sure the carbon papers are destroyed in front of you after a manual transaction has been completed. For any questions about credit cards, visit the Credomatic office in Managua in the Camino de Oriente shopping centre on Carretera a Masaya. Technically it is not legal in Nicaragua to charge an extra fee for credit card purchases and this is rarely attempted at most establishments.

General tips Nicaragua's economy is based heavily on the US dollar, with every Nicaraguan bank offering accounts in US dollars. Changing dollars is quick and painless in any Nicaraguan bank, although there will be long queues on the 15th and 31st of each month and before holidays. Changing on the street is possible and legal though less common outside Managua, Granada and León. The rate of the street changer (*coyote*) is marginally better, but knowledge of current rates is essential. Tell the street changer how much you want to change then he will show you on his calculator the total in córdobas and count the money out. Accept the money and count it before handing the *coyote* your money in exchange. After dark and on Sundays the street changers are not *coyotes*, but *ladrones* (thieves) and con-artists and should not be used under any circumstances. Dollars are almost universally accepted in Nicaragua, so there is no reason to change money at night on the street. The banks in the Metrocentro shopping centre, on the first floor underneath the south side escalator, have long hours that include Saturday into the afternoon and 1300-1600 on Sunday.

NB Though Bancentro will accept Euros as a deposit, it is not possible to change any currency but US dollars and córdobas in Nicaragua. All Costa Rican or Honduran currency must therefore be changed at the border when entering Nicaragua.

Cost of living & travelling

Most visitors to Nicaragua are surprised to find prices higher than expected. The problem stems mainly from the hyper-inflation of the 1980s and the córdoba being adjusted to the US dollar in 1990. The cost of **public transport**, however, ranges from reasonable to very cheap. A normal taxi fare is US$1-2 with buses costing less than a dollar in almost all domestic cases. Local flights range from US$60-105 round-trip from Managua. **Car rental** is comparable with other countries around the world.

Food can be cheap depending on quality: dishes from steet vendors, which are generous, salty and high in fat, cost from US$1-2; moderate restaurants have marginally more healthy fare that ranges from US$3-5; and quality restaurants charge US$5-10 per plate. As a rule, **hotels** in Nicaragua are not good value and those in Managua tend to be overpriced; anything under US$30 in the capital usually means poor quality. Outside Managua, hotels are more reasonable and you can find some very good deals in all price brackets (for more details, see page 28). Living with families outside Managua can be inexpensive, but the cost of renting accommodation in Managua is very high by Latin American standards (a decent apartment costs over US$600 per month), and electricity, water and telephone expenses range from very high to outrageous.

Getting there

Air

Finding reservations to Nicaragua a month in advance is not a problem outside of the Easter and Christmas periods. Flights into Managua are normally crowded, however, due to the lack of carriers serving the country.

From Europe

There are no direct flights from Europe to Managua. All airways lead to Miami in this case, though flights via San José, Costa Rica are another option. One of the most reasonable fares is between Amsterdam and San José on *Martin Air*. The most convenient flight plans to Managua are either with *American* from London or with *Iberia* originating from Madrid, both with a short stopover and plane change in Miami. The average fare ranges from US$750-1,150 dollars.

From North America

Two US carriers fly non-stop to Managua. *American* flies from Miami once a day, seven days a week and twice a day three days a week. *Continental* flies once a day, seven days a week from Houston. The Central American conglomerate *TACA* also flies daily from Miami non-stop to Managua. Flyers from the west coast might opt for *TACA* or *American*'s non-stops from Los Angeles or San Francisco to San Salvador; the connecting *TACA* flight to Managua takes just 35 minutes. Flight costs vary from US$350 from Miami to US$450-650 from most parts of the USA and upwards of US$700 from Canada. From Montreal, cheap charter flights are available during the November to March dry season, but are normally booked full with budget package travellers who spend one or two weeks in the all-inclusive Montelimar Resort.

Essentials

From Australia & New Zealand This is a long trek. The most efficient route, at a cost of around US$1,700, is direct from Sydney to Los Angeles, then changing planes to Houston with *Continental* and non-stop Houston-Managua on the same carrier. From Auckland with the same connections and routes the fare comes to about US$1,400.

From Mexico & Central America There is no direct service from Mexico City to Managua, but connections are easily made with the Guatemalan carrier *Aviateca*, with a plane change in Guatemala City. *TACA* flies to Managua from all countries in Central America, and the Panamanian carrier *COPA* offers a superior service, from Guatemala to Panama and on to Managua, although connections are less frequent. Flights to Managua normally cost around US$237 from Guatemala and US$153 from Costa Rica. From Mexico expect to pay US$50-100 more. COPA is currently offering a US$450 fare that allows for country-hopping flights to Guatemala, Managua, San José and Panamá City.

General tips Airlines limit the amount of luggage you can bring without a surcharge. This is normally one large and one medium checked bags with a weight limit of around 30 kg. Many Nicaraguans visit the United States for shopping and return home laden with goodies, so travellers connected with flights via Houston and Miami should check in as early as possible to ensure that their luggage makes the flight. In case you are unlucky it is a good idea to bring at least one change of clothes in your carry-on bag (if you are allowed one). Tall travellers or people with small children should put in a request well in advance for bulk-head seats or emergency exit rows. Keep in mind that the seats located in the rows in front of the exits often do not recline. **NB** Anyone flying into Managua from El Salvador in the daytime should book a left-side window seat for a breathtaking view of Nicaragua's rugged Maribios volcano range (right-side if flying from Managua).

Road

From Honduras There are three land crossings into Nicaragua from Honduras. For access from Tegucigalpa, the **Las Manos** crossing, entering just north of Ocotal and continuing to Estelí, is the most direct option, though road conditions are unfavourable. The most travelled route into Nicaragua is via the lowlands adjacent to the Golfo de Fonseca using the crossing at **El Guasaule**, north of Chinandega and south of Choluteca, Honduras. This entrance is also the nearest crossing for those coming from El Salvador via Honduras. The other alternative from Choluteca is **El Espino**, which enters via the northern mountains and passes Estelí en route to Managua. International bus services from Guatemala, El Salvador and Honduras are available to Managua via these routes (see Managua chapter for details).

From Costa Rica The only road crossing that connects Nicaragua to Costa Rica and unites Central America via road is at **Peñas Blancas**, 144 km south of Managua on Nicaragua's Rivas Isthmus. Land travel from San José is easiest on international buses (see Managua chapter for details).

Boat

From Costa Rica & El Salvador The only official water crossing into Nicaragua is via **Los Chiles** in northern Costa Rica. There is road access to Los Chiles from La Fortuna. Exit stamps and taxes must be paid in Los Chiles before boarding public boats for the journey down the Río Frío to San Carlos where there is immigration and customs for Nicaragua (see Río San Juan chapter for details). An international ferry is being planned for travel between La Unión in El Salvador and the port of Corinto in Nicaragua, but has yet to open. You can hire or hitch a ride on a boat from La Unión to Potosí, Nicaragua on the Golfo de Fonseca.

Touching down

Official time *Six hours behind GMT (seven hours during daylight savings).*
Hours of business *0800-1700. Banks: Monday-Friday 0830-1600 (sometimes 1700); Saturday 0830-1200 (or 1300 and occasionally 1700).* **Government offices**: *Monday-Friday 0800-1200.*
IDD *505. Equal tones with long pauses indicate it is ringing. Equal tones with equal pauses means engaged.*
Voltage *110 volts AC, 60 cycles.*
Weights and measures *The metric system is official in Nicaragua but in practice a mixture is used of metric, Imperial and old Spanish measurements including the vara, which is equivalent to about 1 m.*

Essentials

Touching down

Airport information

Entrance to Nicaragua via air is through its small, but growing international airport just east of Managua. For details of airport facilities and transport to the city centre, see the Managua chapter.

Hotel Las Mercedes (see page 67) is a good place to kill time near the airport

There is an arrival tax of US$5 payable at the immigration check and an exit tax of US$25 payable at the airline check-in counter.

Airport taxes

Tourist information

Tourism in Nicaragua is promoted by the **Instituto Nicaragüense de Turismo**, located one block south and then one block west of the old *Intercontinental Hotel* in Managua, T222-3333, F222-6610 and www.intur.gob.ni There are also small tourist offices in some towns and cities around the country. See respective destination chapters for addresses. As a rule the representatives are friendly and have some knowledge on their particular city or region, almost exclusively in Spanish.

For information on national parks and conservation, contact SINAP T263-2617

Local customs and laws

Nicaraguans are renowned for their friendliness and, compared with many Latin Americans, are very informal people. To get the most out of your visit, it's a good idea to learn at least some basic greetings in Spanish and to heed local customs and culture.

The traditional greeting for complete strangers is *Mucho gusto* (it's a pleasure) which will be followed by a handshake or a nod and a smile. One kiss to the right cheek (or rather to the air, as the two right cheeks meet) is also common if you are being introduced – though not between men. If in doubt, follow the lead of the person you are being introduced to. In the countryside children often reach up to kiss someone they are being introduced to, as this is the most polite way to greet an adult. The time of day greeting (*Buenos días, Buenas tardes* or *Buenas noches*) is the polite norm when entering a shop or place where you know no one. If you are in a shop or corner store (*pulpería*) and there appears to be no one around, you should call out *¡Buenas!* to receive service. *Hola* (hello) is reserved for people who know each other well and should not be used to greet strangers. If in Nicaragua on business, try not to get down to business right away, even if just placing a business call. Cutting straight to work talk will make everyone think you are rather cold; talk a bit, get to know the person, see how his or her day is going first.

Greetings

Punctuality 'Nicaraguan time' is a place where few find logic and reason. The European or North American sense of punctuality and importance of time is not unknown to the Nicaraguans, but remains a vague and incomprehensible concept for most. Television shows might start at 0714, instead of 0700 as programmed, radio stations often come on the air late or sign off early, one-hour meetings can run the entire afternoon, ferry boats sometimes leave early from the dock and *ya viene* (it's coming now) could mean that the plane is an hour away from arrival. In the countryside this trait is amplified. You may ask how far it is to walk to a given place and receive the answer *una vuelta* (just around the corner); in fact, you may be in for a good five-hour hike.

If visiting Nicaragua on business, it is best to be on time for your meetings and bring something to read while you wait. There is always the outside chance that your appointment might show up on time, as there is always a chance it will snow in hell. If visiting Nicaragua on holiday, relax, don't worry about time; for most Nicaraguans a conversation is almost always more valuable than arriving on time and it and this quality makes for a world with a little more warmth.

Clothing Dress is informal and casual clothes are almost always acceptable. Cool cotton clothes or jeans with some well-ventilated sandals are suitable for most situations. Shorts are fine for hiking in rural areas or at the beach, but are rarely worn in the city (Nicaraguan men do not wear suits either unless it is a special occasion). Although you can wear whatever you want and be treated well, most Nicaraguans take great pride in their appearance and may judge you accordingly. In rural areas or at the beach there is no need to think about dress codes of any kind (although beachwear is inappropriate in all Nicaraguan churches). However, topless bathing is not socially accepted anywhere in Nicaragua and will draw huge attention from local men. Finding a deserted beach isn't too difficult for the dedicated topless tanners, but nude bathing is a very bad idea even on a deserted beach. Both are illegal.

Begging In coming to a country that is considered to be the third poorest in the Americas you would expect to encounter some people asking for a handout. Begging has been practised since pre-Columbian times in the area, when most of the indigenous people were willing to lend a hand to people who had fallen on tough times. In relation to the poverty that exists in Nicaragua today, begging is not a big problem. Most of it will be encountered in Managua while driving and being driven around the capital. There is much debate about whether or not the humane tendency to help out someone who is undoubtedly dramatically poorer than you should be rejected. Most children begging are sent by parents as an additional source of income for the family. What the children are doing is their job, many also go to school with the money they earn. Refusing to give money will not change their day job, just make it longer. A small gift of some use (pens, pencils, small notebooks, etc) could be suggested as an alternative to money.

Tipping The 10% service charge often included in restaurant bills is not mandatory, though most people choose to pay it. A very special service might warrant some extra in the hand of the waiter or waitress. For porters at the airport or in an upmarket hotel the normal tip is US$0.50 per bag. Taxi drivers do not expect tips unless hired out on an hourly or daily basis. About US$0.10 is usual for people who offer to look after your car (usually quite unnecessary, but a way to make a living). The going rate for local guides at national parks is US$5 or more, while kids in the market who help you with translations can expect about US$2. Salaries in Nicaragua are amongst the lowest in the hemisphere, so any extra sum will be very much appreciated. A tip of anything lower than 25 centavos could be considered an insult. **NB** There are miniature paper notes for 25, 10, 5, and 1 centavos; in reality these notes are just used to balance the books and are not accepted by most stores for any kind of purchase.

How big is your footprint?

It is often assumed that tourism only has an adverse affect on the environment and local communities at the more excessive end of the travel industry. However, travellers can have an impact, no matter how few in number they may be, where local people may be unused to their conventions or lifestyles and natural environments may be sensitive. Here are a few tips:

■ *Where possible choose a destination, tour operator or hotel with a proven ethical and environmental commitment – if in doubt, ask.*

■ *Consider staying in local accommodation rather than foreign-owned hotels – the economic benefits for host communities are far greater, as are the opportunities to learn about local culture.*

■ *Learn about local customs and culture – consider local norms and behaviour and dress appropriately for local cultures and situations.*

■ *Always ask before taking photographs or videos of people.*

■ *Spend money on locally produced (rather than imported) goods and services and use common sense when bargaining – your few dollars saved may be a week's salary to others.*

■ *Use water and electricity carefully – travellers may receive preferential supply while the needs of local communities are overlooked.*

■ *To minimize impact during visits to nature reserves, travel in small groups; don't add or take away anything from the environment during the visit, and never feed wild animals in the reserves.*

■ *Protect wildlife and other natural resources – don't buy souvenirs or goods made from these materials unless they are clearly sustainably produced and are not protected under CITES legislation (CITES controls trade in endangered species).*

Recreational drugs of any kind are illegal in Nicaragua and are sure to bring big problems for the user. It is wise to leave any drugs behind and not go looking for them in Nicaragua. Nicaraguan society puts marijuana in the same category as heroin and prosecutes accordingly. Men with long hair, earrings, etc, may arouse more suspicion in local police and run a greater risk of being considered drug users; this is not a problem as long as they are not. — Prohibitions

Responsible tourism

Travel to the furthest corners of the globe is now commonplace and the mass movement of people for leisure and business is a major source of foreign exchange and economic development in many parts of Central America.

The benefits of international travel are self-evident for both hosts and travellers – employment, increased understanding of different cultures, business and leisure opportunities. At the same time there is clearly a downside to the rapidly growing travel industry. Where visitor pressure is high and/or poorly regulated, adverse impacts on society and the natural environment may be apparent. Paradoxically, this is as true in undeveloped and pristine areas (where culture and the natural environment are less 'prepared' for even small numbers of visitors) as in major resort destinations.

The impacts of this supposedly 'smokeless' industry can seem remote and unrelated to an individual trip or holiday. However, air travel is clearly implicated in global warming and damage to the ozone layer. Resort location and construction can destroy natural habitats and restrict traditional rights and activities. With this in mind, individual choice and awareness can make a difference in many instances, and collectively, travellers are having a significant effect in shaping a more responsible and sustainable industry.

In an attempt to promote awareness of and credibility for responsible tourism, organizations such as *Green Globe* (T020-77304428, www.greenglobe21.com) and the *Centre for Environmentally Sustainable Tourism* (CERT) (T01268-795772, F01268-759834, www.c-e-r-t.org) now offer advice on selecting destinations and sites that aim to achieve certain commitments to conservation and sustainable development. Generally the information covers larger mainstream destinations and resorts but the guides are still useful and increasingly aim to cover smaller operations.

Of course travel can have a beneficial impact and this is something to which every traveller can contribute – many national parks are partly funded by receipts from visitors. Similarly, travellers can promote patronage and protection of important archaeological sites and heritage through their interest and contributions via entrance fees. They can also support small-scale enterprises by staying in locally run hotels and hostels, eating in local restaurants and by purchasing local goods, supplies and arts and crafts.

While the authenticity of some eco-tourism operators' claims needs to be interpreted with care, there is clearly both a huge demand for this type of activity and also significant opportunities to support worthwhile conservation and social development initiatives.

Organizations such as **Conservation International** (T1-202-4295660, www.ecotour.org), the **Eco-Tourism Society** (T1-802-4472121, www.ecotourism.org), **Planeta** (www2.planeta.com/mader) and **Tourism Concern** (T020-77533330, www.tourismconcern.org.uk) have begun to develop and/or promote eco-tourism projects and destinations. Their websites are an excellent source of information and details for sites and initiatives throughout most of Latin America. Additionally, organizations such as **Earthwatch** (US/Can T1-800-7760188, in UK on T01865-311601, www.earthwatch.org) and **Discovery International** (T020-72299881, www.discovery-initiatives.com) offer opportunities for travellers to participate directly in scientific research and development projects throughout the region.

Safety

Protecting money & valuables

Crime is not a big issue for visitors to Nicaragua, although the usual precautions for travellers are necessary. Since travellers' cheques are difficult to change and ATM machines are rare outside Managua, visitors will find themselves with a lot of cash to carry. Interior money belts and leg pouches are helpful. Keep a certain amount of cash in your pocket to avoid opening money belts and pouches in public. Neck pouches are not such a good idea as they are almost always visible. Spreading money and credit cards around is a good idea if you are well organized.

Crime in Nicaragua

Current data from the United Nations rates Nicaragua as one of the safest countries in Latin America and Managua as one of the region's safest capitals. That said, Managua has a handful of very unsafe neighbourhoods, some of which are not necessarily the city's poorest. It is impossible to rate all of sprawling Managua's *barrios* for safety, general rules will minimize your chances of running into trouble. Arrival at the airport means a taxi ride to a hotel; don't try to mount Managua's overflowing buses with luggage or packs. Once in a hotel get around town on foot or by taxi in the daytime, or by taxi at night. There are some areas where it is perfectly safe to walk at night, but as a general rule avoid dark areas and places that are not full of people. Bus stops are notorious hotspots for thieves. Avoid the crowded city buses (see below) and the bus stops where possible. Managua's inter-city buses leave from the city's markets. The central market, Roberto Huembes, is safe, but the others are less so. The notorious Mercado Oriental in Managua is considered to be the biggest open-air market in Central America, a mind-boggling labyrinth of sounds, smells, sights – and criminals. It is home to more than 60% of all crime committed in Nicaragua and is not for the faint-hearted. None of the buses to outlying areas leave from the Oriental so either stay away or exercise extreme caution.

Outside Managua, the rest of Nicaragua is very safe indeed. There are, however, pickpockets in León and Granada and youth gangs operate in northern areas, which should be avoided at night (these places are cited in the corresponding chapters).

Rape is not a problem for travellers in Nicaragua, though 'date rape' is just as big a threat here as elsewhere in the world. If rape does occur contact the police at once.

Hotel security Most hotels are small establishments where room theft is rare or non-existent. Don't take this as an invitation to be careless; hide valuables away in cases or in safe deposit boxes. Budget travellers should bring locks for doors and luggage and keep in mind that the main theft threat may come from other travellers. If something goes missing ask the hotel manager to investigate (with ample time to recover what's missing) and then ask him to call the police if nothing can be resolved.

Public transport As mentioned above, the **city buses** in Managua are a sure way to find trouble. They are hot, overcrowded, in bad operating condition and home turf for Managua's finest criminals. As an alternative, walk or use **registered taxis** (they must have red licence plates) which are cheap and reliable. **Inter-city** buses are recommended and generally free of thieves. Sit as close as possible to the driver, not just for safety and the view, but also in case you need to get off before the final destination. Managua **airport**'s domestic terminal is very safe with virtually no reports of thefts. Planes serving domestic routes are small, usually with no overhead bin, so a lock is useful for any bags you need to check in. Keep track of your bags on the runway when you can (normally very easy outside of Managua) to make sure that they get on your flight.

Police Nicaraguan police are seriously underpaid, but on the whole are honest and sincere about their work. As long as you are polite and respectful you should find them to be friendly and helpful. On all major highways there are regular check-points, concerned mainly with illegal traffic in drugs and immigrants headed north to the United States. Papers are checked and you are on your way. If in a taxi or bus keep your passport handy. If driving, make sure you can prove the car was rented by you and that you have a valid driver's licence. If you are pulled over for a driving offence you are likely to lose your licence for at least three weeks, until your violation is processed and you can pay the fine and recover your licence. If you can't wait that long and you speak Spanish, you might ask for a pardon on the grounds that you will be leaving the country soon, can't live without your licence and that you are very sorry to have made a mistake. Another alternative is to carry an international driver's licence that you can leave with the officer in the event of a violation. **NB** Do not offer bribes. This is illegal and can get both the visitor and the police officer in trouble and will contaminate what is one of the most honest police forces in Latin America. If you are asked for a bribe, get the name of the police chief for the area you are travelling in and take down the badge number of the officer in question; that should be more than enough to settle the issue.

Hotel prices and facilities

LL *(over US$150)*, **L** *(US$100-149)* and **AL** *(US$66-99) Hotels in these categories are almost all found in Managua. At the top end of this price bracket are international chain hotels full of businessmen, while the lower end is mostly upscale tourist hotels, discount business establishments and a couple of jungle lodges. With the exception of the jungle lodges, all will include cable TV, hot water in a private bathroom, air-conditioning and laundry service; most have pools, room service and internet access.*

A *(US$46-65)* and **B** *(US$31-45) Hotels at the top end of this category provide most of the services and comforts of the* **AL** *hotels, while the* **B** *category may include good hotels past their prime or upscale budget hotels with air-conditioning and electric showers.*

C *(US$21-30)*, **D** *(US$15-20)* and **E** *(US$12-15) Hotels in this price range* vary from cute, clean and basic to suffocating little boxes. Much of this price range provides poor value for money although there are some clean, decent hotels at the top end. With a couple of key exceptions the **E**-range choices are rather bleak.

F *(US$7-11) Here is where you cross the line into sagging beds, dark boxes and cockroach showers in Managua, and tired low-quality rooms in the outlying towns. However, there are a few clean, good-value exceptions, which have been highlighted in the text.*

G *(up to US$6) Although there are a few decent choices in this price category, most are disgusting and suitable only for those in training to do jail time in Nicaragua. If you are spending more than a few days this close to your shoestrings, a hammock in the park could be a better option.*

Where to stay

If travelling outside the air-conditioned world a mosquito net is a big asset

Nicaraguan hotels are not a reason to visit the country, but there are some very charming lodges in locales that are truly paradisical. In Managua you can either pay more than you would expect for a Latin American hotel or put up with some fairly unpleasant sleeping conditions. Outside Managua the hotels in the low to middle range are often pleasant and some good deals are to be found. In some rural areas there will be only one option, though hanging your hammock in someone's home is always possible, if your language skills are up to the task. A room with private bath usually costs over US$20 per night in the city and US$10 in the country, while air-conditioning and running hot water will push you above US$30 in most cases. In remote areas meals are often included in the price and electricity is produced by a diesel generator that runs for only a few hours after sunset. Water is sometimes scarce outside Managua, particularly at the end of the dry season in the northern mountains and in Bluefields. You should be aware that establishments calling themselves 'autohotel' or 'motel' or displaying 'open 24 hours' signs serve a purpose other than just providing a bed for the night (see box above).

Advice & suggestions
It is always wise to pull the bed away from the wall in the tropics, so whatever is crawling on the wall does not see your head as a logical progression

Always ask to see the room in advance, especially if travelling below the **C** bracket (on page 28 for the classifications). In the more costly **A-C** range, a slight price hike could mean a room overlooking the park instead of the laundry area. Budget travellers should bring a padlock, toilet paper, soap, insecticide and a decent towel. **G**-bracket travellers should remember to shake out the sheets, if there are any. Many hotels on the outskirts of cities will lock up and go to bed early; if you are heading out for a night on the town, check to make sure you can get back in and that you know who has the key. Do not put toilet paper or any non-organic material in any toilet in the country; you will find a little wastebasket for that purpose. This may seem unsanitary, but is much less so than blocked pipes and a clogged and overflowing toilet.

Love shack – automotels in Nicaragua

Many visitors to Nicaragua are confused. What is an 'autohotel' or 'motel'? Why all the romantic imagery on their signs? Is this where Toyotas shack up with Nissans for the night? In reality, the 'auto' reference is a clue, a subtle indicator that the establishment will hide your car, as well as your love partner. Autohotels are for making love; they serve no other purpose. Rooms are sold in two or three-hour blocks and include fresh towels, sheets and a condom. The customers pull quickly into an open parking stall connected to a private hotel room. Whoosh! A big curtain is closed immediately behind their car, effectively hiding the identity of the couple and their vehicle. Each room also has a little blind-box door for the discreet staff to pass ordered beers or soft drinks through. It is not that these hotels are particularly romantic, just part of the Nicaraguan culture. They are used for illicit affairs and by impatient courting couples – most Nicaraguan women must live at home until they are married. Some of them look very inviting from the outside, a lot nicer than many a budget travellers' hospedaje. On occasion, weary travellers have stumbled into an autohotel, looking for a simple night's rest. The hotel staff, confused and at a loss for what to do, will rent them a room for the night. However, if those unsuspecting travellers are not paired off – three men travelling together, for example – the staff might shake their head a bit, perhaps mumbling as they shut the privacy curtain, "whatever happened to tradition?".

NB Electric showers are very common and, if poorly wired, decidedly more effective than Nicaraguan coffee to get the blood pumping in the morning. The shocks are not fatal, but it is best to set the shower head on *tibio* (warm) or *caliente* (hot) with your feet in the dry and then turn on the water; do not touch anything metal or the showerhead until you are outside the shower and dry again.

Amongst the many ugly species of **cockroaches**, there are two main types: indoor and outdoor. The indoor ones are small, run fast and have a million cousins, while the outdoor type is usually quite big, a little slow and much crunchier. The presence of indoor cockroaches means the hotel is dirty and/or rarely sprayed. The outdoor ones can come into any hotel at night, from budget to five-star, and are not a sign of dirtiness, just a feature of the tropics.

Camping

Nicaragua has no official campsites and is so hot that traditional camping - putting yourself inside a tent or, worse, inside a sleeping bag inside a tent - can be a terrifying concept. In more remote areas you can usually find a roof to hang your hammock under (ask for permission first). A mosquito net, which you should bring from home, will keep off the vampire bats as well as the insects. (Hammocks are found in markets all over the country, though the best quality ones are made in Masaya and can be bought at the market there or in Managua at an average cost of US$20.) Some black plastic sheeting (sold by the metre in any city market) will keep the rain off in case there's no roof handy. **NB** If camping in the rainforest, try marking the boundary of your campsite with urine, it's said to keep off the jaguars and other uninvited guests. This is a proven technique used as protection by forest hunters. To be effective, the urine should be collected in empty water bottles in the morning (when it is strongest), then spread around the campsite at night.

Getting around

A decent road system covers the west of Nicaragua and the country's small size makes car or bus travel practical and fairly simple. Buses run between all Pacific and central cities and villages on a daily basis and fares are very cheap. Boat and plane are the only options for long-distance travel on the Caribbean coast and in the rainforest areas of the north and south where roads are very bad to non-existent.

Air

La Costeña and Atlantic Airlines, the local airlines, offer a good number of domestic routes and regular flights

Atlantic Airlines and *La Costeña* both serve the Managua routes than run daily to Bluefields, Puerto Cabezas and Corn Island. *La Costeña* also flies to the Río San Juan capital of San Carlos and other small destinations in the northeastern Nicaraguan interior. Flights are often booked full and early arrival is important as no seat assignments are given on most flights. All flights leave from Managua, so hopping from place to place by plane will mean a lot of returns to Managua. The exception is the *La Costeña* flight between Puerto Cabezas and Bluefields. Details and costs are in the destination chapters.

Bus

This is how most Nicaraguans get around and, outside Managua, the bus drivers are usually friendly and helpful. Routes are not scheduled very rigidly and it is best to arrive early for a bus service that only runs once or twice a day. On routes that leave every hour or half-hour you only need to check the destination above the front window of the bus and grab a seat. You can flag down most buses that are not marked 'Express'. Fares are collected as you board city buses or en route in the case of inter-city buses. Most Nicaraguan buses are 'retired' school buses from the United States and have limited leg-room. Sitting behind the driver may alleviate this problem for tall passengers and in any case is a good idea if you plan to get off before the final destination. Buses often fill up to the roof and can be very hot and bumpy, but they are a great way to meet and get to know the Nicaraguan people. Most principal destinations have an Express service, which makes fewer stops and will be more aggressive on the highway. For longer journeys an Express bus could mean cutting travel times almost in half. For services between Granada, Jinotepe, Masaya, León and several other destinations the Express bus may also be a 12 or 24-seat mini-bus and charge up to double the normal rate.

Truck

In many rural areas flat-bed trucks – usually covered with a tarpaulin and often with bench seating – are used for getting to places that are inaccessible by bus. The trucks charge a fixed fare and, apart from eating a full bowl of dust in the dry season or getting soaked in the wet, they can be a great way to see the country. Communication with the driver can be difficult, so be sure you know more or less where you are going; other passengers will be able to tell you where to jump off. Banging the roof of the driver's cabin is always effective if you find he is passing your destination.

Boat

Public river boats are often slow but are a good way to meet local people; private boats can be hired if you are short on time

In a country with two oceans, two great lakes and numerous lagoons, estuaries and rivers, a boat is never far away and often the necessary means of travel. Apart from regular services between the two **Corn Islands**, boat travel along the **Pacific** and **Caribbean** coasts is difficult, and often the only option is to hire out a boat or convince the fishermen to take you out. Fishermen are also an option in **Lake Managua** where there is no regular service either. In **Lake Nicaragua** you can choose between big ferries and old wooden 'African Queen' models or you can hire a private motor boat. The **rivers** and **coastal lagoons** are home to regular commuter boats, which are long, thin, covered boats with outboards or else cargo boats, which are extremely slow; private motor boats are very expensive to hire but are useful for both wildlife exploration and touring.

Road warrior – driving and surviving in Nicaragua

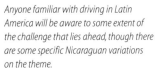

Anyone familiar with driving in Latin America will be aware to some extent of the challenge that lies ahead, though there are some specific Nicaraguan variations on the theme.

Three kinds of driving experiences await you in this tropical state of motoring madness. In the Managua battle-zone the visiting gladiator must steer clear of axle-breaking holes, and city buses. These smoking beasts, filled to the ceiling with sweating commuters and professional thieves, are manned by some of the most aggressive men on earth. The crazed and ruthless bus driver mounts his challenge, horn wailing, sharpened metal spikes spinning from the wheels, and never slows down, gives way or acknowledges anyone, except a boarding or disembarking passenger. That poor paying customer will be lifted on to or tossed off the still moving bus by a hyperactive screaming assistant, whose task it is to collect money and bodies still hanging out of the open door, arms and legs signalling the next life-threatening lane change. Here is where the guest gladiator must yield, brake or just get the heck out of the way, as any counter-challenge will result in sure death.

Taxi drivers too must be respected for what they are, rogue messengers from planet anarchy, routinely breaking every rule of good driving in ways previously unimaginable. Don't be surprised by the crash-the-red-light-by-driving-into-oncoming-traffic-to-overtake-waiting-cars-at-the-junction manoeuvre, the maniacally obsessive horn usage or a host of other dangerous and aggravating practices.

Out of the confines of Managua you can breathe deep, relax and run free ... most of the time. But this game also involves extra finesse and grand prix reaction time to avoid the ox and horse carts, people sitting on the road shoulder, pot holes as deep as the 12th circle of hell, and your fellow road warriors blissfully passing on blind corners and hills. There is no speed limit, just a limit on common sense, patience and judgement. The Nicaraguan driver does, however, give ample room to the oncoming car, the overtaker and the undertaker. No matter how conservative you set out to be, you will be forced into white-knuckle overtaking: use your horn to warn the vehicle you are passing in the daytime and your headlights at night; be decisive and give space to the other gladiators, and they will return the favour.

The real fun of driving in Nicaragua lies beyond the limits of its paved universe. Rock-filled and river-sliced passages lead to places forgotten by earth and roadside services. Driving here is more akin to an off- road endurance test with mud bogs and raging rivers to be forged in the rainy season and relentless banging over rocky dust roads in the dry. The pace is slower though, and when you are not busy coating well-dressed women and children with thick layers of billowing dirt or sheepishly asking for an ox cart to pull you out of a bog, friends can be made and rides offered – even if a horse really would have been a better choice in the first place.

Car
For car hire, see page 75

Four-wheel drive is not necessary, although it does give you greater flexibility in mountain and jungle territory. Wherever you travel you should expect to find roads that are badly maintained, damaged or closed during the wet season, and, delays because of floods, landslides and huge potholes. Don't plan your schedules too tightly. Unleaded and Premium grade fuel are now available everywhere, as is diesel. **NB** The electronic ignition and fuel metering systems on modern emission-controlled cars are allergic to humidity, heat and dust, and cannot be repaired by mechanics outside the main centres. Also, standard European and Japanese cars run on fuel with a higher octane rating than is commonly available in North, South or Central America.

The wearing of seatbelts is not obligatory

Security Use all your ingenuity in making your car secure. Try never to leave it unattended except in a locked garage or guarded parking space. Remove all belongings and leave the empty glove compartment open when the car is unattended. Lock the clutch or accelerator to the steering wheel with a heavy, obvious chain or lock. Street children and car park attendants will generally protect your car in exchange for a tip. Be sure to note down key numbers and carry a set of spares with you (don't keep them inside the vehicle!).

Nicaragua has regular check-points on major highways; just show your paperwork and you will be on your way

Documents Land entry procedures are simple though time-consuming as the car has to be checked by customs, police and agriculture officials. All you need is the registration document in the name of the driver, or, if a car is registered in someone else's name, a notarized letter of authorization. A written undertaking that the vehicle will be re-exported after temporary importation is useful and may be requested. Of course, do be very careful to keep all the papers you are given when you enter the country, to produce when you leave. (An army of 'helpers' loiters at each border crossing, waiting to guide motorists to each official in the correct order, for a tip. They can be useful, but don't give them your papers.) Insurance for the vehicle against accident, damage or theft is best arranged in the country of origin: in all Latin American countries it is very expensive to insure against accident and theft. Get the legally required minimum cover – not expensive – as soon as you can because, if you are involved in an accident and found to be uninsured, your car could be confiscated. If anyone is hurt, do not pick them up (you become liable); instead, seek assistance from the nearest police station or hospital.

Border crossings are about US$20 per vehicle. All borders are free on exit, though you will have to pay the per-person fees.

Motorcycling People are generally very friendly to motorcyclists. Buying a bike in the United States and driving down works out cheaper than buying one in Europe and shipping it over. Choose a comfortable bike that has off-road capability without necessarily being an off-road bike. Motocross is very popular in Nicaragua and a decent bike will be a great conversation piece, especially if it is over 350 cc. The wearing of helmets is required by law (although it isn't always enforced and you will even see motorcycle police without them!).

Security is not a problem, but never leave a fully laden motorbike on its own. An *Abus D* or chain will keep the bike secure. Most hotels will allow you to bring the bike inside, but a cheap alarm will give you peace of mind if you have to leave it outside. Look for hotels that have a courtyard or more secure parking and never leave luggage on the bike overnight or whilst unattended. Also take a cover for the bike.

Documents A passport, International Driving Licence, and bike registration document are necessary. Fees for **border crossings** are the same as for cars (see above).

Cycling Unless you are planning a journey almost exclusively on paved roads – when a high-quality touring bike such as a *Dawes Super Galaxy* would probably suffice – a mountain bike is strongly recommended. The good-quality ones (and the cast-iron rule is never to skimp on quality) are incredibly tough and rugged, with low gear ratios for difficult terrain, wide tyres with plenty of tread for good road-holding, cantilever brakes, and a low centre of gravity for improved stability. Imported bike parts are impossible to find in Nicaragua. Buy everything you possibly can before you leave home. Most towns have a bicycle shop of some description, but it is best to do your own repairs and adjustments whenever possible.

Useful tips   Wind, not hills is the enemy of the cyclist. Try to make the best use of the times of day when it is less windy; mornings tend to be best but there is no steadfast rule. Take care to avoid dehydration by drinking regularly. In hot, dry areas with limited water supplies, be sure to carry an ample supply on the bike. For food, carry the staples (sugar, salt, dried milk, tea, coffee, porridge oats, raisins, dried soups, etc) and supplement these with whatever local foods can be found in the markets. Give your bicycle a thorough daily check for loose nuts or bolts or bearings. See that all parts run smoothly. A good chain should last 2,000 miles/3,200 km or more but be sure to keep it as clean as possible – an old toothbrush is good for this – and to oil it lightly from time to time. Remember that thieves are attracted to towns and cities, so when sightseeing, try to leave your bicycle with someone such as the owner of a café. Country people tend to be more honest and are usually friendly and very inquisitive. However, don't take unnecessary risks; always see that your bicycle is secure (most hotels will allow bikes to be kept in rooms).

Carry a stick or some small stones to frighten off dogs, most of which are more bark than bite. Most cyclists agree that the main risk comes from other traffic, and certainly main roads can be dangerous; it is usually far more rewarding to keep to the smaller roads or to paths if they exist. A rear-view mirror can forewarn you of trucks or cars that are too close behind. You also need to watch out for oncoming, overtaking vehicles, protruding or unstable loads on trucks, etc. Make yourself conspicuous by wearing bright clothing and a helmet; also, displaying a flag of the country you are travelling through helps to keep truckers patient and prompts encouragement.

Recommended reading   *Latin America by Bike – A Complete Touring Guide,* Walter Sienko (The Mountaineers, 1993); *Richard's New Bicycle Book* (Pan, £12.99) makes useful reading for even the most mechanically minded; The **Expedition Advisory Centre**, administered by the Royal Geographical Society, 1 Kensington Gore, London SW7 2AR, T020-7591 3030, www.rgs.org, has published a useful monograph entitled *Bicycle Expeditions*, by Paul Vickers (March 1990), which is available direct from the Centre, price £6.50 plus postage. In the UK there is also the **Cyclists' Touring Club**, CTC, Cotterell House, 69 Meadrow, Godalming, Surrey, GU7 3HS, T01483-417217, www.ctc.org.uk/ for touring and technical information.

Hitchhiking   Hitching is always possible, but is often difficult due to the lack of spare room in the vehicles on the road. It's the done thing to offer to pay, so the low bus fares make it somewhat redundant too. In some very rural areas it may be necessary to hitch and most pick-up trucks that have room will stop and let you jump in the back; offer at least US$.50 for the ride, or more if it is a really long one. **NB** Nicaraguan drivers may refuse to stop for anyone who they think looks like a 'hippie', for fear of the problems that could arise if they were found to be carrying drugs.

Keeping in touch

Internet   The internet has seen an explosion in Nicaragua during the turn of this century. Since many Nicaraguans can't afford computers there is no shortage of internet cafés offering full computer services. Register your web-based email address before leaving home. The internet is a particularly good travel tool in countries like Nicaragua that have a poor telephone infrastructure with very high rates. Apart from contacting friends and family at home and on the road, it can also be useful for checking out destinations and booking hotels. However, response time in Nicaragua is slow and often indifferent, even at some of the more expensive establishments, so do as much of this type of computer work as possible before you arrive. Cybercafés are prevalent in

Managua, Granada and, to a much lesser extent, in León and some other major outlying cities. See destination chapters for details.

Post *Correos de Nicaragua* are slow but reliable. Almost everything reaches its destination sooner or (as is most often the case) later. For some unknown reason, letters to Europe usually arrive in half the time taken by letters to and from the United States and Canada. The average time for a letter to the USA is 18 days while European letters normally take 7-10 days. The cost of mailing normal-sized letters is: US$0.80 to Europe, US$0.55 to North America and just over US$1 to Australia and Asia. **Parcels** should be left open to be inspected and sealed at the post office. **Courier services** from Nicaragua, available from companies like *DHL* and *UPS*, are expensive, with a three-day letter to the USA averaging US$40 and Europe just a bit more; for details see page 79.

Telephone The Nicaraguan telephone company, ENITEL, has offices in all cities and most towns; often the only telephone in a village will be in the ENITEL office. Calls can be placed to local or international destinations with pre-payment for an allotted amount of time. To make a reverse-charge (collect) call to any country in the world you will need to name the country in Spanish and say *una llamada para cobrar*. The average rate for direct calls to Europe or the USA is about US$3 for the first minute and then US$1 a minute thereafter; collect calls cost more.

USA operators: dial 171 for Sprint, 174 for AT&T and 166 for MCI. *European operators*: for Germany dial 169; Belgium 172; Canada 168; Spain 162; The Netherlands 177; and the UK 175.

Public phones are rare and most only accept phone cards, which are available for purchase in petrol station convenience stores.

Phone numbers in Nicaragua have seven digits. In the past it was necessary to add a prefix to a number, but now they are all included in listings around the country. Just dial zero and then the number when calling a city outside the one you are calling from. To make an **international call** from Nicaragua, dial 00 and then the country code. To call into Nicaragua, dial your international access + 505 and the number, without the first zero. All cellphone numbers start with 077 or 088, but if calling from another cellphone you need not dial the zero first (the same holds true for international calls made to a cellphone inside Nicaragua).

Media

One of the great advantages of being able to read or understand Spanish is the chance to tune into the local media. Nicaragua's press is aggressive, conflictive, at times sensationalist and does not pull any punches. It mainly focuses on the high profile political issues and characters, but it also manages to report on the plight of the average man with great compassion.

Newspapers & magazines
The 'Literaria' section of La Prensa's Saturday edition has a good cultural calendar, as well as original poetry, book reviews and interviews

All daily newspapers, costing US$0.20, are published in Managua but are available in most of the country. They are sold at traffic lights and in many shops in Managua and in select stores in outlying cities. The country's oldest and most influential daily is *La Prensa*, centre-right in leaning, but a very vocal critic of Arnoldo Alemán's right-wing administration (1997-2002). It was the murder of *La Prensa*'s director Pedro Joaquín Chamorro that sparked the Revolution of 1978-79 into a struggle of all social classes. His widow, Violeta Barrios de Chamorro, was president of Nicaragua from 1991-97. The family maintains control of the newspaper, which, along with the Catholic church and Channel 2 Television, is the most influential voice in the country.

The other major daily is centre-left *El Nuevo Diario* which, despite a tendency to be sensationalist and focus on crime news, does have some very good provincial news coverage. The third of the dailies, *La Noticia*, is sponsored by the Liberal Party and was created as a response to the now-defunct Sandinista newspaper. The three available weeklies, US$0.50 each, are more difficult to find outside the city (supermarkets and petrol station stores are the best sources): they are *Tiempo del Mundo*, based in South America, *7 Días*, a populist magazine with lots of light news, and *Confidencial*, an investigative news magazine run by Carlos Fernando Chamorro, son of the assassinated *La Prensa* director.

The only English-language publication, *Nicaragua's Best Guide*, is a quarterly magazine offering rather shallow coverage on destinations which may be of interest to the traveller. *Decenio, Revista Centroamericana de Cultura*, published in Managua, is an excellent bi-monthly magazine that deals mainly with Nicaraguan art and culture, though other countries are represented too. You'll find it in Managua's great bookstore, *Hispamer*, *La Colonia* supermarkets and *Casa de Café*.

Essentials

Since the volatile days leading up to the success of the Revolution, when the mobile station *Radio Sandino* kept the rebels and population up to date on the fighting and where to attack next, radio has been an essential means of transmitting the latest in events to Nicaraguans. *Radio Sandino (AM 740)* is still the official station of the Sandinistas and can be seen just north of the *Mirador Tiscapa* restaurant in Managua. The long-time opposition to the Sandinista's radio station has been *Radio Corporación (AM 540)*, which now holds the Liberal Party line. Up and down the AM dial you can hear all kinds of other relevant and irrelevant news programmes. The music stations on FM radio are of huge importance in Nicaragua. Most take a very eclectic approach to programming, though there are stations that specialize in dance music (**FM 95.1**), progressive (**FM 99.9**), classical (**FM 101.1**), Mexican (**FM 93.9**) and romantic (**FM 98.7**). (The romantic station shares towers with the most powerful TV network and it therefore has the best signal around the country.)

Radio
Nicaraguan custom often dictates that radios be played at full volume, so that speakers distort and blow apart, a perfect excuse to go out and buy bigger and louder ones

Visitors are quite often amazed at the penetration of television in Nicaragua. The most out-of-the-way, humble of homes are wired-up and tuned in nightly to the collective passion of after-dark viewing, the *telenovela*, or soaps, produced mostly in Mexico, Colombia, Brazil, Venezuela and Argentina. News is the other most important element of Nicaraguan television, and all stations devote extensive time and effort to news coverage. The most popular and influential is *Canal 2* which has a good morning news and interview programme (0630-0830), and the most-watched nightly news broadcasts (1830 and 2200 weekdays). It also has a great Saturday-afternoon cultural programme (1630) which features folk music and dancing and special cultural and human-interest reports from around the country. *Canal 12* has a morning call-in talk show (0630–0900) that often deals with relevant issues, and one of the better nightly news productions (Monday-Friday 1830 and 2100). As well as the staples of *telenovelas* and news programmes, the other channels – *Canal 4*, government-run *Canal 6* and *Canal 8* – screen anything from music videos and karaoke to bad American movies, interviews and some limited cultural reporting.

Television

Food and drink

Nicaragua has a great selection of traditional dishes that are usually prepared with very fresh ingredients and in generous portions. Anyone looking for international cuisine will be disappointed as both choice and quality tend to be poor. A 15% sales tax is included in all restaurant bills and a 10% service charge is normally added as a tip. Although you are not legally required to pay the service charge most people do, unless the service has been truly awful. Many restaurants offer *comida corriente* (also called *comida casera*), a set menu that works out far cheaper than ordering à la carte. If

Food
Fresh handmade tortillas are available at most central markets and, with a little local cheese, are a great way to fill up for less than a dollar

travelling on the cheap and tired (or literally sick) of street food, ask at a restaurant if they have *comida corriente* and *¿cuánto vale?* (how much does it cost?). Generally speaking the *fritanga* street food, costing about US$1.25, will be for the cast-iron stomach only, while the US$2-3 *comida corriente* is often too salty and/or oily; the really good eating will cost you from US$4-10 a dish. (It may be better to share one good dish with a friend than order two cheap ones.)

A typical Nicaraguan **breakfast** is coffee with *gallo pinto* or *nacatamales. Gallo pinto,* the dish that keeps most of Nicaragua alive, is a mixture of fried white rice and kidney beans, which are cooked apart and then fried together with onions. It can be breakfast, lunch and dinner for much of the population at home and for this reason is not found in all restaurants. *Nacatamales,* similar to the Mexican *tamal* and equally filling, are made of cornmeal, pork or chicken, peppers, onions and lard, all wrapped in a big green banana leaf.

Lunch and **dinner** are more substantial meals, which include a plate full of cabbage salad, white rice, beans, tortilla, onions, fried or boiled plantain and a meat or fish serving. *Asado* or *a la plancha* are key words for most foreigners. *Asado* is grilled meat or fish, which often comes with a mild chilli sauce that is sure to please. *Carne asada,* grilled beef, is popular street food, although Nicaraguan beef tends to be on the tough side. *Pollo asado* or *cerdo asado* (grilled chicken or pork) are very good and always fresh. *A la plancha* means the food is cooked on a sizzling plate or flat grill, and at the more expensive restaurants your beef, chicken or pork will be brought to the table still cooking on its hot plate. At the coast, fresh *pargo rojo* or *pargo blanco* (red or white snapper) is almost always on the menu, and is best prepared fried whole with a tomato, sweet pepper and onion sauce. *Curvina* (sea bass) is also very good, though often served filleted, which means it may have been frozen first. Lobster – the tail only variety – is very good on the Caribbean side but is getting smaller and smaller on the Pacific Coast. Shrimp is good too, especially grilled or sautéed in garlic butter. In the lake or river regions there are good lake fish and *camarones de río* (freshwater prawns) which are prevalent in the Río San Juan region and very tasty in garlic butter (*ajillo*). The lake fish includes *guapote* (a kind of perch) and *mojarra* (carp) as well as *robalo* (snook) and the introduced African *tilapia*. Once again, they are delicious fried whole and served in a tomato, sweet pepper and onion sauce.

There are three basic kinds of cheese, all white: *queso seco* is a slightly bitter dry cheese; *queso crema* is a moist bland cheese; and *queso fresco* is a moist slightly salty cheese. The white Nicaraguan cheese is mild and slightly bitter and excellent fried. If there is any room left, there are three traditional desserts that are well worth trying: *tres leches,* which is a very sweet cake made with three different kinds of milk; *Pío V,* named after Pope Pius the Fifth (though no one seems to know why), is a corn cake topped with light cream and bathed in honey; and if these are too heavy, there is the ubiquitous *cajeta,* which is milk mixed with cane sugar or candied fruit. Look out, too, for *piñonate,* thinly sliced strips of candied green papaya. Other regional dishes are described in the local chapters.

Drink

Water is purified and safe to drink in Managua, Granada, León and other major towns. Bottled water is available throughout the country and is recommended as a simple precaution, though in the cities it's fine to drink frescos and ice cubes made with the local tap water

Since Nicaragua is the land of a thousand fruits, the best drink is the *refresco* or *fresco,* which is fruit juice mixed with water and (almost always) a bit of sugar. If properly made the sugar will not be discernible. *Jugo* means pure fruit juice, but is almost impossible to find in Nicaragua. If you ask the waiter what fresh drinks they have to offer (*¿qué frescos hay?*), you will receive a few suggestions or in some cases a mind-boggling list of choices which may include pineapple, carrot, passion fruit, beetroot, orange, mandarin, lemonade, grenadine, tamarind, mango, star-fruit, papaya, and more. Two notable favourites are *cacao* and *pitaya. Cacao* is the raw chocolate fruit which, when mixed with milk, ice and sugar, is refreshingly cold and filling. *Pitaya* is a cactus fruit, which is blended with lime and sugar and has a lovely, sensual deep purple colour and seedy pulp. The usual fizzy soft drinks are also available and called *gaseosas,* with the Pepsi vs. Coca-Cola war alive and well. For beer lovers there are three national brands (all lagers), the strongest being *Cerveza Victoria,* with *Toña* a softer choice and *Premium* a watery, light version. But Nicaragua is best known for its **rum**. *Flor de Caña* has often been called the finest rum in the world, and its factory – more than 100 years old – is a national institution producing seven different flavours, which mature for between four and 21 years. Nicaraguans often spend a night round the table with a bottle of Flor de Caña, served up with a bucket of ice, a plate of limes and a steady flow of mixers (Coca-Cola or soda water).

Although **coffee** is produced locally, most of the good beans are exported and the Nicaraguans tend to drink instant coffee; sadly, that is what is served in most local restaurants. If you want the real thing, try asking for *café percolado,* which is often quite good if it's available. Finding an *espresso* coffee or *cappuccino* outside the main cities is difficult, if not impossible and hot tea is rare too.

Being paranoid about food safety can ruin your trip and deny you one of the best eating experiences in Central America. Simply stick to a few basic rules. Washing your hands thoroughly before eating is the best way to avoid stomach problems. Portable hand-wash bottles (consisting mostly of alcohol) are a good way to clean up if there's nothing else available. Avoid fried street food as the oil, which has probably been used many times before, may cause stomach distress. The street grills are OK, as long as the meat has been well cooked, but don't eat salads or pre-peeled fruits off the street or market stands. Common traveller's diarrhoea is difficult to avoid, for it is as much a product of travel stress or a radically new diet, as it is of unclean food. In rural areas try to eat in the best restaurants you can afford, and in the cities avoid food from markets or street stalls. For Health, see page 42.

Eating precautions
On the whole Nicaragua is a very safe place to eat and stomach illness is not common

Shopping

Every city and town has its market. Normally, the meats, fruits and vegetables are inside the market, while the non-perishable goods are sold around the outside. Some kind of handmade crafts or products of local workmanship can be found in most markets. It may take some digging to find them as Nicaragua is not a mainstream tourist destination and the markets are not modified for the visitor. The exceptions are the craft market in **Masaya** which is dedicated solely to the talents of the local and national craftsmen, and the central market in **Managua**, Roberto Huembes, which has a big section dedicated to crafts from all over the country. Details of local markets are given throughout the book. **NB** Prices in the Nicaraguan markets are not marked up in anticipation of bargaining or negotiation. A small discount of 5-10% can be obtained if requested, but the prices quoted are what the merchant expects to get.

Markets

The only two shopping malls in Nicaragua, both in Managua (see page 74), stock mostly imported goods and can be useful for getting items that are normally difficult to find. Both have cinemas and food courts with local establishments and international chains.

Malls

All over Nicaragua street vendors set up stands or roam the streets selling everything you can possibly imagine and more. You'll find all sorts of interesting items that aren't available in most stores and these vary from region to region. This informal industry is critical to the survival of a large part of the population and visitors need not hesitate to buy from street merchants.

Street vendors

Camera equipment is almost impossible to buy in Nicaragua, so be sure that your gear is in good condition and with fresh batteries. Video film is very difficult, if not impossible, to find so bring with you whatever you will need. Print or negative film for still

Photography

photography is cheap and widely available in most markets and many general stores (*pulperías*). APS film is not available. Slide or positive film is very rare and almost twice as expensive as elsewhere. If shooting slide film bring all that you could use, or else buy in Managua at Kodak or Fuji.

Holidays and festivals

Public holidays
Local celebrations of each town's patron saint are listed throughout the book

1 January, *New Year's Day*. *Holy Week*, the week leading up to Easter Sunday, most businesses close at 1200 on Wednesday and don't reopen until the following Monday. **1 May**, *Labour Day*. **30 May**, *Mother's Day*, many businesses close after 1200. **19 July**, anniversary of the 1979 Revolution. **14 September**, Battle of San Jacinto (first victory against William Walker). **15 September**, Independence from Spain. **2 November**, *Día de los Muertos* (All Souls' Day), most businesses close after 1200. **7 and 8 December**, *La Purísima* (celebration of the Immaculate Conception of Virgin Mary), most businesses close at 1200 on 7 December and don't reopen until 9 December. **24 and 25 December**, most businesses close for *Christmas* at 1200 on 24 December and reopen on 26 December, although some stay closed from 23 December-2 January. **31 December**, *New Year's Eve*, most businesses close at 1200.

Sport and special interest travel

Despite tremendous potential, Nicaragua has little to offer in the way of organized special interest travel. No companies can offer the equipment, training or supervision facilities necessary for sports like windsurfing, diving and whitewater rafting, although some tour operators can organize excursions for trekking, surfing and fishing (see page 74). For the experienced adventure traveller who wants to explore and does not need a lot of infrastructure this is truly a blessing. Some activities highlighted below do have precedent and are not new to the country, but much ground-breaking "I did it first" activity is still possible in Nicaragua.

Archaeology & architecture
Although the archaeology is not as inspiring as the Mayan temples further north, Nicaragua's pre-Columbian history is fascinating. Nicaragua was at the centre of a trading block that stretched from Peru to Mexico and was home to several interesting cultures such as the Nicaraguas, Chorotegas, Maribios and Miskitos. Around the country, museums display artefacts that have been discovered in each region; the best are at the **National Museum** in Managua and the **San Francisco Convent** in Granada. In Lake Nicaragua, there are some interesting remains on the islands of **Zapatera** and **Ometepe**, where you can see some large basalt statues. Petroglyphs are also present on many islands in Lake Nicaragua as well as numerous sites around the mainland. For tour operators offering archaeological programmes see page 74.

Colonial-era architecture is best in León and Granada and there are some fine examples in small villages all around the countryside. The country's only UNESCO World Heritage Site, **León Viejo**, has the partially excavated ruins of a colonial town.

Bird-watching
According to the latest official count Nicaragua is home to just under 700 species of bird, including boat-billed flycatcher, collared aracari, black-headed trogan, wood stork, limpkin, roseate spoonbill, kingfisher, great white egret and orprey. In addition to this diversity, the sheer number of birds in Nicaragua is amazing. The **Indio-Maíz Biological Reserve** in Río San Juan area has primary rainforest and river habitats. The **Los Guatuzos Wildlife Reserve** has gallery and rainforest as well as ample wetlands. The **Solentiname Archipelago** has two islands that are nesting sites. In the northern

mountains of **Jinotega** the cloud forest is home to many prize birding species, some of which can also be found in the cloud forest reserves on the **Mombacho** and **Maderas** volcanoes in the Pacific Basin. For tropical dry forest the **Chocoyero Reserve** just outside the capital offers a chance to see many interesting species. For tour operators offering bird-watching trips, see page 74.

Nicaragua offers little in the way of serious climbing and most climbs are non-technical in nature. There are some places where the use of climbing gear is an advantage, but it will have to be your own as none exists in Nicaragua. There are no climbing outfitters or stores here. Although the maximum elevation of the Pacific volcanoes is just under 1,700 m, the climbs are not all easy. Most start just above sea level, so the actual elevation tackled is more than it initially seems. What's more, the steep grade of the cones, difficult footing conditions with sharp rocks, sand and loose terrain, combined with serious heat, make some of the ascents a good physical if non-technical challenge. From north to south there are several interesting cones that present good, somewhat challenging climbs, depending on your condition. These are described in the appropriate chapters or, for a run down, see page 39. Climbing **San Cristóbal**, the country's highest, is for the very fit and somewhat brave due to loose footing, steep ascents and regular eruptions. Further south is the little **Cerro Negro** which, although easy climbing, is through deep sand that gives a good leg burn. This little cone is the most violent of the Nicaraguan volcanoes and if you are on it when it erupts it'll all be over. **Concepción** and **Maderas** on the island of Ometepe can both be climbed. Concepción is active and a steep windy climb once above tree level. Maderas is a muddy slog in virgin cloud forest with the serenade of howler monkey screams and parrot songs. For companies offering climbing tours, see page 74.

Diving is of the true adventure variety, with no dive centres or dive shops anywhere in the country and the available air of questionable quality. The conditions for diving around **Pearl Cays**, off the coast of Bluefields in the Caribbean, are reported to be good, if difficult to access. Diving for lobster is very common in the Caribbean and the locals have gear, but much of it looks like it's come from a Second World War garage sale, and deaths are not uncommon amongst the local divers.

Nicaragua is a fisherman's paradise, with its rivers, lakes and seas. Deep-sea fishing can be arranged in San Juan del Sur or Corinto in the Pacific and bone fishing is possible on the Corn Islands. Lake Nicaragua is great for bass and perch fishing, not to mention the chance (though small) to hook one of the world's only lake sharks. The Island of Zapatera and its archipelago are home to Central America's biggest annual freshwater tournament. In Pearl Lagoon on the Caribbean side as well as on the Río San Juan tarpon and snook fishing is very good. See page 74 for tour operators who offer lake and river fishing excursions.

There are some very good opportunities for snorkelling in Nicaragua. Bring your own gear, though it can be rented on the Corn Island. The **Pearl Cays** and **Corn Islands** are great places for snorkelling. Little Corn, the smaller of the two islands, was spared much of the hurricane damage that Big Corn suffered during the 1980s and 90s and it reefs are teaming with life and very accessible. Much has yet to be explored in this area; all you need is some gear, a sense of adventure and a rented motor boat. Most Nicaraguan tour operators (see page 74) offer excursions to Corn Islands, while trips to Pearl Cays can be arranged in Bluefields or Pearl Lagoon.

Nicaragua's Pacific Coast is home to some beautiful breaks that are empty almost any day of the week. Most surfing is done along the coast of Rivas, using San Juan del Sur as

Climbing

Diving

Fishing

Snorkelling

Surfing

Essentials

a jumping-off point to reaches breaks to the north and south. The country's biggest and most famous break is at Popoyo in northern Rivas. On big days Popoyo can be higher than 18 ft, and even when the rest of the Pacific looks like a lake it still has a 3-ft swell. It is possible to rent a board in San Juan del Sur, but in most cases you will need to bring everything with you, as even wax can be impossible to find at times. Most people who have surfed in Nicaragua have been amazed at the tube rides and point breaks that lie empty all year round. Surf programmes can be organized with tour operators in Managua (see page 74).

Trekking   Most of Nicaragua's Pacific Basin is great walking country. The trekker will need to speak some Spanish to get by, but once outside the city a whole world of beautiful landscapes and friendly people await the adventurer. Fences in Nicaragua are for animals, not people (with the exception of the walled-in homes of Managua's wealthy neighbourhoods) and you need not worry about trespassing or other problems. Respect the privacy of the people, but be friendly and they will almost always welcome you into their homes like a long lost friend. Local guides are useful and you should ask around each village to see who can take you and how far. Lodging will be in hammocks (see Camping page 29). Due to wild driving habits it is best to get off the roads as soon as possible and use the volcanoes as landmarks to arrive at desired destinations. It is possible to trek the **Maribios volcano range** in northwestern Nicaragua, starting at the extinct lake-filled crater of Volcán Cosigüina, which is the most westerly point of Nicaragua, and continuing to all 21 cones, five of which are active. The route passes through many ranches and farms, where you can ask for directions if you need to.

Another great place for trekking is the **Island of Ometepe** with its breathtaking beauty, friendly people and many dirt trails. Here it would be quite difficult to get lost with the two cones and lake as reference points. Local guides are available at the hotels in the two main villages if you intend to do any climbing.

NB Despite the beauty of Nicaragua's northern mountains, they are not recommended for trekking. The last of the land mines set by government and rebel forces during the conflicts of the 1980s are still being removed and, sadly, a small percentage of the mines (which were well mapped) were washed downstream by Hurricane Mitch in 1998. They are now being re-mapped to be detonated and removed, and the region along the border with Honduras (the last in Nicaragua to have land mines) should be free of all mines by 2004.

Spectator sports

Baseball   The national sport in Nicaragua with the first league games being organized over 100 years ago and a very hard-fought national championship for the first division and many minor divisions. Nicaraguans follow the major leagues in the United States with more fervour than many Americans. The regular season begins in November and runs until the championships in February. Games are played all over the country during the dry season on Sundays in stadiums that are in themselves a cultural experience. Nicaragua has put several players into the North American professional league and usually finishes in the top five of the world championships.

Basketball   Basketball is very popular in the parks and streets of Managua. There is no league of note to watch, but the possibility to join in a game always exists in Managua, particularly on the park courts located on Avenida Bolívar, across from the parliament building.

Boxing   Another big passion for Nicaraguans, with four world champions in the lighter categories to be proud of. Though most fights of importance take place outside Nicaragua, it may be possible to watch low-level Nicaraguan fights as well as quality boxers in

Fear in the afternoon – the Nicaraguan bullfight

The small 20x20-m bullring, surrounded by splintering wood fencing, was lined with people waiting under an infernal sun for the bulls to arrive: ground level was packed with children; mid-level was all men; and, straddling the top of the fence, a mixture of young men and women. I too was waiting, in the bar, or at least what passes for a bar in the small settlement known as La Orilla (the edge), an isolated row of rural homes at the base of the massive Mombacho Volcano. I had come to photograph the patron saint festival of Nandiame, a cowboy town along the Pan-American Highway south of Granada. Their festival is for Santa Ana, the mother of the Virgin Mary, abuelita (granny) of Jesus.

Part of the tradition is a noisy and chaotic pilgrimage to La Orilla. Male dancers dressed in psychedelic costumes accompany the long procession, with a life-size image of Santa Ana in tow. The 40 or so dancers spin and hop in a spectacular, punk-like dance to a traditional chichero band (brass and drum). They are accompanied by devout pilgrims who, fulfilling a promise, make the journey of several kilometres entirely on their knees, in the hope of receiving Santa Ana's help.

The main event, as with many patron saint festivals, is the bullfight, which is really one man riding the back of the bull and other brave young men running around the ring tempting fate with red capes.

When the procession arrives, they put Santa Ana in a small chapel, and anyone who is not already lining the bullring looks for a spot to view the event. It was time to leave the bar. Like any documentary photographer, I had to get very close. No matter that a 26-year-old man had been killed the day before, hooked in the neck by a charging bull. I entered the ring.

The game is simple. The bull is brought inside the ring roped by a few mounted cowboys and tied to a bare tree in the centre. Someone mounts its back using a leather strap to hold on and the angry bull is released from the tree. The rider tries to stay on top and a few others show the animal some red capes for as long as they dare, before cutting sharply out of its path. Uninspired, the first two bulls just wanted to go back to pasture; they ran a bit and then looked for shade. The third bull wanted blood. Now I had my subject. The beast was frothing at the mouth and running wildly, sending cowboys up high on the fencing around the ring. I was also running wildly - to get into the bull's path. Finally I found the set-up. I waited behind two outstretched red capes, crouching in the dirt to get the best angle. In a traditional bullfight, men on horses wound the bull. Then others come into the ring to tire the beast. Finally, when the famous hero steps into the ring, to tease it a bit and kill it, the bull is bleeding and damaged, slowed. In a Nicaraguan bullfight the bull is not killed, nor injured, nor slowed, just completely pissed off. The bull picked up a good head of steam and charged towards the outstretched capes. The two capes parted, as the young men holding them dived out of the bull's path. That was the perfect shot, framed low, with the bull coming into the lens and the bullfighters exiting the frame left and right. Bravo!

Now I was left with a small dilemma. I was in a deep crouch, with a snorting, bloodthirsty bull coming at me full speed. I had got close, too close. By the time I was up on my feet the bull was nearly upon me. I did what anyone else would do. I ran like hell. The massive crowd grew silent, holding their breath. After six or seven desperate running strides with the bull's hot breath on my lower back, I cut hard left, and the beast's horn passed within millimetres of my left buttock. The crowd let out its breath at once, erupting in a collective "Ooooaaaahhhh!!!" followed by hysterical laughter. The guys in the ring thought it was pretty funny too, patting me on the back, with laughter all around. For me it looked like a perfect time to go back to the bar.

Essentials

training at the Alexis Argüello gymnasium in Managua (Barrio San José Oriental, de la Clínica Santa María, 2 c al sur, 1 c arriba).

Bullfighting/ riding Another aspect of the patron saint festivals is the bullring. The 'fighting' that goes on inside (see box page 41, is a strange hybrid of bullfighting and bull rodeo. The bulls are not injured, just made very angry by being mounted and then having some young men who show them capes and then run off before (in most cases) being impaled. After the bull gets too tired, a fresh one is brought in, mounted and shown more capes and running targets. Occasionally there are mortal injuries for the young men.

Cock fighting Cock fights are legal and take place every Sunday all over the country. The biggest time for the fights (*pelea de gallo*) are during the patron saint festival of each town. To find the fight rings you will need to ask around as they do not have signs. The fight ring in Estelí is one of the most serious in the country, with bets of over US$3,000 being waged.

Football Nicaraguan *futból* is among the poorest and least developed in Latin America. The passion for baseball is mainly to blame. There are several fairly unprofessional leagues; the most notable teams in the country come from the central plateau and coastal areas, though the Nicaraguan national team is always the weakest in Central America. Games can be watched on Sundays in several decent stadiums such as Estelí and Diriamba.

Motocross Very popular with those that can afford it. There are two national championships, one for natural terrain and another for stadium motocross. Nicaraguan riders are good, but are usually beaten by other Central American riders who compete in the international races. If you have your own dirt bike, there is a small practice track located in the touristic centre of Granada's lakefront. At the moment dirt bikes are not available for rent, although there are four-wheel ATC rentals at some beaches.

Health

Staying healthy in Latin America is straightforward. With the following advice and precautions you should keep as healthy as you do at home. Most visitors return home having experienced no problems at all beyond an upset stomach. However, the health risks in Latin America, especially in the lowland tropical areas, are different from those encountered in Europe or the USA. The level of risk also depends on how you travel, and where. Clearly, there are differences between the various countries of Latin America and between the risks for the business traveller staying in international-class hotels in large cities, the backpacker trekking from country to country and the tourist heading for the beach. There are no hard and fast rules to follow: you will often have to make your own judgement on the healthiness or otherwise of your surroundings. There are English (or other foreign language) speaking doctors in most major cities who have particular experience in dealing with locally occurring diseases. Your embassy representative will often be able to give you the name of reputable local doctors and most of the better hotels have a doctor on standby. If you do fall ill and cannot find a recommended doctor, try the outpatient department of a hospital – private hospitals are usually less crowded and offer a more acceptable standard of care to foreigners. It is worth remembering that, apart from mosquitoes, the most dangerous creatures are men, be they bandits or behind steering wheels. Think carefully about violent confrontations and wear a seat belt if you are lucky enough to have one available to you.

Take out medical insurance. Make sure it covers all eventualities especially evacuation to your home country by a medically equipped plane. Before leaving, have a dental check up, obtain a spare glasses prescription, a spare oral contraceptive prescription (or enough pills to last) and, if you suffer from a chronic illness (such as diabetes, high blood pressure, ear or sinus troubles, cardio-pulmonary disease or nervous disorder), make an appointment with your doctor. Ask for a letter explaining the details of your condition and have it translated into Spanish. Check the current practice in countries you are visiting for malaria prophylaxis (prevention). If you are on regular medication, make sure you have enough to cover the period of your travel.

Before travelling
Visit the Medical Advisory Services for Travellers Abroad website www.masta.org

More preparation is probably necessary for babies and children than for an adult and perhaps a little more care should be taken when travelling to remote areas where health services are primitive. This is because children can become more rapidly ill than adults (although, on the other hand, they often recover more quickly). Diarrhoea and vomiting are the most common problems, so take the usual precautions, but more intensively. Breastfeeding is best and most convenient for babies, but powdered milk is generally available and so are baby foods in most countries. Papaya, bananas and avocados are all nutritious and can be cleanly prepared by peeling. The treatment of diarrhoea is the same as it is for adults, except that it should start earlier and be continued with more persistence. Children get dehydrated very quickly in hot countries and can become drowsy and uncooperative unless cajoled to drink water or juice plus salts. Upper respiratory tract infections, such as colds and catarrh, and middle ear infections are also common and if your child suffers from these normally, take some antibiotics against the possibility. Outer ear infections after swimming are also common and antibiotic ear drops will help. Wet wipes are always useful and sometimes difficult to find in Latin America, as, in some places, are disposable nappies.

Children

Essentials

There is very little control on the sale of drugs and medicines in Latin America. You may be able to buy any and every drug in pharmacies without a prescription. Be wary of this because pharmacists can be poorly trained and might sell you drugs that are unsuitable, dangerous or old. Many drugs and medicines are manufactured under licence from American or European companies, so the trade names may be familiar to you. This means you do not have to carry a whole chest of medicines with you, but remember that the shelf life of some items, especially vaccines and antibiotics, is markedly reduced in hot conditions. Buy your supplies at the better outlets where there are more refrigerators, even though they are more expensive, and check the expiry date of all preparations you buy. Immigration officials occasionally confiscate scheduled drugs (Lomotil is an example) if they are not accompanied by a doctor's prescription. Self-medication may be forced on you by circumstances so the information given here contains the names of drugs and medicines which you may find useful in an emergency or in out-of-the-way places.

Medicines & what to take

Sunglasses: a type designed for intense sunlight; **earplugs**: for sleeping on aeroplanes and in noisy hotels; **suntan cream**: with a high protection factor; **insect repellent** containing DET for preference; **mosquito net**: lightweight, permethrin-impregnated; **tablets**: for travel sickness; **water sterilizing tablets**; **antimalarial tablets**; **anti-infective ointment**: for example, Cetrimide; **dusting powder** for feet, etc containing fungicide; **antacid tablets**: for indigestion; **sachets of rehydration salts plus anti-diarrhoea preparations**; **painkillers**: such as paracetamol or aspirin; **antibiotics**: for diarrhoea, etc. **First-aid kit**: Small pack containing a few sterile syringes and needles and disposable gloves. The risk of catching hepatitis, etc, from a dirty needle used for injection is now negligible in Latin America, but you may feel safer carrying your own supplies – available from camping shops and at airports.

Medical kit checklist

Vaccination & immunization Smallpox vaccination is no longer required anywhere in the world and cholera vaccination is no longer recognized as necessary or effective for international travel by the World Health Organization. Nevertheless, some immigration officials are still demanding proof of vaccination against cholera in Latin America, and in some countries outside Latin America, following the outbreak of the disease that originated in Peru in 1990-91 and subsequently affected most surrounding countries. Although it is very unlikely to affect visitors to Latin America, the cholera epidemic continues to make its greatest impact in poor areas where water supplies are polluted and food hygiene practices are insanitary.

Vaccination against the following diseases is recommended:

Yellow fever This is a live vaccination not to be given to children under nine months or persons allergic to eggs. Immunity lasts for 10 years, an International Certificate of Yellow Fever Vaccination will be given and should be kept because it is sometimes asked for. Yellow fever is very rare in Latin America, but the vaccination is practically without side effects and almost totally protective.

Typhoid A number of new vaccines against this condition are now available; the older TAB and monovalent typhoid vaccines are being phased out. The newer versions, for example Typhim Vi, cause fewer side effects, but are more expensive. For those who do not like injections, there are now oral vaccines.

Poliomyelitis Despite its decline in the world this remains a serious disease if caught, but is easy to protect against. There are live oral vaccines and in some countries injected vaccines. Whichever one you choose it is a good idea to have a booster every 3-5 years if visiting developing countries regularly.

Tetanus and other routine vaccinations One dose should be given, with a booster at six weeks and another at six months, and 10 yearly boosters thereafter are recommended. Children should already be properly protected against diphtheria, poliomyelitis and pertussis (whooping cough), measles and HIB, all of which can be more serious infections in Latin America than at home. Measles, mumps and rubella vaccine is routinely given to children throughout the world, but those teenage girls who have not had rubella (German measles) should be tested and vaccinated. Hepatitis B vaccination for babies is now routine in some countries. Consult your doctor for advice on tuberculosis inoculation: the disease is still widespread in Latin America.

Infectious hepatitis This is less of a problem for travellers than it used to be because of the development of two extremely effective vaccines against the A and B form of the disease. It remains common, however, in Latin America. A combined hepatitis A and B vaccine is now licensed and has been available since 1997 – one jab covers both diseases.

Other vaccinations These might be considered in the case of epidemics, for example meningitis. There is an effective vaccination against rabies, which should be considered by all travellers, especially those going through remote areas or if there is a particular occupational risk, for example for zoologists or veterinarians.

Further information Further information on health risks abroad, vaccinations, etc, may be available from a local travel clinic. If you wish to take specific drugs with you such as antibiotics these are best prescribed by your own doctor. Be aware, however, that not all doctors are experts on the health problems of remote countries. More detailed or more up-to-date information than local doctors can provide is available from various sources. In the UK there are hospital departments specializing in tropical diseases in London, Liverpool, Birmingham and Glasgow and the Malaria Reference Laboratory at the London School of Hygiene and Tropical Medicine provides advice about malaria, T0891-600350. In the USA the local Public Health Services can give such information and information is available centrally from the Centre for Disease Control, in Atlanta, T404-332 4559, www.cdc.gov In Canada contact IAMAT, 40 Regal Road, Guelph, Ontario, N1K 1B5, www.sentex.net/~iamat/index.html There are in addition computerized databases which can be accessed for destination-specific, up-to-the-minute information. In the UK, try MASTA (Medical Advisory Service to Travellers Abroad), T0906-822 4100 – calls cost 60p per minute. The Scottish Centre for Infection and Environmental Health has an online database providing information for travellers at www.fitfortravel.scot.nhs.uk Detailed information on medical problems overseas can be obtained from *Travellers' Health, How to Stay Healthy Abroad* (Oxford University Press 1992 £7.99), edited by Dr Richard Dawood. We strongly recommend the new, revised and updated edition (publication imminent), especially to the intrepid traveller heading for the more out-of-the-way places. General advice is also available in the UK in *Health Information for Overseas Travel* (Department of Health) available from HMSO, and *International Travel and Health* (WHO). Handbooks on First Aid are produced by the British and American Red Cross and by St John's Ambulance (UK).

For most travellers a trip to Latin America means a long air flight. If this crosses time **On the way** zones then jetlag can be a problem. The main symptoms are tiredness and sleepiness at inconvenient times and, conversely, a tendency to wake up in the middle of the night feeling like you want your breakfast. Most find that the problem is worse when flying in an easterly direction. The best way to get over jetlag is to try to force yourself into the new time zone as strictly as possible. This may involve, on a westward flight, trying to stay awake until your normal bedtime and, on an eastward flight, forgetting that you have lost some sleep on the way out and going to bed relatively early but near your normal time on the evening after you arrive. The symptoms of jetlag may be helped by keeping up your fluid intake on the journey, but not with alcohol. The hormone melatonin seems to reduce the symptoms of jetlag but is not presently licensed in most of Europe, although it can be obtained from health food stores in the USA. On long-haul flights it is also important to stretch your legs at least every hour to prevent slowing of the circulation and the possible development of blood clots. Drinking plenty of non-alcoholic fluids also helps. If travelling by boat sea sickness can be a problem – this is dealt with in the usual way by taking anti motion-sickness pills.

Staying healthy on arrival

The thought of catching a stomach bug worries visitors to Latin America but there have **Intestinal** been great improvements in food hygiene and most such infections are preventable. **upsets** Travellers' diarrhoea and vomiting is due, most of the time, to food poisoning, usually passed on by the unsanitary habits of food handlers. As a general rule the cleaner your surroundings and the smarter the restaurant, the less likely you are to suffer.

Foods to avoid: uncooked, undercooked, partially cooked or reheated meat, fish, eggs, raw vegetables and salads, especially when they have been left out and exposed to flies. Stick to fresh food that has been cooked from raw just before eating and make sure you peel fruit yourself. Wash and dry your hands before eating – disposable wet-wipe tissues or portable alcohol-based hand-wash bottles are useful for this.

Shellfish eaten raw are risky and at certain times of the year some fish and shellfish concentrate toxins from their environment and cause various kinds of food poisoning. The local authorities notify the public not to eat these foods. Do not ignore the warning. Pasteurized or sterilized heat treated milk (UHT) is becoming more widely available in Latin America as is pasteurized cheese. On the whole matured or processed cheeses are safer than the fresh varieties. Fresh unpasteurized milk can be a source of food poisoning germs, tuberculosis and brucellosis. This applies equally to ice-cream, yoghurt and cheese made from unpasteurized milk, so avoid these home-made products – the factory made ones are probably safer.

Tap water is rarely safe outside the major cities, especially in the rainy season. Stream water, if you are in the countryside, is often contaminated by communities living surprisingly high up in the mountains. Filtered or bottled water is usually available and safe, although you must make sure that somebody is not filling bottles from the tap and hammering on a new crown cap. If your hotel has a central hot water supply, this water is safe to drink after cooling. Ice for drinks should be made from boiled water, but it rarely is, so stand your glass on the ice cubes, rather than putting them in the drink. The better hotels have water-purifying systems.

Travellers' diarrhoea
This is usually caused by eating food that has been contaminated by germs or eating with dirty hands. Drinking water is rarely the culprit. Sea water or river water is more likely to be contaminated by sewage and so swimming in such dilute effluent can also be a cause.

Infection with various organisms can give rise to travellers' diarrhoea. They may be viruses, bacteria (such as *Escherichia coli*, probably the most common cause worldwide), protozoa (such as Amoeba and Giardia), salmonella and cholera. The diarrhoea may come on suddenly or rather slowly. It may be accompanied by vomiting or by severe abdominal pain; the passage of blood or mucus is a sign of dysentery.

Diagnosis & treatment
If you can time the onset of the diarrhoea to the minute ('acute') then it is probably due to a virus or a bacterium and/or the onset of dysentery. The treatment, in addition to rehydration, is an antibiotic such as ciprofloxacin 500 mg every 12 hours; the drug is now widely available and there are many similar ones. If the diarrhoea comes on slowly or intermittently ('sub-acute') then it is more likely to be protozoal, that is caused by an amoeba or Giardia. Antibiotics such as ciprofloxacin will have little effect. These cases are best treated by a doctor as is any outbreak of diarrhoea continuing for more than three days. Sometimes blood is passed in amoebic dysentery and for this you should certainly seek medical help. If this is not available then the best treatment is probably tinidazole (Fasigyn) one tablet four times a day for three days. If there are severe stomach cramps, loperamide (Imodium) and diphenoxylate with atropine (Lomotil) may help but are not very useful in the management of acute diarrhoea. They should not be given to children. Any kind of diarrhoea, whether or not accompanied by vomiting, responds well to the replacement of water and salts, taken as frequent sips of some kind of rehydration solution. Proprietary preparations consist of sachets of powder that you dissolve in boiled water, or you can make your own by adding half a teaspoonful of salt (3½ g) and four tablespoonsful of sugar (40 g) to a litre of boiled water.

Thus, the linchpins of treatment for diarrhoea are rest, fluid and salt replacement, antibiotics such as ciprofloxacin for the bacterial types and special diagnostic tests and medical treatment for the amoeba and giardia infections. Salmonella infections and cholera, although rare, can be devastating diseases and it would be wise to get to a hospital as soon as possible if these are suspected. Fasting, peculiar diets and the consumption of large quantities of yoghurt have not been found useful in calming travellers' diarrhoea or in rehabilitating inflamed bowels. Oral rehydration has on the other hand, especially in children, been a life saving technique and should always be practised, whatever other treatment you use. As there is some evidence that alcohol and milk might prolong diarrhoea they should be avoided during and immediately after an attack. So should chillies. Diarrhoea occurring day after day for long periods of time (chronic diarrhoea) is notoriously resistant to amateur attempts at treatment and again warrants proper diagnostic tests (most towns with reasonable sized hospitals have laboratories for stool samples). There are ways of preventing travellers' diarrhoea for short periods of time by taking antibiotics, but this is not a foolproof technique and should not be used other than in exceptional circumstances. Doxycycline is possibly the best drug. Some preventatives such as Enterovioform can have serious side effects if taken for long periods.

Constipation can also be a problem, probably induced by dietary change, inadequate fluid intake in hot places and long bus journeys. Simple laxatives are useful in the short term and bulky foods such as maize, beans and plenty of fruit are also useful.

There are a number of ways of purifying water in order to make it safe to drink. Dirty **Water** water should first be strained through a filter bag available from (camping shops) and **purification** then boiled or treated. Bringing water to a rolling boil at sea level is sufficient to make the water safe for drinking, but at higher altitudes you have to boil the water for a few minutes longer to ensure that all the microbes are killed.

Sterilizing methods include proprietary preparations containing chlorine (for example Puritabs) or iodine (for example Pota Aqua) compounds. Chlorine compounds generally do not kill protozoa (for example Giardia). There are a number of water filters now on the market available in personal and expedition size. They work either on mechanical or chemical principles, or may use both. Make sure you take the spare parts or spare chemicals with you and do not believe everything the manufacturers say.

Insects are mostly more of a nuisance than a serious hazard and, with a bit of prepara- **Insects** tion, you can prevent being bitten entirely. Some, such as mosquitoes, are of course carriers of potentially serious diseases so it is sensible to avoid their attentions. Sleep off the ground and use an insecticide-impregnated mosquito net or some kind of insecticide. Preparations containing pyrethrum or synthetic pyrethroids are safe. They are available as aerosols or pumps and the best way to use these is to spray the room thoroughly in all areas (follow the instructions rather than the insects) and then shut the door for a while, re-entering when the smell has dispersed. Mosquito coils release insecticide as they burn slowly. They are widely available and useful out of doors. Tablets of insecticide which are placed on a heated mat plugged into a wall socket are probably the most effective. They fill the room with insecticidal fumes in the same way as aerosols or coils. You can also use insect repellents, most of which are effective against a wide range of pests. The most common and effective is diethyl metatoluamide (DET). DET liquid is best for arms and face (take care around eyes and with spectacles – DET dissolves plastic). Aerosol spray is good for clothes and ankles and liquid DET can be dissolved in water and used to impregnate cotton clothes and mosquito nets. Some repellents now contain DET and the insecticide permethrin. Impregnated wrist and ankle bands can also be useful.

If you are bitten or stung, itching may be relieved by cool baths, antihistamine tablets (care with alcohol or driving) or mild corticosteroid creams, for example hydrocortisone (great care should be exercised: never use if there is any hint of infection). Careful scratching of all your bites once a day can be surprisingly effective. Calamine lotion and cream have limited effectiveness and antihistamine creams are not generally recommended – they can cause allergies themselves. Bites that become infected should be treated with a local antiseptic or antibiotic cream such as Cetrimide, as should any infected sores or scratches.

When living rough, infestations of the skin with body lice (crabs) and scabies happen easily. Use whatever local commercial preparation is recommended for lice and scabies. Crotamiton cream (Eurax) alleviates itching and also kills a number of skin parasites. Malathion lotion 5% (Prioderm) kills lice effectively, but avoid the use of the toxic agricultural preparation of malathion, more often used to commit suicide.

Ticks Ticks usually attach themselves to the lower parts of the body, often while walking in areas where cattle have grazed. They take a while to attach themselves strongly, but swell up as they start to suck blood. The important thing is to remove them gently, so that they do not leave their head parts in your skin because this can cause infections or an allergic reaction some days later. Do not use petrol, vaseline, lighted cigarettes, etc, to remove the tick, but, with a pair of tweezers, remove the beast gently by gripping it at the attached (head) end and rock it out in very much the same way that a tooth is extracted. Certain tropical flies which lay their eggs under the skin of sheep and cattle also occasionally do the same thing to humans with the unpleasant result that a maggot grows under the skin and pops up as a boil or pimple. The best way to remove these is to cover the boil with oil, vaseline or nail varnish so as to stop the maggot breathing, then to squeeze it out gently the next day.

Other animal bites & stings It is a very rare event indeed for travellers, but if you are unlucky (or careless) enough to be bitten by a venomous snake, spider, scorpion or sea creature, try to identify the creature, without putting yourself in further danger. Snake bites in particular are very frightening, but in fact rarely poisonous – even venomous snakes bite without injecting venom. What you might expect if bitten are: fright, swelling, pain and bruising around the bite and soreness of the regional lymph glands, perhaps nausea, vomiting and a fever. The following would be symptoms of serious poisoning: numbness and tingling of the face, muscular spasms, convulsions, shortness of breath or a failure of the blood to clot, causing generalized bleeding. Victims should be taken to a hospital or a doctor without delay. Commercial snake bite and scorpion kits are available, but are usually only useful for the specific types of snake or scorpion. Most serum has to be given intravenously so it is not much good equipping yourself with it unless you are used to making injections into veins. It is best to rely on local practice in these cases, because the particular creatures will be known about locally and appropriate treatment can be given.

Treatment of snake bite Reassure and comfort the victim frequently. Immobilize the limb by a bandage or a splint or by getting the person to lie still. Do not slash the bite area and try to suck out the poison – this sort of heroism does more harm than good. If you know how to use a tourniquet in these circumstances, you will not need this advice. If you are not experienced, do not apply a tourniquet.

Precautions Avoid walking in snake territory in bare feet or sandals – wear proper shoes or boots. If you encounter a snake stay put until it slithers away, and do not investigate a wounded snake. Spiders and scorpions may be found in the more basic hotels. If bitten or stung, rest, take plenty of fluids and call a doctor. The best precaution is to keep beds away from the walls, look inside your shoes and under the toilet seat and soap every morning, and shake out wet swimsuits.

Marine bites & stings Certain tropical sea fish when trodden upon inject venom into bathers' feet. This can be exceptionally painful. Wear plastic shoes when you go bathing if such creatures are reported. The pain can be relieved by immersing the foot in extremely hot water for as long as the pain persists.

Sunburn The burning power of the tropical sun, especially at high altitude, is phenomenal. Always wear a wide brimmed hat and use some form of suncream or lotion on untanned skin. Normal temperate zone suntan lotions (protection factor up to seven) are not much good; you need to use the types designed specifically for the tropics or for mountaineers or skiers, with protection factors of 15 or above. These are often not available in Latin America. Glare from the sun can cause conjunctivitis, so wear sunglasses especially on tropical beaches, where high protection factor sunscreen should also be used.

In Latin America AIDS – called SIDA – is increasing and is not wholly confined to the well-known high-risk sections of the population (homosexual men, intravenous drug abusers and children of infected mothers). Heterosexual transmission is now the dominant mode and so the main risk to travellers is from casual sex. Of 33,600,000 adults and children affected by HIV worldwide, an estimated 1,700,000 live in Latin America and the Caribbean. The same precautions should be taken as with any sexually transmitted disease. The AIDS virus (HIV) can be passed by unsterilized needles which have been previously used to inject an HIV-positive patient, but the risk of this is negligible. It would, however, be sensible to check that needles have been properly sterilized or disposable needles have been used. If you wish to take your own disposable needles, be prepared to explain what they are for. The risk of receiving a blood transfusion with blood infected with HIV is greater than from dirty needles because of the amount of fluid exchanged. Supplies of blood for transfusion should now be screened for HIV in all reputable hospitals, so again the risk is very small indeed. Catching the AIDS virus does not always produce an illness in itself (although it may do). The only way to be sure if you feel you have been put at risk is to have a blood test for HIV antibodies on your return to a place where there are reliable laboratory facilities. The test does not become positive for some weeks. `AIDS`

In Central America malaria is more common in jungle zones, and is now on the increase again. Mosquitoes do not thrive above 2,500 m, so you are safe at altitude. There are different varieties of malaria, and some are resistant to the normal drugs. Make local enquiries if you intend to visit possibly infected zones and use a prophylactic regime. Start taking the tablets a few days before exposure and continue to take them for six weeks after leaving the malarial zone. Remember to give the drugs to babies and children also. Opinion varies on the precise drugs and dosage to be used for protection. All the drugs may have some side effects and it is important to balance the risk of catching the disease against the (albeit rare) problems they may cause. The increasing complexity of the subject is such that, as the malarial parasite becomes immune to the new generation of drugs, it has made concentration on the physical prevention of being bitten by mosquitoes more important. This involves the use of long-sleeved shirts or blouses and long trousers, repellents and nets. Clothes are now available impregnated with the insecticide permethrin or deltamethrin or it is possible to impregnate the clothes yourself. Wide meshed nets impregnated with permethrin are also available, are lighter to carry and less claustrophobic to sleep under. `Malaria`

Prophylaxis and treatment If your itinerary takes you into a malarial area, seek expert advice before you go on a suitable prophylactic regime. This is especially true for pregnant women who are particularly prone to catch malaria. You can still catch the disease even when sticking to a proper regime, although it is unlikely. If you do develop symptoms (high fever, shivering, headache, sometimes diarrhoea), seek medical advice immediately. If this is not possible and there is a great likelihood of malaria, the treatments are as follows.

If the local strain is likely to be sensitive to it, then the treatment is Chloroquine, a single dose of four tablets (600 mg) followed by two tablets (300 mg) in six hours and 300 mg each day following.

If it is falciparum malaria or the type is in doubt, take local advice. Various combinations of drugs are being used such as Quinine, Tetracycline or Halofantrine. If falciparum malaria is definitely diagnosed, it is wise to get to a good hospital as treatment can be complex and the illness very serious.

The main symptoms are pains in the stomach, lack of appetite, lassitude and yellowness of the eyes and skin. Medically speaking there are two main types. The less serious, but more common is hepatitis A, against which the best protection is the careful preparation `Infectious hepatitis (jaundice)` of food, the avoidance of contaminated drinking water and scrupulous attention to toilet hygiene. The other, more serious, version is hepatitis B, which is acquired usually as a sexually transmitted disease or by blood transfusion. It is less commonly transmitted by injections with unclean needles and possibly by insect bites. The symptoms are the same as for hepatitis A. The incubation period is much longer (up to six months compared with six weeks) and there are more likely to be complications.

Hepatitis A can be protected against with gamma globulin. It should be obtained from a reputable source and is certainly useful for travellers who intend to live rough. You should have a shot before leaving and have it repeated every six months. The dose of gamma globulin depends on the concentration of the particular preparation used, so the manufacturer's advice should be taken. The injection should be given as close as possible to your departure and, as the dose depends on the time you are likely to spend in potentially affected areas, the manufacturer's instructions should be followed. Gamma globulin has really been superseded now by a proper vaccination against hepatitis A (Havrix), which gives immunity lasting up to 10 years. After that boosters are required. Havrix monodose is now widely available, as is junior Havrix. The vaccination has negligible side effects and is extremely effective. A gamma globulin injection can be a bit painful, but it is cheaper than Havrix and may be more available in some places.

Hepatitis B can be effectively prevented by a specific vaccine (Engerix) – three shots over six months before travelling.

If you have had jaundice in the past it would be worthwhile having a blood test to see if you are immune to either of the two types of hepatitis, because this might avoid the discomfort and costs of vaccination or gamma globulin. There are other kinds of viral hepatitis (C, E, G etc), which are fairly similar to A and B, but vaccines are not available as yet.

Other afflictions   **Athlete's foot**   This and other fungal skin infections are best treated with Tolnaftate or Clotrimazole.

Chagas' disease (South American trypanosomiasis)   This is a chronic disease, very rarely caught by travellers and difficult to treat. It is transmitted by the simultaneous biting and excreting of the reduvid bug, also known as the vinchuca or Barbeiro. Somewhat resembling a small cockroach, this nocturnal bug lives in poor adobe houses with dirt floors often frequented by opossums. If you cannot avoid such accommodation, sleep off the floor with a candle lit, use a mosquito net, keep as much of your skin covered as possible, and use DET repellent or a spray insecticide. If you are bitten overnight (the bites are painless) do not scratch them, but wash thoroughly with soap and water.

Dengue fever   This is increasing worldwide, including in Nicaragua. It can be completely prevented by avoiding mosquito bites. No vaccine is available. Dengue is an unpleasant and painful disease, with symptoms of high temperature and body pains, but at least visitors are spared the more serious forms (haemorrhagic types), which are more of a problem for local people who have been exposed to the disease more than once. There is no specific treatment for dengue – just painkillers and rest.

Intestinal worms   These are common and the more serious ones, such as hookworm, can be contracted from walking barefoot on infested earth or beaches. Some cause an itchy rash on the feet 'cutaneous larva migrans'. Schistosomiasis (bilharzia) is also present in some lakes – take local advice before swimming in them.

Leishmaniasis   A parasitic disease carried by sandflies, which tend to bite at dawn and dusk, through all forested areas. It causes a persistent crusty sore or ulcer on the skin, sometimes followed by destructive lesions in the nose, mouth or throat (Espundia) and a nasal discharge. Protect against sandfly bites by wearing impregnated long trousers and long-sleeved shirt, and DET on exposed skin. Sleep under an impregnated bed net. Seek advice for any persistent skin lesion or nasal symptom. The treatment is daily injections for three weeks.

Leptospirosis   Various forms of leptospirosis occur throughout Latin America, transmitted by a bacterium that is excreted in rodent urine. Fresh water and moist soil harbour the organisms which enter the body through cuts and scratches. If you suffer from any form of prolonged fever consult a doctor.

Prickly heat   A very common intensely itchy rash is avoided by frequent washing and by wearing loose clothing. It is cured by allowing skin to dry off (through use of powder and spending two nights in an air-conditioned hotel!).

Rabies   Avoid dogs that are behaving strangely and cover your body with netting at night from the vampire bats, which also carry the disease. If you are bitten by a domestic or wild animal, do not leave things to chance: scrub the wound with soap and water and/or disinfectant, try to have the animal captured (within limits) or at least determine its ownership, where possible, and seek medical assistance at once. The course of treatment depends on whether you have already been satisfactorily vaccinated against rabies. If you have (this is worthwhile if you are spending lengths of time in developing countries) then some further doses of vaccine are all that is required. Human diploid vaccine is the best, but expensive: other, older kinds of vaccine, such as that derived from duck embryos, may be the only types available. These are effective, much cheaper and generally interchangeable with the human-derived types. If not already vaccinated then anti-rabies serum (immunoglobulin) may be required in addition. It is important to finish the course of treatment whether the animal survives or not.

Typhus   This can still occur and is carried by ticks. There is usually a reaction at the site of the bite and a fever. Seek medical advice.

Other tropical diseases and problems in jungle areas   These are usually transmitted by biting insects. They are often related to African diseases and were probably introduced by the slave trade. Onchocerciasis (river blindness) carried by blackflies is found in parts of Mexico. Leishmaniasis (Espundia) is carried by sandflies and causes a sore that will not heal or a severe nasal infection. Wearing long trousers and a long-sleeved shirt in infected areas protects against these flies. DET is also effective. Epidemics of meningitis occur from time to time – a vaccination is available. Be careful about swimming in piranha- or caribe-infested rivers. It is a good idea not to swim naked: the candiru fish can follow urine currents and become lodged in body orifices. Swimwear offers some protection.

Remember to take your antimalarial tablets for six weeks after leaving the malarial area. If **When you** you have had attacks of diarrhoea it is worth having a stool specimen tested in case you **return home** have picked up amoebas. If you have been living rough, blood tests may be worthwhile to detect worms and other parasites. If you have been exposed to bilharzia (schistosomiasis) by swimming in lakes, etc, check by means of a blood test when you get home, but leave it for six weeks because the test is slow to become positive. Report any untoward symptoms to your doctor, explaining exactly where you have been and, if you know, what the likelihood is of having contracted the disease to which you were exposed.

Essentials

Further reading

Nicaragua has given birth to a long list of great poets, some very fine novelists and an interminable list of political history books. Sadly most of the Nicaraguan works have not been translated into English. The fiction and poetry works below are examples of some that have been translated and a good indication that, with some searching, other works by the same authors can be found in translation, as well as some works that were written in English by foreign authors. **Gioconda Belli**, *The Inhabited Women* (translated by Kathleen March, Warner Books, 1994). One of Nicaragua's most famous writer/poets. Her work is always very sensual and this story is no exception. A yuppie turns revolutionary after being filled with native Indian spirits story. The hero joins an underground rebel group for a story based partially upon historic events, which works well, at least until its action-film ending. A very enjoyable read, with some beautiful and magical prose. **Sergio Ramírez**, *To Bury Our Fathers* (translated by Nick Caistor, Readers International, 1993). Nicaragua's finest living author recounts life in the Somoza García period of Nicaragua, from the viewpoint of exiled rebels in Guatemala. Sergio Ramírez paints a detailed picture of the Nicaraguan character and humour. Vice-President of Nicaragua during the Sandinista period, Ramírez is recognized as one of Latin America's finest writers and this one of his best-known works. Translations of other classic works, and his newest award-winning novels, can only be hoped for. **Rubén Darío**, *Selected Poems* (translated by Lysander Kemp, prologue by Octavio Paz, University of Texas, 1988). Darío is one of the great poets of the Spanish language, a founder of the modernist movement and Nicaragua's supreme national hero. This attractive collection of some of his best-known poems has the original Spanish and English translations on facing pages and an enlightening introduction by the great Mexican poet/essayist Octavio Paz. **Omar Cabezas**, *Fire from the Mountain* (translated by Kathleen Weaver, Crown Publishers, 1985). This very honest first-hand account of a revolutionary rebel in the making and later in action was dictated into a tape recorder and reads like a long tragic and often hilarious confession. If you can read the original Spanish, it's a study on Nicaraguan use of the language. A must-read for those who wish to get the feel of this time in Nicaraguan history and the irreverent Nicaraguan humour. **Salman Rushdie**, *The Jaguar Smile* (Penguin Books, 1988). A diary of sorts, this is a detailed and entertaining account of this famous writer's visit to Nicaragua during the volatile Sandinista years. Rushdie's attention to detail and powers of observation are a pleasure but, sadly, the book serves as an apology for the Sandinista government, while claiming objectivity. Taken with a pinch of salt, a very interesting read. **David Gullette**, *Gaspar, A Spanish Poet/Priest in the Nicaraguan Revolution* (Bilingual Press, 1993). A sentimental, but balanced look at the Spanish Jesuit rebel-priest who died in action during the Revolution. A great hero amongst the poor of Nicaragua's southern Pacific Coast during the 1970s, Gaspar was one of many unusual heroes the Nicaraguan Revolution produced. This thin volume includes many of his very compassionate poems about the plight of the Nicaraguan *campesino*, in the original Spanish with English translations, as well as a biographical sketch and some humorous accounts of early botched battles. **Thomas Belt**, *The Naturalist in Nicaragua* (University of Chicago, 1985). This reprint of 1874 classic is very enlightening in its observations of insect life and acute observations of 19th-century Nicaragua. Described by Charles Darwin at the time of its publication as 'the best of all natural history journals which have ever been published', this book by a mining engineer also sheds light on the mentality of a naturalist 125 years ago. In the text, amongst brilliant and sensitive analytical observation, Belt freely admits beating his pet monkey and shooting dozens of birds, and laments not bagging a giant jaguar encountered in the forest. **Mark Twain**, *Travels with Mr Brown* (Alfred A Knopf, 1940). Although his observations on Nicaragua make up a small part of this book, Twain's irrepressible humour and use of the language make this memoir a very fun read. Twain describes in detail the Nicaraguan inter-oceanic steamship route from San Francisco to New York, using the Río San Juan and Lake Nicaragua as a crossing from ocean to sea, which was so popular with gold-rushers at that time. This book is only available in its original edition. **Christopher Dickey**, *With the Contras* (Simon and Schuster, 1985). This is a mixture of journalism and lowbrow comedy, its theme the *Contra* insurgency and the US government's role in the war. Despite being flippant at times, the book manages to highlight many key characters in the conflict and exposes the difficulty of defining good and bad guys in real-life war dramas. **Donald C Hodges**, *Intellectual Foundations of the Nicaraguan Revolution* (University of Texas, 1986). An in-depth study of Nicaragua's 20th-century political players and the lead-up to the Revolution of 1978-79. A very good account of the Sandinista's namesake, the nationalist hero Augusto Sandino. Written with a rare combination of balance and eloquence, this book is a must for those who wish to understand 20th-century Nicaraguan politics. **Fredrick W Lange**, *The Archaeology of Pacific Nicaragua* (University of New Mexico, 1992). Dr Lange is one of the foremost experts on Nicaraguan archaeology. Though not meant as an introduction for the layman, this book is very interesting in its descriptions and observations about Nicaraguan archaeology in the extraordinarily ceramic-rich Pacific region. **Joseph Mulligan**, *The Nicaraguan Church and the Revolution* (Sheep and Ward, 1991). This subject deserves better treatment, for it is undoubtedly a fascinating one. Mulligan's book deals with liberation theology and its direct effect on the Nicaraguan Revolution and the local Catholic church. Unfortunately the book doubles as a platform for blindly defending everything that was Sandinista. Interesting, but difficult to take seriously amongst all the gushing. **Les W Field**, *The Grimace of Macho Ratón* (Duke University, 1999). A cultural anthropological look at Nicaragua's national play, *El Güegüence* and how it relates to Nicaraguan identity, in particular its effect on definitions of indigenous and *mestizo* people in Pacific Nicaragua. This curious, wandering work also focuses on Nicaragua's ceramic artisans as a model for understanding Nicaraguan social-behavioural traits and occasionally slips into being a travel diary.

Essentials (side tab)

Films

Under Fire, **Roger Spottiswoode** (1983, USA). Hollywood does the Nicaraguan Revolution. This film starring Nick Nolte and Gene Hackman is a hearty attempt at historical drama, with a lot of factual events being massaged to keep the necessary love story plot thumping along. Some interesting details in the film like authentic Nicaraguan beer and street signs of obscure villages are made all the more impressive by the sad fact that not one scene was shot in Nicaragua. The murder by the Somoza's army of a US journalist is factual, if twisted, and gives the movie a surprise element. *Walker*, **Alex Cox** (1987, USA). This obscure film was actually filmed in Nicaragua and deals with the infamous North American filibuster William Walker, perhaps the worst of many players in US interventions in Nicaragua. Impossible to find here in Nicaragua, I have yet to see it. Find it and let us know how it is. *Carla's Song*, **Ken Loach** (1996, Scotland). With big points for originality, this film ends up playing like a Sandinista party film. Aside from political axes being ground, there are some great elements of Nicaraguan life in the 1980s. Also featured is Nicaragua's unique use of the Spanish language (which at the film's opening in Managua had the audience in tears of laughter), along with many other fine details, which, for Nicaragua, have never appeared before or since on the silver screen. The obligatory love story is between a Glasgow bus driver and a Nicaraguan immigrant woman who lives off performing folkloric dancing in the streets for coins. The fact that a Nicaraguan woman who spoke English (and even understood the Scots) would be begging was particularly offensive to many women here, who used every possible skill to survive those years. In any case, the film is the best yet made using Nicaragua as an authentic stage for drama. *Pictures from a Revolution – A Memoir of the*

Nicaraguan Conflict, Susan Meiselas, Richard Roberts and Alfred Guzetti (1991, USA). In 1978 30-year-old Susan Meiselas was an inexperienced documentary photographer with a degree in education from Harvard. She had never covered a major political story. After just being admitted to the most prestigious photo agency in the world, Magnum, she read about the assassination of the *La Prensa* editor Pedro Joaquín Chamorro and soon found herself in Managua with no ability to speak Spanish and doubts about what she was even to photograph there. By the time she returned from shooting the Nicaraguan Revolution, she had became a world-famous, award-winning war photographer and her images stand today as some of the defining ones of the struggle. In this film she returns 10 years later to Nicaragua, with a film crew in tow, to shoot the 'where are they now' of her photo subjects.

Maps

If you want to pick up a map to study before arrival the only decent one made internationally, *Nicaragua – An International Travel Map*, is published by International Travel Maps (1995) in Vancouver. Despite some glaring errors, the map is head and shoulders above other foreign attempts thus far. The Nicaraguan Institute of Tourism has finally made a good map, which is available in the country for US$1.50 at the institute's main office in Managua (from the entrance to the old *Intercontinental*, one block south and one block west, T222-3333) or at branch offices around the country. Detail maps (1:50,000) can be bought at the government geological survey office, INETER (across from Policlínica Oriental, T249-3590). Many maps are sold out and waiting for funding to reprint, but those that remain are useful if you are planning to escape the beaten track and/or go trekking.

Managua

3

Managua

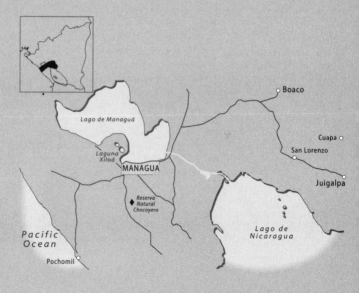

If, as the local saying goes, Nicaragua is the country where 'lead floats and cork sinks', then Managua is its perfect capital. It's certainly hard to make any sense of this lakefront city which ignores its lake – you can drive around for hours without ever even seeing the water. Managua has 20% of the country's population, yet there is no crowding; it has no centre and lots of trees (from the air you can see more trees than buildings); this is the place where city parks are concrete, not green spaces – there are plenty of those already – and where directions are given referencing buildings that haven't existed for 20 years. Managua is the capital without a city, a suburb of a million people. There was once a downtown but it was swept away in the 1972 earthquake. Despite having no centre, no skyline and no logic, Managua is still a good place to start your visit. It is a city full of energy, the heartbeat of the Nicaraguan economy and psyche.

The extinct volcanoes and crater lakes surrounding the city provide a dramatic setting, and the central mountains and warm Pacific waters lie an hour away in either direction: to the east are the cowboy departments of Boaco and Chontales, famous for their great cheese, sprawling cattle ranches and numerous pre-Columbian remains; to the west is the wave-swept Pacific Coast, which has everything from fishermen in rustic villages to expensive vacation homes and a five-star resort.

Ins and outs

Getting there
Colour map 3, grid B3
Population: 1,028,695
Altitude: 40-200 m

Managua International Airport is small and manageable (information: T233-1624 ext. 2309). Upon landing you will need to pay US$5 at the immigration counter, before retrieving your bags and passing through customs. If you want to rent a car, there is a small office just to the right as you leave the airport building. Taxis to Metrocentro, Bolonia or Martha Quezada should charge US$15 (less if you speak Spanish and know exactly where you are going). If you can lug your bags to the highway, the taxis that wait along the Carretera Norte just 100 m from the building will normally charge half the price. Be sure to have accurate directions to your desired destination. When returning to the airport from the capital, a taxi hailed on the street will charge US$5-6. If leaving early, a radio-taxi costing US$8-9 is safer and will not make stops on the way. (For more on hiring taxis, see box page 77).

Taking a bus from the airport is not recommended, but if you just can't resist the adventure, buses can be boarded westbound on Carretera Norte in front of *Las Mercedes* hotel (on the hotel side of the road). Take a bus marked '*Tipitapa*' to Mercado Roberto Huembes and then change to the mini-ruta No 4 and get off on the main street that runs past Barrio Martha Quezada (ask the driver to tell you where). The other option is to take a city bus on Route 14 to the UCA (Universidad Centroamericana) and then change to Route 102 to arrive in the same street of Martha Quezada. To return to the airport by bus, take any bus marked 'Tipitapa' from Mercado Huembes.

Related maps
A Barrio Martha
Quezada page 67
B Metrocentro page 63

Three of the four international bus companies (*Ticabus*, *Cruceros del Golfo* and *Nicabus*) arrive and leave the city from in or around the easily accessible Barrio Martha Quezada (see map page 67). The fourth, *Transnica*, is 150 m east of the Santo Domingo roundabout (the one with the big Jesus Christ) in Centro Commercial Lucila No 8.

Managua

Sleeping
1 Casa de Fiedler

Lakefront and the old centre The only place in the city to see Lake Managua is around
the small *malecón* (waterfront) in what used to be the city centre. From the *malecón*,
Avenida Bolívar runs south away from the lake past the main tourist attractions of
Managua (Teatro Nacional, Casa Presidencial, Catedral Vieja and Palacio Nacional de la
Cultura). The boulevard then crosses the Carretera Norte past the revolutionary statue to
the workers, to the park-like area that surrounds the parliament building.

Martha Quezada to Plaza España Two blocks south of the government offices is
the old *Intercontinental Hotel* and its newer shopping centre. Directly west from the
pyramid-shaped *Intercontinental* is the Barrio Martha Quezada, home to budget lodging and two of the international bus stations. Avenida Bolívar runs up the hill from the
Intercontinental and down to a traffic signal which is the road that runs west to Plaza
España or east for Carretera a Masaya and Metrocentro. Plaza España, marked by the
grass mound and Indian statues of Rotonda El Güegüence, is a series of small stores,
banks, airline offices and a big supermarket. Just to the north of Plaza España and west
of Martha Quezada is Managua's gallery district, which provides some more comfortable hotel lodging as well.

Metrocentro and Carretera a Masaya On the south side of the Tiscapa crater lake is
the Carretera a Masaya, which runs through the closest thing Managua has to a centre.
The bizarre New Cathedral stands on the north side of the big fountains of Rotonda
Rubén Darío, which marks Metrocentro – a shopping complex and a new *IntSsconti-
nental Hotel*. The Carretera a Masaya runs south past single-storey shops and restaurants and the monstrous new headquarters of Casa Pellas to the plain grass
roundabout of Rotonda Centroamérica, and further south past the Camino de Oriente.

The Nicaraguan Institute of Tourism, *INTUR*, is 1 block south and 1 block west of the old
Intercontinental Hotel, T222-3333, www.intur.gob.ni Open Mon-Fri, 0800-1200,
1400-1700. They sell a very good map for US$1 and provide free brochures in English. The

airport INTUR office is inexplicably in the
waiting lounge for the outbound only
flights. Information on national parks and
conservation should be obtained from
Sistema Nacional de Areas Protegidas
(SINAP), at Ministerio de Medio Ambiente
y Recursos Naturales (*MARENA*), Km 12.5
Carretera Norte, T263-2617.

Managua shares the Pacific Basin weather
pattern of rain and sun from mid-May to
late Nov and a very dry season the rest of
the year. The average temperature is 27°C
with dry season highs reaching 36-38°C
and rainy season lows dipping to 20°C in
the early morning. It gets windy at the
end of the dry season.

    As with all of Nicaragua's Pacific Basin
the best time of year to visit is during the
rainy season. After Feb the land dries, the
heat rises and Mar and Apr can be down-
right miserable at times thanks to the dry
winds and farmers burning their fields.

Roundabout directions in Managua and beyond

How do you find anything in a country without street names or numbers? Sometimes visitors feels as if they are going in circles, especially in Managua, with the epidemic of dizzying rotondas (roundabouts) that has invaded the capital. In fact, the Nicaraguan system is foolproof, as long as you know every landmark that exists, or used to exist, in the city. This means that, more often than not, foreigners are completely lost.

In Managua, directions are based around the lake, so it is essential to know where the lake is and keep a bird's eye view of the city in your mind. With the location of Lake Managua you have north (al lago); away from the lake is south (al sur). Then you need to use basic Spanish and common sense with sun. Where the sun comes up (arriba) is east and where it goes down (abajo) is west. City blocks are cuadras (abbreviated in this book as 'c'), and metres are better known here as varas. The only other

element is the landmark, which can be a hotel, park, pharmacy, factory or, in worst-case scenarios, where a factory or cinema used to be 20 years ago. Once you find the landmark, getting to your ultimate destination is simple. Here is an example: Restaurante Italia, viejo Hotel Intercontinental, 2 c al sur, 1 c abajo, 20 varas al lago. *For that tasty seafood linguini you will have to find the old Intercontinental Hotel, go 2 blocks south, 1 block west and 20 m to the lake (north).*

Outside Managua many directions are given from the town's Parque Central *or* Iglesia *(main church). It is useful to remember that almost all Catholic churches in Nicaragua face west; so when stepping out of the church the north is to your right, south to the left, etc. The rest of the directions in any town in Nicaragua use the same compass directions from landmarks. If the worst comes to worst, hire a taxi, give the driver the co-ordinates and let him figure it out.*

History

This shore of Lake Managua has been inhabited for at least 6,000 years and was once an area of major volcanic activity with four cones, all of which are now extinct. Managua means 'place of the big man' or 'chief' in the Mangue language of the Chorotega Indians. It was a large village that extended for many kilometres along the shores of Lake Managua (whose indigenous name is Ayagualpa or often-used Xolotlán). When the Spaniards first arrived it was reported to have 40,000 inhabitants, but shortly after the conquest, the population had dropped to about 1,000. This may have been the result of the tough battle waged in 1524 against Francisco Hernández de Córdoba, the founder of León and Granada. Managua remained a stopping-off point on the road between León and Granada, and so avoided some of the inter-city wars that plagued the country after Independence. In 1852 it was declared the capital of Nicaragua as a compromise between the parties of León and Granada, even though its population was still only 24,000.

Much seismic activity remains in the area and the city experiences a big earthquake every 50 years or so, with those of 1931 and 1972 generating widespread damage. Following the troubled years of the 1980s and the resulting migrations from the countryside, the capital now has an inflated population of over one million and is the economic and political heart of the country.

24 hours in Managua

*Early birds can watch the heavy tropical
sun rise over muddy Lake Managua before
setting off on the popular 3-km circuit
around Laguna de Tiscapa which has fine
views of lake and city. A well-earned
breakfast at the* Hotel Intercontinental
*will set you up for a morning of museums
before the heat sets in: the 6,000-year-old
footprints at Museo Acahualinca can be
followed by the fine pre-Columbian
collection at the Museo Nacional.*

For a people-watching lunch, try El
Guapinol *in the noisy Metrocentro food
court. After lunch browse the Roberto
Huembes central market for the best
crafts in Managua, and everything else
from a haircut to shoe repair. More
refined, perhaps, would be a visit to some
of the Bolonia galleries to see the very*

latest in Nicaraguan art.

*In the early evening, catch the sunset at
the Catedral Nueva (New Cathedral) before
dinner at* Las Brasas, *a good outdoor place
on Camino de Oriente, with fair prices, a
happy local crowd and roaming musicians
(the traditional centre-piece is a half-litre
of rum, a bucket of ice, cut limes and a
steady flow of Cokes or sodas). With the
night just beginning, you can take to the
dance floor and work up a sweat at* Bar
Chamán. *Then cool off with some live jazz
or folk at the Café Amatl, just two blocks
from the old* Intercontinental *on the
Tiscapa loop. When the* Amatl *closes
(0200-0300) it's a short walk (or stumble)
to* Bar La Chocoya *for yet more locally
made refreshments until dawn tells you it's
time for that early morning jog.*

Sights

Attractions for the visitor in Managua are fewer than you might expect. There
are two good museums, two very different and interesting cathedrals, a nice
lookout park and a good market. The city also has many interesting private art
galleries which provide the only available public view of modern Nicaraguan
painting and sculpture. Performances in the national theatre are usually good,
if you are lucky enough to be in town when there is a show on.

At the northernmost end of Avenida Bolívar is the *malecón* (waterfront), or **Lakefront &**
what remains of it after Hurricane Mitch in 1998 when most of it was lost to **old centre**
the rising lake. This is a popular place to spend a Sunday afternoon with a lot
of cheap food and drinks in the little establishments that line the lakefront.
The **Península Chiltepe** jutting out into the lake is part of the ancient volcanic
complex that includes two beautiful crater lakes, Apoyeque and Xiloá. The
stage next to the *malecón* is used for political speeches and rallies. The area in
front of the stage, **El Parque Juan Pablo II**, has been turned into a monument
and park in honour of Pope John Paul II who preached here in 1983 and again
in 1996. Past the statue of Simón Bolívar is the 30-year-old **Teatro Nacional**, a
project of the last Somoza's wife (see page 267), which survived the earthquake of 1972 and provides the only quality stage in Managua for plays, concerts and dance productions. ■ *US$1.50-US$20, depending on show.* There
are usually temporary art exhibitions in the theatre so, in the day, ask at the
window to view the exhibit and you can probably look inside the auditorium
as well. Just south of the theatre is the **Parque Rubén Darío**, a small park with
one of the most famous monuments in Nicaragua. Sculpted from Italian marble in 1933 by Nicaraguan architect Mario Favilli and restored in 1997, it is
said to be the aesthetic symbol of modernism, the poetry movement which

☛ ## Managua – the invisible city

I landed in August 1995, found an airport taxi and crawled inside. "Take me to the centre, please." The Managua sun beat down on the ancient Lada's windshield, it was an oven inside. The taxista looked at me with sympathy. "¿El Centro? First time in Managua?" I smiled back and we took off in a hurry, on a road to nowhere. I had imagined the city centre: concrete high-rise buildings, narrow streets filled with too many cars, smoke and noise. After all Managua, with more than a million people, is home to 20% of the country's populace.

We arrived at what is called Parque Central; *the driver pulled over and glanced in his rear-view mirror, looking for acceptance. There stood the park, alone with a couple of old buildings and surrounded by open fields. "No my friend, I mean the centre, you know, where all the tall buildings and people are?" He was losing patience with my ignorance and bizarre Spanish, but was a kind sort, and took me down the open highway, past green fields, a pyramid-shaped hotel and rows of homes, to a little shopping centre next to a petrol station and one-storey shops. "Bueno, gracias," I told him, somewhat frustrated, and slid out. The shopping centre was closed. A lone Chinese couple stared into a store window, while a stray dog trotted though the uncovered centre. "This is it? Where is Managua? Help!"*

What I had asked the kind taxista *to do was to deliver me to another dimension, one that has not existed since 1972. To a place called Managua, which existed only until the Tiscapa fault ruptured, less than 5 km beneath the lakefront, sending forth a 6.6 earthquake that rocked the city and crumbled (and later burned) all that could be considered downtown. The quake came cruelly just after midnight on Saturday, December 23, a day before Christmas. Most of Managua was inside, enjoying big parties; many were never found. Half the population (then 200,000) was left homeless, and at least 5,000 Nicaraguans were killed.*

There are ample reasons not to rebuild the high-rises. In fact, 14 good reasons, in the form of 14 seismic fault lines that run underneath greater Managua. Today's 21st-century Managua is still one of the greenest capitals in the world, wide-open spaces in every direction, with sprawling barrios and a couple of new low-rise office and hotel buildings looking very much out of place. Much of what was downtown became a sort of monument valley, home to a confused garden of statues, concrete parks and a few new government buildings. With a proper sense of Nicaraguan irony, the new presidential office was built directly over the epicentre of the 1972 quake.

Darío founded. Passages from some of his most famous poems are reproduced on the monument. In front of the Darío statue is the **Parque Central**; now central to almost nothing, it was once surrounded by three- to five-storey buildings and narrow streets that made up the pre-1972 Managua. The Templo de la Música is at the centre of the park and there's a monument to the revolutionary Sandinista ideologue, Carlos Fonseca. Next to the park is a dancing, musical fountain complete with its own bleachers and an ample, romantic crowd on weekend nights. Around the fountain are two of Managua's most historic buildings and the garishly painted **Casa Presidencial**, with its own 'oval office' facing the lake, that has been described (generously) as 'post-modernist eclectic'. Directly across from the presidential office is the attractive neoclassical **Palacio Nacional de la Cultura**. Finished in 1935 after the original had been destroyed in an earthquake in 1931, the cultural palace was once the seat of the Nicaraguan Congress and the site of Edén Pastora's (*Comandante Cero*) famous 1978 revolutionary raid and hostage taking. The elegant interior houses the **Museo Nacional de Nicaragua**,

Metrocentro

Laguna de Tiscapa

Not to scale

N

✝ New Cathedral

To Plaza España

La UNI (University)

To La UCA (University)

Av Colón

Rubén Darío (Metrocentro) Roundabout

Metrocentro Shopping Centre

To Bar Charman

⑪

To Legends Hotel & Hard Rock Café

ℹ

2

3

Lacmiel

1

⑦ ⑩

④ ①

⑤ Alianza Francesa

@ Mi Oficina

⑥ Optica Matamoros

Mexican Embassy

@ Kafé

⑨

Distribuidora Vicky ✉ @

Coconut Grove Plaza & Cyber Café

② @ Sirca Bus

ℹ Kodak

Carretera a Masaya

Banic ⑤ Forex

To Rastipollo Restaurant

To Mercado Roberto Huembes

BAC ⑤

Ⓜ La Colonia

Centroamérica Roundabout

Pista Portezuelo

Camino de Oriente Shopping Centre

⑧

To Masaya & Granada

■ Sleeping
1 Colón
2 Princess
3 Real Intercontinental Metrocentro

● Eating
1 Astillero
2 Bongó
3 Casa del Café
4 Indigo & Café

5 La Casa del Pomodoro
6 La Cocina de Doña Haydée
7 La Fonda
8 Las Brasas
9 María Bonita
10 Pizza Valenti

● Bars & clubs
11 Guantanamera

as well as the national archive and national library. The National Museum has a fine pre-Columbian collection, some of which is on permanent display in the Pacific and Northern archaeology display halls; there's also a statue exhibit from the islands of Ometepe and Zapatera, as well as a natural history hall. The museum also has changing temporary exhibits and several murals, including a very dramatic one depicting the history of Managua and the earthquake. ■ *Sun-Fri 0800-1700, US$1 (guided tour only, sometimes available in English) US$2.50 extra to photograph. T222-4820.* Next to the Palacio de la Cultura is the Old Cathedral. Baptized as *La Iglesia Catedral Santiago de Los Caballeros de Managua*, it is now known simply as **La Catedral Vieja**. The church was almost finished when it was shaken by the big earthquake of 1931, and when the earth moved again in 1972 it was partially destroyed. It has been tastefully restored; only the roof of narrow steel girders, and side-window support bars were added to keep it standing. There is something romantic about this old and sad cathedral in ruins; a monument to what Managua might have been. Recent tremors have closed the old church indefinitely and it appears that it may in fact come down soon. On the south side of the Palacio de la Cultura is the **Centro Cultural Managua**, which was built out of the ruins of the *Gran Hotel de Managua*, the best hotel in Managua from the 1940s-60s. Now, as a cultural centre, it has a good selection of before and after photos of quake-struck Managua in 1972 and many small artists' studios upstairs. The centre is also home to the national art school and the national music school. There are some antique and craft shops and art exhibits in galleries downstairs. The central area downstairs is used for performances (check with the

Managua

newspapers or entrance staff to see what is coming up). On the first Saturday of every month an artisans' fair gives craftsmen from outside Managua a chance to show and sell their wares.

Across the Carretera Norte from the Centro Cultural is the **Parque de la Paz**, a graveyard for weapons and a few dozen truckloads of AK-47s which are buried there; some can be seen sticking out of the cement. The park was built as a monument to the end of the Contra conflict, with a big lighthouse, a mini-amphitheatre and a tank with a palm tree growing out of it. The plaques on the northern wall include names of most of the big players in the conflict and its resolution.

Heading south from the old centre is the government seat, next to the **Asamblea Nacional** (congress building), a square red-roofed building. The complex is marked by a white 16-storey building, a true giant in Managua and by far the tallest in Nicaragua. It served as the Bank of America before the Revolution and is now an office building for the *Diputados* (parliamentary members).

Just south of the government administrative offices that accompany the congress is the **Arboretum Nacional**, which, in spite of being a bit neglected, houses 180 species of plants including Nicaragua's national flower, the *sacuanjoche* and the national tree, the *madroño* (strawberry tree).

Laguna de Tiscapa & Metrocentro

Parque Nacional de la Loma de Tiscapa has a fabulous panoramic view of Managua and is great for photographing the city and trying to figure out its layout. It is reached by the small road that runs directly behind the old *Intercontinental Hotel*, passing a Somoza-period monument to Franklin D Roosevelt and following it up the hill to the summit. ■ *0800-1630 daily*. At the top, a giant black silhouette of Sandino stands looking out over the city and the crater lake, **Laguna de Tiscapa**, on the south side of the hill. This spot, the site of the former presidential palace, has much historical significance. Sandino signed a peace treaty here and was abducted on the same day (and later killed) at the entrance to the access road. Underneath the park facing the crater lake (blocked off by a fence) are the cells used during the Somoza regime for political prisoners, who were said to have been tortured and then tossed into the lake. Avoid taking photographs until you're at the top of the hill, as the access road passes the important military installations next to the *Intercontinental*.

Some 500 m south of the Laguna de Tiscapa is the New Cathedral, designed by the Mexican architect Ricardo Legorreta, who has said his inspiration was found in an ancient temple in Cholula, Mexico. Begun in 1991 and finished in September of 1993, it is known as **La Catedral Nueva** or by its full name of **Catedral Metropolitana de la Purísima Concepción de María**. This very unusual mosque-like Catholic church faces south-north, instead of the usual west-east, and is basically a squat, anti-seismic box with a beehive roof. Each of the roof's 63 domes has a small window, which means that the interior is cool and very well lit. In addition, a row of side doors that are opened for Mass allow the east to west trade winds to ventilate the church. The stark concrete interior has a post-nuclear feel with a modern altar that looks like a futuristic UN Security Council meeting room. Many visitors are fascinated by the Sangre de Cristo room, which vaguely recalls a Turkish bath and holds a life-size, bleeding Christ icon encased in a glass and steel dome, illuminated by a domed roof with hundreds of holes for the sun to filter through. At night, the dome sparkles with the glow of light bulbs in the holes. The belltower holds the bells from the ruins of the Catedral Vieja. The church has capacity

Museo Las Huellas – Managua, 4000 BC

Most of the world looks to the Mediterranean or China for ancient history. Few think of little 'New World' countries like Nicaragua when looking for mankind's ancient footprints. Yet our human family was well established on this part of the Central American isthmus over 18,000 years ago. Virtually nothing is known about these ancient peoples. However, in 1874, during digging for quarry stone near the shores of Lake Managua, one of the oldest known evidences of human presence in Central America was found: footprints of men, women and children left in petrified volcanic mud, 4 m beneath the topsoil. Las Huellas de Acahualinca ('the footprints of the land of sunflowers') were radiocarbon-dated as being made in 4000 BC. Archaeologists from around the world have come to examine the site and in 1941 another site was found, with prints made by the same prehistoric people as well as tracks made by birds, deer and racoons.

The tracks and footprints were imprinted in fresh volcanic mud, the product of a burning cloud eruption, characterized by a discharge of ashes, gases, water and volcanic fragments. Such clouds destroy vegetation upon descent and form mud capes, which may take several days or months to harden.

What were these ancient ancestors doing when they made these perfectly preserved footprints? After numerous theories, some of which involved dramatic images of natives fleeing a volcanic eruption, the Nicaraguan National Police made an anthropometric study of the footprints. They determined that they had been made by 10 different people, with an average height of 140-150 cm, walking normally, some weighed down, perhaps with children or supplies. The volcanic mud was most likely from one of Managua's now-extinct volcanic cones. The footprints were undoubtedly covered in volcanic sand shortly after and therefore preserved for all time.

Managua

for 1,500 worshippers at any one time, but is filled well beyond that when the famous Cardinal, Miguel Obando y Bravo gives Mass, every Sunday at 1100. ■ *Access for pedestrians is from the Metrocentro junction and for automobiles from the east side entrance.* **NB** *Avoid flash photography and entering during Mass via the side doors.*

These ancient footprints (see box above), discovered when stone was being quarried to build homes in the area, represent some of the oldest evidence of human occupation in Nicaragua. A museum has been created around the original site and the 6,000-year-old footprints have been left exactly as they were found in excavation. The museum also has a small display of ceramic artefacts found at the site (the oldest ceramics date from 1000 BC, 3,000 years later than the footprints) and a crude illustration of the estimated height of the people who made the footprints. This little museum, located along the lake due west of the Museo Nacional, is a must for lovers of archaeology and indigenous history). ■ *Mon-Fri, 0800-1700 and Sat, 0800-1600. US$1 (additional US$2.25 to take photographs and US$3.00 to use video cameras). T266-5774.* Taxi or car recommended as this is not a nice neighbourhood. From the Portón de Gadala María, 1½ blocks towards the lake, buses 102, 12 or 6 pass the site; look out for a concrete tower and a huge stone slab by a small red footbridge. Sign off main road. By road, take the street that leads west (*abajo*) from the Parque Central and continue to the big building of López Richardson International Inc. Turn right (*al lago*) immediately before López Richardson; the road follows a big wall, crosses a small bridge and then the red metal gates on the right mark the entrance to the museum.

Museo Las Huellas de Acahualinca

Mercado Roberto Huembes For shopping the Roberto Huembes market or **Mercado Central** is the place. It is an interesting visit just for the produce and meat sections, which are found inside the structure proper, along with flowers and other goods. At the parking northwest corner of the market is a very big craft section with goods from all over the country. While the market in Masaya is more famous and more pleasant to shop at, the artisan section of Huembes is in some ways more complete, if more jumbled and difficult to move about. The market is located a few kilometres north of the Centroamericano roundabout and the shopping entrance is located next to the fire station.

Galleries

Managua has several good private galleries that are of interest for art lovers who wish to see what is happening in the Nicaraguan scene. Many have permanent collections as well as temporary exhibitions, and most are located in the Bolonia neighbourhood, just west of the Barrio Martha Quezada and north of Plaza España. Probably the most famous is **Galería Codice**, Colonial Los Robles, *Hotel Colón*, 1 c al sur, 2½ c arriba, No 15, with art from Nicaragua and the other parts of Latin America, and a small 'coffee garden'. ■ *Mon-Sat 0900-2000, T267-2635, www.galeriacodice.com* Also in Los Robles, on the other side of Carretera a Masaya, is the gallery of the famous poet/sculptor/priest/politician Ernesto Cardenal, **Galería Casa de los Tres Mundos**, *Restaurante La Marseillaise*, 2½ c al norte, T267-0304, with *primitivista* paintings from Solentiname, crafts from the islands and some works of the controversial *padre* himself.

In the upscale Villa Fontana neighbourhood in the southern part of Managua is **Galería Pleyades**, Club Villa Fontana, 2 c abajo, No 40, T278-1350, pleyades@nic.gbm.net, with a good selection of Nicaraguan painters. In Bolonia, near Plaza España is **Galería Praxis**, Plaza España, 2 c al norte, 1 c abajo, ½ c norte, T266-3563, with a small café and works of member artists and visiting exhibits. Near by is **Galería Josefina**, Embajada de Japón, ½ c abajo, T268-5809, museogaljosefina@teran.com.ni, which has permanent and changing exhibits in a very attractive space. Also in Bolonia is the **Epikentro Gallery**, Canal 2, 75 varas abajo, T268-5953, with an emphasis on modern styles. Just half a block west of the Epikentro is the beautiful new space of the **Añil, Galería de Artes Visuales**, Canal 2, 1 c abajo, 5 varas al sur, T266-5445, anil@cablenet.com.ni, featuring an impressive list of artists, including all the Nicaraguan greats.

Essentials

Sleeping

■ *on maps, pages 58, 63 and 67*
For price codes, see inside front cover

LL *Real Intercontinental Metrocentro*, Metrocentro shopping plaza, T271-9483, www.gruporeal.com 157 rooms, hot water, a/c, telephone, TV, pool, secretary service, internet, restaurant and bar. Nicaragua's finest hotel, built in 2000, with a great central location and friendly professional service. Special weekend rates, favourable multi-day rates with some tour operators. Recommended. **LL** *Hotel Princess Managua*, Km 4½ Carretera a Masaya, T270-5045, www.hotelesprincess.com A/c, cable TV, 2 telephones in every room, laundry service, restaurant, bar, internet service, secretary service, friendly front desk, centrally located, some rooms with view of lake.

L *Hotel Intercontinental*, 'El Inter', in front of the Plaza Inter shopping centre (and not to be confused with the *Real Intercontinental Metrocentro*), T228-3530, F228-3087, www.interconti.com Some rooms with lake view, rooms small for the price, slow service, good location, sauna, use of swimming pool for non-residents on Sun for US$18. Bookshop, handicraft shop, buffet, breakfast and lunch. A legendary hotel for journalists (see box, page 68). L *Hotel Legends*, from *Real Intercontinental Metrocentro*, 1 c abajo, 1 c al sur, T270-0061. Private bath with hot water, opened in 2001, TV, a/c, telephone, small swimming pool, restaurant and bar, upstairs the *Hard Rock Café Managua*, very nice hotel in the shadow of a giant guitar, rooms for disabled travellers. **L-AL** *Las Mercedes*, Km 11 Carretera Norte, T263-1011, F263-1083, www.lasmercedes.com.ni Excellent food, but expensive, charming open-air restaurant, pool, tennis court, barber shop, all rooms have cable TV, a/c, bath, fridge, phone, 3 levels of room (standard, premiere and executive – avoid standard if possible). Local phone calls can be made here when airport office is shut; the outdoor café is the best place to kill time near the airport. **L-AL** *Mansión Teodolinda*, Bolonia, T228-1050, F222-4908, www.teodolinda.com.ni A/c, private bath with hot water, kitchenette with refrigerator, cable TV, telephone, pool, bar, restaurant, laundry service, very clean, often full with business people, good location.

AL *Casa Real*, de la Rotonda Rubén Darío 2 c al sur 1½ c arriba. T278-3838, F267-8240, casareal@ibw.com.ni Private bath, hot water, a/c, telephone, cable TV. Recommended. **AL** *Hostal Real*, Bolonia, opposite German Embassy, T266-8133. Private bath with hot water, breakfast included, internet, cable TV, very clean, interesting and unusual airy rooms decorated with antiques and art. Very popular, so book in advance. Centrally located. Highly recommended. **AL** *Hotel Los Robles*, 30 m south of *Restaurante La Marseillaise*, T267-3008, F270-1074, losrobles@bigfoot.com Private bath, hot water, cable TV, a/c, very classy furnishings, interior courtyard, owner Guy Mathews speaks French and English and is very helpful. New in 2001.

At Km 8.5 on Carretera Sur is **A** *Hotel César*, T265-2760, cesar@ibw.com.ni Big rooms, a/c, private bath, cable TV, balconies, garden, safe, very good food, garage, swimming pool for children. This Swiss-run hotel is great value and often fully

If you are going to splurge on a room during a visit to Nicaragua, this is the place to do it, as hotels below the 'C' category are usually quite bad

Managua

Barrio Martha Quezada

■ **Sleeping**	6 Hospedaje Meza	● **Eating**
1 Casa Azul	7 Hospedaje Quintana	1 Café Amatl
2 Casa de Huéspedes	8 Hospedaje Tica Nica	2 Delicias del Mar
Santos	9 Intercontinental	3 Italia
3 El Dorado	10 Jardín de Italia	4 Las Anclas
4 El Molinito	11 La Fragata	5 Mirna's
5 Hospedaje Carlos	12 Mansión Teolinda	

N

0 metres 100
0 yards 100

Hotel Intercontinental – a room with a view, on history

Built in 1969 Managua's pyramid-shaped Hotel Intercontinental has more associations with contemporary history than the majority of the buildings in Nicaragua. Best known to the world's international press corps, which used the hotel as a home base while covering the Revolution and, later, the Contra War, the pyramid has also seen its share of action as a hostel for the eccentric and as the central seat of the Nicaraguan government.

Despite the fact that it was built right on the Tiscapa fault, the hotel was one of the few buildings that withstood the great earthquake that devastated Managua in 1972. At the time of the earthquake, the mysterious North American millionaire Howard Hughes and his many employees occupied the seventh and eighth floors of the hotel. Legend has it that Hughes spent most of his days sitting naked on his favourite leather chair engrossed in his complete collection of James Bond movies. When the earthquake hit, the millionaire ran downstairs in a robe to his car, and was driven to his private plane,

never to return to Nicaragua again.

On 17 July, 1979, after Somoza Debayle resigned from power and fled to the United States, the Nicaraguan legislature met on the top floor of the hotel and chose Francisco Urcuyo Maliaños as the new provisional President. He would rule for one day. For several weeks after 19 July, the eight-storey 200-room building became the offices for the Junta del Gobierno de Reconstrucción Nacional *(JGRN), which had taken control of a country in ruins. At the Intercontinental, the new authorities carried out government business, received foreign visitors and diplomats, and held emergency cabinet meetings.*

The hotel was reportedly built in 18 months at a cost of four million dollars. The Somoza family (see page 267) had 25% interest in the project. The original blueprints called for a larger building, but the design was radically changed to an eight-storey pyramid shape – to expand its centre of gravity – after an earthquake in Venezuela destroyed a newly constructed 25-storey building. Today the hotel is owned by Taiwanese investors.

---

booked, so you will need to call ahead. **A** *Hotel El Almendro*, Rotonda Rubén Darío, 2 c abajo, ½ al sur, T270-1260, F277-5745, www.el-almendro.com Private bath with hot water, a/c, cable TV, telephone, internet access, each room has mini-kitchen with refrigerator, microwave, plates and utensils. Private and central location, good value. Recommended. **A** *La Posada del Angel*, opposite Iglesia San Francisco, Bolonia, T/F266-1347, pdelangel@interlink.com.ni Private bath with hot water, cable TV, a/c, mini-bar, telephone, laundry service. Lots of character, quiet location. Recommended. **A** *El Conquistador*, *Hotel Intercontinental*, 1c al sur, 1c abajo, T222-4789, F222-3657, elconquistador@ ideay.net.ni 11 rooms, a/c, private bath, cable TV, refrigerator, lake-view *terrraza*, good value and location. **A-B** *Europeo*, Bolonia, Canal 2, 75 m abajo, T/F268 5999, europeo@ibw.com.ni A/c, private bath, hot water, cable TV, includes continental breakfast, restaurant, bar, fax, secure parking, laundry service, internet, very clean, interesting furnishings, each room different, very friendly and helpful staff, quiet but central location. Highly recommended. Hotel proceeds go to a drug rehabilitation programme.

B *Hotel Colón*, Lacmiel 2 c arriba, T278-2490, hcolon@ibw.com.ni With bath and a/c (**C** with fan), cable TV, secure, clean, good restaurant. **B** *La Fragata*, Estatua Simón Bolívar 1 c al abajo, 50 varas al sur, a block west of the *Intercontinental*, T222-4179, F222-4133. Good value though getting older, includes full breakfast, good restaurant, new beds, hot showers (not electric), cable TV, a/c, central location, disabled access. Recommended. **B** *Ejecutivo*, 1 block north of Ticabus, T/F222-2816. Smart and clean with comfortable beds, but lacking in character. **B** *Las Cabañitas*, near Plaza 19 de

Julio, T278-3235, F277-2740, hoteleco@interlink.com.ni Good, helpful, with pool and decent restaurant next door. **B** *María La Gorda*, Iglesia El Carmen, 1c al sur, ½ c arriba, ½ c al sur, T268-2455, F268-2456. 8 rooms, a/c, private bath with hot water, email access, cable TV, telephone, just west of Martha Quezada, nice.

C *Ay Caramba*, Montoya 2 c al lago, T266-6284, F266-2194. 10 rooms, a/c, private bath, cable TV, telephone, not ideal location but good service and value, often recommended. **C** *Casa de Fiedler*, CST bus terminal, 2 blocks south and 1½ blocks west, T266-6622. With bath and a/c or fan, comfortable, soft mattresses, clean, friendly, popular, accepts travellers' cheques, cold Victoria beer, good breakfasts, coffee all day, has interesting collection of pre-Columbian ceramics. **C** *Casa San Juan*, Calle Esperanza 560, T278-3220, F267-0419, sanjuan@nicanet.com.ni Shared or private bath, clean, owner's family sleeps in, safe, excellent breakfasts for US$3, friendly, good value. Highly recommended.

Managua

D *Casa de Huéspedes Castillo*, Casa del Obrero 1 c arriba, 1½ al sur, 2 blocks from Ticabus, also known as *Casa Ramiro*, with bath, fan, some with a/c, clean, quiet, safe.
There are many hotels west of *Hotel Intercontinental* in the Barrio Martha Quezada and near the Cine Dorado (now called *Casino Royal*, but still ask for 'Cine Dorado'). To get there from *Hotel Intercontinental*, walk west for 10 mins to a main north-south road, Av Williams Romero; Cine Dorado is just south. **E** *Jardín de Italia*, Ticabus 1 c arriba, ½ al lago, T222-7967. Some rooms with a/c (more expensive), with bath, basic but friendly, not good value. **E** *El Pueblo*, 3 blocks north, 2 blocks east from *Intercontinental*, simple, old house, big rooms, private bath, friendly. **E** *Hospedaje Carlos*, ½ block north of Ticabus, rooms on left at the back better than on right, cold shower, fan, a/c extra, good value, clean, *Comedor Las Anclas on opposite corner*.

Most hotels in this price range have very thin walls and are noisy

F *Hospedaje Meza*, from Ticabus 1 block north, 1 east, OK, laundry facilities, TV. **F** *El Dorado*, turn left out of Ticabus station, clean, small rooms of varying standard, key deposit charged. **F** *Hospedaje Quintana*, from Ticabus 1 block north, then ½ block west, rooms with fan, shared shower (cold), laundry, clean, good value, family-run. Recommended for longer stays. **F** *Hospedaje Tica Nica*, 1½ blocks north of Ticabus, with or without bath, noisy, use of kitchen. **F** *Sultana*, at the Ticabus terminal, dormitory accommodation, friendly, clean, fan, handy if you have an early bus, otherwise noisy from 0500 and overpriced. The owners of **F** *Hospedaje Mangaia* often wait at Ticabus, free transfer to and from terminal, 1 block south then about 5 towards Plaza España, turn left in C Gabriel Cardinal Cabrera, 2nd house on right, No 930, T268-0480 (Optica Nicaragüense). In the same block as Ticabus is **F** *Casa Azul*, which is popular but pushy. **F** *El Molinito*, ½ block from Ticabus, meals available, good value, basic, clean, hot in the day. **F** *Casa de Huéspedes Santos*, from Ticabus 1 block north, 1½ west, with bath but washbasins outside, no soap, towel or toilet paper, clean, bright, basic, good value, spacious courtyard with hammocks, friendly, serves meals, including breakfasts and snacks. Very popular, good place to meet other travellers.

Eating and drinking

Hotel César, Km 8½ Carretera Sur, T265-2760, good, try duck in orange sauce, best place for those craving real Euro-food, cheeses, wines, etc. *Las Delicias del Bosque*, Colegio Centroamericano 5 Km al sur, T0883-0071, restaurant for the Nicaraguan power brokers, lovely setting in hills, good food, Wed-Sat only. *El Mesón Español*, *Mansión Teodolinda* 3 c al sur, Spanish dishes, very good, either totally empty or completely full with high level of government employees. *La Marseillaise*, Calle Principal Los Robles, T277-0224, closed Sun, daily specials, French cuisine, good wine list, very expensive. *La Casa del Pomodoro*, Km 4.5 Carretera a Masaya, Italian, average pasta,

Expensive
● *on maps, pages 58, 63 and 67 Almost all establishments accept Visa cards and many accept Mastercard and American Express*

very good *calzone*. **Rincón Español**, Iglesia El Carmen, 2 c al lago, 1 c abajo, good Spanish. **El Churrasco**, Rotonda El Güegüence (Plaza España), expensive and very good beef dishes, try the restaurant's namesake. **Harry's Grill Argentino**, in Las Colinas behind Texaco station, T270-2382, very expensive Argentine dishes with imported beef, very good. **El Cartel**, across Carretera a Masaya from Metrocentro, T277-2619, traditional fare, moderately priced lunch specials, nice setting, popular with Miami crowd. **Las Lugo**, Km 4 Carretera a Masaya, best seafood, expensive but worth it, octopus US$13, lobster US$17, sea bass US$11.

Mid-range *Restaurante Italia*, Bolonia next to Institute of Tourism, Managua's best Italian food, try spaghetti *mariscos*, seafood pizza or octopus in tomato and garlic sauce, also excellent soups and pastas. Highly recommended. **El Astillero**, Lacmiel 1½ arriba, T267-8110, good ceviche of shrimp, fish, octopus, quiet setting. **Kameleón**, Colonial Los Robles, T277-2700, interesting varied menu, Swiss owners. Recommended. **María Bonita**, Altamira, de la Vicky 1½ c abajo, T270-4326, Mexican, closed Mon, try the *carnitas*, wildly popular on weekend nights with live music and a noisy, happy crowd, good food and service, lethal margaritas, fun. Recommended. **Tacos al Pastor**, Carretera a Masaya across from Camino de Oriente, T278-2650, Mexican, delicious make your own tacos dish with pork, chicken, beef, beans and hot tortillas that feeds at least 2 or 3 for US$11, but horrible fish tacos. **La Hora del Taco**, Monte de Olivos, 1 c al norte, T277-5074, traditional Mexican fare, decent, nice setting. **Martín Fierro**, de Lacmiel 1 c arriba, best steak, Argentine grill, excellent. **La Plancha**, various locations, T278-2999 for nearest one, good value, very generous portions, good beef, very popular, one Nicaraguan serving can often feed 2 foreigners. Recommended. For the best value, **Rostipollo**, just west of Centroamérica roundabout, T277-1968, headquarters for Nicaraguan chain that is franchised across Central America and Mexico, great chicken, Caesar salad, very good. **La Cocina de Doña Haydée**, opposite *Pastelería Aurami*, Planes de Altamira, T270-6100, once a popular family-kitchen eatery that has gone upscale, traditional Nicaraguan food at higher prices than elsewhere, very popular with foreign residents, good, try the *surtido* plate for 2 US$6.50, good *indio viejo* US$3, and a great the carrot/orange *fresco* drink. **Bongó**, Carretera a Masaya across from Colegio Teresiano, Cuban, food not special but good cocktails, classy crowd, good live music at weekends. **China de Asia**, Lacmiel 1 c arriba, ½ sur, Taiwanese specialities, salty but good. **La Ballena que Cayó del Cielo**, next to *Camino de Oriente*, T277-3055, Nicaragua's best hamburgers, good grilled chicken, overpriced but good, salsa and merengue videos.

   Plaza España/Barrio Martha Quezada area *Las Anclas*, 1 block from *Casa Santos*, good seafood, mid-range to expensive. **Delicias del Mar**, ½ block from *Santos* on Santos Vargas Chávez, good but not cheap.

Cheap *Pizza Valenti*, Colonial Los Robles, best cheap pizza, US$4.50, home delivery, most popular in Managua, try pizza with garlic, green olives and fresh tomatoes. **Rincón Salvadoreño**, Enel Central, 1 c al lago, *pupusas*, *tamales* and *quesadillas*, very cheap, simple and good in cool setting. **Topkapi**, Camino de Oriente, across from *Alhambra* cinema, pizza (US$2.50), tacos, Nicaraguan food, if low on funds the *cacao con leche fresco* is a meal in itself, US$.90, good people-watching, outdoor seating. Recommended. **La Fonda**, Lacmiel 1 c arriba, good, try *quesadilla suprema*, also has vegetarian. **Las Brasas**, behind Cinema 1 and 2, Camino Oriente, good Nicaraguan fare, traditional, outdoors, great atmosphere, very popular, sea bass US$5.50, *churrasco* steak US$5, best deal to drink rum with friends, half-bottle comes with bowl of ice, limes, a Coke and 2 plates of food, US$9.50. **Tacos Charros**, Plaza el Café, 1 c abajo, cheap, generous servings, delicious *enchiladas*, good value. Highly recommended. **Rincón Chino**, Km 4½ Carretera Norte, T244-0155, popular, best of the poor Asian choices. *La Crema Batida*, Camino de Oriente, T277-2517, North American-style foods with many ice cream combinations, family crowd. The **Metrocentro** shopping centre has several good restaurants in its food court, the best being *El Guapinol*, with grilled beef, chicken and fish. Try *copinol*, with grilled beef, avocado, fried cheese, salad, tortilla and *gallo pinto*, US$4. *Las Sazón*, Cine Cabrera, 3 c al sur, 1½ abajo, T222-2243, 1200-1500 only, buffet US$2, great value, often very crowded. *Café Amatl*, Plaza Inter, 3 c al sur, ½ c abajo, good lunches Mon-Fri, 1200-1400 for US$1.50 with Coke included.

Plaza España/Barrio Martha Quezada area *Comedor Sara*, next to Ticabus, cheap, popular with gringos, serves breakfast, noticeboard. *Eskimo*, ice cream, on 27 de Mayo before ex-*Cine Cabrera*. Near *Santos*, *China Bien Bien*, on 27 de Mayo, 1 block south and 1 block down from CST bus terminal, excellent fast food, Chinese. *Mirna's*, near *Pensión Norma*, open 0700-1500, good economic breakfasts and *comidas*, popular with travellers and Nicaraguans, friendly service. *Fruitilandia*, Rotonda El Güegüence, 1 c al lago, T266-1256, fruit drinks and shakes, bakery, decent coffee, breakfast and lunch.

Café Jardín, Galería Códice, Colonial Los Robles, *Hotel Colón*, 1 c al sur, 2½ c arriba, No **Cafés** 15, T267-2635, Mon-Sat 0900, here you can sip espresso in the confines of an art gallery, and eat sandwiches and salads. *Café y Té Jordan*, first floor Plaza Inter, T222-3525, although the atmosphere and décor is very hotel-like, they do have a salad bar, *café veneciano* and are unique in that they offer Earl Grey tea. *Café Van Gogh*, Plaza España, 2 c al norte, 1 c abajo, ½ c norte, T266-3563, we are not sure how Vincent took his coffee, but here is another gallery offering paint fumes and caffeine for the same low cost. *Casa de Café*, Lacmiel, 1 c al arriba, 1 ½ c al sur, T278-0605, the king of cafés in Managua, very popular with a nice, airy upstairs seating area that makes the average coffee taste much better. Good turkey sandwiches, desserts and *empanadas*, Mon-Sun, 0700-2200. There's another branch on the second level of the Metrocentro shopping plaza, but it lacks the charm and fresh air. *Cyber Café*, across from *Cine Dorado* in Martha Quezada, T222-5283, Mon-Sat, 0900-2100, the only way to get completely wired. *Don Pan*, Km 4 Carretera Norte, across from *El Nuevo Diario*, T249-0191, Mon-Sat, 0700-1900, right across from the country's two biggest newspapers, this is the place to go to share the morning news buzz with the country's finest hacks, a good working man's café. *Indigo & Café*, Lacmiel, 1½ c arriba, T270-6470, indigocafenic @yahoo.com Mon-Fri 1000-2200, Sat 0900-1800, this little blue café has very good food and 20 variations of coffee, nice sandwiches with salad, soup of the day, all at reasonable prices.

Guantanamera, El Cartel, 1 c abajo, by Metrocentro, T277-5875, Cuban drinks and **Bars** food with *Noche Guajira* and live music every Fri night of live music, try *yuca con mojo* *If you can't find a fun* US$5.50, good fun and attentive service, open Mon-Sat from 1000. *La Ruta Maya*, de *bar in Managua, you* Montoya 150 m east, entrance US$5, good bands Thu-Sun, often with reggae on Thu, *are inside your room* some good folk concerts. *El Parnaso*, la UCA 1 c arriba, 1 c al lago, bohemian crowd, live *with the lights out.* music Thu-Sat, bookshop across from la UCA. *El Quetzal*, Colonia Centro América, *This is a very short list* opposite Shell, Thu-Fri after 1800, fun crowd who fill big dance floor and dance *of some favourites* non-stop, no entrance fee, loud live music, ranchera, salsa, merengue. *La Chocoya*, *Hotel Intercontinental*, 2 c al sur, 1 c abajo, open 25 hours, simple greasy food, cheap, very loud crowd and music, outdoor seating, heavy drinking and laughing. *Café Amatl*, 2 blocks south of old *Intercontinental*, open Thu-Sat, 2000-0300, terminally hip crowd, bookshop and café open during the day, nice outdoor setting under a giant tree, good crêpes, good live music at weekends, Brazilian, reggae, folk. Recommended. *Hard Rock Live*, top floor of the *Hotel Legends*, behind *Hotel Princess*, T270-0061, happy hour Mon-Fri, 1800-2000, with half-price national drinks and free *bocas* (snacks), Wed-Fri live music, generic. *La Casa de los Mejía Godoy*, Plaza El Sol, 2 c al sur, T278-4913,

Managua

Thu-Sat, opens 2100, this is a chance to see 2 of Nicaragua's favourite sons and most famous folk singers. A very intimate setting, check with programme to make sure either Carlos or Luis Enrique is playing. Fri is a good bet, entrance US$10. *La Cavanga*, trendy bar in Centro Cultural Managua, live jazz and folk music weekends. *Shannon Bar Irlandés*, Ticabus, 1 c arriba, 1 c al sur, international crowd, recommended, excellent food, whisky, expensive Guinness, internet. *El Quelite*, Entitel Villa Fontana, 5 c abajo, daily 1400-0200, live music Thu-Sun, good traditional place, open-air with dance floor, spacious, very good sea bass (*curvina a la plancha*) for US$4, nice unpretentious crowd. *Mirador Tiscapa*, on Laguna de Tiscapa, daily 1700-0200, open-air restaurant and bar with dance floor, live band on weekends, overpriced slow service, but very nice setting above crater lake.

Entertainment

Cinemas

Unlike most cinemas the information lines are manned by human beings, not a tape recording, so you can actually ask what the movie's like as well as what time it's playing

Cinemateca Nacional, Parque Central south corner, US$2, non-mainstream movies, T222-6560, Mon-Fri 1830, 2000, Sat, Sun 1600, 1800, 2000. *Alianza Francesa*, Altamira, 1 block north of Mexican Embassy, Fri 1900, French films, free, art exhibits during the day. *El Coro de Angeles*, Km 5 Carretera a Masaya, BanExpo, 100 varas abajo, small cultural centre with a European flavour, showing non-Hollywood films with video projector, Thu-Sun, US$2. *Cinemas 1 & 2*, Camino de Oriente, T267-0964, US films, Spanish subtitles. *Alhambra 1, 2 & 3*, Camino de Oriente, T270-3842, mostly US films with Spanish subtitles, occasional Spanish and Italian films, US$3, bring sweater for polar a/c. *Plaza Inter*, T222-5090, 4 screens, American films, subtitles in Spanish, buy tickets in advance for weekend nights. *Metrocentro Cinemark*, 6 screens, small theatres with steep seating, very crowded so arrive early, impossible to see well from front rows, US$3. **NB** Flyers with film schedules are free at supermarkets and petrol station mini-markets. If possible see a comedy; the unrestrained laughter of the Nicaraguan audience is sure to make the movie much funnier.

Dance & theatre

To find out what's on in Managua and throughout the country, look in Thu and Fri newspapers for listings

Ballet Tepenahuatl, one of many folkloric dance companies in Managua, gives regular performances in the Centro Cultural Managua as well as the Teatro Nacional Rubén Darío. Check *La Prensa's Revista* page for what's happening. Folkloric, salsa and merengue dance classes take place at the *Escuela de Danza*, across from UNI. The *Teatro Nacional* also has plays in the main theatre and a small one downstairs. You could call the country's best-known theatrical group, *Comedia Nacional*, T244-1268 to see what's on.

Discos

You don't need to go to a disco to dance in Nicaragua; almost anywhere that has music and a bar is appropriate

Dancing is an integral part of Nicaraguan life at any age. The discos are mostly for people of 18-30 years and the music is played at a deafening volume, always. If your ears can take the pain, the party is always good and, as long as there is music, Nicaraguans will take to the floor. Most discos play a variety of dance music, though salsa and merengue are almost always an essential element. Some of the establishments in the Bars section (see page 71) also offer dancing. *Amnesia*, Metrocentro Intercontinental, 1 c abajo, T270-2409, salsa, merengue, some modern music, sleek yuppie disco, clientele aged 18-40, Wed-Sun, opens 2000, entrance US$4. *Bar Chamán*, on street behind new *Intercontinental*, US$3 entrance which includes US$1.50 drink coupon, young, devout dancing crowd, salsa, rock and disco on tape, lots of dancing and sweating, great fun. *La Iguana Club*, Plaza Coconut Grove, T278-8542, Wed-Sat, from 2000 until you drop, Thu is male strip night. *Island's Taste*, Km 6 Carretera Norte, T240-0010, Wed-Sun, 1800-0400, reggae, Garífuna music, the only place to dance to Nicaraguan Caribbean music this side of Bluefields. *KTV*, first floor Plaza Inter, T222-4593, daily from 1800, a fancy, but generic place, a Las Vegas hotel bar in the tropics. *Salsa's Bar*, Pista de Resistencia, T249-1515, daily until sunrise, this is *the* place for merengue and salsa lovers, there is always a whole lot of shaking going on, bust or move. *Stratos Disco Bar*, La Vicky 2 c abajo, T278-4013, US$5 entrance, very elegant, 1970s and 80s music, mixed crowd from 18-60.

Festivals

19 Jul is the anniversary of the fall of the last Somoza in 1979, a big *Sandinista party* in front of the stage at the *malecón*. The 2001 party had a turnout of 800,000 plus from all over the country; don't forget to wear black and red. *Santo Domingo* is the patron saint of Managua and his festival is from **1-10 Aug**. On 1 Aug he is brought from his hilltop church in the southern outskirts of Managua, in a crowded and heavily guarded procession, to central Managua. With party animals outnumbering the devotees, this may be the least religious and least interesting of any of the Nicaraguan patron saint festivals. Domingo must be the smallest saint celebrated in Nicaragua, too about the size of a Barbie doll and reported to be a replica, with the original in a safe box. On the Sun of the festival week is the country's biggest *hípica*, a huge parade of very fine horses and very drunk riders from all over the country. The festival ends on 10 Aug with a return journey to the Iglesia Santo Domingo.

Shopping

Bookshops *Editorial Vanguardia* in the Centro Antonio Valdivieso, C José Martí, near *Mirador Tiscapa* also sells records. *Hispamer*, UCA, 1 c arriba, 1 c al sur, 1 c arriba, is the best Spanish-language bookstore in the country, with a great selection of Nicaraguan authors and informative books.

Handicrafts The best place for handicrafts in Managua is the central market, *Roberto Huembes*, which offers an ample selection from most of the country. On the 1st Sat of every month there is a craft fair at the **Centro Cultural Managua**, which gives some more unusual crafts a chance to be seen and sold. *IMPYME*, the Nicaraguan Institute for Small and Medium Enterprise has a store a few blocks behind the *Intercontinental Metrocentro*, 2 c arriba, 1 c norte, ½ abajo, T277-0599, inpyme@ibe.com.ni, with a good variety of crafts such as hammocks and ceramics. There are also little shops around the city that sell specialized products. **NB** All the markets have some crafts, but avoid the *Oriental Market*. Possibly the biggest informal market in Latin America, this is the heart of darkness in Managua, with some 60% of the crimes in the *country* being committed here. Its dark labyrinths are for hard-core adventure travel and survival television programmes, but not worth the risk for simple shopping.

Photography Fuji, AGFA and Kodak all have distributors in Managua. *Fuji* is next to the *Holiday Inn* and *AGFA* is 2 blocks east and a block north from the El Güegüence roundabout of Plaza España. There is a *Kodak* next to AGFA, as well as branch stores all over the city. The main office is the only one that has slide and black and white film; it is located behind the BANIC building on Carretera a Masaya just north of the Centroamérica roundabout. Slide film is very expensive in Nicaragua, at US$12 or more per roll. Print film is more reasonable with prices from US$4 per roll. Don't have slides or black and white film developed in Nicaragua; if it is urgent, the AGFA lab in Bolonia, near Plaza España, is highly recommended, with a quality that rivals any 1-hr lab in the world. When shopping for film at home, keep in mind that anything lower than 400 ASA in the rainforest is impossibly slow.

   Camera repair *Mecánica Fotográfica de Róger Bermudez*, near Mercado Huembes. *Foto Castillo*, ½ c al sur, 1 c abajo, E-185, Villa Don Bosco, T249-0871, Mon-Fri 0800-1700, good for basic repairs of still equipment and video.

Shopping malls The 2 big shopping malls are the Plaza Inter and Metrocentro, always full on weekends and a good place to people-watch. The *Plaza Inter* has better deals, with some low-price stores and good cinemas. They often programme events on the patio to the east of the mall. The *Metrocentro* is bigger and broader and attracts a more affluent crowd and prices reflect it. The cinemas are better in Plaza Inter, but the food court is much better in Metrocentro, where several good Nicaraguan restaurants offer good prices and quick service. Metrocentro also has a little area of banks underneath the southern escalator with 4 banks that are open late on Sat and also on Sun afternoon for a couple of hours (most 1200-1600).

Supermarkets Three big chains are represented in Managua, with *Supermercado La Colonia* being the best. It is located in Plaza España and at the roundabout in the Centroamérica neighbourhood. The Plaza España branch has a Kodak and both branches have a salad bar with some cheap *cafetería*-style dishes for lunch, and a good selection of Nicaraguan books and magazines. *Supermercado La Unión* is a few blocks east of the Plaza Inter and *Supermercados Pali* is the cheapest with goods still in their shipping boxes and no bags supplied at the checkout counter; they can be found scattered around the city. *Supers* have good prices for coffee and rum if you are thinking of taking some home, and they are great for finding imported goods such as tea.

Sports

The national sport and passion is **baseball**, which has been established in Nicaragua for more than 100 years. Games are on Sun mornings at the national stadium, *Estadio Denis Martínez*, just north of the Barrio Martha Quezada. It was in front of this stadium that one of the most symbolic scenes of the 1978-79 Revolution occurred – the destruction of the statue of Somoza on horseback, which is depicted on the back of older 50 córdoba notes. The pedestal remains empty in front of the stadium. The season runs from Nov-Feb, with good seats US$4 and a cheap one at US$1. For further information see page 38. **NB** Golf and tennis are rarely played in Nicaragua: there are a couple of tennis courts at the park by the parliamentary building, and only two golf courses in the whole country.

Tour operators

All the tour operators listed are members of ANTUR, the Nicaraguan tour operators' association and are licensed with the Nicaraguan Institute of Tourism

Careli Tours, Plaza El Sol, 3 c al sur, T278-2572, F278-2574, info@carelitours. com Focused on large groups and mass tourism, but with programmes for individual travellers, good guides, professional service. *Munditur Tours*, Km 4.5 Carretera a Masaya, T278-5716, fishing and dove hunting programmes, very funny owner/guide Adán Gaitán speaks English and is president of the tour operators' association. *Millennium Tours*, Altamira D'Este, casa 455, T278-9759, miltours@ideay. com.ni Friendly owner Maria Ofelia, Spanish only. *Nicarao Lake Tours*, Bancentro Bolonia, 120 m arriba, T266-1694, F266-0704, nlr@nicaraolake. com.ni Owner of several hotels and tourist properties, including a nice hotel in Las Isletas de Granada; fishing and other programmes also offered. *Nicaragua Adventures*, Planes de Altamira 103, T267-4406, nica-adv@nicanet. com.ni Owner/guide/driver Pierre is charming, speaks French and English, and offers low-price 1-day tours of the Pacific. *Tours Nicaragua*, old *Hotel Intercontinental*, 1 c al sur, Av Bolívar, T228-7063, F228-7064, nicatour@nic.gbm.net, www.toursnicaragua.com Tours to all parts of the country with English-speaking guides, volcano trekking, cultural and archaeological programmes, Corn Island, Ometepe Island, Pacific surfing, Indio Maíz and Los Guatuzos wildlife reserves; best company for Río San Juan. Prices based on group size. Discount hotel reservations, English spoken, owner and devout trekker Mike Newton is very helpful.

Turismo Joven, Calle 27 de Mayo, del Cine Cabrera 3 c arriba, (inside Nicabus station), T222-2619, F222-2143, turjoven@munditel.com.ni Travel agency and representative for international student identity cards, affiliated to Youth Hostel Association. *El Viajero*, Plaza España, 2 c abajo, No 3, T268-3815, manager Karola is very helpful, cheap flights to all parts. Recommended. *Continental*, across from *La Cocina de Doña Haydée*, T278-1233. *Globo*, across from AGFA Bolonia, Edificio Policlínica Nicaragüense, T266-4515, contact Alfredo. In Plaza España area are *Aeromundo*, T266-8725, *Atlantida*, T266-4050 and *Capital Express*, T266-5043, F266-3583, capital@ibw.com.ni

Travel agencies
All travel agencies sell domestic and international flight tickets

Transport

Bus City buses in Managua charge US$0.25 per ride; pay when you get on. They run every 10 mins 0530-1800, and every 15 mins 1800-2200; buses are frequent but their routes are difficult to fathom. The main bus routes are: **101** from Las Brisas, passing CST, *Intercontinental Hotel*, Mercado Oriental, then on to Mercados San Miguel and Mayoreo; **103** from 7 Sur to Mercado Lewites, Plaza 19 de Julio, Metrocentro, Mercado San Miguel and Villa Libertad; **109** from Teatro Darío to the Bolívar/Buitrago junction just before *Intercontinental*, turns east, then southeast to Mercado Huembes/bus station; **110** from 7 Sur to Villa San Jacinto passing en route Mercado Lewites, Plaza 19 de Julio, Metrocentro, Mercado Huembes/bus station and Mercado San Miguel; **113** from Ciudad Sandino, Las Piedrecitas, CST, *Intercontinental*, to Mercado Oriental; **116** runs east-west below *Intercontinental*, on Buitrago, also passing CST; **118** takes a similar route but turns south on Williams Romero to Plaza España, thence to Israel Lewites bus station; **119** from Plaza España to Mercado Huembes/bus station via Plaza 19 de Julio; **123** from Mercado Lewites via 7 Sur and Linda Vista to near Palacio Nacional de Cultura, and Nuevo Diario. **NB** Beware of pickpockets on the crowded urban buses. Crime is prevalent at bus stops and on city buses, if there are no seats available (which is normal) you are at more risk.

Local
City buses are usually very full and try not to come to a full stop for only one or two people getting on or off; they slow down and the assistant yanks you on

Car hire There are more than 15 car rental agencies in Managua. The rates are all very similar, though vehicles from the more successful agencies tend to be in better condition. It is not a good idea to rent a car for getting around Managua as it is a confusing city and fender benders are common (you will pay the excess). Outside the capital roads are well marked and a rental car means you can get around more freely. (Taxis can also be hired by the hour or by the day, see below.) For good service and 24-hr roadside assistance, the best rental agency is *Budget*, with rental cars at both the old *Intercontinental*, T222-2336, in the Texaco station across from the new *Intercontinental*, T278-9504, the airport, T263-1222, and *Holiday Inn*, T270-9669. Their main office is just off Carretera Sur at Montoya, 1 c abajo, 1 c al sur, T266-7222. Average cost of a small Toyota is US$45 per day while a 4WD (a good idea if exploring) is around US$85 per day with insurance and 200 km a day included. Check website for details: www.budget.com.ni Also at the airport is *Avis*, T233-3861, avis@ibw.com.ni, and at the *Hotel Camino Real*, T263-1381. *Hertz*, hertznic@interlink.com.ni, is at the airport, T233-1237, the *Holiday Inn*, T270-4069, *Intercontinental Metrocentro*, T270-0283, and old *Intercontinental*, T222-2320. Another respectable agency is *Toyota Rent a Car*, www.toyotarentacar.com, which has cars to match its name and is at the airport, T233-2192, the *Hotel Princess*, T270-4937, *Camino Real*, T263-2358, and old *Intercontinental*, T222-2269. *Rent-a-Jeep*, Colonial Los Robles, semáforos de la nueva pista, 1 c al lago, 1 c abajo, T267-0147, slivan@cablenet. com.ni, specializes in renting 4WDs. They have chauffeurs and waive the deposit if you hire one.

Managua

Taxis without red licence plates are 'piratas' (unregistered); avoid them if possible

Taxis The Managua *taxista* has an unparalleled knowledge of the city. Taxis can be flagged down in the street. They also cruise the bus stations and markets looking for passengers. Find out the fare (*¿por cuánto me lleva?*) before entering (fares range from US$0.80-US$1 for a short trip, US$1.50-US$2.50 across town, US$8 to airport). Fares are always per person, not per car. For tips on the art of taxi hire in Managua, see page 77. **NB** It may be handy to have the telephone number of your hotel with you. Street names and numbers are not universal in the city and the taxi driver may not recognize the name. Make sure you know the co-ordinates if you are heading for a private residence. If you are going to Barrio Martha Quezada, ask for the Ticabus terminal if you do not know your exact destination.

Some recommended **radio taxis** are: *Cooperativa 25 de Febrero*, T222-5218, *Cooperativa 2 de Agosto*, T263-1512, *Cooperativa René Chávez*, T222-3293, *Cooperativa Mario Lizano*, T268-7669. Get a price quote on the phone (normally 80-100% more expensive) and reconfirm the cost when the taxi arrives.

Radio taxis can also be hired by the hour or by the day for use inside Managua and for trips anywhere in the country. This should be done with a radio taxi company, negotiating the fare per hour, per day or per journey. Some guidelines are: US$10 per hour inside Managua; US$50 per day inside Managua; a trip to Volcán Masaya, US$50, Granada US$65; León US$75, Estelí US$100, border with Honduras US$150. Despite his love of hard braking (3 sets of brake pads a year) *Santos Andino* is a very safe, reliable and friendly driver (book via *Cooperativa René Chávez*, see above, or direct on mobile T0881-3085. Other good *taxistas* (both members of *Cooperativa 2 de Agosto*, see above) are **León Germán Hernández**, home T249-9416, mobile T0883-3703, and **Dionisio Ríos Torres**, T263-1838.

Long distance

Foreigners can pay in dollars or córdobas for domestic flight tickets, but dollars only for international tickets

International flights You must reconfirm your flight out of Nicaragua 48 hrs in advance (call the airline office during business hours Mon-Sat). There's a US$25 exit tax on all international flights. Cheap food is available upstairs at the airport (after check-in) and there are also some stalls for last-minute shopping for crafts. Once through security, in duty free, everything except the rum is imported, so spend your last córdobas before you get there. BanPro, downstairs, is the only bank in the airport, open 0900-1200, 1400-1600. They do not change travellers' cheques, but will change cash. There is also an ATM machine that accepts Visa. The X-ray machines at the security check-point are not recommended for film above 200 ASA (pass film around the machine).

The 50-min flight in the 15-seat Cessna from Managua to San Carlos is a beautiful adventure, with great views over Lake Nicaragua. The gravel and mud landing strip in San Carlos has been described as resembling "an Irish country road". What has been said about the alternative, a treacherous 9-hr bus ride is unprintable

Domestic flights Two domestic carriers serve the Caribbean coast destinations of Corn Island, Bluefields and Puerto Cabezas: *La Costeña*, T263-1228, F263-1281 and *Atlantic Airlines*, T222-3037, F228-5614; both have flights daily. For flights to San Carlos in the Río San Juan you will need to use *La Costeña*. Tickets can be bought at the domestic terminal, which is located just west of the exit for arriving international passengers, or from city travel agents or tour operators. *La Costeña* flights are in single-prop Cessna Caravans or 2-prop Short 360s. In the Cessna there is no room for overhead lockers, so pack light and check in all you can. For checked luggage on all flights there is a 15-kg (30-lb) weight limit per person for 1-way flight, 25 kg (55 lb) for round-trip tickets. There is a US$1.25 exit tax on domestic flights.

La Costeña schedules are subject to change at any time; all flights run daily, Mon-Sun. **Managua-Corn Island**, 0630, 1400 and **Corn Island-Managua** 0810, 1540, US$103.00 round-trip. **Managua-Bluefields**, 0630 (2 flights at same time), 1400 and **Bluefields-Managua**, 0740, 0840, 1610, US$81 round-trip. **Managua-Puerto Cabezas**, 0730, 1030 and **Puerto Cabezas-Managua**, 0820, 1220, US$94 round-trip. **Puerto Cabezas-Bluefields**, 1110 (no flight Sun) and **Bluefields-Puerto Cabezas** 1210 (no flight Sun), US$50 one-way. **Managua-San**

The art of taxi hire

Despite the Managuan taxi driver's spirited interpretation of Nicaraguan driving laws, his knowledge of the city is second to none and taxis are often the best way to travel in the cities of Nicaragua.

The main point to understand is that the taxi hailed on the street is really a colectivo, with all seats inside available for hire to the same destinations and to places en route. After flagging down a taxi in the street, lean into the passenger window and state your desired destination (your best Spanish accent should keep the rates down). If the driver nods in acceptance, ask him how much – '¿por cuánto me lleva?' There are no set rates so, unless his quote is outrageously high (see guide lines below), get in. It is normal for most drivers to quote the going rate plus two to 10 córdobas extra for foreigners. When you reach your destination pay the driver with the most

exact money possible (they never seem to have change for 20 córdoba notes – a good way of making a few extra centavos).

The minimum charge is 10 córdobas (US$0.70) per person (there will be a discount for two people riding together); within the same area the fare should be about 12-15 córdobas (US$1); halfway across town no more than 20 córdobas (US$1.50); and all the way across town 25-30 córdobas (US$2). The exception is journeys to the airport, which cost 50 córdobas (US$4) from Managua city centre. Radio taxis from the airport into the city charge US$10-12 and do not stop for other passengers.

For an early or late-night journey it may be wiser to call a radio taxi, which normally charges double the going rate, but is private and in most cases in better condition than the other taxis.

Managua

Carlos, 0900 (Fri and Sun at 1200) and **San Carlos-Managua** 1000 (Fri and Sun at 1300), US$94 round-trip.

Inter-city buses Buses for destinations south of Managua leave from **Mercado Roberto Huembes** (also called **Mercado Central**). **Managua-Masaya**, every 30 mins, 0415-2200, US$0.40, 1 hr; *Express*, every 30 mins, 0500-2100, US$0.80, 40 mins. **Managua-Granada**, every 20 mins, 0500-2100, US$0.70, 1½ hrs; *Express* from **La UCA**, every 30 mins, 0500-2200, US$1, 1 hr. **Managua-Rivas**, every 20 mins, 0400-1830, US$1.50, 2 hrs 45 mins. **Managua-San Jorge** (dock), 0830, 1500, US$2, 2½ hrs. **Managua-San Juan del Sur**, every hour, 0400-1600, US$2.25, 3½ hrs. **Managua-Peñas Blancas**, 0400, US$3.50, 3½ hrs. **Managua-San Carlos**, daily, 0500, 0600, 0700, 1300, US$7, 9½ hrs.

For return times see individual destinations

For destinations east and then north or south, the buses leave from **Mercado Mayoreo**. **Managua-Boaco**, every 30 mins, 0430-1800, US$1.50, 2½ hrs. **Managua-Juigalpa**, every hour, 0500-1700, US$2.25, 3 hrs. **Managua-El Rama**, every hour, 0400-1100, US$5.25, 8-10 hrs. **Managua-San Carlos**, every hour, 0505-1310, US$5.25, 9 hrs. **Managua-Matagalpa**, every hour, 0500-1800, US$2.25, 2½ hrs. **Managua-Jinotega**, every hour, 0500-1730, US$3, 3½ hrs. **Managua-Estelí**, every hour, 0545-1745, US$2.25, 2¾ hrs; *Express Luxury*, 1315, 1515, US$3, 2¾ hrs. **Managua-Ocotal**, every hour, 0510-1700, US$3.25, 3½ hrs. **Managua-Somoto**, 1330, 1530, 1645, US$3, 3½ hrs.

For destinations west and northwest, buses leave from the **Mercado Israel Lewites** (also called **Mercado Boer**). **Managua-Pochomil**, every 30 mins, 0600-1830, US$0.75, 2½ hrs. **Managua-Diriamba**, every 20 mins, 0530-2130, US$0.80, 1 hr 15 mins. **Managua-Jinotepe**, every 15 mins, 0500-2100, US$1, 1 hr 20 mins. **Managua-León**, every 30 mins, 0500-1900, US$1, 2½ hrs. **Managua-El Sauce**, 1400, US$4, 3½ hrs. **Managua-Chinandega**, every 30 mins, 0500-1800, US$2.25, 2½ hrs. **Managua-Corinto**, every hour, 0500-1715, US$3, 3 hrs. **Managua-Guasaule**, 0300, US$3, 4 hrs.

International buses If time isn't a critical issue, international buses are a cheap and efficient way to travel between Nicaragua and other Central American countries. Buses are available to and from Honduras, El Salvador and Guatemala in the north, Costa Rica and Panama to the south. When leaving Managua you will need to check in 1 hr in advance with passport and ticket. Four companies operate the international routes to and from Managua. The buses all have a/c, toilet, reclining seats; most have television screens and offer some sort of snacks. The most famous is *Ticabus*, which parks in Barrio Martha Quezada (this is why the barrio has so much budget lodging), from Cine Dorado, 2 c arriba, T222-3031. Leaving next door are the buses of *Cruceros del Golfo*, T228-1454. Just across from the Plaza Inter shopping plaza, behind the DHL office, is *Nicabus*, T228-1383, while *Transnica* is a long-haul bus option, 150 m east of the Santo Domingo roundabout (the one with the big Jesus Christ) in Centro Comercial Lucila, No 8, T278-2090.

Travel time 15½ hrs **Guatemala-Managua / Managua-Guatemala** *Ticabus* leaves Guatemala City at
(not including 1300 or Managua at 0500, US$30 (plus overnight costs in El Salvador). *Cruceros de*
overnight stop) *Golfo* leaves Guatemala City at 0530 or Managua at 0430, US$53 (plus overnight costs in El Salvador).

Travel time 11½ hrs **El Salvador-Managua / Managua-El Salvador** *Transnica* leaves El Salvador at 0500 and Managua at 0500, US$25. *Ticabus* leaves El Salvador at 0500 and Managua at 0500, US$20. *Cruceros del Golfo* leaves El Salvador at 0530 or Managua at 0430, US$30.

Travel time 9 hrs **Honduras-Managua / Managua-Honduras** *Ticabus* leaves Tegucigalpa at 0800 and Managua at 0800, US$20. *Cruceros de Golfo* leaves Tegucigalpa at 0600 and Managua at 0430, US$20.

Travel time 9 hrs **Costa Rica to Managua / Managua to Costa Rica** *Ticabus* leaves San José at 0600 or Managua twice daily at 0545 and 0700, US$10. *Transnica* twice daily from San José at 0530 and 0700 and Managua at 0530 and 0700, US$12.50. *Nicabus* from San José at 0600 and from Managua at 0600, US$10.

Travel time 22 hrs **Panamá-Managua / Managua-Panamá** *Ticabus* leaves Panamá at 1100 to con-
(with 1 hr stopover) nect with 0600 from San José to Managua and leaves Managua at 0545 to connect with 1600 bus in San José to Panamá, US$35.

Directory

Airline offices Around Plaza España: *Aeroflot* T266-3588; *Air France* T266-2612; *American Airlines* T266-3900; *British Airways*, in the Grupo Taca office, T266-3136; *Grupo Taca* T266-3136; *Iberia* T266-4440; *Japan Airlines* T266-3588; *KLM* T266-8052; *LanChile* T266-6997; *Alitalia*, Los Pipitos 1½ c abajo, T266-6997; *Continental*, Km 4 Carretera a Masaya, T270-3403; *Copa*, *Sorbet Inn*, 1 c abajo, Carretera a Masaya, T267-5438.

Banks The best 2 banks for foreigners are *Banco de América Central (BAC)* and *Banco de Finanzas (BDF)*; their acronyms are used regularly. BAC offers credit card advances, uses the Cirrus debit system and changes all travellers' cheques with a 3% commission. BDF changes American Express travellers' cheques only, also with a 3% commission. Any other bank can be used for changing dollars to córbobas or vice-versa. See page 19 for more details on street changing and ATMs. *BDF* central office across Av Bolívar from the old *Intercontinental*. Other locations include: across the Carretera a Masaya from Metrocentro, T277-0343, at the Mayoreo market, T233-4350, in Martha Quezada next to *Cine Dorado*, T268-5662, and at immigration, T248-6272. *BAC*'s slick new office headquarters is at Casa Pellas, Km 4 Carretera a Masaya, T277-3624. There is a BAC in Plaza España, T266-7062, and at Metrocentro, with long hours including Sun afternoon, T278-5510.

Internet Internet cafés are being opened monthly in Managua. Near *Cine Dorado* in **Martha Quezada**, *Kafé@Internet*, CST, 120 m al sur, T0860-5103, charges US$2 for ½ hr. In **Plaza Inter** there is a small stand on the top floor, next to the food court, which charges the same rate, and a new internet café, phone and mail service on the bottom floor across from BanPro. **Metrocentro** shopping centre has the best (but most expensive) one in the country, with a direct satellite connection: *Café@TMX*, upstairs next to *Casa de Café* , US$3 for ½ hr, some English spoken, daily 0930-2000. There are also 2 cybercafés along Carretera a Masaya, one in the blue office complex just north of *Subway* sandwiches, *Kafé@Internet*, US$2 for ½ hr, Mon-Fri 0800-2000, Sun 0900-1800, and another 2 blocks east of *El Bongó*, **Cyber-Café**, Distribuidora Vicky 1 c abajo 2 c al sur, Plaza Coconut Grove, T278-8526, servicio@cybercafe.com.ni, Mon-Sat 0900-2200, US$2 for ½ hr. All offer snacks, coffee and soft drinks. **NB** You will get a slightly better rate at most if you pay in córdobas.

Post office and telephone *Correos de Nicaragua*, www.correros.com.ni, is at 21 locations around Managua. The main office for the country is 1 block west of Parque Central. The tall building was a survivor of the 1972 earthquake, but is looking the worse for wear. Inside, *Enitel* has telephone, fax and internet services, as well as a postal service and stamps for collectors, T222-4149. There is also a small office just before security check at the international airport. *Enitel*, T278-4444, telephone offices are spread around Managua; most are next to or near the Correos office.

See page 34 for details on making phone calls in Nicaragua

   Courier and express mail Correos de Nicaragua is slow so you may want to use an express courier. *DHL* is across from the Plaza Inter, T228-4081, with letters to the USA and Europe costing between US$35-50. A little cheaper is *UPS*, inside Plaza España, next to La Colonia, upstairs, No A-3B, T266-4289. The best deal is *SkyNet*, which is 400 m south of the roundabout at Plaza España inside the KLM office, T266-8052, prices start at US$23 to the USA and US$30 to Europe.

Embassies and consulates *Costa Rica*, Montoya 1½ c east, Calle 27 de Mayo, T266-3986, F266-3955, open 0900-1500. *Guatemala*, just after Km 11 on Carretera a Masaya, T279-9609, F2799-610, fast service, 0900-1200 only. *Honduran Consulate*, Km 12.5 Carretera a Masaya, T279-8231, F279-8228, open Mon-Fri, 0830-1530 (bus 118 from *Hotel Intercontinental*); *Honduran Embassy*, Planes de Altamira 64, T267-0184, F267-0183. *Mexico*, from Km 4.5 on Carretera a Masaya, take 2nd left and it's at the 1st crossroads on your right, in Altamira, T277-5886. *Panamá*, Colonia Mantica, el Cuartel General de Bomberos, 1 c abajo, No 93, T/F266-8633, open 0830-1300, visa on the spot, valid 3 months for a 30-day stay, US$10, maps and information on the Canal. *Venezuela*, Km 10.5 Carretera a Masaya, T276-0267, F267-8327.
   Canada, east side of Casa Nazaret, 1 c arriba, El Nogal No 25, T268-0433, F268-1985, open Mon-Thu 0900-1200. *Denmark*, Rotonda El Güegüence 1 c abajo, 2 c al lago, ½ c abajo, T268-0250, F266-8095, open 0800-1400. *Finland*, Hospital Militar 1 c north, 1½ c west, T266-7947, open 0800-1200, 1300-1500. *France*, Iglesia El Carmen 1½ c abajo, T222-6210, F228-1057, open 0800-1600. *Germany*, 200 m north of Plaza España (towards lake), T266-3917, F266-7667, open Mon-Fri 0900-1200. *Italy*, Rotonda El Güegüence 1 c al lago, T266-6486, F266-3987, open 0900-1200. *Sweden*, from Plaza España, 1 c west (abajo), 2 c to the lake, ½ c west (abajo), Apdo Postal 2307, T266-0085, F266-6778, open 0800-1200. *Switzerland*, Restaurante Marseillaise 2 c lago, Apdo Postal 166, T277-3235, F278-5263. *UK*, Reparto Los Robles, Primera Etapa,

Managua

main entrance from Carretera a Masaya, 4th house on right, T278-0014, F278-4083, Apdo Aéreo 169, open 0900-1200. *USA*, Km 4½ Carretera del Sur, T266-6010, F266-3865, open 0730-0900.

Hairdressers There are many salons and barber shops around Managua, but a really good haircut can be found in the Barrio Ciudad Jardín at the *Prestige Hair Studio*, BanPro, ½ c arriba, T244-2066. Ask for Irina Kudriavtseva who cuts with Russian precision, US$8.

See Estelí and Granada for more Spanish-studying opportunities

Language schools *Universidad Centroamericana*, better known as *La UCA*, T278-3923 and 267-0352, www.uca.edu.ni, runs Spanish courses that are cheaper than some private institutions, but with larger classes.

Libraries Managua's main **universities** have big libraries although the texts are almost all in Spanish. The following university websites have more information: www.uca.edu.ni, www.unica.edu.ni, www.uni.edu.ni, www.unicit.edu.ni, www.aum.edu.ni The country's finest library is inside the *Nicaraguan Central Bank*, 150 m east of Km 7 of Carretera Sur, T265-0131. They also publish many important books on Nicaragua's history, culture and economy.

Medical facilities Hospitals: the best are *Hospital Bautista*, near Mercado Oriental, T249-7070, F249-7327; *Hospital Militar*, T222-2172, F222-2391 (go south from *Intercontinental* and take 2nd turn on left); and *Hospital Alemán-Nicaragüense* Km 6 Carretera Norte Siemens, 3 blocks south, 249-3368, operated with German aid, mostly Nicaraguan staff. Make an appointment by phone in advance if possible. Private clinics are an alternative. *Policlínica Nicaragüense*, consultation US$30. *Med-Lab*, 300 m south of Plaza España, is recommended for tests on stool samples, the director speaks English. **Doctors: Internal medicine**, Dr Enrique Sánchez Salgado, T278-1031, Dr Mauricio Barrios, T266-7284. **Paediatricians**, Dr Alejandro Ayón, T268-3103, Dr César Gutiérrez Quant, T278-6622, T278-5465 (home). **Gynaecologists**, Dr Walter Mendieta, T278-5186, T265-8543 (home), Dr Edwin Mendieta, T266-6591. **Ophthalmologist**, Dr Milton Eugarrios, T278-6306. **Dentists**: Dr Claudia Bendaña, T277-1842 and Dr Mario Sánchez Ramos, T278-1409, T278-5588 (home).

Translations The Managuan tour operators have guides who can act as informal translators, but for precise, professional translation, English-Spanish and Spanish-English, contact *Thomas Lee*, T278-2465, tomlee@ibw.com.ni, who is expensive but good.

Useful numbers **Police**, dial T118 in an emergency. The local police station number will depend on what *distrito* you are in. Start with the Metrocentro area number, T265-0651. **Fire**, dial T115 in an emergency; the central number is T265-0162. **Red Cross**, dial T128 in an emergency, to give blood T265-1517.

Excursions from Managua

Laguna de Xiloá

Colour map 3, grid B3 Some 18 km northwest of Managua, off the Carretera Nueva a León (turn right at Texaco station), is the extinct volcano of Xiloá and its lovely water-filled cone. The laguna de Xiloá (meaning 'corn lake' in Náhuatil) is one of Nicaragua's most beautiful crater lakes with extraordinary turquoise-blue waters. It was badly flooded during the 1998 hurricane and is only just recovering. The flooding damaged the small whitesand beaches and the ageing Sandinista-era infrastructure, but there are plans to clean it and build a resort. North American biologists are studying the crater lake fish at the ecological research station . The wreck of an aeroplane in the lake dates from the US occupation of Nicaragua in the early 1930s. There are paddleboats for rent, some tired restaurants around the lake, and a motel, used primarily for hidden liaisons.

Take bus 113 to Las Piedrecitas for Xiloá, Sat and Sun only (US$0.35); admission **Transport** US$1.60 for cars, US$0.30 for pedestrians. Taxi one-way from the city centre should be about US$10.

Carretera Sur to the Sierras de Managua

Carretera Sur is the continuation of the Pan-American as it travels south out of Managua (as it enters the city, the Pan-Am becomes the Carretera Norte). At Km 6 is the little park **Las Piedrecitas**, which fills up at weekends with children and couples and has a cheap *cafetería* serving horrible hamburgers. The park has a view of **Laguna de Asososca** (meaning 'blue waters' in Náhuatl), the principal reservoir for Managua. It is a pretty lake and the view extends to Lake Managua and the Chiltepe Peninsula. At Km 9 on the Carretera Sur is another crater lake of an extinct volcano, **Laguna de Nejapa** (meaning 'ash waters' in Náhuatl), in the wooded crater of an old volcano that is almost dry during the summer. The highway continues south and turns right at a traffic signal 1 km past the final petrol station. From there the road rises gradually past some of the wealthiest homes in Nicaragua. The section of road from Km 19-21 has no development, this may seem like a coincidence, but some might tell you otherwise, as there is a **haunted house** at Km 20 (see box page 82). Past the haunted house the highway twists and climbs to the summit filled with transmitter towers called **Las Nubes**. You can turn left at the summit, just beyond the towers and take a narrow road that runs along the ridge. Close to the end of the paved road, a small turn-off leads to a spectacular view of the valley of Lake Managua, Peninsula Chiltepe, the Pacific Ocean and the northern volcanic chain, Los Maribios.

Continuing along the Carretera Sur is the small village of **El Crucero**, home of Arnoldo Alemán, President of the Republic until 2002. The climate here is remarkably fresh and there's a pleasant, moderately priced restaurant and hotel at the end of the town, *Hotel Capri*. Before the big white sculpture that marks the highway to San Rafael del Sur and Pochomil, a road branches off the Carretera Sur to the coast. The superb highway, built by President Alemán to provide easy access to his many coffee plantations, gave rise to much controversy and criticism in the local media. The Carretera Sur continues south to Cuatro Esquinas, Diriamba and the area known as the Meseta de los Pueblos.

Carretera Sur to the Pacific Coast

The Carretera Sur turns left to climb to the Sierras de Managua; continuing straight on over the traffic lights along the **Carretera Vieja a León** is not the recommended route to León, as its condition deteriorates further on, but it is the fastest way to the Nicaraguan Pacific. The Carretera Vieja a León climbs out of Managua and over a pass of fields and rolling hills. At Km 32, beyond the baseball and football pitches, is the turn-off to the **Carretera a**

La Casa Embrujada – a legend?

The Pan-American Highway twists its way up into the fresh forested highlands south of Managua, past many luxurious residences, the big walled-in homes of wealthy Nicaraguans. It seems strange that, suddenly, on one of the most beautiful stretches of the highway, the luxurious residences give way to the green goodness of Mother Nature. Then out of the blue, at around Km 20, the road passes La Casa Embrujada ('the haunted house') a two-storey house in ruins which, it is said, is not just haunted, but evil and possessed.

Some 35 years ago the owner of this hilltop house in paradise killed everyone in his family and then took his own life. For some strange reason the bodies were buried around the house, and this monument to insanity and murder stood empty for years. It was used again, at the time of the Revolution in the late 1970s, by Somoza's National Guard, who took Sandinista rebels to the empty house to be executed. Later, the Sandinistas got their revenge by taking captured members of the National Guard up the hill to the house to be shot and left to the vultures. The Devil could not have written a better script

himself. The house was not torn down, nor was it rebuilt: it remained there in full view of all who passed by, a monument to man's darker side. People talked about it, its ghosts, the strange cries, and the danger of going inside, especially at night.

The Sandinista government was not amused by this nonsensical ghost talk, and the army received orders to set up a 'base' there. A battalion of 200 soldiers was dispatched to the concrete red and white skeleton of a home. Their aim was to make a point to the Nicaraguan people: have no fear; the state is in control. Darkness fell and the soldiers settled down for the night. The nervous chatter and laughter died out and one by one they fell asleep. In the early morning the first soldier woke to a smell of tarmac and the deafening noise of an angry bus horn. Startled, he jumped to his feet to find that he had been sleeping in the middle of the road. He had no idea how he had got there. He looked down the road and, to his befuddled amazement, saw the other 199 soldiers waking from a deep sleep – all in the middle of the highway.

Masachapa. Another 25 km of fields, forest and sugar cane on a cobblestone road leads to the paved highway (turn right) that will take you to Masachapa. The first exit to the right is for the private beaches of the Montelimar Beach Resort (see page 83); carry straight on for the little fishing village of Masachapa, or turn left for the broad public beaches of Pochomil.

Pochomil Beach

Colour map 3, grid B2 The touristic centre of Pochomil (entrance is US$1.50 per car, free if you come by bus) has countless restaurants (mostly poor value) and a main beach that is not very clean. Further south the beach is cleaner, the sand lighter in colour and more beautiful. The huge, garishly painted presidential summer-house is here, and President Arnoldo Alemán has often been seen (usually with a smile on his face and a cocktail in hand, cruising the beach on his four-wheel drive, en route to a party with friends further down the beach). Along a rocky break at high tide natural waterfalls, created by waves crashing over the rocks, are great for cooling off. Further south is a cove with more very expensive homes and beyond **Pochomil Viejo** is another long beach. At low tide it is possible to drive in a four-wheel drive for almost an hour along this stretch of sand from Masachapa to just short of La Boquita in Carazo. North of the touristic centre is the rocky shore of Masachapa with many tide pools for cooling off at low tide. The surf here is strong and swimming far out is a considerable risk.

In Pochomil A *Ticomo Mar*, just south of the presidential beach house on a nice part of the beach, T265-0210. A/c and bath. (Best beach hotel in the region apart from Montelimar (see below) but still not very good value).

   In northern Pochomil A *Cabañas de Mar*, 300 m north from centre, T276-2137. Private bath, a/c, nice, restaurant and bar. **B** *Villas del Mar*, just north of Pochomil centre, T269-0426. Rooms with private bath, a/c, crowded, overpriced food at restaurant, fun party atmosphere, use of swimming pool $5 per person. **E** *Alta Mar*, 50 m south of bus station, T269-9204. Situated on a bluff with a great view of the ocean, rooms with fan, shared baths. Very good restaurant serving fish at tables on the sand. Hotel poor value, with suffocating rooms, dirty baths. Go to eat. Popular with backpackers because of lack of choice.

   In Masachapa A *Ecológico*, Petronic 300 m south, T248-3958. 10 rooms with private bath, a/c, swimming pool, TV. **C** *La Bahía*, behind Petronic, T0887-3489. Private bath, a/c, TV, parking, nice little rooms, not great locale, swimming pool, friendly staff, bar and restaurant.

   LL *Montelimar Beach Resort*, Apdo Postal 1262, Managua, T269-6769, F269-7757, www.barcelo.com Just 3 km north of Masachapa, Nicaragua's only all-inclusive resort. Price includes all meals and national drinks. Most of the rooms are in single-storey bungalows surrounded by towering palms. Rooms have a/c, minibar, cable TV, bathroom, supposedly the largest swimming pool in Central America, four restaurants, several bars, disco, fitness centre, shops, laundry, tennis, casino (US$50 per person for use of all facilities for 6-hr day, including buffet lunch). This was once the sugar plantation of German immigrants. During the Second World War the first General Somoza confiscated the land. His son made the estate into the family's favourite beach house, built an airstrip and turned the sugar plantation into one of the best in the country. The Sandinista government then took over and after the Revolution, the Tourism Ministry, led by Herty Lewites (currently Managua's Mayor), turned the vacation home into a very attractive beach resort. After the Sandinistas lost the elections in 1990, new President Violeta Barrios de Chamorro sold the resort to the Spanish hotel chain Barceló, which runs it today. It is set along an impressive beach with 3 km of uninterrupted sand. The beach is good for swimming with a very gradual shelf and weak current. The resort is normally full with Canadian tourists between Nov and Mar. For luxury on either Nicaraguan coast, there is no other option. The nearest public transport is at Masachapa; taxi from Managua US$30 (70 km), or hire a car.

Managua-Pochomil, every 30 mins, 0600-1830, US$0.75, 2½ hrs. **Pochomil-Managua**, every 30 mins, 0600-1800, US$0.75, 2½ hrs. This is a tedious ride.

Sleeping & eating
Early risers can go to north Masachapa to see the fishermen pull their boats on to the sand with the morning catch

Managua

Transport

Reserva Natural Chocoyero

This tiny reserve is one of Managua's best-kept secrets. Without a car the walk to the reserve from the highway is a long one – about one dusty or muddy hour. With four-wheel drive transport, it is the most accessible wildlife park in Nicaragua, just 29 km from downtown Managua and full of interesting wet-tropical forest wildlife. Chocoyero, meaning 'land of *chocoyos*' (the indigenous name for Pacific green parakeets, smaller versions of the Amazon parrot) is home to at least 800 parakeets. The park is also home to many other interesting species such as toucans, deer, snakes, lizards and howler monkeys. The *chocoyos*, which nest in holes in the steep rock face of the **Chocoyero waterfall**, spend most of the day flying around gossiping and eating fruit as far

Colour map 3, grid B3
Area 184 ha
Don't bathe in the park waterfalls, as they supply the drinking water for the region

as 30 km away. When they begin to arrive home at around 1530, the sight is spectacular and the noise of their incessant chatter is deafening. The local guides at the park are very enthusiastic about its importance, have a birding book and binoculars and work for tips. ■ *The entrance to the park is US$4 and a normal tip for a guide's job well done would be about the same again. T279-9774. Yáder Peralta is a recommended guide.* Another waterfall, **El Brujo**, is reached along a different trail where the forest is prettier but there are no *chocoyos*. To get there, take any bus from Roberto Huembes market towards La Concepción. Ask the driver to let you off at the entrance to the park and walk, staying to the left and then following the signs.

Managua to Boaco

East of the great lakes of Lago de Managua and Lago de Nicaragua are two infrequently-visited departments which produce most of the country's milk, cheese and beef. They are worth visiting for anyone who wants to see the Nicaraguan cowboy culture or anyone interested in pre-Columbian archaeology and the little-understood but impressive Chontales.

Exiting Managua on the Carretera Norte (Panamericana), the highway leads north to the small town of San Benito (Km 35). To the north lie the northern mountain ranges (see page 84) and to the east begins the Carretera a Rama highway that leads to the town of El Rama (270 km away) and the Río Escondido that drains into Bluefields Bay (see page 84). A very good paved highway leads past the **Las Canoas** lake, created by damming the Río Malacatoya that drains into Lake Nicaragua. The water is used to irrigate thousands of hectares of sugar cane that is cultivated just south of the highway. Here there are several places to eat a tasty lake perch (*guapote*) fried up whole. *Restaurante El Viajero*, fried *guapote* plate is US$3, with rice and cabbage salad. At Km 74 the road forks: to the left is the highway to Boaco, which is paved to Muy Muy and then continues to the Caribbean town of Puerto Cabezas (see page 84) – more than 400 km of unpaved adventure and the only road link from the Pacific to the Caribbean. At the fork in the road – called **El Empalme de Boaco** – there are girls who sell delicious *guirilas* (sweet, very coarse tortillas) with *cuajada* (home-made cheese) for US$0.30, extra cheese US$0.10.

At Km 88 is the pleasant hilltop town of Boaco, capital of the department of the same name.

Boaco

Colour map 3, grid A4
Population: 20,000
Altitude: 365 m

Surrounded by mountains and perched on a two-level hill, Boaco's setting is impressive and its high-low division gives it the nickname **Ciudad de Dos Pisos** ('city of two floors'). The relaxed cowboy atmosphere is reminiscent of some northern mountain towns, but the city is actually a commercial meeting place for the workers and owners of the sprawling cattle ranches that make up the department. Ask if you can watch cheese being made at the factory and store, by the entrance to Boaco, next to the open-air saddle workshop. They usually start making the cheese at 1100 daily. You can also buy good locally made cowboy boots. (The town of **Camoapa**, 20 km further on, also makes good cheese, saddles and traditional woven agave hats.) There are pre-Columbian statues in the parochial church of Boaco, which dates from the mid-19th century. Above the church is a lookout park with a fabulous view of the town and the surrounding hillsides and the streets of the upper level are nice to walk around.

Managua

F *Hotel Boaco*, across from Cooperativa San Carlos, T842-2434. Private bath, tiny rooms with tired beds, but clean, the best in town, with parking. **G** *Sobalvarro*, on Parque Central, T842-2515, shared bath, very basic, good location. There are lots of little places to eat, including *La Casona*, next to Texaco, T842-2421, 0800-2300 daily, serving surf 'n' turf, traditional dishes, grilled chicken, good, moderate prices.

Sleeping & eating

From Mercado Mayoreo, **Managua-Boaco**, every 30 mins, 0430-1800, US$1.50, 2½ hrs. From the central market in **Boaco-Managua**, every 30 mins, 0430-1800, US$1.50, 2½ hrs.

Transport

San Lorenzo

Back on the main Carretera a Rama, the right fork at the *Empalme de Boaco* passes a paved turn-off to the left (Km 88) which leads to San Lorenzo, one of the cutest villages of the region. Nestled in a narrow mountain pass, surrounded by lush green hills, this little village of 1,400 people has a pleasant air to it and its cleanliness and beauty make it well worth a stop if you have your own vehicle. The locals here are a bit amazed to see foreigners, but are friendly and welcoming. There is a small church and the Parque Central is half-way up the cobblestone ridge. The church was remodelled in 1977 and has a white-tiled floor contrasting with its dark wood ceiling. Across from the church, *El Taurete* serves cheap *carne asada* and tacos. Down the hill, 50 m from the little Parque Central, is *Restaurante El Mirador* with very cheap chicken and taco plates, very friendly owners and lukewarm beer. There is a lookout with little benches across from the eatery. You can get some extremely crunchy but excellent *rosquillas* in the village. 10 August is the feast day of San Lorenzo.

Colour map 3, grid B4

Managua

Cuapa

Continuing on the highway to Rama, the striking, extraterrestrial-looking, 600-m monolith of **Cerro Cuisaltepe** ('eagle's mountain' in Náhuatl) appears to the east of the highway beyond Km 91. It is believed to be part of an ancient volcano that was thrust upwards. In fact, the whole region is geologically one of the oldest in Nicaragua and volcanic activity ceased millions of years ago. The highway passes a prison and, later, a large slaughterhouse before reaching the dirt road turn-off to the small but famous village of Cuapa marked by a monument to the Virgin Mary. The road passes through pleasant countryside and at Km 134 the impressive **Piedra de Cuapa** appears to the south, reminiscent of Cerro Cuisaltepe and equally mysterious in form and appearance. At Km 149 is a monument to more than 70 Sandinista government troops who died in a lethal ambush by the Contras in 1985, remembered by Chilean poet Pablo Neruda (see page 85).

At Km 152 another Virgin marks the entrance to an access road to a monument and open-air church at the spot where the Virgin appeared to a priest helper, Bernardo Martínez (known as Bernardo de Cuapa) on 8 May, 1983. At the time Nicaragua was suffering from Contra rebel attacks against the Sandinista military, while personal liberties were vanishing rapidly all over the country. The Virgin, known as **La Virgen de Cuapa**, appeared on a cedar tree and told the man that the Nicaraguan people must unite their families and pray for peace. "Nicaragua has suffered much since the earthquake", she said. "It is in danger of suffering even more. You can be sure that you all will suffer more if you don't change." The man told of his experience publicly and there was a media frenzy. In Nicaragua everything becomes political, and

Colour map 3, grid B5

Barnardo's vision was no exception. The Sandinista administration, dealing with a big Contra problem in an area that was very unsympathetic to its cause, saw it as an anti-Sandinista threat and denounced Barnardo as a *maricón* (homosexual) and, worse still, a counter-revolutionary. The experience changed his life and he went on to become a priest until his death at the end of 2000. An elaborate monument stands on the beautiful hillside where the Virgin appeared in 1983; the only noise is the wind rustling the trees and parrots squawking in the distant forest. Even an atheist would find the setting special. On 8 May every year, some 5,000 pilgrims celebrate the happening with mass, prayers and confessions, in the hope of seeing her again. Mother Teresa of Calcutta visited the site twice. The village itself just 1 km down the main road is sleepy and uninteresting, though pleasant enough. The local church holds the official icon representing the Virgen de Cuapa, which is brought to the site of her appearance every 8 May.

Just a few kilometres past the entrance to Cuapa is Juigalpa, head of the Chontales department and cattle capital of Nicaragua.

Juigalpa

Colour map 3, grid B5
Population: 41,000
Altitude: 117 m

A hot and sprawling rural capital, Juigalpa is not terribly attractive, but its setting is beautiful and it is a great base for exploring the **Sierra de Amerrique** mountain range, which lies to the east. Nineteenth-century naturalist Thomas Belt lived in the valley to the east and wrote about this area in his book *The Naturalist in Nicaragua* (see Further reading page 52). You'll get a great view of the Río Mayale, the Valle de Pauus and the Amerrique range if you go to the east end of the street on which stands the museum. There, up on the left, is the lookout park, **Parque Palo Solo**, 'one tree park', which has an endless view of the mountains and valley. On Parque Central, the very modern **Catedral de Nuestra Señora de la Asunción**, constructed in 1966, appears starkly modern for Nicaragua with its two giant grooved bell towers. The cathedral has an interesting stained-glass treatment on the façade that is illegible from the outside; from inside the images appear to represent cowboys, women and Christ. On the south side of the church is a health centre and a post office. *Enitel* is three blocks north of the park and there is a *BDF* bank on the west side. Juigalpa has a raucous patron saint festival on **14-15 August**, when the image of the Virgin is taken from the hospital (where she stays all year long to help with healing) to the cathedral at the head of a procession of cowboys and about 30 bulls. As in the rest of the country the bulls are mounted and brave young men run around in front of them with capes. Juigalpa, like most towns in this region, has a brightly painted, very well-kept and attractive cemetery, on the main highway.

Juigalpa's claim to fame, and rightly so, is its superb **Museo Gregorio Aguilar Barea** or **Museo Arqueológico**. Founded in 1952, the museum has more than 100 pre-Columbian statues, of all different sizes, and with varying reliefs, but always in the same cylindrical form. Many are in excellent condition, despite being carved out of relatively soft rock and having been exposed to the rain and sun for more than 600 years. The works date from 800-1200 AD and include one that, at over 4 m in height, is believed to be the tallest statue of its kind in Nicaragua and perhaps in Central America. Their smooth cylindrical form differentiates these statues from pieces found on the other side of Lake Nicaragua and its islands. They are sublime works, depicting men, women, priests, gods and warriors. The warriors hold knives; others hold hatchets or, if idle, their hands are crossed.

The effort of this private museum is staggering considering its limited funds. The curator, Carlos Villanueva, is a young, enthusiastic and sincere protector of national heritage, who knows the surrounding hills and their pre-Columbian treasures better than anyone in Chontales. It was Carlos who discovered the biggest ceremonial *metate* (used to crush corn for tortillas) encountered anywhere in Nicaragua (87cm long and 46 cm tall). It is on display at the museum, along with many others. He has recently discovered a previously unknown ceremonial site with eight statues. The museum also has colonial relics, taxidermy of native species and historic photography. One of the most beautiful statues – **La Chinita** also known as the **Mona Lisa Chontaleña** (Mona Lisa of Chontales) – is currently on loan to the Louvre in Paris though she's due to return in April 2002. ■ *Mon-Fri 0800-1130, 1400-1630, Sat 0800-1130. Entry US$0.25. T812-0784. From bus station, ½ c south, ½ c east. Carlos Villanueva will take visitors on archaeological expeditions (including camping and 2-3 days on horseback). Contact him at the museum or T812-0511 at home.*

The nearest archaeological site is just a few kilometres outside of Juigalpa at the entrance to the highway to Cuapa, where numerous burial mounds and the ruins of some ancient homes lie behind a small school.

There are not very many good sleeping options in Juigalpa; most of the establishments are set up for love liaisons rather than overnight stays. This holds true for the best hotel in the department, **D** *Hotel La Quinta*, across from the hospital on the highway, T812-0812. 38 rooms, private bath with hot shower, a/c, TV. There is also a restaurant which is not very popular, with moderately priced steak dishes. The *La Quinta* disco charges US$2 entry for dancing, with a nice upper-view deck, complete with stuffed bulls' heads and wagon wheels. **E** *Hotel Rubio*, 2 ½ c south of the cemetery on highway, T812-0630. Private bath, fan, clean and basic, best value in town, parking. From Parque Central ½ c west is the **E** *Hospedaje Angelita*, T812-2408, with shared bath, outhouse toilets, small airless rooms with mosquito netting. They are nice people and the grandmother makes some interesting crafts. At the Parque Palo Solo is the *Restaurante Palo Solo*, with the same good view of the valley and mountains, good fruit juices, fruit salad in a milkshake glass and *Plancha Palo Solo*, a *carne asada* served with onions. For spice lovers, *pollo a la diabla* ('devil's chicken'), is made in a burning hot chilli sauce; moderate prices. There are 2 cheap places to eat in Parque Central. The best cheap meal in town is at the wildly popular **Comedor Quintanilla**, just past the cemetery opposite *Hotel Rubio*, 3 meals a day, all less than US$2, with generous servings, fruit juices, *sopa huevos de toro* (bull's ball soup).

Sleeping & eating

Join the locals on Sun at the Comedor Quintanilla (see below), who cure their hangover with a good bowl of bull's balls soup

From Mercado Mayoreo in **Managua-Juigalpa**, every hour, 0500-1700, US$2.25, 3 hrs. From the terminal **Juigalpa-Managua**, every hour, 0330-1700, US$2.25, 3 hrs. **NB** If you are staying on the highway and don't want to go into town to catch the bus you can wait at Esso petrol station on the highway exit to Managua.

Transport

Managua

Masaya and Los Pueblos

4

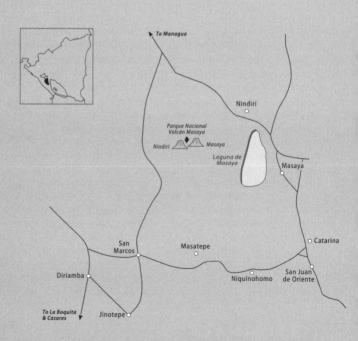

The inhabitants of this, the country's smallest, most densely populated department, are descendants of the Chorotega peoples who, despite having lost the use of their Mangue language, maintain a strong indigenous identity that is mixed with a deep Catholic faith. They are also famous for their manual skills and the Masaya area is considered to be Nicaragua's cradle of tradition, folklore and crafts. Most of the villages in this region were built in colonial times on the sites of important Chorotega settlements and their histories date back hundreds of years.

In Parque Nacional Volcán Masaya the very active smoking cone of Santiago exhales tons of sulphur every day from its molten lava pool. The active crater is easily accessible and there is good hiking in the park. In addition there are two crater lakes: Laguna de Masaya is inside the Masaya volcanic complex; Laguna de Apoyo, the country's largest, is home to a nature reserve with extraordinary eagle's-nest vistas from the rim of the extinct crater. The mesa of the highland villages, Los Pueblos, extends all the way from Laguna de Apoyo to the Pacific Coast, where there are sandy beaches and sleepy fishing villages.

Carretera a Masaya

This region of Nicaragua is easily accessible: Masaya itself is less than 30 km from Managua and travel distances between villages are less than 10 km

Leaving Managua on the **Carretera a Masaya**, a newly amplified highway of six lanes narrows down to two at the entrance to Ticuantepe and the Valle de las Piñas. Here, in the fertile soils of the back side of the Masaya Volcano, most of Nicaragua's pineapples are grown (hence the name, which means 'pineapple valley'). The highway leads past the exit to the Reserva Natural Chocoyero (see page 83) and into the department of Masaya and the village of **La Concepción de Masaya**, known simply as **La Concha**. It is a small, industrious highland village, very typical of this part of Nicaragua, where few travellers go. The area is rich in coffee, mandarins, oranges and *pitaya* fruit as well as pineapples, and the people are very welcoming. Access is by bus from Jinotepe, every 20 minutes, US$0.50, or from Managua's Roberto Huembes terminal, every 30 minutes, US$0.75. Accommodation can be found at the house of Jacinto Caldero, a former barber who lives next to the now-closed *Banco del Café* on the Carretera (**E** with full board, **F** without). Don Jacinto also shows visitors around on foot for US$20 per day, to see farms, wood shops and the countryside and to meet the local people (including the blind guitarist and songwriter Santiago). The highway continues to the university village of San Marcos (see page 104).

Past the entrance to Ticuantepe at Km 15 the Carretera begins to climb, passing an extremely popular restaurant, *Mi Viejo Ranchito*, Km 17, which is very good and cheap with typical Nicaraguan food like *quesillo* and *tiste* (see 92). The road continues to rise on to a small plateau, then dips down at Km 21 where the limits of the national park can be seen. The Carretera cuts its way through solidified lava from the 1772 eruption, which continues almost all the way to the runway of the international airport in Managua. At Km 23 is the entrance to the Parque Nacional Volcán Masaya.

Parque Nacional Volcán Masaya

Colour map 3, grid B3
Altitude: 635 m
Area: 54 sq km

Masaya is one of the most active volcanoes of the Americas and is reported to be one of only four on earth that maintain a constant pool of lava (neither receding nor discharging) in its open crater. Just 24½ km from the Metrocentro in Managua, with a 5-km paved road that reaches the edge of its active crater, this is undoubtedly one of the most accessible active volcanoes in the world. It is a beautiful place with a rugged landscape, delicate plant life and a stunning view of the great lake valley.

Ins and outs

Park hours are 0900-1700, though you will have trouble getting in after 1630. The US$4 admission includes entrance to the museum. The visitors' centre (the *Centro de Interpretación Ambiental*) is 1½ km in from the entrance. Shortly after is a beautiful area with toilets, picnic facilities and *asadores* (barbecues). Camping is possible here but there are no facilities after the visitors' centre closes. There are guided hikes to the fumaroles at Comalito, the coyote trail to Laguna de Masaya (at the moment you are not allowed all the way to the lake), or to visit the lava tubes of Tzinancanostoc (the bat cave) cost US$0.40 per person. If hiking, bring plenty of water, sunscreen and a hat. The hike up the hill is without shade, but hitching is possible. At the summit parking lot (Plaza de Oviedo) there are soft drinks for sale and usually coconut water (ask the woman to break open the coconut for eating after you drink the water).

History

At first glance it's not obvious that the park is actually located inside a massive extinct crater, **Ventarrón** (10 x 5 km) which includes all the park's cones and the crater lake. From the summit of the active cone, you can see the ancient walls of the Ventarrón crater sweeping around the outside of the park. Ventarrón is believed to have erupted in 4550 BC in a massive explosion. Since then, successive lava flows have filled in the cauldron and mountains have risen in its centre, the lake being the last remaining part of the original crater that has not been filled with rock and earth. The current active complex was called **Popogatepe** ('burning mountain') by the Chorotega Indians. In 1529 the Spanish chronicler **Gonzalo Fernández de Oviedo y Valdés** (known simply as Oviedo) visited the volcano and wrote that there were many ceremonies at the base of the mountain, with the Chorotegas sacrificing young women and boys to appease **Chacitutique**, the goddess of fire. In the adjacent village of Nindirí, Chief Tenderí of the Chorotegas told Oviedo that they would go down into the crater to visit a magical fortune-teller who lived there. She was a very ugly old woman, naked, with black teeth, wrinkled skin and tangled hair (there is a beautiful rendition of her in the park's museum painted by the Nicaraguan master Rodrigo Peñalba). The old fortune-teller predicted eruptions, earthquakes, the quality of the coming harvest, wars and victories; she even told the chief that he should go to war with the Christians (the Spaniards). Oviedo needed to hear no more to be convinced that this horrible woman was the Devil. After visiting the volcano, he commented that any Christian who believed in Hell would surely fear the crater and be repentant for his sins. Around the same time **Friar Francisco de Bobadilla** was sent to place a cross above the lava pool, in the certain knowledge that the magma was the door to Hell. The cross still stands in its original place above the crater, though it has been replaced several times. Another friar, less religious perhaps, or at least more capitalistic, **Friar Blas de Castillo**, organized an expedition into the west crater. Holding a cross in one hand and a flask of wine in the other and wearing a conquistador's helmet, Friar Blas descended into the crater to extract what he was sure was pure gold. With the help of his assistants and a metal bowl dangling on a long chain, he managed to extract some molten lava, which, to his profound disappointment, turned into worthless black rock when exposed to cool air.

Masaya and Los Pueblos

Masaya & Los Pueblos

★ Things to do in Masaya and Los Pueblos

- Watch squawking parrots dive into the smoke-filled crater of Santiago in the Parque Nacional Volcán Masaya as they return home to their wall nests.
- Find out about the fascinating indigenous history of the area at the small Museo Nindirí, in the peaceful and pretty pueblo of the same name.
- Shop for local crafts at the restored craft market in relaxed Ciudad de Masaya.
- Enjoy one of the country's finest views from the rim of the volcano at Mirador de Catarina; you can see across Laguna de Apoyo (the biggest crater lake in Nicaragua) all the way down to Lake Nicaragua, Granada, Las Isletas and Volcán Mombacho.
- Have lunch at *El Tunel*, Mirador de Catarina, and while you're waiting for that *pollo a la plancha* you can peer across the lake through their old army binoculars.

The final eruption of the Nindirí crater occurred in 1670 and the lava flow can still be seen on the left side of the access road when climbing the hill to the summit. Volcán Masaya burst forth on 16 March 1772 with a major lava flow that lasted eight days. The eruption threatened to destroy the town of **Nindirí** until, according to legend, the lava flow was stopped in its path by **Cristo del Volcán**, the church icon, and diverted into the Laguna de Masaya, thus saving the city. A colourful mural depicting the event can be seen in the park museum. Another violent eruption occurred in 1853 (though the park brochure says 1852), creating the Santiago crater as it stands today, some 500 m in circumference and 250 m deep. The crater erupted again in 1858 and fell silent until the 20th century, when it erupted in 1902, 1918, 1921, 1924, 1925, 1947, 1953, and 1965, before collapsing in 1985. The resulting pall of sulphurous smoke made a broad belt of land to the Pacific uncultivable. From 1996-2000 the crater has been showing increasing signs of life, with sulphur output rising from 150 to over 400 tonnes per day and a noticeable increase in seismic activity. For reasons of safety, the west side of the Santiago crater has been closed since 1997. (The photographs you see on posters and brochures of the famous lava pool are taken from that side of the crater.) In early 2001 the crater's gaseous output came almost to a complete stop and on **23 April 2001** the resulting pressure created a small eruption. Debris pelted the parking area of the park with flaming rocks at 1427 in the afternoon, and exactly 10 minutes later the crater shot some tubes of lava on to the hillside just east of the parking area, setting it ablaze. There were some minor injuries and several vehicles were badly damaged by falling stones.

Sights and trails

The Masaya National Park was created in 1979 and is the country's oldest

The park boasts 20 km of trails that meander around this intense volcanic complex. This area includes fumaroles at the base of **Comalito**, a small extinct cone, the crater lake of Laguna de Masaya, two extinct craters, **Masaya** and **Nindirí**, whose cones support the active crater of **Santiago**, along with three smaller extinct cones. The park is beautiful, its surreal moonscape punctuated by orchids and flowers such as the sacuanjoche (*Plumeria rubra*), Jesus flower (*Laelia rubescens*), and many species of small lizards. Racoons, deer and coyote share this rockscape, and motmots, woodpeckers and magpie jays nest in the trees. The real heroes of the park are the bright green parakeets, which nest in the truly toxic environment of the active Santiago crater. They can be spotted late in the afternoon returning to their nests on the interior walls. With only one egg to lay per year, protection against predators becomes essential, but vulcanologists who have travelled the world's active craters are amazed at this bird's ability to adapt to this kind of environment.

A short path from the visitors' centre leads up to **Cerro El Comalito** and the fumaroles there, with good views of Mombacho, the lakes and the park's extraordinary volcanic landscapes. **Sendero Los Coyotes** is a 5½-km trail that accesses Laguna de Masaya. **Sendero de las Pencas** is a hike through lava flows that is interesting in the dry season because of the flowers to be found in the area. The **San Fernando crater**, straight up the hill from the summit parking area (Plaza de Oviedo), offers great views of the Ciudad de Masaya and the lake, as well as the interior of the forested crater. The easiest and most accessible hike is up the 184 stairs to the **Cruz de Bobadilla** which also has a wonderful view of the park and Volcán Momotombo, Lake Managua, Río Tipitapa and the very northern tip of Lake Nicaragua. The **Cueva Tzinancostoc** is a gaseous cave formed by lava and full of bats. ■ *Los Coyotes, Comalito and La Cueva can only be visited with a park ranger and all tickets must be bought at the museum, US$0.40 per person. The rangers there can tell you what is open, depending on activity in the crater.*

Essentials

C *Hotel Volcán Masaya*, Km 23 Carretera a Masaya, T522-7114, F522-7115. 4 rooms with private bath, a/c, fridge, cable TV, and lobby area for relaxing, very comfortable. Spectacular view of the park and the volcano. There are several places to eat right at the entrance of the park. Just north of the entrance to the park is *Sabores de Mi Tierra*, T522-5428, 1130-2100, a funky restaurant serving traditional Nicaraguan food. All the traditional dishes like *indio viejo* US$2.50 with some good sampler plates of traditional meats, cheese and fruits that serve two for US$4-6. Good seafood cocktails, like the

Sleeping & eating

Masaya and Los Pueblos

Volcán Masaya

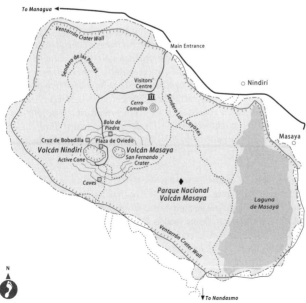

To Managua

Ventarrón Crater Wall

Main Entrance

Sendero de las Pencas

Visitors' Centre

Cerro Comalito

Nindirí

Sendero Los Coyotes

Bola de Piedra

Cruz de Bobadilla   Plaza de Oviedo

Volcán Nindirí

Volcán Masaya
San Fernando Crater

Active Cone

Masaya

Caves

Parque Nacional Volcán Masaya

Laguna de Masaya

Ventarrón Crater Wall

N

To Nandasmo

Not to scale

vuelve a la vida ('back to life') – black clams, shrimp, sea bass and avocado marinated in lemons and onions, US$3. Very nice garden setting, full of cactus, palms, with stuffed black iguanas as décor and a view of the smoking Santiago crater out the back. Recommended. Across from the park entrance is the open-air, ranch-style eatery, *Sopas Dina #2* with traditional meat dishes, fruit juices and of course soup, moderate to expensive.

Shopping Next to *Sabores de Mi Tierra* is the store selling religious icons and supplies, *La Inmaculada, SA, Artesanías Religiosas*, where you can buy a life-size fibreglass Virgin Mary (US$1,200) should you want to have your own procession, as well as authentic priests' shirts and robes. Some nice woodcarvings of Jesus, but most images are made of fibreglass and imported from Costa Rica. Smaller images are US$20-100. This is where the Nicaraguan Catholic Church comes to shop to clothe their priests and pick up new images for the local parish.

Transport **Bus** Take any non-Express bus between Managua and Masaya and get off at park entrance, Km 23. **Taxi** from Managua US$25 one-way or US$50 to wait.

Nindirí

Colour map 3, grid B3
Population: 37,317
Altitude: 220 m

At Km 25 on the east side of the Carretera a Masaya is the historic village of Nindirí with a cemetery marking the first entrance; the third or southernmost entrance leads directly to Parque Central. Inhabited continually for the last 3,000 years, this attractive, well-kept village is built in one of Central America's richest areas for pre-Columbian ceramics. A quiet place, Nindirí makes quite a contrast from the hustle and bustle of Masaya just down the road. The leafy and colourful Parque Central is marked by a tall monument to **Tenderí**, the legendary Chorotega chief who was in charge of this area when the Spanish arrived in 1526. In 1528 Diego Machuca laid the plans of the town, which was not officially named a city until 468 years later. The town church is a charming primitive-baroque structure with ancient tile floors, cracking adobe walls and a traditional tile roof. It has a comfy, well-worn feel, and is home to the patron saint Santa Ana as well as the famous **Cristo del Volcán**, credited with stopping the lava flow of 1772 from annihilating the village (see page 94). The **Museo Tenderí**, so overflowing with relics that it is difficult to distinguish one piece from another, is home to more than 1,500 pre-Columbian pieces and a few very interesting colonial-period artefacts. The elderly woman who owns the museum will show you around and can be coaxed into playing an ancient Indian flute that represents three different animals. Her deceased husband accumulated the collection. If she is not around ask the neighbours to help you find her. ■ *0800-1600 Mon-Fri, donation requested. The museum is the corner house, 1 c north of the Biblioteca Rubén Darío (which is located on Parque Central).*

Eating There are a couple of good places to eat in Nindirí if you want to stay and enjoy its timeless ambience: *Restaurante La Llamarada*, ½ c north of the church, T522-4110, daily 0900-2100, try the *lomo relleno*, cheap to mid-range. Quiet in the daytime, but filling up at night, *Restaurante La Quinta*, Alcaldía, ½ c north, T522-3675, serves great *plato típico* that includes pork, fried pork skins, blood sausage, beans and cream, fried cheese, fried plantains, grilled beef and tortilla. Mon-Fri 1000-2400, Sat-Sun 1000-0200.

Transport **Buses** between Masaya and Managua pass every 15 mins along the Carretera.

Masaya and Los Pueblos

Fortaleza del Coyotepe

Past Nindirí the highway rises again to the ancient southern wall of the Ventarrón crater where Masaya City is located, above the Laguna de Masaya. Just before the city limits is the extinct cone of Coyotepe and the Fortaleza del Coyotepe, which is open to visitors. The fort was built in the 19th century to defend Masaya. In 1912 it saw action during a battle between the US Marines and national troops. Though donated to the boy scouts during the 60s, it was used by the second General Somoza as a political prison and saw battle between Sandinista rebels and Somoza's National Guard. With the Sandinistas in power it remained a political prison, until it was finally returned to the boy scouts after the Sandinista electoral defeat in 1990. The cells below can be visited and screams can still be heard, if you listen closely. The top deck offers a 360° view of the department of Masaya and on to Granada and its Volcán Mombacho. ■ *0900-1600, US$0.75. Bring a torch/flashlight, or offer a volunteer US$1-2 to show you below.* The access road is a steep but short climb from the Carretera a Masaya; if you drive you will have to pay a US$0.50 parking fee. At Km 29 the main entrance to Masaya City is marked by a silhouette of Sandino. If travelling by bus you should get off here and walk into town; otherwise you can walk or take a taxi from the new market's bus station.

Ciudad de Masaya

Masaya has long been a vibrant centre for Nicaraguan culture and is home to several beautiful churches. Shaken by a 5.5 earthquake in July 2000, this attractive town suffered damage to some 80 houses and most of its churches. Many beautiful homes remain and the city is full of bicycles and traditional horse-drawn carriages, the latter used as taxis by the local population. Protected from the volcano by the Laguna de Masaya, the city is renowned across Nicaragua for its folklore and craftsmen.

Colour map 3, grid B3
Population: 140,000
Altitude: 234 m

History

Masaya has always been home to many skilled craftsmen. The first tribute assessments of 1548 for the Spanish crown stipulated that Masaya was to produce hammocks and *alpargatas* (cloth shoes). When US diplomat and amateur archaeologist E Squier visited Masaya in 1850 he noted that, along with Subtiava (León), Masaya was a centre of native handicraft production. Composed of at least three pre-Columbian villages – Masaya, Diriega and Monimbó – Masaya was briefly the colonial capital of Nicaragua when Granada rose up in rebellion, and it has always been involved in major political events in Nicaragua.

Sights

Most people come to Masaya to shop, and the country's best craft market is here in the newly refurbished 19th-century **Mercado Nacional de Artesanías**, one block east of the south side of Parque Central. The late Gothic walls of the original market were damaged in air attacks carried out by the National Guard during the Revolution in 1979. A newer market opened to replace the old one, which sat in ruins for 15 years until the walls were repaired and it was reopened, dedicated exclusively to handmade crafts. Masaya and its surrounding villages house an abundance of talent, which is clearly evident

Masaya and Los Pueblos

here. There are 80 exhibition booths and several restaurants inside the market and it's a great place to shop without the cramped conditions of a normal Latin American market. Every Thursday night from 1700-2230 there is a live performance on the stage in the market, which may be by one of Masaya's five professional folkloric groups with beautifully costumed dancers and live marimba music accompaniment, or a mediocre salsa band (you can call the office to see what's on). The market sells local leather works, wood, ceramic and clothing. ■ *Daily 1000-1700. T522-6000, F522-6129. Young boys will greet you at the market with the handful of words they know in English; they can help you find what you are looking for and will translate with the merchants for a tip of US$1-2.*

Masaya is famous for its locally produced, handmade **hammocks**, which are perhaps the finest in the world. The tradition pre-dates the arrival of the Spanish. The density of weave and quality of materials help determine the hammock's quality. Most are made of the same gauge thread, but you should compare; stretching the hammock will reveal the density of the weave. You can watch the weavers making the hammocks (normally in very cramped conditions) in their homes just a block from the *malecón*; with a deposit and 48-hours notice, you can custom-order a hammock in the workshops.

If the old market feels too sterile you can walk to the new one, which also has some crafts and is marginally cheaper on some items (but beware of pickpockets, as the surroundings are more cramped).

Ciudad de Masaya

Sleeping	3 Maderas Inn	Eating
1 Cailagua	4 Montecarlo	1 Alegría
2 Hospedaje Rex	5 Regis	2 La Jarochita

El Güegüence – comedy and identity

El Güegüence, the name of a 17th-century play set in Masaya, is everywhere in Nicaragua and has come to symbolize the very essence of what it means to be Nicaraguan.

Originally a verbal piece performed in Mangue, the language of the Chorotegas, the play was first written down between 1683 and 1710. Later it was translated into Náhuatl, the Indian lingua franca for the Spanish colonizers, and into Spanish.

As well as being a superb humourist, the anonymous Indian author was, without a doubt, a master of languages and colonial law. The plot is simple. El Güegüence (the buffoon) is an Indian trader in a variety of goods, some of which are contraband. He is called in by the local colonial chief of police for a bribe. In a very funny 'who's on first?' type of skit, he pretends first to be deaf, then stupid, so as to avoid the subject of

payment. Eventually he is brought in to meet the governor whom he befriends with wit, humour and brilliantly funny lies. In the end, feigning immense wealth, the struggling Indian merchant manages to marry off his son to the daughter of the powerful governor.

The play is laced with crude jokes and double meanings, many at the expense of the Spanish colonial ruler who plays the sucker. The great José Martí called it a "master comedy" and León vanguard poet Salomón de la Selva said it was, "as good as or better than what we know of Greek comedy before Aristophanes". The work has been analyzed by just about every Nicaraguan intellectual of any note. Each and every one has their own conclusion as to the plays deeper meaning. The average Nicaraguan calls it the master play of indigenous theatre, a source of cultural pride for Nicaragua.

The view of **Laguna de Masaya** and the Masaya volcanic complex is great from the *malecón*, or waterfront, always populated with romantic couples. There is also a baseball stadium, named after the Puerto Rican baseball star Roberto Clemente, who died in an aviation accident in Florida while en route to Nicaragua with earthquake relief aid in 1972. The lake is 300 m below, down a steep wall. Until a pump was installed in the late 1800s all the town's water was brought up from the lake in ceramic vases on women's heads, a 24-hour-a-day activity according to British naturalist Thomas Belt. There are some interesting petroglyphs on the walls of the descent to the lake that can also be seen in reproduction in the *Museo Nacional* (see page 99) in Managua. There is not a reliable source for a guide to see them, but you can try the *Masaya Club Social*, located on the lakefront at the far south side of the *malecón*.

Nearly every barrio in Masaya has its own little church, but two dominate the city. In the centre of Parque Central, **La Parroquia de la Asunción**, a late-baroque church constructed from 1893, is currently being restored. The work on the exterior is almost finished and the scheduled opening date is early 2002, though the earthquake of 2000 may have set that date back. The **Iglesia de San Jerónimo**, though not on Parque Central, is the heart of Masaya. This attractive domed church is visible from kilometres around and is home to the city's patron saint and a focal point for his two-month long festival. The celebration begins on 30 September and continues until the end of November, by far the longest in Nicaragua and perhaps in Latin America, with processions, folkloric dances and many bizarrely costumed dances and parades. You can check at the craft market to find out what is coming up next; there is sure to be some activity on a Sunday during the two-month period. San Jerónimo was badly damaged by the earthquake in 2000 and in 2001 it is still closed and being held up by four sets of temporary, exterior supports.

Masaya and Los Pueblos

Monimbó is the famous Indian barrio of Masaya. During Spanish rule the Spanish and Indian sections of major cities were well defined. Nearly all the lines have now been blurred, yet in Monimbó (and in the León barrio of Subtiava) the traditions and indigenous way of life have been maintained to some extent. The people of the southern barrio are masters of all kinds of crafts. In 1978, the people of Monimbó rebelled against Somoza's repressive Guardia Nacional; entirely on their own, without Sandinista planning, they held the barrio for one week and, with crude arms, fought against what was then a mighty army of modern weapons and tanks.

Essentials

Sleeping
■ on map, page 98
For price codes, see
inside front cover

Lodging in Masaya is very limited, due mainly to its proximity to Managua and Granada. On the Carretera a Masaya there is one good option. **C** *Cailagua*, Km 30, T522-4435. 22 rooms, secured parking, private bath, a/c, cable TV, swimming pool, restaurant. Noisy location with overpriced restaurant; only for the exhausted driver. **C** *Hotel Montecarlo*, Cuerpo de Bomberos, 1 c south, T522-2166. Private bath, cable TV and a/c, **F** with shared bath. Clean, good location, this is Masaya's best choice, good hamburgers in restaurant. **D** *Maderas Inn*, 1 c south of Montecarlo, T522-5825. Private bath, a/c, **F** with shared bath, very friendly owners. **E** *Hotel Regis*, from the church on Parque Central, 3½ c north, T522-2300. Clean, shared bath with fan, friendly, helpful owner. Highly recommended. **G** *Hospedaje Rex*, Iglesia San Jerónimo, ½ c south. Dark and dirty, this is for liaisons of the hidden kind.

Eating
● on map, page 98

Restaurante Che Gris, ½ block south around corner from *Regis*. Very good food in huge portions, excellent *comida corriente* for US$2.50, nice garden. Recommended. *Alegría*, C Real San Jerónimo, ½ block north of Parque Central. Good, clean, comfortable, not expensive, good pizzas. Inside **craft market** are several small places to eat, best during day is *Sacuanjoche* with chicken tacos US$2. *Coconut Sports Bar* is a trendy bar, good for a beer, hamburger and cable TV. *La Jarochita*, 75 m north of Parque Central, T522-4831. Daily 1030-2300, best Mexican in Nicaragua, excellent, some drive from Managua to eat here, mid-priced, try *sopa de tortilla*, and chicken *enchilada* in *mole* sauce. *Pochil*, near park, good food, ask for vegetarian dishes. *Xochild*, 50 m north of *Hotel Regis*. Has good *comida corriente*. A host of places on the southwest corner of the main plaza. *Panadería Corazón de Oro*, 2-3 blocks towards highway from the church, excellent cheese bread (*pan de queso*), US$0.50 a loaf. There are 2 *Fuentes de Soda* near the northeast corner of the Parque Central, both good, and 5 blocks north of the Parque Central is a small park with a Pepsi stand that sells excellent fresh 'Tutti-Frutti' fruit juice. **NB** Every Thu night during the festival there are many stands inside and outside the craft market selling very cheap, traditional Masaya food.

Dancing is very good at *Cocojambo*, next to the *malecón*, T522-6141, Fri-Sun from 1900. US$2 entrance, very popular disco, lots of fun.

Transport

Bus Buses leave from the new market or you can also catch a non-express bus from the Carretera a Masaya towards Granada or Managua. Express buses leave from Parque San Miguel to *La UCA* in Managua when full or after 20 mins. **Masaya-Managua**, every 30 mins, 0400-1800, US$0.40, 1 hr. **Express Masaya-Managua**, every 30 mins, 0400-2100, US$0.80, 40 mins. **Masaya-Jinotepe**, every 30 mins, 0500-1800, US$0.40, 1½ hrs. **Masaya-Granada**, every 30 mins, 0600-1800, US$0.40, 45 mins. **Masaya-Matagalpa**, 0600, 0700, US$2.25, 4 hrs.

Taxi Fares around town are US$0.30-0.80. Taxi to Granada, US$15 Managua US$20, airport US$25. Horse-drawn carriages (*coches*) US$0.30.

Banks Both banks that change travellers' cheques are just off Parque Central, *BDF*, **Directory**
T522-3204, changes Amex and *BAC*, T522-6395, changes all types. **Communica-tions** Internet: next to the bakery 20 m east of old market. Post office: *Correos de Nicaragua* is 1 block north of police station, T522-2631, F522-4747. **Telephone:** *Enitel* is on Parque Central, next to Palí, T522-2891. **Shopping** There is a *Palí* supermarket on Parque Central and of course the many craft workshops and the new and old markets. **Tourist office** Inside the craft market, T522-7615. **Useful numbers** Fire: T522-2313. **Hospital:** T522-2778. **Police:** T522-2521. **Red Cross:** T522-2131.

Carretera a Los Pueblos

Leaving Masaya the Carretera a Masaya becomes Carretera a Granada, which leads to the colonial city on Lake Nicaragua (see page 113). There is a secondary highway at the end of Masaya City limits that heads south to Los Pueblos. This highway can also be accessed via the main street of Monimbó that passes through the cemetery of Masaya. The highway to Los Pueblos rises continually to an average elevation of 500 m above sea level. It is one of the most agreeable and beautiful areas in Nicaragua. This *mesa* is cooler than the valley of the lakes and remains green even at the end of the dry season.

This, like Monimbó in Masaya, is the land of the Chorotegas. Although you will not hear indigenous languages nor see a particular style of dress (as in Guatemala for example), most of the people of Los Pueblos are of Chorotegan ancestry. The **Chorotega Empire** stretched from just north of Lake Managua into what is today the Nicoya Peninsula of Costa Rica. Made up of 28 chiefdoms, the capital for this large, loosely held empire was here in the high-lands behind Masaya. It is believed that the chiefs from all 28 local governments came to meet here every seven years to elect a new leader. Today the local people have a quiet but firm pride in their pre-Conquest history.

Catarina

This attractive hillside colonial-period village was built on top of a Chorotega *Colour map 3, grid B3* settlement and has a mid-17th-century church in front and an obvious love of *Population: 8,350* potted plants. The town climbs the extinct cone of the Apoyo volcano from *Altitude: 520 m* the highway until its highest point overlooking the majestic deep blue crater lake of Laguna de Apoyo. Between the highway and the lookout park are numerous horticultural nurseries, and Nicaraguans come here from around the country to buy their houseplants. Up the hill from the church the road has little potted plants on every lamp-post and the town is a pleasant one to walk in. The lookout, or **Mirador de Catarina**, has an entrance fee of US$0.80 if you come by car. There is a row of restaurants that share the magnificent view across the lake. From the lookout you can see the dormant Mombacho Volcano and its cloud forest as well as the city of Granada, Lake Nicaragua and part of the Las Isletas archipelago. This area is crowded on Sundays with families and romantic young couples, but for most of the week it is quiet. Due to its perch-like position it is breezy all year round but in the dry season the wind can be a bit strong for eating on the lookout decks. The eating places are all independently owned and, as you walk down the deck, will invite you to sit in their section. Try the last of the restaurants on the long deck, *El Túnel*, T558-0303, 1100-2000, where the view is best. Order *a la plancha*, which comes on a sizzling plate, with either pork, beef or chicken, and is served with fried plantains, fried cheese, rice and salad, US$5. They also have about five or six delicious *frescos* (fruit juices) to choose from. There are some small shops selling jewellery and crafts from neighbouring San Juan de Oriente in the parking lot. It is possible to hike down into the crater from the Mirador. The hike down is easy, with spectacular vistas; the hike back up is not so easy – it's only about 500 m, but a very steady climb. Ask at the Mirador for the trailhead and then keep asking on the way down, as there are several forks in the path that make getting lost a possibility (for the road entrance and lodging in Laguna de Apoyo see page 112). Catarina's patron saint, Santa Catalina, is celebrated on 26 November, but the town's big fiesta is for San Silvestre, on 31 December.

Transport **Buses** pass in front of Catarina every 15 mins to Masaya or San Marcos or Rivas. Buses to Granada are less frequent; take a bus towards Masaya and get off on the highway to Granada for a connecting bus.

San Juan de Oriente

Colour map 3, grid B3
Population: 3,770
Altitude: 495 m

Across the highway from Catarina and just south is San Juan de Oriente. This traditional little Chorotega village was called **Namotivá** before the arrival of the Spanish. It is now known around Nicaragua and internationally for its elegant ceramic earthenware. Until about 25 years ago, San Juan de Oriente was a village of indigenous clay and plant fibre houses. Stone-block construction is now the norm, and the last clay house in San Juan was ruined in early 2001 by a local boy who accidentally crashed into it while learning how to drive. Today, the distinguishing feature of the village is the tremendous creativity and dexterity of the predominantly indigenous population. San Juan's fame in ceramics is an old one and the local clay has been used to make hand-shaped pottery for at least 1,000 years. After the Spanish conquest, much of the ornamental expertise evident in the pre-Columbian pieces was lost, but the tradition continued until the 20th century. For many years, the village was known as **San Juan de los Platos**, because of the rustic ceramic plates that were made there. The villagers also used to sell pots for plants and storing water, of the type still used today all around the Nicaraguan countryside. In 1978 the Nicaraguan Ministry of Culture and the country's Central Bank initiated a programme of training scholarships. Eleven people from the village learned how to use a potter's kick-wheel, how to mix the clay with a product superior to sand, and how to polish and paint pieces in the pre-Columbian style that had been lost after the conquest. These 11 artists formed **Artesanos Unidos**, the town's first co-operative. After the success of the Revolution, the Sandinista administration helped support and promote the co-operative's work and the influx of foreigners who came to help the revolutionary government provided a more affluent clientele. In the most Nicaraguan fashion, the knowledge was unselfishly passed on to family members and to other families, and today at least 80% of the villagers who are old enough work in pottery production. The creativity of their designs and the quality of their work is excellent and their products can be found in markets and shops all over Nicaragua. To buy from the source or to see the artisans at work there are many houses with small storefronts or go to the artisans' co-operative, **Cooperativa Quetzal-Coatl**, 25 m inside the first entrance to the town. ■ *Daily 0800-1700*. Some of the more famous ceramic artists will sell direct and may invite you into their shop if you call ahead of your visit: **Francisco Calero**, Taller Escuela de Cerámica, ½ c east, T558-0300; **José Ortiz**, main entrance, 1 c west, on the left side, T558-0290; **Helio Gutierrez**, second entrance, 1 c west, 300 m south, T558-0338.

San Juan's small and precious early 17th-century church was shaken badly by the Laguna de Apoyo earthquake in 2000, which was followed a week later by the earthquake in Masaya. Work began in 2001 to reinforce the structure and reopen it. The main day for the often-wild festival for patron saint **San Juan Bautista** is 24 June.

Buses pass in front of the village's main entrance for Masaya every 20 mins; buses for Granada, Managua and Rivas are less frequent.

Transport

The highway to San Marcos begins at the exit of Catarina and is the carretera that takes you into the heart of Los Pueblos. Just 3 km from Catarina is another town built on top of a Chorotega settlement, the village of Niquinohomo.

Niquinohomo

This quiet colonial-period village is best known for its famous son, **Augusto Sandino** (perhaps the only Nicaraguan who claims more attention is the country's great poet Rubén Darío). The town's entrance is marked by a tiny church and a new statue of Sandino, installed in 2001, a bronze relief of the nationalist warrior who finally receives more than a silhouette to show for his legendary determination and integrity. His father's house – today the public library, on Parque Central, opposite the gigantic cross that guards the church – houses a small display on the life of Sandino (see box page 105). ■ *Mon-Fri, 0900-1200, 1400-1800.* The pride of the village is the town's stately church, finished in 1689. Both the classic exterior and clean simple interior of this long and elegant colonial church are pleasing to the eye, despite the unfortunate and monstrous new cross on its front patio. Apart from a few cynical men with drinking problems who hang around Parque Central, most of the village is pleasant, if a bit lacking in energy. Niquinohomo does come to life – in a big way – for its patron saint festival for **Santa Ana**, with folkloric dancing on 26 July. The Niquinohomo cemetery, on the far west side of the town, is well kept, brightly painted and pretty. Buses pass between Catarina and San Marcos every 15 minutes.

Colour map 3, grid B3
Population: 16,031
Altitude: 440 m

Several kilometres west of Niquinohomo is the entrance to the village of **Nandasmo**, which borders the south side of the beautiful Laguna de Masaya. The village itself is sad and rather neglected; it is a place that few outsiders see and wide eyes will greet any foreigner who walks through town. The climate is fresh, with the breeze coming off the lake. From the highway it is a 5-km walk to the **Laguna de Masaya**, where the views of the volcanoes and the city of Masaya are spectacular. It is possible to walk to Masaya from here although you will have to rely on local farmers to keep you on the right path.

Past the entrance to Nandasmo the highway leads to Masatepe and becomes an endless roadside market, with furniture makers displaying their wares in front of their workshop-homes.

Masatepe

This colonial-period village, once a Chorotega Indian settlement, is now the capital of furniture production in Nicaragua. There are small shops around the country, but Masatepe is overflowing with talented wood and wicker furniture makers. Great dining room sets and wicker baby cribs, hardwood bed frames and dressers, and the fabulous rocking chairs that are found in

Colour map 3, grid B3
Population: 28,870
Altitude: 455 m

almost every house in Nicaragua are made here in every style and type of wood imaginable. This is when many travellers wish they were going home on a boat rather than a plane. Aside from the countless roadside workshops that sell their products there is a big store at the entrance to the town, in the old train station. The town itself is hotter than most of the other *pueblos* of the region. Rickshaw taxis wait at the entrance and the *carretera* to take visitors on a small tour of the village for US$3. The patron saint festival for **Santísma Trinidad** is on 5-6 June.

Eating   There are many popular restaurants on the highway in Masatepe. The best is at Km 54, *Mi Terruño Masatepino*, T0887-4949, daily 0900-2100, where the menu features many traditional dishes. *Sopa de iguana,* though not on the menu, can often be found here as a special on the blackboard. Most prices are in the US$3-5 range and they offer a very big plate of assorted traditional foods for US$10 that feeds two. It has a cool and breezy patio next to a nursery with the kind of hardened and cured raw earth floor that is common in many Nicaraguan homes. The sign outside says simply *Platos Típicos*.

Transport   Buses pass on the highway every 15 mins en route to Catarina or San Marcos.

San Marcos

Colour map 3, grid B3
Population: 30,917
Altitude: 552 m

Continuing west 8 km, the highway enters the scenic coffee-growing department of Carazo and the university town of San Marcos. An active and optimistic village, San Marcos is known as the home of the country's only English-speaking university, once an extension of the University of Mobile and now a Catholic institution, still dominated by North American professors. **Ave María College of the Americas** (www.avemaria.edu.ni) is the university's new title and its location in the south of the town means there's a large student population (mostly well-off Nicaraguans) which adds an interesting atmosphere different to the rest of the *mesa*. The town was a big ranch until the mid-19th century and is very clean, with much life in its Parque Central, especially during the patron saint festival for San Marcos, which culminates on 24 April with the **Tope de las imágenes de San Marcos**. This is the famous meeting of the icons of the four main saints of the region: **San Sebastián** (from Diriamba), **Santiago** (from Jinotepe), the black **Virgen de Montserrat** (from La Concepción) and San Marcos himself. They are paraded around in pairs until they all finally meet at El Mojón (on the highway between Diriamba and Jinotepe). It is a huge party with great folkloric dancing. The next day there is dancing in the Parque Central and the four saints come out of the church together to tremendous fireworks with confetti and processions.

   The rather plain-looking church is happy and colourful inside with a series of murals on the aqua ceiling and over the altar is a fresco of Jesus in tropical surroundings, complete with Nicaragua's volcanic range in the distance. San Marcos is also the birthplace of **Anastasio Somoza García** (the first of the two rulers), whose mother owned a bakery in town and whose father had a coffee farm just outside the village. Somoza's home town is just a few kilometres down the road from Niquinohomo, the birthplace of his nemesis, Augusto Sandino. There is a rustic, 100-year-old coffee plantation outside San Marcos that welcomes visitors. **Café Natural**, on the highway between Cuatro Esquinas and San Marcos at Km 39.5, T432-2200, sndionis@ibw.com.ni , offers guided tours of its plant cultivating process and nursery which includes coffee plant species from all over Latin America, as well as mature plants. It may

General Augusto César Sandino

The man from who the revolutionary Sandinistas took their name is the Nicaraguan hero for armed opposition to external and internal domination in the 20th century. His shadow looms large over the Nicaraguan political landscape, as his giant silhouette does above the Tiscapa crater lake in Managua.

Sandino was born the illegitimate son of a white middle-class landowner and his Indian housekeeper in the small village of Niquinohomo in 1895. He spent his first 11 years living with his mother until his father agreed to accept him into the family house, where he was treated like a second-class citizen, eating at the servants' table. He grilled his father on life and equality. His father replied, "If I don't exploit, I will be exploited". Sandino would dedicate the rest of his life to a search for justice, defending the exploited while trying not to become the exploiter.

From 1923-26 Sandino learned about the conflict between big business and revolutionary ideas while working for a US-owned oil company in Mexico, where anarchist, socialist and communist ideas were commonly discussed. The Mexican Revolution had also created a strong society of Freemasons. In 1926 Sandino returned to Nicaragua with new ideas and in time for the Liberal Party revolt against Conservative Party ruler Emiliano Chamorro. The Nicaraguan Liberals shared many ideals with the Mexican Liberal Party and nationalism was one of its strongest elements. When Sandino showed up at Liberal Party headquarters asking for arms from Liberal General Moncada and Anastasio Somoza García, they were suspicious of his ideologies. Somoza, particularly, pointed to Sandino's use of the anarchistic phrase 'property is theft'. Despite the difficulties with Moncada and Somoza, Sandino managed to get an army together to fight the Conservative regime under the Liberal Party command. Later the US Marines intervened, pressured Emiliano Chamorro to resign and installed their perennially faithful president, Adolfo Díaz. The US threatened war against the Liberals unless they agreed to their appointment and terms. All of the Liberal generals capitulated, except Augusto Sandino. From 1927-33 Sandino fought a war of anti-occupation from Nicaragua's northern mountains, first against the puppet government of Adolfo Díaz and the US Marines, then, with the election of General Moncada in 1928, against the US occupation. His army won the respect of the Marines, who could not defeat their mountain guerrilla tactics. Sandino's strategies would later be used in Cuba to win the Revolution and with the Sandinistas to fight Somoza García's son, years after Sandino's death. When the US Marines left Nicaragua in 1933 Sandino signed a peace treaty with the Nicaraguan government; one year later he was abducted and shot on the order of Somoza García.

Much has been written about Sandino's religious and political theories. The truth seems to be that he was eclectic in his beliefs, combining bits and pieces of numerous theories, from socialism to Freemasonry. One thing everyone does agree on is that Sandino was a nationalist and today he is a national hero.

Masaya and Los Pueblos

also be possible to arrange a visit to a *beneficio* (coffee processing plant) as well if you contact them in advance and are visiting during the drying and roasting season (from late November to January). Coffee plantation visits can also be booked with *Careli Tours* in Managua (see page 74).

B *Hotel Casa Blanca*, across from the Baptist church, T432-2717. 16 rooms with private bath and hot showers, fan, clean. Next to the park is **F** *Hotel Castillo*, 7 rooms, shared baths, basic with cheap *comida corriente*.

Sleeping & eating

Transport   **Buses** run from San Marcos to Managua via La Concepcíon highway and to Jinotepe (south) and Masatepe (east). The buses west connect with the Carretera Sur (Carretera Panamericana), which can be used to catch buses south to Diriamba or north to Managua.

Directory   San Marcos also has a **BAC** (*Banco de América Central*) for changing money and all travellers' cheques, next to the main entrance of the university, T432-2339.

South from San Marcos is the highway to the Carazo department's two principal towns, Jinotepe and Diriamba. One kilometre before Jinotepe is the Nicaraguan version of Disneyland. To be specific the Herty Lewites version – **Hertylandia**. Herty Lewites, ex-Minister of Tourism from the 1980s Sandinista administration, is currently the Mayor of Managua. Hertylandia is a very simple amusement park in a green and spacious setting. The rides are specifically aimed at children and are of no interest to adults. There are two separate sections, one with a big swimming pool and water slide and the other with mechanical rides. There is also a mid-range to expensive restaurant with dishes ranging from chicken in mushroom sauce to lobster in a hot chilli sauce. ■ *Wed-Sun, 0900-1800. US$5 entry to both sections, US$2 entry to amusement section only, with additional charges for each ride (US$0.50-US$2). T412-2155.*

Jinotepe

Colour map 3, grid B3
Population: 42,566
Altitude: 569 m

Another pleasant highland town built on top of a Chorotega village, Jinotepe has a coffee- and agriculture-based economy and some pretty, older homes. The town prides itself on being the cleanest of the *pueblos*, although conditions at the bus station do little to support that theory. On the whole though it is clean and attractive. The city has a fine neoclassical parochial church that is said to be a scale mock-up of the Cathedral of León. The modern stained-glass windows are from Irún, Spain. The patron saint festival for **Santiago** runs from 24-26 July. The city makes a good base for exploring the *pueblos* of the *mesa*.

Sleeping   **B** *Casa Grande Hotel*, Enitel, 1 c north, 1 west, T412-3284, F412-3512. Private bath, hot water, cable TV, some rooms with a/c, nice building, central location, very clean and comfortable, with expensive restaurant. Recommended. **C** *Montreal*, Esso station, 3 c south. 8 rooms with private baths and hot water, fan. **F** *Hospedaje San Carlos*, no sign, ask around for it.

Eating   The most popular place in town to eat is *Pizzería Colisseo*, Parque Central, 1 c north, T412-2150, colisseo@ibw.com.ni Tue-Sun 1200-2200, simply the most famous pizza in Nicaragua, with 18 different toppings. Some customers drive from Managua to eat here. Pastas too. Recommended. Next door is *Buen Provecho*, T412-1145, Sun-Fri 1100-1500 only, baked chicken, beef in asparagus. *Casa Blanca*, Cruz Lorena, 1 c east, T412-2379. Daily 100-2200, Chinese food, wonton soup.

Transport   **Bus**   As the capital of the Carazo region, Jinotepe has very complete bus routes with many express options to Managua, some of which go to the centrally located *la UCA* (university stop) next to Metrocentro. The rest use Mercado Israel Lewites (also called Mercado Boer.) **Express Jinotepe-Managua**, every 15 mins, 0500-2000, US$1, 1 hr 15 mins to Mercado Boer. **Express Jinotepe-Managua (la UCA)**, every 15 mins, 0600-2000, US$1.25, 1 hr 25 mins to la UCA. **Jinotepe-Rivas**, every 30 mins, 0540-1710,

Iguana soup

Hung over? Love life not what it used to be? What you need is a good soup, one that picks you up, rejuvinates the body. For a few dollars you can be a new person. Iguana is a very traditional dish in Nicaragua. Its meat is soft and tender and it is prepared in all kinds of imaginative ways. In fact, when asked to describe what chicken tastes like, a Nicaraguan will say "hmm, you could say it tastes a bit like iguana" (well, not really).

First you must choose your species; most iguanas in Nicaragua are black or green. The black ones (called garrobos) have meat that is higher in protein thanks to a diet that includes many insects; however, this also means they are more prone to parasites. The preferred meat is that of the green iguana (called simply

iguana), which is a vegetarian and has bigger eggs. Iguana eggs can be removed and cooked, and are said to be better than chicken eggs (really); perfect for that relaxing Sunday morning coffee, with toast and a Jurassic omelette.

The most traditional dish is iguana en pinol, which means the meat is bathed in cornmeal and then fried. The lizard can also be grilled over a wood fire and smothered in tomatoes and onions. But other people prefer their iguana in a sopa levanta muerto (back from the dead soup) which is said to aid recovery after a heavy night's drinking and love-making. The recipe is simple: boil water and add salt, onions, sweet pepper, garlic, yucca and peppermint. Then add the iguana, boil until tender and serve ¡Buen provecho!

US$1, 1 hr 45 mins. **Jinotepe-Granada**, 0630, 1200, US$0.75, 1 hr 25 mins. **Jinotepe-Masaya**, every 30 mins, 0500-1800, US$0.45, 1 hr 15 mins.

Banks *BDF* (*Banco de Finanzas*), one block north of the church, can change cash or Amex travellers' cheques, T412-2110. **Tourism office** is located 1 block east of the Esso station with friendly Dr Fabio Sánchez at the helm, T412-0298. **Directory**

Diriamba

In comparison with many other pueblos on the *mesa*, Diriamba is a slightly grungy, disorganized place. Here the locals are a bit different from the rest. The bicycle-powered taxis that are prevalent from Nindirí to San Marcos have been modified to use little motors and the population tends to hang out more in the streets. The town's people are famously good-looking, open and friendly. Diriamba was one of the most important settlements in Nicaragua when the Spanish first arrived in 1523 and the town is named after Nicaragua's most famous Indian rebel, **Chief Diriangén**, who has become a symbol of resistance to outside intervention. Though the great chief has recently been taken off Nicaragua's 20 córdoba note, he still stands proudly over Parque Central, albeit with the spear missing from his outstretched hand. Perhaps Diriamba is the land of rebels, for it is here that the anti-establishment play and focal point of Nicaraguan culture **El Güegüence** may have originated. During the spectacular patron saint festival for **San Sebastián**, on 20-27 January, dances from this extraordinary play (see box page 99) are performed in the streets along with many different masked performances that have come to represent the very identity of Nicaraguan culture. Perhaps the most attractive of all the *pueblos'* churches is here in front of Diriamba's tired-looking Parque Central. Around the park most of the buildings were destroyed in the war against Somoza, but the church stands proud with an elegant, well-lit, domed interior and much fine woodwork. The **Museo**

Colour map 3, grid B3
Population: 57,682
Altitude: 580 m

Masaya and Los Pueblos

Ecológico Trópico Seco, ENEL, 4 c west, provides an interesting ecological and geographical overview of the region and deals with conservation issues, particularly the effect of agriculture on local ecosystems. ■ *Mon-Fri 0900-1200, 1400-1700. T422-2129.*

Sleeping & eating	**E** *Diriangén*, Shell station, 1 c east, ½ c south, T422-2428. 12 rooms with private bath, fan, parking. *2 de Junio*, very good fish. *Mi Bohio*, INE, 3 c west, T422-2437. Chicken in wine sauce, soups, ceviche, good.
Transport	**Buses** run to Jinotepe every 15 mins for US$0.25. **Diriamba-Managua**, every 20 mins, 0530-2030, US$0.80, 1 hr 15 mins.
Directory	**Banks** *BDF*, next to Texaco station, T422-3124, will change cash and American Express travellers' cheques.

La Boquita The department of Carazo has 40 km of Pacific Ocean coastline with crashing waves and light grey sand. La Boquita, 25 km on rough but paved highway from Diriamba, is a popular beach during the dry season and particularly Semana Santa (Easter Week); for the rest of the year it is quiet with a touristic centre and many little ranch-style restaurants that serve fresh fish against the background of the sound of the sea. If you are driving, there is a US$1.50 entrance fee to the parking area. **C** *Palmas del Mar*, T552-8716. 25 rooms with private bath and a/c, tiny swimming pool. Palmas is at the centre of the tourist centre, which means it can be noisy at night, not least because of its own discotheque. It does have a lovely patio on the beach and good seafood.

Casares South of La Boquita, where the Río Casares drains into the Pacific, is the friendly fishing village of Casares. At the north part of the beach are the homes of wealthy Managuans. There are a few very cheap places to eat. Fishing is done in little fibreglass boats with outboards. The ocean has strong currents here and it is not unusual for the odd bather to be caught too far out. Travel further south is possible, but even four-wheel drives in the dry season are known to get stuck attempting the river crossings. For access further south it is best to use the entrance from the Pan-American Highway.

Granada

5

Granada

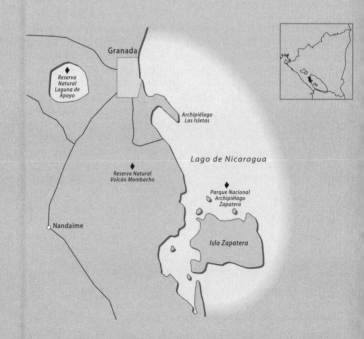

Granada

Reserva Natural Laguna de Apoyo

Archipiélago Las Isletas

Lago de Nicaragua

Reserva Natural Volcán Mombacho

Parque Nacional Archipiélago Zapatera

Nandaime

Isla Zapatera

If there is one destination inside Nicaragua that has finally been discovered by the outside world it is Granada. In fact, for the first three centuries of its existence, it was almost too well known, especially to pirates and adventurers. Today, instead of marauders, it is tourists who are attracted to the peaceful and timeless beauty of this historic city. With an ever-improving tourist infrastructure, Granada can be used as a base and jumping-off point for exploring most of southern Nicaragua. Within easy reach of any Granada hotel room is the Volcán Mombacho, a sleeping giant with a pristine cloud forest and the country's best-managed nature reserve. In the shadow of the volcano is the tiny tropical paradise of Las Isletas, a freshwater archipelago with a water-bound community on its rocky isles. Beyond Las Isletas is another archipelago, which contains Lake Nicaragua's most important Indian ceremonial site, the mysterious Isla Zapatera. Granada also shares the deep blue crater lake of Laguna de Apoyo with its neighbouring department of Masaya.

Reserva Natural Laguna de Apoyo

Colour map 3, grid B3
Area: 3,500 ha

At Km 37½ of the highway between Masaya and Granada is the only road access to the shores of Nicaragua's largest and, many people believe, its most beautiful crater lake. The water of the lake, which is slightly salty and very clear, turns a deep azure colour when the sun shines across it. Created by a massive volcanic explosion some 20,000 years ago, the drop from the extinct crater's highest point to the lake is more than 400 m and the lake itself is 6 km in diameter. Although the exact depth of the water is unknown, it is considered the deepest natural well in the country and the sudden drop off from the shoreline means that many a tipsy bather has drowned in its depths.

When the Spanish arrived, Laguna de Apoyo, then known as **Norome**, was a central point for the Chorotega Indian tribes, whose capital is thought to have been at Diriá, on the south side of the lake. The basalt used for many of their ceremonial statues came from inside the crater. The stone was partially carved on the lakeshore and then hauled up the steep rim of the crater for the detail work. Two elderly carvers who have hung on to this 1,200-year-old tradition are still at work here, although they use a lighter stone and no longer haul the basalt up the mountain.

There is a 5-km dirt access road from the Granada highway leading to a settlement called **Valle de Apoyo** that sits at the edge of the crater's north rim. The road is paved on the steep descent, though it was badly damaged by landslides in an earthquake in July 2000. At the bottom of the crater an earth road circles the lake partially on both sides. To the left is one of the many vacation homes of ex-President Arnoldo Alemán and a small research centre founded by North American biologists to study the flora and fauna of this nature reserve. **Proyecto Ecológico Espacio Verde** has documented more than 145 species of birds in the crater's tropical dry forest, including the boat-billed flycatcher, collared aracari and the black-headed trogon. The forest is also home to an equal number of butterfly species, and howler and whiteface monkeys. The scientists have diving gear at the site and have been investigating the fish of this extraordinary lake. They have a language school at the research lodge that helps fund research and educational projects in the reserve and local community.

The walk from the **Mirador de Catarina** down to the interior of the crater finishes just south of *Hotel Norome*; a good way to earn a big lunch and a beer is to climb from the lake up to the summit restaurant (then roll back down).

Sleeping
A-B *Norome*, T0883-9093, noromeresort@yahoo.com, accessed by the shore road to the east, this charming lakefront lodge has 8 rooms, a/c, bar, restaurant, very clean, smartly decorated rooms, great views and setting, jacuzzi, and a small dock. **C-E** *Monkey Hut* bottom of the lake access road, 100 m west, T552-4028. Can be booked with transfer from Granada, dormitory and private rooms, breakfast and dinner included, canoe, kayak and sailboat rentals. It's also possible to stay at the *Proyecto Ecológico Espacio Verde* (see *Apoyo Intensive Spanish School* in Directory, below).

Transport
Buses to Valle de Apoyo from Masaya once a day for US$0.70, then walk down the road that drops into the crater. Buses also run between Masaya and Granada every 15 minutes. You will have to get off at Km 37½ and walk down the 5-km access road (it's very dusty in the dry season, so bring a bandanna). Hitchhiking is possible though traffic is sparse during the weekdays. *Monkey Hut* offers transfers from their Granada hotel, *The Bearded Monkey* (see page 112) for US$1.25 twice weekly (**Granada-Laguna de Apoyo**: Tue 1200, Fri 1000; **Laguna de Apoyo-Granada**: Wed 1100, Fri 1400). The other alternative is a taxi from Granada, US$15-20, or from Managua, US$35-40.

> ### Things to do in Granada
>
> - Bathe in the salty crater-lake waters of Laguna de Apoyo, one of the most unusual swimming experiences in Nicaragua.
> - Ride through the charming streets of colonial Granada in a horse-drawn carriage, the city taxis since 1524.
> - Enjoy the pre-Hispanic treasures from Isla Zapatera (especially the large basalt Chorotega figures) on display in the restored Convento de San Francisco.
> - Visit Las Isletas de Granada in the late afternoon for a bird-lover's feast of gnat catchers, oropendulas, kingfishers, osprey, egrets and parrots.
> - Hike the well-kept cloud-forest trails in the Reserva Natural Volcán Mombacho if you want misty jungle without the mud.
> - Explore the wild and remote islands of the Archipiélago Zapatera, rarely seen by visitors and home to many archaeological treasures.

Directory *Apoyo Intensive Spanish School*, T0882-3992, econic@guegue.com.ni, groups of 4, 5 hrs' tuition per day. 5-day programme, US$195, US$230 for a week including accommodation and food (vegetarians catered for) or US$750 per month, family stays available. It is also possible to stay in the lodge without enrolling in the school, prices start at US$16 plus meals, contact the *Proyecto* for information.

Granada

Few cities can match the beauty, charm and setting of Granada, one of the oldest European settlements in the Americas. In the shadow of the Mombacho volcano, Granada is a city of nostalgia and romance, a place to relax and wander through the streets. It's hard not to be voyeuristic and steal glances beyond the vast doors of the brightly painted homes where lovely interiors with high-ceilinged rooms face out on to patio gardens lush with tropical plants.

Colour map 3, grid B4
Population: 111,506
Altitude: 60 m

Ins and outs

Getting there The **ferry** from San Carlos to Granada takes 15 hrs or more, depending on lake conditions. Boats are very crowded and may include a good dose of quality time with some pigs or chickens. Get on the boat as early as possible if you want to get a seat.

There are regular **bus** services to and from Granada from all points south of Managua, and international buses coming from San José in Costa Rica stop in Granada very briefly.

Getting around Granada's city centre is small and manageable on foot. As in most Nicaraguan towns the **Parque Central** is the focal and reference point and the cathedral is visible from most of the city. There are three main streets: leading from the Fortaleza de La Pólvora, at the western extreme of the old centre, the **Calle Real** runs east (*al lago*) past several churches to the central square. The road continues as **Calle El Calmito** east of the park past the city's two Spanish restaurants and on to the lake. Running perpendicular is the **Calle Atravesada**, one block west of Parque Central, behind the *Hotel Alhambra*. This street runs from the old train station in the north of the city past Parque Central and south to Granada market. It has most of the cheap eating and night entertainment. The other important route, **Calle Calzada**, starts at the big cross on Parque Central and runs east towards the lake, past many beautiful homes and small *hospedajes*, ending at Lake Nicaragua and the city port. Much of the city's beauty can be appreciated within an area of five blocks around the centre. The east side of the Parque Central is generally much quieter with dramatically fewer cars and trucks.

Tourist office The local INTUR office, on Parque Central next to the cathedral, has good maps of Nicaragua and the usual array of information on the country.

Best time to visit Granada shares the climatic characteristics of the Pacific Basin at close to sea level: this means it is hot. There is a bit of relief with the breezes of Jan and Feb, but the median temperature is 27°C. Annual rainfall is 1,350 mm with the usual tropical pattern of short hard bursts of rainfall preceded and followed by sunshine or partially cloudy skies. Although there is no bad time to visit Granada, it is probably best to avoid the very hot and dusty late dry season (Mar to mid-May), and the rainiest months of Sep and Oct.

History

Granada claims to be the oldest, continuously inhabited city on mainland America

The Chorotega population encountered by the first Spanish explorer, Captain Gil González Dávila, inhabited important settlements on both north and south sides of the Volcán Mombacho. **Nochari**, on the south side of the volcano, was later moved further southeast and became modern-day **Nandaime** (see page 127). Today's Granada was in the northern Lake Nicaragua province of **Nequecheri**, and was dominated by the heavily populated settlement of **Jalteva** (or Xalteva). According to most estimates Granada was founded by **Captain Francisco Hernández de Córdoba** on or around 21 April 1524 (the same year as León, and Nicaraguan historians have been arguing ever since to establish which was the first city of Nicaragua). The original wall, which divided the Spanish and Indian sectors of Granada, can be seen today just south of the Jalteva church. In 1585 a French chronicler described a religious procession in the city as rich in gold and emeralds, with Indian dances that lasted, without rest, for the duration of the procession, and a line of very well-dressed Spaniards, with the total Spanish population estimated at only 200. Granada became a major commercial centre and when the Irish friar Thomas Gage visited in 1633 he marvelled at the city's wealth, most of which came from trade with Peru, Guatemala and Colombia.

It was not long before these reports of wealth began to reach the ears of the English pirates who were able to use the recently acquired possession of Jamaica, which they wrested from Spain in 1665. Edward Davis and **Henry Morgan** entered via the Río San Juan and took the city by surprise on 29 June 1665 at 0200 in the morning. With a group of 40 men he sacked the churches and houses before escaping to Las Isletas. In 1670 another band of pirates led by Gallardillo visited Granada via the same route. After destroying the fort at San Carlos, they sacked Granada and took with them men and women hostages. In 1685, a force of 345 British and French pirates, led by the accomplished French pirate William Dampier, came from the Pacific, entering near where the Chacocente wildlife refuge is today (see page 132). The local population, armed and waiting to fight off the pirates, was easily overwhelmed by the size of the pirate army. After taking the riches of the city the invaders burned the **Iglesia San Francisco** and 18 big houses, then retreated to the Pacific with the loss of only three men. Granada saw even more burning and destruction in what was the biggest uprising during the War of Independence from Spain in 1812 and the persistent post-Independence battles between León and Granada. The defeat of León's Liberal Party in 1854 in Granada led them to invite the North American filibuster **William Walker** to fight the Conservatives of Granada, thus initiating the darkest days of Granada's post-colonial history (see page 132).

Since the days of William Walker Granada has lost its importance as a commercial centre for inter-oceanic travel, but its Conservative Party supplied the country with presidents from 1869-94. The 20th century saw little action for Granada other than a celebration in 1965 for 100 years of peace. It was also spared significant damage during the Revolution of 1978-79. The city has undergone many facelifts in the last 10 years to rebuild and preserve its architectural heritage.

Sights

Despite the repeated ransackings and burnings, Granada has maintained an unmistakable colonial charm. The style has been called a mixture of Nicaraguan baroque and neoclassical. Granada's history has given the city a delicious visual mix of Spanish adobe-and-tile roof structures and Italian- inspired neoclassical homes with ornate ceiling work and balconies (Italian architects were contracted by the Granada élite to reconstruct the city after the many foreign-led assaults). However, most of the houses maintain the southern Spanish trademark interior gardens and large, airy corridors. It is interesting to compare the architecture of Granada with that of León, which was spared much of the colonial and post-colonial destruction and has maintained its classic Spanish colonial forms and lines.

Churches & museums As a result of Granada's troubled history, its churches have been rebuilt several times. Sadly they have not retained much in the way of grace, beauty or charm. Last rebuilt and amplified after William Walker's flaming departure in 1856, the **Catedral de Granada** on Parque Central has become a symbol for Granada, and its impressive size and towers make it a beautiful backdrop to the city. The interior is nothing short of boring. At the edge of the old city, on Calle Calzada, the **Iglesia Guadalupe** was also burnt down by Walker, who used it as a stronghold before escaping on the lake. Originally constructed in 1629, it has a rustic charm, although once again the post-Walker rebuild lacks character inside. The most attractive of the Granada churches is **Iglesia La Merced**, which is part of a very nice walk from Parque Central down the Calle Real to the old Spanish Fortaleza de la Pólvora (see below). La Merced, built between 1751 and 1781 and also destroyed by William Walker, has maintained its colonial charm and part of the original belltowers and façade. The pretty interior, painted an unusual tropical green colour, has an attractive altar and deceiving three-dimensional painting of the Virgin on its north side. In front of the church is a cross constructed in 1999 as a symbol of hope for peace in the 21st century. Further down the street is the interesting **Plaza de Xalteva**, which has unusual stone lanterns and walls said to have been erected in tribute to ancient Indian constructions. Unlike León and Masaya, Granada no longer has an Indian barrio of any kind, yet you can see the remains of the walls from the colonial period that separated the Spanish and indigenous sectors: to the west of the park is Jalteva and, to the east, Granada proper. The church on the plaza, **Iglesia Jalteva**, was yet another Walker burn victim, rebuilt at the end of the 19th century and reminiscent of a New England

Granada

church, without a trace of creativity. Further west along the Calle Real is the cute little **Capilla María Auxiliadora**. This church has some interesting features on its façade and some lovely detail work inside and is worth a visit (its worshippers are decidedly less stuffy than those found in some of the other Granada churches).

At the end of the street, as it turns to raw earth, is the 18th-century fort and ammunitions hold, **Fortaleza de la Pólvora**. The fort was later used as a military base and then a prison. Today it is open to visitors. In the ruins of the original weapons and gun powder hold are barrels from the Nicaraguan rum producer used to represent gun powder kegs (though which of the two is more explosive has yet to be determined) and it is interesting to note the thickness of the walls. You can climb up inside the southeastern turret on a flimsy ladder to have a good view down the Calle Real. Note the turret bathroom that was cleverly installed below. ■ *Open to visitors during daylight hours. US$1-2 donation to the caretaker.*

There are two sights of interest along the Calle Atravesada. The **old train station**, a beautifully restored structure, is now a trade school and next to it is the **Parque sin Nombre** (park with no name). It seems this little park was called Parque Somoza until the Revolution, when it was changed to **Parque Sandino**, and when the Sandinistas lost in the 1990 elections, the poor park was caught again on the wrong side of the fence. The locals have since decided it best to allow the park to remain anonymous (although most addresses still use 'Parque Sandino' to avoid even further confusion). Past Parque Central on the same street is the bustle and hustle of Granada's market. This is a good place to pick up some new shoes, buy a side of pork, or enjoy a cheap meal! Next to the Parque Central is the **Plaza de Independencia**, which has a

Granada

Sleeping
1 Alhambra
2 Another Night in Paradise
3 Central
4 Colonial
5 Hospedaje Cocibolca
6 Hospedaje Esfinge
7 La Barba del Mono
  (Bearded Monkey)
8 Posada Don Alfredo

Eating
1 Café Conveso
2 Doña Conchi's
3 Las Bocaditas
4 Mediterráneo

0 metres 100
0 yards 100

movie-set quality to it. The bishop of Granada lives in the red house, the telephone office is next door and just a few doors down is the historic **Casa de los Leones** (or Casa de Los Tres Mundos) with an early 17th-century Moorish stone door frame that survived all the burning. It is now a cultural centre and a good place to see the inside of a Granada house. ■ *Daytime exhibitions free of charge; admission charged for live concerts on weekend nights.* The Plaza de Independencia is home to a street concert every Friday night, known as **Noches de Serenatas** (Nights of Serenades), although the quality of music is very variable. One block west from the end of the plaza is the bright blue **Iglesia San Francisco**, Nicaragua's oldest standing church with original steps, although it was burnt down like most others in Granada. The legendary 'human rights' priest Fray Bartolomé de las Casas preached here while visiting Granada. The church, founded in 1585 on top of two more earlier temporary structures, was reconstructed in 1868 and is now being remodelled. The work has been slowed by the discovery of a possibly important pre-Columbian site underneath the main altar.

Connected to the church is the mustard yellow **Museo Antiguo Convento de San Francisco**. Originally founded as a convent in 1529, it was burnt down in 1685 by the French pirate Dampier. In 1836, after the religious orders of Central America had been given their marching orders by the Central American Federation, it became a university, and then, in 1856, it was used as a garrison by William Walker, who burned it down once again before leaving the country. The old convent was rebuilt and became the most important secondary school in town, the Colegio de Granada, which later became the Instituto Nacional de Oriente until it closed in 1975. Restoration began in 1989 with help from the Swedish government. There is a new mural in the entrance that leads to a small

5 Osteria Pane e Vino
6 Pizza Hot

shop and café. The interior garden is dominated by towering 100-year-old palms, often full of squawking parakeets. It is possible to peep inside the church and see the restoration work there. In the east wing of the building is one of the country's most interesting pre-Columbian museums, housing large religious sculptures from the island of Zapatera in Lake Nicaragua (see page 123). The sculptures date from AD 800-1200, and especially worthy of note are the double standing or seated figures bearing huge animals, or doubles, on their heads and shoulders. The significance of the animals that accompany the human figures or sometimes take the place of a human head has been the subject of much discussion (the most popular theory is that they are alter egos or protectors, although it is impossible to know for certain). The museum also has changing exhibitions, historic photography of Granada, some colonial period religious art and a gallery of Solentiname naïve painting.

Granada

■ *Daily 0900-1800, US$1 with a US$2.50 additional charge for permission to photograph. T552-5535.*

Parque Central
During mango season, the Parque Central is raided by beautiful and noisy Amazon parrots from nearby Volcán Mombacho

Parque Central is officially called Parque Colón (Columbus Park), though no one uses that name. Its tall trees and benches are a good place to while away some time and there are small food stalls selling the famous and tremendously popular Granada dish *vigorón* (big and vigorous), which consists of a big banana leaf filled with cabbage salad, fried pork skins, yucca, tomato, hot chilli and lemon juice.

Next to the Cathedral of Granada is a big cross, installed in 1899, with a time capsule buried underneath. The hope was that the burying of common artefacts and personal belongings from the 19th century could be a way to ensure a peaceful 20th century. And, despite the fairly violent 100 years that followed for much of Nicaragua and the rest of the world, Granada did enjoy a reasonable amount of peace. The people of Granada have not given up the idea of total peace, and, in 1999, they buried the 20th century under a new cross in front of La Merced.

Essentials

Sleeping

■ *on map, page 116*
For price codes, see inside front cover

L *Hotel Colonial*, 25 m west from Parque Central, Calle La Libertad, T552-7299, F552-6029, hotelcolonialgra@nicanet.com.ni 27 very nice, compact, well-decorated rooms, private bath with hot water, a/c, cable TV, telephone, pool, bar, breakfast served daily, US$4-6, dinner upon advance request. French owned and operated. **L** *La Casona de los Estrada*, 50 m west of the Convento San Francisco, T552-7393, F552-7395, www.casonalosestrada.com Pleasant well-lit rooms, most luxurious in Granada, decorated with antiques, expensive restaurant, Tania speaks English.

AL-B *Hotel Alhambra*, Parque Central, T552-4486, F552-2035, hotalam@tmx. com.ni This is Granada's landmark hotel, with a/c, cable TV, hot water, swimming pool, restaurant, bar, and a wonderful terrace for drinks and meals. Rooms vary dramatically in quality and price, 3rd floor rooms are most expensive and new, hotel is currently undergoing renovation. Restaurant is not owned by hotel and receives mixed reviews with much criticism for its service. Parked cars guarded by night watchman. **B** *Posada Don Alfredo*, from La Merced 1 block north, T/F552-4455, charlyst@ tmx.com.ni With bath and hot water, **C** without, beautifully maintained 165-year-old house with much of its original flavour, high ceilings, dark rooms, English and German spoken by friendly, very helpful owner Alfred, clean, good location, kayaks and bicycles for rent US$12 and US$10 per day respectively, buffet German breakfast for US$7. **B** *Italiano*, La Calzada, T/F552-7047, next to Iglesia Guadalupe. Italian owned, with bath and a/c, **C** without, nice patio, restaurant and bar, good value.

D *Another Night in Paradise*, La Calzada, near Iglesia Guadalupe, T552-7113, donnatabor@hotmail.com Bath, fan, Spanish, English, Danish and German spoken, no sign so look for the mural, very helpful. **E** *Hospedaje Cocibolca*, La Calzada, T552-7223. Clean, bath, use of kitchen, family-run, friendly, internet access. **E** *Hospedaje Esfinge*, opposite market, T552-4826. Rooms with character, 50 years old, patio with washing facilities for extra charge, friendly, clean, motorcycle parking in lobby. Recommended. **E** *La Calzada*, La Calzada near Guadalupe church. Huge rooms with bath, fan, clean, friendly, great breakfasts.

F *Central*, La Calzada. Friendly, clean, laundry facilities, popular with backpackers, no mosquito nets, good restaurant. **G** *La Barba del Mono* (*The Bearded Monkey*), 14 de Septiembre, near the fire station, T552-4028, www.thebeardedmonkey.com Dormitory accommodation with lockers, shared bath, also private rooms, relaxed common areas, food and excellent breakfasts, bar, cable TV, internet access, great atmosphere, comfortable and very friendly, free transfer to dock in Granada, transfers to Laguna de Apoyo, Wed 1200, Fri 1000, US$1.25, also in Laguna de Apoyo, *Monkey Hut* (see page 112).

Eating

Café Converso, next to La Casa de Los Leones, T552-5626. Very good, great outdoor and indoor setting, Granada's best salads (washed in chlorinated water), great espresso, omelettes, beef dishes; also sea bass, prawns, pasta and a large selection of fresh fruit drinks, open 0700-2200, closed Mon. *Pizza Hot*, next to *Hotel Alhambra*, T552-6732. Daily 1100-2300. Good mid-priced pizza, nice setting. *TelePizza*, Calle Caimito, T552-4219. 0900-2130 daily, great pizzas and quick service. On the same street is *Mediterráneo*, T552-6764. Open daily 0800-2300, lovely colonial house, quiet garden setting, expensive, Spanish owners and menu, very good seafood, bad paella. Also on Calle Caimito, *Doña Conchi's*, T552-7376. 0800-2300, closed Tue, expensive, beautiful restaurant with antique décor and hundreds of candles at night, Spanish, Mediterranean, seafood, home-made bread, Manchego cheese, very good. Recommended. *Osteria Pane o Vino*, Calle Atravesada north, T552-2953. Italian food, *carpaccio, panna cotta, filete al vino*. 1200-1500, 1800-2400, closed Wed. *El* Volcán, 1 block south of La Merced. Run by Danielo, friendly, good *brochetas*, breakfasts, plans for future accommodation. *Eskimo's*, Calle La Calzada. Good ice cream. Between *El Ancla* and *Eskimo's* is a cheap, good chicken place. *Tasa Blanca*, near market, friendly, good coffee. Nearby is *Restaurant Querebe's*, popular with locals, set menu for lunch (US$1.50). Cheap food at the friendly *Café Astoria*, near Parque Central. *Las Bocaditas*, near Parque Central, popular and recommended. *Las Portales*, Parque Central, opposite *Enitel*. Simple, good. *Cafetín Amigo*, near cathedral towards lake. Good food, good value. Good breakfasts at the market. On Calle Atravesada behind the *Hotel Alhambra*, are: *El Prix*, ice cream, fried chicken, beer, snacks, cheap; and *Dragón Dorado*, mid-priced Cantonese fare, attentive service, mediocre food. *Bullpen*, from Los Cocos, 1 block east, very cheap drinks and good soups. Near the Shell station, *Tito Bar*, good local place, with inexpensive typical Nicaraguan food. Also *La Colina del Sur*, T552-3492. Daily 1200-2200, Tue lunch only 1200-1500, seafood specialities, excellent lake perch, boneless fillets, avocado salad, expensive but worth it. Recommended.

● *on map, page 116*

In the **Complejo Turístico** on the lakeshore there are many places for dancing and eating (although it can be a miserable place at the beginning of the rainy season because of flying insects). For meals, recommended are *El Cubano*, mid-range bar and restaurant with Nicaraguan and Cuban food, and *La Terrazza La Playa*, mid-range, great *cerdo asado* and *filete de guapote*. *César*, open Fri and Sat only, recommended for dancing and drinking very popular, inexpensive bar, merengue and salsa music. *Cocibolca* restaurant on Isla Cocibolca is reached by lancha.

Entertainment

The street that runs behind the *Hotel Alhambra*, Calle Atravesada, is the centre of most of Granada's nightlife and restaurants. On this street, next to the cinema, is the very popular *Flamingo*, cheap canteen with cheap beer and a very diverse clientele, particularly at night. Upstairs is *Charley's Disco Bar*, more upscale with dancing and popular with international crowd. Also along Atravesada is *El Túnel*, good cheap bar with snacks, dark interior, popular for extramarital romance! Just before the *Complejo*

Granada

Turístico (see Eating) is *Caribbean Blue*, reggae music, Thu-Sun. *Cinema Karawala*, 1 block behind *Hotel Alhambra*, is good, modern, with 2 screens.

Festivals

Granada's patron saint festival is for *La Virgen de la Asunción* and is from **14-30 Aug** with the most important date **15 Aug**; on first Sun of the festival cowboys bring roped bulls into the central plaza, let them free and catch them again. There are also processions, folkloric dancing and a free bull-running through the Parque Central. *Noches de* Serenata, live music in the Plaza de Independencia, with food stalls every Fri night. *Folklore, Artisan and Food Festival* on 3rd weekend in Mar. *Holy Week* celebrations are also good in Granada.

Shopping

Antiques Granada is the best place to hunt for antiques in Nicaragua. Keep in mind that pre-Columbian pieces cannot be taken out of Nicaragua and colonial period relics may also be considered national patrimony and subject to the same laws made to protect Nicaragua's history. The highest profile of the antique stores is *La Piedra Bocona*, 2 c north of La Merced church, T552-2718, English spoken. *Mercedes Morales* is 1½ c south of La Merced, call to see if someone will be there to attend you, T552-4983 or cell phone 0887-1488. *Felicia Sandino*, Calle El Beso, Casa 114, T552-4677.

Cigars There is some rolling going on in Granada although the wrap and filler are brought down from Estelí (see page 226). You can ask to enter the factory, or just pick up some *puros*. *Doña Elba Cigars*, Calle Real, Iglesia Xalteva, 1 c west, T552-3217 and *Compañía Nicaragüense de Tabacos, SA* Parque Sandino, 1 c south, 20 *varas* west, T552-3453.

Furniture Granada is not the place to shop for cheap handicrafts (go to Masaya for that). The exception is the high-quality rattan (*mimbre*) furniture, which is better here than anywhere else. The rattan rocking chairs made in Granada's workshops are famous around Nicaragua and are sold in exclusive shops in Europe too. The real thing does not come cheap, but these handmade pieces are made to last at least 50 years. The most famous workshop is at the entrance to Granada, on the *carretera* between Masaya and Granada. Call in advance if you want to visit: *Muebles de Mimbre Auxiliadora*, at Km 45, and its sister shop *Muebles de Mimbre Granada*, at Km 45½, both reached on T522-2217. *Muebles de Mimbre El Hogar*, half a block from the cathedral towards the lake, La Calzada 409, T522-2366. *Mimbre y Ratan Kauffmann*, from Parque Sandino, 4 c south, ½ c east, T552-2773.

Markets *Granada Market*, 1 block west and then south on Calle Atravesada, is a large green building surrounded by many street stalls. It's dark, dirty and packed and there have been plans to move it for years but for now it remains in its claustrophobic locale. Just south of the market is *Supermercado Palí* with low-price goods; bring your own bags *Supermercado Lacayo*, just west of Parque Central on Calle Real, has purified water and everything else you could need and is a good place to stock up on goods before heading out of town.

Photography There is a *Kodak Express* 1 block north of *Cine Karawala*, T552-5455.

Sweets Granada is also well known for its traditional handmade sweets made from local fruits. There are many *dulcerías* (sweet shops), so ask around, these are a few examples:

Dulcería El Encanto, Jobonería Chamorro, 50 *varas* south, T552-2668; *Dulcería El Buen Gusto*, Calle Santa Lucía, Casa 327, T552-5352; *Dulcería La Miel*, Calle Atravesada, Ixchen 2 c west, T552-3908.

Sports

During the **baseball** season from Nov to Feb you could check out the Granada Sharks who play in a nice stadium at the exit of Granada for Masaya, US$0.80-4, though it has been some time since they have had a competitive team. There is a stadium **motocross** series in the baseball park in the off season and also concerts. **Bike** (US$12) and **kayak** (US$10) rentals are available from *Posada Don Alfredo*, from La Merced, 1 block to the north, T/F552-4455, charlyst@tmx.com.ni

Tour operators

The best is *Oro Travel*, ½ block west from Convento San Francisco's north corner, T552-4568, F552-6512, orotravel@tmx.com.ni Owner Pascal speaks French, German and English. He offers good tours to the Mombacho volcano and around the country, very professional, information for travellers, car rental, book exchange, domestic and international flight tickets. *Servitur*, in the *Hotel Alhambra*, also has lots of good information, T552-4390.

Auxiliadora Travel Agent, Iglesia La Merced, 1 c west, Calle Real Xalteva, Apdo 180, T552-3304. Most helpful and efficient. *Viajes Griffith*, Calle Real No 414, T552-4358, F552-6262. English spoken.

Transport

Horse-drawn carriages (*coches*) are for hire and are used here, as in Masaya, as taxis **Local** by the locals. Normal rate for a trip to the market or bus station should be no more than US$1.50. The drivers are also happy to take foreigners around the city and actually make very good and willing guides if you can decipher their Spanish. Rates are normally US$4.50 for 30 mins, US$9 for 1 hr. You can see most of the city's sights in a ½-hr rental unless you want to enter the fort, churches and museum. A good carriage ride starts from La Pólvora and continues down Calle Real, past La Capilla María Auxiliadora, La Jalteva, and La Merced to Parque Central. From the cathedral you can then continue to La Virgen de Guadalupe and to the lakefront along the La Calzada, returning via a visit to the Iglesia San Francisco.

Taxis The Granada taxi driver is a happy and relaxed type and useful for finding places away from the centre, average fare US$0.75-1.50. Rates to Masaya US$15-20 and Managua US$45, but make sure the taxi looks strong enough to make the journey.

Buses Leaving from the Shell station, 1 c south of the Mercado: **Granada-Masaya**, **Long distance** every 30 mins, 0500-1800, US$0.40, 40 mins; **Granada-Rivas**, every 45 mins, 0540-1510, US$1, 2 hrs; **Granada- Niquinohomo**, every 45 mins, 0430- 1610, US$1, 45 mins, use this bus for visits to Diriá, Diriomo, San Juan de Oriente, Catarina; or **Granada-Jinotepe**, 0630, 1200, US$0.80, 1½ hrs, for visits to Los Pueblos, including Masatepe and San Marcos.

From the bus terminal next to the old hospital: **Granada-Managua**, every 20 mins, 0400-1900, US$0.75, 1½ hrs; **Granada-Nandaime**, every 20 mins, 0500-1800, US$0.70, 1 hr. Express mini- buses to Managua leave from Parque Sandino and from a small lot just south of BAC on Parque Central, US$1.25.

Granada

International buses Offices for the international bus companies are on Av Arellano. Nica Bus, T552-529, Ticabus, T552-4301, see Transport in Managua for complete schedules, and add 1 hr for the departures for Costa Rica.

Car hire *Budget Rent a Car*, at the Shell station near the north city entrance, T552-2323, provides very good service. If you rent a car in Managua you can leave it here, or you can hire it in Granada and drop it off in Managua or other northern destinations. However, cheaper rates can be found in Managua with other companies.

Ferry The ferry from Granada to **San Carlos** leaves the main dock on Mon and Thu at 1400. It also stops in **Altagracia**, Ometepe, after 4 hrs of sailing (see page 122 for departure times on Tue and Fri).

Directory

Banks For travellers' cheques, cash advances and cash exchange, the *BAC* (*Banco de América Central*) is in the historic yellow corner house on the southwest corner of Parque Central. The building was the original *Casa Pellas* in Granada and today *BAC* is one of the many Pellas family businesses. On the south side of the *Cine Karawala* behind the *Hotel Alhambra* is *BDF* (*Banco de Finanzas*), which is another option for American Express TCs. For changing cash there are several other banks, such as *BanCentro* (also in a beautiful restored building) and *Banic* across from *BDF*.

Communications **Internet**: There has been an epidemic of internet café openings in Granada, most are within 2 blocks of the centre. *Computer Internet Service*, from Casa Pellas 75 m west of Enitel (see below), T552-2544, F552-3061, US$5 per hour. Other places include *Compunet* beside cathedral, US$5.50 per hour; 1 place across from *Hotel Colonial*, also in several *hospedajes* and many, many more. **Post office**: *Correos de Nicaragua*, in front of *Cine Karawala*, T552-3331, F552-2776. **Telephone**: *Enitel* is next to the bishop's house, on Plaza Independencia, T552-2288.

Medical facilities *Bernardino Díaz Ochoa* is just off the highway at the entrance to Granada at Km 45, T552-2719. There are also clinics and laboratories on Calle Atravesada, including *Laboratorio de Análisis y Clínica Fletes Aguilar* across from the *Cine Karawala*, T552-6366.

Language schools *Casa Xalteva*, Calle Real Xalteva 103, T/F552-2436, www.ibw.com.ni/~casaxal Small Spanish classes, 1 week to several months, home stays arranged, voluntary work with children. Recommended. *GLSN*, Calle Real Xalteva, 6½ blocks west of Parque Central, 1 block from Jalteva church, US$55 per week, or US$85 with accommodation, 4 hrs' tuition per day. Recommended. (See also Laguna de Apoyo, page 113.)

Useful numbers Fire: T552-4440. **Police**: T552-2929. **Red Cross**: T552-2711.

Excursions from Granada

Archipiélago Las Isletas

Colour map 3, grid B4 Just five minutes outside Granada, in the warm waters of Lake Nicaragua, is the chain of 354 islands called **Las Isletas**. The islands are really big piles of basalt rock and incredibly they are covered in lush vegetation growing in the fertile soil that fills in the islands' rocky surface. The quantity of mango trees on the archipelago is staggering and there are some big older trees that dominate the little islands. Bird life is rich, with plenty of egrets, cormorants, ospreys, magpie jays, kingfishers, oropendulas, various species of knat and flycatchers, parrots and parakeets, as well as the occasional mot-mot. The age of the islands is unknown, but it is generally agreed that they were created by a massive discharge of the Mombacho volcano that watches over the lake and islands to the west.

The islands are well populated with a mixture of super-wealthy and very humble residents; the well-off use the islands as a weekend escape while the poorer inhabitants live full time in this water-bound community. The school, cemetery, restaurants and bars are all on different islands and the locals commute mostly in rowing boat or by hitching rides from the tour boats that circulate in the calm waters. Fishing is the locals' main source of income and you may well see the fishermen in the water laying nets for the lake's *guapote* (perch) or *mojarra* (carp). Also, many find work building walls or caretaking on the 'private islands' that are owned by the wealthy weekenders. The abundant fruit is an important part of the local diet.

The peninsula that jets out between the islands has small docks and restaurants on both sides. The immediate (north) side of the islands is accessed by the road that runs through the touristic centre of Granada and finishes at the docks and three restaurants. This is the more popular side of the archipelago and boat rides around the islands are cheaper from here (US$11 per hour per boat). As well as the many luxury homes on this side, the tiny, late-17th-century Spanish fort, **San Pablo**, on the extreme northeast of the chain, can be visited from the north side of the peninsula. Real estate companies have moved into this side of the archipelago and it is not unusual to see 'For sale' signs in English on the islands.

There is a turn-off before the road ends with big signs for **Puerto Assese**, which is a larger, more luxurious marina with a big restaurant. The boats from Puerto Assese also offer one-hour rides around the islands, though there are fewer canals and this part of the archipelago is populated almost entirely by locals. An hour on this side is normally US$12 with both sides charging US$1.50 for parking. To arrive at the docks without a car, you can hire a taxi (not more than US$3) or horse carriage (not more than US$3).

In Puerto Assese there are boats for **A** *Nicarao Lake Resort*, on the island of La Ceiba, T266-1694, F266-0704, nlr@nicaraolake.com.ni Includes all meals, a/c, good beds, part-time generator, delightful setting, fresh perch in restaurant kept live in a water cage until lunch. You can also visit the island for the day to use their facilities, with the cost of lunch (US$15); best to arrange visits in advance. The best of the restaurants is at the marina *Restaurante Puerto Assese*, T552-2269, Tue-Sun, 1100-1800, good value, fish specialities, relaxed service. There are many little bars and eateries on the islands; negotiate a drop-off and pick-up price and ask the boat driver to recommend.

Sleeping & eating

Parque Nacional Archipiélago Zapatera

Although many of the important relics have been taken to museums, this archipelago of 11 islands remains one of the country's most important pre-Columbian sites. **Isla Zapatera**, the centrepiece and Lake Nicaragua's second largest island, is a very old and extinct volcano that has been eroded over the centuries and is accompanied by 10 satellite islands.

Colour map 3, grid B4
Area: 5,227 ha

Granada

👉 Lake Nicaragua – El Mar Dulce

A lake so vast the Spanish conquistadors dubbed it the 'Freshwater sea' (Mar Dulce), Lago de Nicaragua or Cocibolca covers 8,264 sq km. In a little country like Nicaragua, this is massive. The lake is fed by numerous rivers in Nicaragua and northern Costa Rica and its waters drain into the Caribbean Sea, via the Río San Juan. Lago de Nicaragua is home to more than 430 volcanic islands. This is the earth as it was being formed millions of years ago, for Cocibolca is actually a 160 x 65 km floodplain with the earth rising up around it and inside it. Its average depth is 20 m with some deep sections near Ometepe at 60 m. The two continents were finally connected on the lake's west coast, some four or five million years ago, blocking off the Caribbean from the Pacific and forming a land bridge that allowed the flora and fauna of the two great continents to mix.

For an estimated 30,000 years, the bridge has been used by humans too.

Some of the lake's islands were, without a doubt, very important religious sites, places of organized worship, human sacrifice and ritual cannibalism. Indeed, getting to the islands in canoes must have been a religious experience in itself. Thanks to its shallow floor, Cocibolca's waves change by the hour. The lake can go from calm to swells, and from swells to rough in no time at all.

Lake Nicaragua is also unique in its freshwater sawtooth fish, sharks, sardines and the prehistoric gaspar fish. A visit to Nicaragua without a visit to its freshwater sea is like touring Egypt without visiting the pyramids or Peru without the Andes. Still free of resorts, pleasure yachts, jet skis and commercial fishing boats, Cocibolca, the world's second biggest lake in the tropics, remains as it has been for thousands of years: a place of volcanoes, mysteries and murmurs from the past; a huge body of clean, fresh water, teeming with fish, asleep under an endless sky.

Ins & outs The islands are reached by *panga* (outboard motorboat) in 1 hr or more depending on lake swells. At times the passage between the protected waters of Las Isletas and Zapatera is very rough with a short interval, big swell that is common in the lake and can make boating a real adventure. The average cost of a rented boat to visit the islands is US$200-250 leaving from Puerto Assese. Several tour companies offer 1-day trips to the islands that include lunch, boat and guides. *Tours Nicaragua* in Managua offer the trip with the guidance of a National Museum archaeologist, aided by an English- language translator.

The island system is located 40 km south of Granada. Isla Zapatera has both tropical dry and wet forest ecosystems depending on elevation, which reaches a maximum height of 625 m. It is a beautiful island for hiking, with varied flora. Zapatera also has a crater lake that is easily accessed due to its proximity to the northwest shore of the island; the lake is 300 x 500 m and has been negatively effected by recent settlement on the islands (see below). The big island is best known for what must have been an enormous religious infrastructure when the Spanish arrived, though many of the artefacts were not 'discovered' until the mid-19th century. There are conflicting reports on the island's indigenous name, ranging from *Xomotename* (duck village) to *Mazagalpan* (the houses with nets). Archaeological evidence dating from **500 BC** to **AD 1515** has been documented from more than 20 sites on the island. Massive basalt images attributed to the Chorotega Indians were found at three of these sites and some can be seen in the Museo Convento San Francisco in Granada and the Museo Nacional in Managua. US diplomat and amateur archaeologist **Ephraim George Squier**, on his visit to the island in 1849, uncovered 15 statues, some of which he had shipped to the US where they are in a collection at the Smithsonian Museum in Washington, DC. Another 25 statues were found by the Swedish naturalist **Carl Bovallius** in 1883, in what is the most interesting site, **Zonzapote**, which appears to have been part of an ancient ritual amphitheatre. In 1926, the US archaeologist Samuel Kirkland Lothrop theorized that Bovallius had uncovered a **Chorotega temple** consisting of several sacred buildings each with a separate entrance, idols and sacrificial mounds. But the evidence is not conclusive and much study still needs to be done here.

Equally impressive is the broad, flat rock that sits on the highest point of a small island to the north called **Isla el Muerto**. This 100 m x 25 m rock is one of the most interesting of Nicaragua's hundreds of petroglyph sites. The extraordinary array of rock drawings is believed to have been a very important burial site (hence the name 'Death Island').

Isla Zapatera has several hundred inhabitants who came during the 1980s from the northern extremes of Nicaragua to escape fighting there. They are not legally on the island, which enjoys national park status, and this makes them very shy. Isla el Muerto has one family living on it who can show the way to the massive petroglyph site in the island centre. There are no facilities on the islands or shops of any size, so an expedition must take all supplies, including food and water.

Reserva Natural Volcán Mombacho

Just 10 km outside Granada is one of only two cloud forests found in Nicaragua's Pacific lowlands. As well as the forest reserve, the volcano is home to coffee plantations and some ranches. The summit has five craters in all: four small ones – three of which are covered in vegetation and one that is along the trails of the nature park – and one big one that lost one of its walls in a tragic mudslide in 1570 (see Nandaime, below).

Colour map 3, grid B4
Area: 2,487 ha
Altitude: 850-1,344 m

Buses en route between Nandaime or Rivas and Granada or Masaya. Get off at the Empalme Guanacaste and walk 1 km to a parking area. You could hire a taxi or car to the park. To make it to the top you have to go in a big truck with a covered bed and seating (great view), 25 mins. They leave every couple of hours, from the parking area, with the last trip at 1500, though if enough people accumulate (or you come in a group) they will make another trip to the top of the volcano. You could walk to the top using the steep cobblestone road. The parking area is at 450 m, then you pass through a large coffee farm at 700 m before reaching the biological station at 1,100 m. The road winds upwards and is steep, 5½ km in all. Bring lots of water for the hike, which should take 2-4 hrs.

Ins & outs

The nature reserve is administered by the non-profit **Cocibolca Foundation** and is the best organized in Nicaragua. Paths are so well kept and labelled and the park so well run that it almost has a 'Costa Rica' feel to it. For those who want to see a pristine, protected cloud forest without getting muddy, or without an athletic adventure, this is a perfect place. However, there are opportunities to do some long hikes too. Most visitors opt for a one-hour or two-hour walk that leads through magnificent cloud forest vegetation full of ferns, bromeliads and orchids (752 species of flora have been documented so far). The forest has many species of butterfly and the **Mombacho salamander** (*Bolitoglossa mombachoensis*) is found nowhere else in the world. The forest is also home to 119 species of birds and a further 49 species that are migratory visitors. The biologists have counted some 60 species of mammals, 28 reptiles,

Granada

Cloud forest trekking – Volcán Mombacho

The well-managed park on the Mombacho volcano reserve offers an easy way to appreciate the flora of the cloud forest. However, to really commune with the jungle you need to explore, get a little dirty and sweaty. An alternative route to the summit runs from Granada through rural ranches and directly into the forest of the sleeping cone. A mixture of four-wheel drive travel, good physical condition and guided machete hiking is required, but the pay-off is coffee ranches, howler monkeys and virgin cloud forest. You will need to get an early start (sunrise or before), leaving Granada via La Sabanetta *and* Reparto Adelita *and arriving at the scenic coffee farmhouse at* Finca Las Delicias. *With permission from the farm the four-wheel drive path leads to the organic coffee farm,* Finca La Locura *('madhouse farm'). It was so named for the tradition of Granada families exiling insane family members to the fresh climate of this Mombacho jungle farm. The hope was that a little fresh air and robust communication with resident howler monkeys might help them regain their senses (so if you feel in need of a little primal screaming, the locals here can usually find a family of howler monkeys in the trees). The dirt track continues to an abandoned house from where the journey continues on foot. Total travel time by four-wheel drive is about one hour. After the last house, located at about 700 m above sea level, there is a quarter of an hour of remaining footpath before the jungle closes in and clearing with machete becomes necessary. The forest here is home to numerous species of reptile and bird, as well as howler and white-faced monkeys. There are also pumas and ocelots further up the trail (850 m). The going is tough with plenty of steep mud-filled ascents where you need to grab roots to push forward. Alongside the groaning and sweating of the jungle climb is the marvel of the ever-changing ecosystem, as the temperature drops 1°C every 150 m, modifying the forest flora. Mombacho's primary forest is full of bromeliads, lianas and ferns as well as orchids. After 2½ hours of true grit, you reach a 1,250-m summit. From the top of the cone you can go back down to the vehicle, or continue on a 1½-hour hike on the new park trail called* Sendero El Puma *to the Mombacho park station. You will need to pay admission to the park at the research station and can use their transport to take you down the south face of the mountain and catch a bus back to Granada. If using a tour operator (recommended) they can send the vehicle around to the park to take you back to Granada. Transport and a guide for the hike can be found at* Oro Travel *in Granada (see page 121).*

10 amphibians and some 30,000 insect species. The volcano has terrific views of extinct craters and, if cloud cover permits, of Granada, Lake Nicaragua and Las Isletas. The cloud often clears for a few hours in the afternoon, with 1400-1530 being your best bet for a good view. A walk to the micro-desert on the cone where the fumaroles are will reveal a breathtaking view not just of the lake and Granada City, but also of the Laguna de Apoyo and Volcán Masaya. It is easy to spend a full day hiking on the dormant volcano and there are park guides (Spanish only) to assist. The main beauty of the park is its flora, but if you wish to examine the amphibian, reptile and bird life of the reserve, you will have to sleep in the **research station** and go out at night and in the early morning. They have one big room with several beds, shared baths, kitchen and an outhouse. Cost per person with meals is US$25. The research station offers simple, cheap sandwiches and drinks to visitors and has a good model of the volcano and historical explanations. Bring hiking shoes and a light sweater or better still a rain jacket or poncho.

■ *Park hours are 0830-1700 Tue-Sun. US$6.50 adult and US$3.25 for children which includes the transfer to the reserve from the parking area and the aid of a park guide. Tickets are sold at the parking area at the base, along with purified water and snacks. Cocibolca Foundation can be contacted in Granada T552-5858 or Managua T277-1681, F270-0578, fcocibol@ibw.com.ni*

Tours

Canopy tours are all the rage in touristic countries like Costa Rica, and Nicaragua has seen two tours open in the last two years. They are not designed for nature watching, but to get a bit of a rush and live for an hour like the birds and monkeys up in the trees. For most people it takes a long while for their smile to wear off. Mombacho has one canopy tour with another planned to open soon. The current one has 14 platforms from which the visitor can buzz along a cable from platform to platform, high up in the trees. The Mombacho tour is over coffee plants and includes some very big trees. The service includes some refreshments in a little viewpoint overlooking the valley after your adventure. You need to book at least 24 hours in advance with a tour operator or direct at T0888-2566. They will pick you up at the same parking area as the truck for the forest reserve, but if you want to see both you will have to pay again for the reserve entrance fee. The canopy tour is located just below the house of the coffee plantation, cost is US$25 per person, which includes lessons on a practice cable at ground level, assistance of one of the company guides, and all gear. **NB** There is no relation between the canopy tour and the park administration, and admission for one does not relate to the other.

Travelling south from Granada, the highway meets up with the **Carretera Panamericana**, which travels north to Los Pueblos and on to Managua. To the south the highway continues to the departments of Granada and Rivas and on to the border with Costa Rica. A few kilometres south of the junction is the ranching town of Nandaime, which lies just west of the highway.

Nandaime

Nandaime is the department of Granada's second most important town with interesting history and traditions. The name means, roughly, 'well-irrigated lands'. Little or nothing is known of the original settlement which was near the shores of the lake in front of the Zapatera Archipelago and was visited by the Spanish explorer Gil González Dávila. It was known to be the most important town for the Chorotega southern federation and could have been responsible for administering the religious sites on Isla Zapatera (see above). The city was moved for unknown reasons to a second location further west along the base of the Mombacho volcano. This could have grown to be a sister-city to Granada had it survived. It was reported to have been a town with the same classic colonial design as Granada and was home to a "formal and solid Catholic church". Fate would not allow this, however, for in 1570 an earthquake caused the rim of the Volcán Mombacho crater lake to collapse and the village was annihilated in a massive landslide. A third settlement was established at Nandaime's current position.

Colour map 3, grid B3
Population: 37,596
Altitude: 140 m

At the time of the arrival, and well into the Spanish occupation of the land, it was a place for cultivation of the **cacao** fruit, the raw ingredient from which chocolate is made. Cacao was used by the indigenous population as a monetary unit for a thousand years or so and later came to be known in Europe as the 'food of the gods'. Today the area is home to big ranches and sugar cane and rice farms. Nandaime has two pretty churches, **El Calvario** and **La Parroquia** (1859-72). It is a peaceful cowboy town for most of the year, but becomes a

Granada

raucous party town for the patron saint **festival of Santa Ana** in the last week of July (the most important day is 26 July). The festival includes the dance of the **Diablos de al Orilla**, which is a colourful, spectacular dance of more than 40 men, who accompany the saint on an annual pilgrimage to the tiny settlement of La Orilla, closer to the southern face of Volcán Mombacho. There is a bullfight in La Orilla and much dancing and drinking, and the following days in Nandaime include more dancing in colonial period costume, male cross-dressing, and more drinking and parading around on horseback.

South of Nandaime the *carretera* passes over the region's most important river, Río Ochomogo, the ancient border between the Chorotega Indian world and that of the Nicaraguas Indians to the south. Today it marks the end of Granada and the beginning of the isthmus department of Rivas.

Granada

Ometepe Island and Rivas Isthmus

6

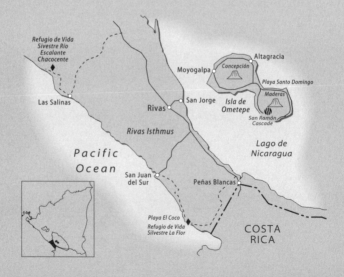

The department of Rivas is blessed with fertile land, a rich cultural history and two long coasts. The 110-km eastern coast hugs the warm shores of the mighty Lake Nicaragua, with long dark sand beaches and huge ranches that give way in the south to dense jungle. The west coast is rugged and empty, with a low mountain chain and more than 130 km of virgin Pacific Coast bays and beaches.

Rising towards the lake's endless sky is Isla de Ometepe, two pyramids of volcanic power and surely one of the world's most beautiful lake islands. It was here, eight or nine million years ago, that Rivas rose from the sea and connected the two great land masses: northern and southern Americas became one continent.

On the Pacific Coast, south of the popular beach town of San Juan del Sur, you can visit two of the most important sea turtle nesting sites in the world, where thousands of turtles make an annual journey of reproduction that has been practised for thousands of years.

In pre-Columbian times, Rivas was home to Nicaragua's most sophisticated society, the Nicaraguas, whose brilliant Chief Niqueragua lent his name first to the department (which was called Valle de Nicaragua), then to the entire country. Today the people of Rivas are very organized and proud, and there is a great tradition of hospitality and warmth in the region.

Carretera Panamericana along the Rivas Isthmus

The dirt roads that lead to the Pacific in Rivas are for 4WD only; some are passable to a certain point with normal cars in the dry season, but eventually become impassable

At Km 80 is the bridge over the **Río Ochomogo**; on the south side of the bridge a rough dirt road runs west to the Pacific Ocean. This is the easiest access to the little-seen and beautiful wildlife reserve of Chacocente. A high-clearance, four-wheel drive vehicle is necessary for the 40-km journey through small friendly settlements to Las Salinas. Here you must turn north and pass through the scenic fishing village in the **Bahía de Astillero** before reaching the entrance to the park. There are two major rivers and several secondary ones to cross; the biggest and hairiest is **Río Escalante**. Crossing this river can be a challenge in the rainy season, with a fair share of speed, bravado and skill necessary to make it to the other side. There are plans to pave this road and build bridges. Expect to ask directions during this trip.

Refugio de Vida Silvestre Río Escalante Chacocente

Colour map 3, grid C3
Area: 4,800 ha
Altitude: 40-200 m

This long-winded name marks the tropical dry forest and beach that make up **Chacocente Wildlife Refuge**. The real fame of the beach and the reason for its protected status are the sea turtles that come to nest every year. This is one of the four most important sea turtle nesting sites along the entire Pacific seaboard of the American continent (another of the four, the La Flor Wildlife Refuge, is further south, see page 150). The park is also a critical tropical dry forest reserve for the Nicaraguan Pacific and a good place to see giant iguanas and varied bird life during the dry season, when visibility in the forest is at its best. The beach itself is lovely too, with a long open stretch of sand that runs back into the forest, perfect for stringing up a hammock. Camping is permitted (in fact this spot is a personal favourite), but no facilities are provided and you will need to come well stocked with water and supplies. ■ *There is a US$3 entrance fee to the park.*

The Pan-American Highway is in excellent condition here as it continues south past sprawling ranches and farmland, with the highlands of Isla Zapatera visible to the east and the cone of Volcán Concepción on Isla de Ometepe coming into view to the southeast. The dry season here is very brown, but most of the year the landscape is fluorescent green, shaded by rows of mango trees and dotted with small, attractive ranch homes and flowered front gardens. Roadside stalls offer many fruits, such as watermelon and some of the biggest papaya seen anywhere. The arrival in San Jorge and Rivas, two separate cities that run together, is marked by a tiny roundabout at Km 111. To the west lies Rivas and to the east San Jorge and the dock for boats to Ometepe.

Rivas

Colour map 3, grid C4
Population: 41,764
Altitude: 139 m

The capital of the department that carries its name, Rivas is a pleasant city with two beautiful churches, a happy, friendly population and lots of horse carriages with car tyres, particular to this area. It carries the nickname of City of Mangos for the tree that seems to be growing everywhere in and around the city. Few travellers bother to visit Rivas town, preferring to head straight for San Jorge along the route that leads to Isla de Ometepe. Founded in 1720 and named after a high-level Spanish diplomat in Guatemala, Rivas was and still is a ranching centre. For the filibuster William Walker (see page 132), who fought and lost three battles here, the last a 53-day siege, it was never a very happy place. The **Templo Parroquial de San Pedro** on Parque Central is the

Sea turtles – the miracle of life

Every year between July and February thousands of beautiful Olive Ridley turtles (Lepidochelys olivacea) arrive at La Flor and Chacocente, two wildlife refuges set aside to aid in their age-old battle against predators with wings, pincers, four legs and two. The sea turtles, measuring up to 80 cm and weighing more than 90 kg, come in waves. Between August and November as many as 7,000 sea turtles may arrive to nest in a three-night period and this is just one of many arrivals during the nesting season. Each turtle digs a hole with her rear flippers and patiently lays up to 100 eggs, covers them and returns to the water: mission complete. For 45 days the eggs incubate under the tropical Nicaraguan sand. Then, all at once, they hatch and the little turtles run down to the sea. If they survive they will travel as far as the Galapagos Islands where Olive Ridleys tagged in Nicaragua have been recovered. The massive leatherback (Dermochelys coriacea), which can grow up to 2 m and weigh over 300 kg, is less common than the Olive Ridley and arrives alone to lay her eggs.

Turtle eggs are a traditional food for the Nicaraguans, and although they are not eaten in large quantities, poaching is always a threat. Park rangers and, during peak times, armed soldiers protect the turtles from animal and human threats in both Chacocente and La Flor wildlife refuges. If you have the chance to witness the arrival, take it and get talking to the rangers who have a great passion for their work. Extreme caution must be exercised during nesting season as, even if you see no turtles on the beach, you are most likely to be walking over nests. Limit flash photography to a minimum and never aim a flash camera at turtles coming out of the water.

Camping will be essential to see the turtles in Chacocente, but from San Juan del Sur to La Flor, an 1800-2000 night trip or 0400 morning trip are also viable ways to see them without roughing it. If you're in Nicaragua during the season, you can call the Cocibolca Foundation to see when they think the next arrival might occur, T278-3224.

city's principal church of the, with a design that is very reminiscent of León cathedral; inside there is a famous fresco depicting the heroic forces of Catholicism defeating a withered Communism in a rather one-sided looking sea battle. There is also the gaily painted **Iglesia San Francisco** to the west of the park, which is the older of the two temples. **Museo de Antropología y Arqueológico**, Escuela International de Agricultura 1½ c north, T453-000, the region's best museum, has a dwindling, but precious collection of archaeological pieces as well as taxidermy and some ecological information. It might be worth the visit just for the views and the charm of the old hacienda.
■ *Mon-Fri 0800-1200, 1400-1700, Sat 0800-1200.*

Rivas is famous around Nicaragua for the indigenous drinking cups made from the dried, hard case of the fruit that grows on the native *jícara* tree. The *jícara* fruit is oval shaped like a very big egg and has been used for cups since long before the arrival of the Spaniards; each has its own base or can be hung on a cup rack. Archaeological digs have found that early ceramic cups were also egg-shaped and accompanied by a base, moulded on the shape of the *jícara*. In Monimbó in Masaya the *jícara* is used to make maracas, and both the cups and maracas can also be found in the Masaya market.

A-C *Hotel Cacique Nicarao*, next to cinema, T453-3234. 18 rooms, private bath, a/c (**C** with fan), cable TV, parking, bar, restaurant, clean, friendly, best in town, prices include breakfast. Recommended.

Sleeping

Ometepe Island and Rivas Isthmus

F *Español*, behind the Iglesia San Pedro, T453-0006. 4 rooms, private bath, fan, laundry service, restaurant. **F** *Hospedaje Lidia*, ½ c west of Texaco, T453-3477. 12 rooms, family atmosphere, clean, some with private bath, close to bus stop. Recommended. **F** *El Coco*, on Highway near where bus from border stops, T453-3298. Noisy, basic, small rooms, some with private bath, interesting bar, *comedor* with vegetarian food, nice garden. **G** *Laureles*, northeast side of market. 9 rooms, shared bath, fan, billiards.

Eating   *Chop Suey*, opposite *Enitel*, T453-3235. 1000-2100 daily, Chinese food at Nicaraguan prices, for those intent on a change. *El Mesón*, Iglesia San Francisco, ½ c west, T453-4535. Very good, try *pollo a la plancha* or *bistec encebollado*, open daily 1100-2300. *Restaurante El Ranchito*, near *Hotel El Coco*. Friendly, serves delicious chicken and *churrasco*. *Rinconcito Salvadoreño* in the middle of the Parque Central. Open-air, charming. *Restaurante Moimar*, *Enitel*, 1½ c west, T453-4363. Daily 1100-1200, popular place, with typical food, good. *Rayuela*, across from police station, T453-3221. Prices here are a steal; very cheap tacos, *repochetas*, sandwiches, open 0730-2100 daily except Sun 0730-1300, 1700-2200.

Transport   **Bus**   Rivas-Managua, every ½ hr, 0330-1800, US$1.50, 2 hrs 45 mins. **Rivas-Granada**, every 45 mins, 0530-1625, US$1, 1 hr 45 mins. **Rivas-Jinotepe**, every ½ hr, 0540-1710, US$1, 1 hr 45 mins. **Rivas-San Juan del Sur**, every ½ hr, 0600-1830, US$70, 45 mins. **Rivas-Peñas Blancas**, every ½ hr, 0500-1600, US$.60, 1 hr. **Taxi** to **San Jorge**, the best way to get to the dock, US$1.50.

Directory   **Banks** *BDF (Banco de Finanzas)* for changing cash and American Express travellers' cheques, from the fire station, 1 c south, 75 *varas* east, T453-0743. **Communications** *Enitel* is 3 blocks south of Parque Central, or 7 blocks south and 3 blocks east from bus terminal, T453-0003. **Post office:** *Correos de Nicaragua*, Gimnasio Humberto Méndez, ½ c west, T453-3600. **Tourism office** *INTUR* is located 3½ c west of the Texaco station, T453-4914, ask for Sr Francisco Cárdenas. Good maps of Nicaragua and general information. **Tour operators** *Tour Nicarao*, 1 block south from Plaza, T453-4157, F453-3371, arranges local tours, good place to send faxes. **Useful numbers** Fire: T453-3511. **Hospital:** T453-3301. **Police:** T453-3631. **Red Cross:** T453-3415.

San Jorge

Colour map 3, grid C4
Population: 7,675
Altitude: 50 m

It looks like an extension of Rivas, but San Jorge is a separate town, one that most see on their way to the ferry for Ometepe. To catch the ferry you must go from the roundabout on the highway directly east towards the lake as far as the little Parque Central and Iglesia de San Jorge, a little Gothic-Mudéjar church, with the ruins of an ancient convent behind. From the church it is two blocks north, then east again all the way to the *muelle* (dock). The cross over the road between the highway and the church is known as **La Cruz de España** and, together with a small mural painting and a few plaques, commemorates the fateful arrival of the Spanish. The cross marks the assumed spot where the Spanish explorer Gil González Dávila met Chief Niqueragua (see box), the leader of the most developed indigenous society in the region. In those days San Jorge was known as *Nicaraocalli*. The festival for San Jorge is 23 April.

Sleeping   If you miss the last boat, there are some small *hospedajes* in San Jorge, though it may be more interesting to sleep in Rivas. About 500 m south of the dock is **D** *Mar Dulce*, T453-3262. 6 rooms, bath, TV, parking, restaurant and bar. If you wish to be close to the fatal first meeting place between the great chief and González Dávila you could sleep

Things to do in Ometepe and Rivas

- Wade out into the warm gentle waves off Santo Domingo beach, Ometepe, for a magical view of the two volcanoes.
- Follow a local guide through the ruggedly spectacular scenery to see ancient rock paintings at one of the island's many pre-Columbian petroglyph sites.
- Witness the sea turtles arriving to lay their eggs at Playa La Flor wildlife refuge, as they've been doing between August and November for millions of years.
- Try a dish of fresh red or black snapper at the beach-front bar and restaurant *El Timón* in San Juan del Sur, then wash it down with a cold Victoria beer.
- Watch bobbing boats silhouetted against the sunset in the bay of San Juan del Sur.

at the **E** *Hotel Cruz de España*, roundabout, 400 metres east (towards the lake), T453-4995. Private bath, a/c or **F** with fan. **F** *El Farolito*, northeast side of la Portuaria, T453-4738. 6 rooms, private bath, fan, *comida corriente*.

Eating There are plenty of little places to eat around the dock area, most of them serving very cheap food, one or two of which are good. *El Faro*, across from the Portuaria, T453-4738. Beef, pork and chicken, open daily 0700-2300. *El Refugio*, 200 m south of the Portuaria, T453-4631. Good beef dishes, daily 0900-2200. For a good fish soup or shrimp and fish ceviche you might try *Restaurante Ivania*, Alcaldía Municipal, 1 c west, 2½ c south, T453-4764. To toast the great chief Niqueragua, you can stop just 60 m east of the Cruz de España at *La Cabaña*, T453-4952. Cold beer, tacos, open daily after 1100.

Transport **Bus** The ride to or from the bus station in Rivas is US$1.50. There are buses direct to Managua's Roberto Huembes market, **San Jorge-Managua**, 0745, 1445, US$2, 2½ hrs. Otherwise use bus station at Rivas for connections.

Car If you have a high-clearance 4WD you may want to take it across on the ferry to use on the island (US$17 each way). You need to arrive at least 1 hr before the ferry departure to reserve a spot (if possible call the day before, T459-4284, to make an initial reservation). You will need to pay, fill out some paperwork, and buy a boarding ticket for each person travelling. Make sure you reserve your spot as close to the ferry ramp as possible, but leave room for trucks and cars coming off the ferry.

Ferry *El Ferry* is the best of the five boats that make the crossing (the others offer varying degrees of fear and smoke inhalation, but therein lies the adventure, depending on the severity of the lake conditions and the strength of your sea legs).

The lake crossing: San Jorge to Ometepe

There are five boats that make the one-hour journey from the dock at San Jorge to the dock at Moyogalpa on the island (see box page 138). The best choice is *El Ferry*, which has three levels, a toilet, snack bar, TV (with the *telenovela* of the hour being blasted through concert speakers over the noise of the motors) and room for six cars, or two trucks full of plantains and two cars. The best reasons to time your crossing for the ferry are the '*African Queen*' conditions of the other boats and the great viewing deck on top of *El Ferry*, which offers a panoramic view of the lake and islands. If it's a clear day, the Zapatera Archipelago is visible to the north, with Volcán Mombacho rising

Those prone to seasickness should buy Nausil from the farmacia before the crossing

Ometepe Island and Rivas Isthmus

Fatal embrace – Chief Niqueragua and Conquistador Gil González

The image is forever embossed in the minds of the Nicaraguan people. It adorns murals, plaques, paintings and postage stamps: the first meeting of the European explorers and the Nicaragua natives on 12 April 1523. The cagey money man Gil González holds out a linen shirt as an offering to the most powerful chief of the land, Niqueragua, who looks on, somewhat suspicious yet welcoming. It is said that González traded his shirt, a silk jacket and a red hat for 18,506 gold pesos. The pillage of Nicaragua had begun, with one of the worst deals in history. Yet Chief Niqueragua lives on as a symbol of nobility and intelligence. He welcomed the Spaniard peacefully, perhaps out of curiosity, and he sat for one week with González in philosophical discussion. With the help of an interpreter Niqueragua grilled the Spaniard thoroughly on all subjects, from astronomy and geology to

philosophy and especially religion. González later admitted sheepishly that Chief Niqueragua was a "linguistic engineer", and that he, González, had to excuse himself for his lack of expertise. Yet destiny was on the side of greed, not reason.

Not only was trade with Chief Niqueragua good for the Spanish, but his land was also a treasure. The chronicler Oviedo described it just after the Conquest: "its healthful and soothing climate, its fine waters and fisheries and its abundance of hunting and game, there is nothing in all the Americas, that feature for feature, surpasses it."

Further north, Gil González would soon come across real trouble with the less philosophical Chief Diriangén of the Chorotega Indians. However, the first bricks had been laid for the destruction of the indigenous world of western Nicaragua.

up behind it, and on super clear days you'll see the smoke surging out of Volcán Masaya.

The approach to the island is one of the best photo opportunities in Nicaragua, particularly on the afternoon crossings

If you look carefully at Isla Zapatera and its westerly islands, the form of a man, face down, becomes apparent. The head starts in the east and then a long back, rump, then calf and heel. This shape, combined with the obvious female shape of Ometepe, is essential to understand the beautiful legend about the formation of the lake and island (see box page 139). If your travel diary lacks colour (hard to believe in Nicaragua) you may want to take a non-ferry boat to spice up your text. The smaller boats really shake, rattle and roll in the lake swells that can reach up to 2½ m on really rough and windy days. That, combined with their rustic, on-the-verge-of-falling-apart appearance and the smoke that inevitably billows into the water-logged passengers' deck, makes a trip on boats like the Santa María or *Reyna del Sur* quite a bit of fun. Still, if the lake is rough you are definitely advised to take *El Ferry*, which has a big steel hull that cuts the swells (don't sit outside in the first level bow or you will be soaked). But take note when the deck hands tie down the trucks full of plantains (*plátanos*) to the sides of the ferry; in the open lake the trucks will rock menacingly from side to side, threatening to take the whole boat over with them.

NB If you have some heavy bags you can leave them on the bottom level against the front wall under the TV. If you are on the upper deck stay clear of the centre, as the ferry captain will need a clear view as he backs the ferry into dock. Boys will come on board to help with bags in Moyogalpa; they are honest but aggressive. If you need a hand, US$0.50 per bag. When the ferry departs the boys will hitch a partial ride, then use the boat as a moving diving platform and swim back to the Moyogalpa dock.

Isla de Ometepe

Ometepe is a place of history, legends and stunning vistas. There is a rustic beauty to the island and the people are famously friendly and welcoming. The Ometepinos celebrate their island's fortune of being left out of centuries of wars by calling it the Oasis de Paz (Oasis of Peace), for none of the big battles of Nicaragua's post-Conquest history have been played out on Ometepe (two mountains) Island.

Colour map 3, grid C4/5
Population: 32,000
Area: 276 sq km
Altitude: 60-1610 m

History

Ceramic evidence shows that the island has been inhabited for at least 3,500 years, though some believe it could be as much as 12,000 years or more. Little is actually known about the pre-Conquest cultures of the island. From ceramic analysis done by US archaeologist Frederick W Lange and published in 1992, it appears the people of 1500 BC came from South America as part of a northern immigration that continued to Mexico. They lived in a settlement in what is today the town of Los Angeles, Ometepe. They were followed by waves of settlement both from the Pacific and Caribbean sides of the island. A certain mystery surrounds the people who inhabited the island at the time of the conquest. A visiting priest reported in 1586 that the Indians of the island spoke a language different from any of those spoken on the mainland. Yet the large basalt statues found on Ometepe appear to be of the same school as the ones found on Zapatera and attributed to the Chorotegas. The lack of research seems surprising. **Dr J F Bransford**, a medical officer for a US Navy survey team, came to Nicaragua in 1872 as part of an inter-oceanic exploratory team. His observations (published in 1881 by the Smithsonian Institute) remain one of the few sources of information about this mysterious place. This is despite him declaring that "there can be no more interesting field for archaeological research than in Nicaragua". Bransford made several excavations uncovering the **Cerámica Luna** school of pottery found nowhere else in Nicaragua (named after the owner of the excavation site land). During his digs in 1876 and 1877 near Moyogalpa he noted that the Concepción volcano was forested to the top and 'extinct' (it would become very much alive in five years' time) and that the isthmus between the two volcanoes was passable by canoe during the rainy season. The island's population was estimated at 3,000 with most living in Altagracia and some 500 others scattered around the island. Most fit the description of an *Ometepino* today, basically Chorotega in appearance. However, in the very sparsely populated Maderas side of the island lived a tall people, with many men over 6 ft in height, tall women and decidedly unusual facial features. These same people were suspicious and reluctant to talk or share the location of the big basalt idols of the islands with Dr Bransford. This led Bransford to speculate that they still worshipped the gods represented in the statues. In contrast, the other inhabitants of the island would happily reveal the location of the statues and point them out as meaningless sculptures. There seems to be little evidence of these people today, but their idols can be found next to the church in Altagracia and in the National Museum in Managua.

Ometepe Island and Rivas Isthmus

 Ferry timetable

San Jorge – Ometepe:	Ometepe – San Jorge:
0930 Karen María, US$1.20	0530 Karen María, US$1.20
1030 El Ferry, US$1.50	0600 Señora de Lago, US$1.35
1130 Señora de Lago, US$1.35	0630 Santa María, US$1.20
1230 Santa María, US$1.20	**0645 El Ferry**, US$1.50
1400 Karen María, US$1.20	0700 Reyna del Sur, US$1.20
1430 El Ferry, US$1.50	1130 Karen María, US$1.20
1530 Reyna del Sur, US$1.20	**1230 El Ferry**, US$1.50
1630 Señora del Lago, US$1.35	1330 Señora de Lago, US$1.35
1730 El Ferry, US$1.50	**1600 El Ferry**, US$1.50.

During the colonial period, Ometepe was used as a refuge for pirates, en route to or returning from pillaging Granada. The bandits would often steal food supplies, livestock or even women, and some of the population was forced to move inland. With the decline of the pirates, the Isla de Ometepe was left alone with its thousand-year-old mysteries, untouched by battles of Independence, wars against Somoza and the Contras. Today, all that remains of the island's past are symbols yet to be decoded, legends and enigmas.

Sights

Climbing is good on both volcanoes, with the flora and fauna of Maderas being superior in both quantity and diversity

Ometepe's two volcanoes rising up out of Lake Nicaragua seem improbable, prehistoric and almost otherworldly. The two cones are nature reserves and they are connected by a 5-km wide lava-flow isthmus. Travel on the island is always in the shadow of one of its two Olympian volcanic cones. The dominant mountain is **Volcán Concepción** (1,610 m high, 36½ km maximal diameter), an active volcano that last threw forward ash in December 1999 with its most recent major lava flow occurring in 1957. The volcano was inactive for many years before it burst into life in 1883 with frequent, lava-filled eruptions until 1887. Concepción also erupted from 1908 until 1910, with further significant activity in 1921 and 1948-72. It was a Nicaraguan postage stamp of the volcano in eruption that doomed a proposed inter-oceanic canal project that would have had to pass by the burning mountain. In fact, thanks to its hot lava outbursts, one of the cone's indigenous names was **Mestlitepe** (mountain that menstruates), the other well-known name being **Choncotecihuatepe** (brother of the moon) and an evening moonrise above the volcano is an unforgettable sight. Concepción, one of the most symmetrical cones in the world, is covered by 2,200 ha of protected forest.

Volcán Maderas (1,394 m high, 24½ km maximal diameter) last erupted about 800 years ago and is now believed to be extinct. The mountain is wrapped in thick forest and is home to the ohly cloud forest in Nicaragua's Pacific Basin other than Volcán Mombacho. The Nicaraguas called the mountain **Coatlán** (land of the sun). The 400 x 150 m cold, misty crater lake, **Laguna de Maderas**, was only discovered by the non-indigenous population in 1930. On the western face of the cone spurts a lovely waterfall. Maderas has 4,100 ha of forest set aside and protected in a *reserva natural*.

Isla de Ometepe is also home to many freshwater beaches, the most beautiful and accessible of which is **Playa Santo Domingo**, a long stretch of grey sand on

Romeo and Ometepetl – a lake story

Centuries ago, there was no Lake Nicaragua and no islands. Instead, there was a lush valley with fruit-bearing trees, full of deer and serenaded by the songs of beautiful birds. This was a valley of the gods. Tipotani, the supreme god, sent Coapol to watch over the valley and for that it was called the Valle de Coapolca. Coapol was not alone in his duties; other gods such as Hecatl, Xochipilli, Oxomogo and Cachilweneye helped tend the garden. But despite all the lush trees, green fields and healthy animal life, there was no source of water in the valley. Its lushness was created and maintained by the gods. Several tribes lived around the edge of the Valle de Coapolca and entered the valley often, to use its forests for hunting, to pick its wild fruits and for romance.

One summer afternoon the beautiful Ometepetl from the Nicaraguas tribe met the brave and handsome warrior Nagrando, from the neighbouring Chorotega tribe, and it was love at first sight. The god Xochipilli sent harmonious breezes across the pastures, while other gods offered gentle rain and singing birds. The gods married them for this life and the afterlife.

But Ometepetl and Nagrando had to keep their love secret as their tribes were rivals and war was possible at any moment. The tribal chiefs had long since

passed laws that their sons and daughters could not mix. One day when they came to the valley to make love, they were seen by some soldiers and Nagrando was sentenced to death for his insolence. The supreme god Tipotani warned the couple of impending danger and the couple were led to a safe hiding place. Still, they knew that the chief's pronouncement was inexorable, and they decided they would rather die together than live apart.

After reciting a prayer to the gods, they held each other tightly, kissed an eternal kiss, and then they slit their wrists. Their blood began to fill the valley; the skies went dark and opened in torrential rains. Thunder clapped across the sky and rain filled with meteorites, as shooting stars ran across the heavens. Nagrando, delirious and writhing in pain, rose to his feet, stumbled and fell away from Ometepetl. The valley filled with water. The gods looked on and Nagrando's body came to rest as the island of Zapatera, while Ometepetl became the island of Ometepe, her breasts rising above the waters of the torrential floods. The instigators of the tragedy, those who put politics above love, were drowned in the floodwaters and the punished bodies from each tribe formed the archipelagos of Las Isletas and Solentiname.

the **Isthmus of Istián** (where two waters meet) that connects the two volcanoes' round bases. This is the centre of the island's figure-of-eight shape and there are several lagoons and creeks that are good for bird-watching. On the northeast side of the isthmus there are a couple of islands that also house a rich bird life, as well as the legendary **Charco Verde** (see box page 145) on the southern coast of Concepción. Both cones house monkey populations, with the Maderas residents being almost impossible to miss in a full-day hike on the cone. The forest of Maderas has a great diversity of butterfly and flower species, as well as a dwarf forest. The entire island is home to many parrots and magpie jays; the latter are almost as common as the pigeons in the squares of European cities.

Apart from its unusual geology, flora and fauna, Ometepe has much to offer the culturally curious. There are numerous pre-Columbian sites and a way of living that most of the outside world has long since forgotten. A guided visit is recommended to one of the many **petroglyph sites**, which are known according to the name of the farm they are found on. To name but a few: **San Marcos** has an eagle with outstretched wings; **Hacienda San Antonio** has geometric figures; **Altagracia**, in the house of Domnigo Gutiérrez, shows a rock with an 'x' and a cross used to make sacrifices to the cult of the sun; **Hacienda La Primavera** has various images; **La Cigueña** shows the southern cross and various animals; and **El Porvenir** has a sundial and what some believe to be an alien being and a representation of the god of death. **La Palmera**, **Magdalena**, **San Ramón** and **Mérida** all have interesting petroglyph sites and **Soccoro** has some sun calendars. This is only a small selection of sites; Ometepe really is a playground for the archaeologically curious.

Moyogalpa

Colour map 3, grid C4
Population: 9,117
Altitude: 60 m

The 'place of mosquitoes' is how the name of the village would translate, but there aren't really any more here than elsewhere in the region

Moyogalpa is the port of entry for arrivals from San Jorge. It is a bustling town of commerce and travel, with a decidedly less indigenous population than the rest of the island. There is not much to do in Moyogalpa, but due to its port status it has many hotels. You may decide to spend a night here if leaving on an early boat, otherwise Altagracia, Santo Domingo and San Ramón are all more attractive options with excellent hiking and cultural touring opportunities.

One interesting excursion would be to walk or rent a bicycle to visit **Punta Jesús María**, 4-5 km away, but well signposted from the road just before Esquipulas. Jesús María has a good beach, a panoramic view of the island and a small café; in the mornings you can watch the fishermen on the long sandbar that extends into the lake. (The beach is smaller at the end of the rainy season.) From Altagracia you can continue to Santo Domingo, Balgues and San Ramón. The patron saint festival for **Santa Ana** is a very happy affair. Processions begin on 23 July in the barrio La Paloma and continue for several days. On 25 July there is a lovely dance with girls dressed in indigenous costume and on 26 July there's a huge party with bullfights.

Sleeping & eating

C *Ometepetl*, on main street from dock, T459-4276, F459-4132. Bath, a/c, rooms dirty, very friendly, poor food, best rental cars on the island. **D-E** *Hotel Cari*, 1 block from pier next to fountain, T459-4263, F459-4283. Best location, poor service, some a/c, run down, car rental, restaurant.

E *El Pirata*, from *Hotel Cari*, 3 c east, T459-4262. Private bath, a/c or fan, dark rooms, very pleasant staff, good value. **F** *El Colonial*, on main street from dock. With bath, clean, balcony, good food. Recommended. **F** *Pensión Aly*, opposite Shell. Clean, uncomfortable beds, helpful, poor value and service in restaurant. **F-G** *Los Ranchitos*, on same street as telephone company. 4 rooms, excellent food, including vegetarian pasta, vegetable soup, chicken in garlic butter, reasonable prices, 2 branches, both good. Highly recommended. **G** *Pensión Jade*, good atmosphere, friendly, water problems, meals available, good value. There are several bars that serve cheap food from the dock up the hill to the church, such as *Bar-Soda El Chele* with breakfast, cheap food, sandwiches.

Transport

Buses wait for the boats in Moyogalpa and run to Altagracia, the principal town on the eastern side of the island. **Moyogalpa-Altagracia**, 0600, 0730, 0830, 1130, 1230, 1300, 1700, 1800, US$0.50, 1 hr. **Moyogalpa-Santo Domingo-Balgue**, 1030, 1400, 1530, 1630, US$0.75, 2 hrs. **Moyogalpa-Mérida**, 1400, 1800, US$0.75, 2 hrs.

Pick-up truck taxis wait for the ferry, price is per journey not per person, some have room for four passengers others two, the rest go in the back, which is the far better view, but dusty in dry season. **Altagracia**, US$15-20, **Santo Domingo**, US$20-25.

Car hire Toyota Rent a Car, *Hotel Ometeptl*, T459-4276, a good strong 4WD is a must, US$35-50 for 12 hrs, US$60 for 24 hrs. They can also find a driver, though advance notice is best. A bit cheaper and in worse condition, the little jeeps at *Hotel*

Cari, T459-4263, US$30 for 8 hrs and US$50 for 24 hrs, driver also possible. Most drivers will charge US$20 per day plus meals; they can also serve as a guide unless they have recently arrived on the island.

Communications Post office and telephone: *Enitel*, T459-4100, from the dock 2 c east, 1½ south, for both postal and telephone services. **Shopping** On the road from the dock to the church there are some general stores. It is best to buy what you need here or in Altagracia. **Tours and tourist information** There is a tourist office up the hill from the harbour in Moyogalpa, which offers good information, tours, horse rental, bus timetables, etc. *Fundación Entre Volcanes* (postal address: de la Gasolinera Esso 1½ c al Sur, Moyogalpa, Ometepe, Nicaragua) runs the organization *Ecotur*, from the dock, 2 c east, 1½ c south, T/F459-4118, which is useful for finding local guides, have an excellent guide (in Spanish) to Ometepe parks and can arrange home stays. (*Ecotur* is also in the museum in Altagracia.) *Ometepe Tours*, in Moyogalpa, ½ block north of *BND*, T459-4105, sells a useful booklet with maps and information, also in San Jorge, next to the dock, T453-4779. Most of the Managuan tour operators offer Ometepe packages that can be useful if travelling in a group. **Guides**: *Rommel Gómez*, *Restaurante Los Ranchitos*, T459-4112. *Horacio Galán*, *Hotel Ometeptl*, T459-4276.

Directory

This is an alternative route up Volcán Concepción from behind the church in Moyogalpa. A guide is seriously recommended for finding the route in jungle sections (machete useful) and cloud. The climb takes eight hours and camping is possible near the top. Guides from *Villa Paraíso* in Playa Santo Domingo are the most expensive and most responsible (see below). **NB** When looking for a guide always ask as many questions as you can about his experience with the trail or climb and never pay in advance of the journey, as Moyogalpa now has a con artist who demands payment in advance. However, some guides have been ripped off by travellers after a hard day's work, so you may have to pay a deposit once the journey has begun, but not before you are en route.

Volcán Concepción from Moyogalpa
This route is much more dangerous than the Altagracia route due to the very high landslide risk

Ometepe Island and Rivas Isthmus

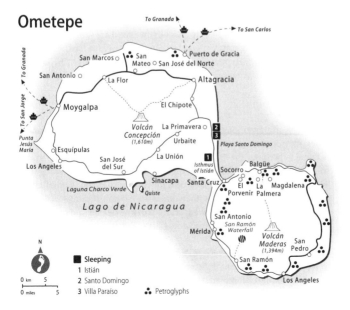

Ometepe

Sleeping
1 Istián
2 Santo Domingo
3 Villa Paraíso

∴∴ Petroglyphs

Lago de Nicaragua

0 km   5
0 miles   5

N

Routes to Altagracia

There are two equally interesting routes that pass the flanks of Concepción to the sleepy village of Altagracia. The **north route** is more scenic; it runs along the north shores of the island through the tiny settlements of La Flor and San Mateo. There are commanding views of the volcano with its eastern erosion zones and 1957 lava flow visible beyond rock-strewn pasture and highland banana plantations. The road is unpaved and at times very rough. A fork leads to the coast and the small, very indigenous settlement of **San Marcos** to the left, and on to Altagracia on the right, past a baseball field (Sundays) and a school. A tiny church marks your arrival in Altagracia. The town entrance lies just southeast of the cemetery, perhaps the most scenic in Nicaragua for its imposing backdrop of Volcán Concepción. This is also the entrance to one of the routes up the volcano.

The **south route** is more heavily populated, has some paved stretches and is the quickest route to Playa Santo Domingo and the Maderas side of Ometepe. The *carretera* passes the town of **Esquípulas** (place of flowers), where it is believed the great chief Nicaragua may have been buried, and the village of **Los Angeles**, which has some of the oldest known evidence of ancient settlers on the island, dated at 1500 BC. The fairly developed **San José del Sur**, evacuated in 1998 under threat of massive mudslides from Concepción, is further along the skirt of the volcano, and the road rises to spectacular views of Volcán Maderas across the lake. Just past San José del Sur is the rough and narrow access road to **Charco Verde**, a big pond with an even bigger legend (see box, page 139), and one of the most scenic parts of the island. At the end of the road are a petrol storage tank and a twiggy beach. There is some very rustic lodging near the legendary pond, F *Finca Venecia*, T453-3878, meals and transportation available. Just east is the **Bahía de Sinacapa** (meeting place) that hides an ancient volcanic cone under its waters, along with an island named **Quiste**. La Unión is the highway's closest pass to the active cone and a good place to see howler monkeys. The road then passes through the happy little village of **Urbaite** where the belltower, typical of a design peculiar to the island, is separate from the church, built alongside it so as to ride out the island's seismic events. After Urbaite, there is a right turn to the isthmus and Maderas (see below). The road to Altagracia then passes the delightful little church at **El Chipote** and enters the south of Altagracia.

Altagracia

Colour map 3, grid C4
Population: 20,704
Altitude: 70 m

This calm, unpretentious town is the most important on the island and it hides its population well, except when there is a festival and holiday. Altagracia predates the arrival of the Spanish and was once home to two tribes who named their villages **Aztagalpa** (egrets' nest) and **Cosonigalpa**. The tribes were divided by what is now the road from Parque Central to the cemetery. Thanks to a less than amiable relationship the people of Cosonigalpa had to escape to what is now San José del Sur and to the bay of Sinacapa. The Spanish renamed the village, but the population remains largely indigenous.

In the shade of the trees next to Altagracia's attractive church, built in 1924 to replace the colonial temple, is a sculpture park which contains some of the most famous pre-Columbian statues in Nicaragua. They are estimated to date from around AD 800 and represent human forms and their alter egos, the eagle being most famous, and as the jaguar, which is believed to have been the symbol of power. West of the plaza, the **Museo de Ometepe** has displays of archaeology and covers local ethnographic and environmental themes; the guide is enthusiastic and sincere (Spanish only). ■ *Tue-Sun 0900-1200, 1400-1600, US$1*. Altagracia has inexpensive lodging and good access to the preferred ascent of Concepción and there is even some dancing on Saturday nights, although fights often break out among the local cowboys in the early morning hours. The town's patron saint, **San Diego de Alcalá**, is celebrated from 28 October-18 November with many dances and traditions, particularly the Baile del Zompopo (the dance of the leaf-cutter ant), which is famous around the country but is only danced here. The indigenous population of the zone celebrated their harvest god, Xolotl, every November. The story goes that one year, no one is sure when, the harvest was being annihilated by red ants, the tribe shamans practised some ritual sacrifices and instructed the people to do a special dance to drums with branches of various trees. The disaster and starvation was averted and a tradition was born. When the Franciscans arrived in 1613 they brought with them an image of the saint of San Diego whose days coincided with that of the annual celebration for Xolotl and the red-ant dance. Over time, the friars convinced the Indians to substitute one god for another, and the dance is still performed on 17 November. The Purísima celebrations to the Virgin Mary on 7 December are a marathon affair here of singing to a large, heavily decorated image of Santa María on the back of a pick-up truck in what is truly a Felliniesque setting.

Sleeping & eating
There are several small eateries and food in the hotels

B *Hotel Central*, 2 c south of church, T552-6072. 17 rooms, attractive courtyard, charming bungalows in garden with private bath, **F** with shared bath, both good value, dining room, good friendly service, nice patio. Recommended.

F *Hospedaje Castillo*, 1 c south, ½ west, T552-6072. Shared bath, 3 meals, real coffee, friendly, good food, talkative 80+year-old owner is legendary source of information for the island, slow service, water problems, petroglyph trips US$4 per person or US$12 for a group guide, internet available a couple of hours per day. **F** *Hospedaje Astagalpa*, Parque Central, 1 ½ c east, T552-6082. Shared bath, basic and clean, also restaurant.

Transport

Bus Altagracia-Moyogalpa, 0430, 0710, 0900, 1200, 1315, 1530, 1630, US$0.50, 1 hr. Altagracia-Balgue, 0430, 0500, 1130, 1400, 1630, US$0.45, 45 mins.

Ferry The port of Altagracia is called **San Antonio** and is located 2 km north of the town; pick-up trucks meet the boat that passes between Granada and San Carlos. Altagracia-San Carlos, Mon and Thu at 1820, 11 hrs. **Altagracia-Granada**, Tue and Fri at 0130, 3½ hrs. See Chapter 5 for departures from Granada.

Directory

Post office and telephone are in *Enitel* building, ½ c south of southwest corner of Parque Central.

Volcán Concepción

This climb without a local guide is not recommended under any circumstances and can be very dangerous. Leave from Cuatro Cuadras, 2 km from Altagracia, and make for a cinder gully between forested slopes and a lava flow. There are several farms on the lower part of the volcano. The ascent takes 5 hours, though a good athlete can do it in 3½ hours (take water and sunscreen), with tropical dry and wet forest, heat from the crater and the howler monkeys as added attractions. The view from Concepción is breathtaking. The cone is very steep near the summit and loose footing and high winds are common. **NB** Follow the guide's advice if winds are deemed too strong for the summit.

Tour guides **Neftali Paisano**, Shell Altagracia, 100 m south. **Eduardo Ortiz** and son, **José**, Cuatro Cuadras. Guides from *Hotel Villa Paraíso* in Playa Santo Domingo (see below) are most expensive and most responsible. **NB** When looking for a guide always ask as many questions as you can about his experience with the trail or climb and never pay in advance of journey. Some guides have been conned by travellers, so you may have to pay a deposit once the journey has begun, but not before you are en route.

From Altagracia to Playa Santo Domingo

The sweeping sandy beach at Santo Domingo is reached via the southern road from Moyogalpa (see above) or from Altagracia's southern exit. There are signs, which mark the turn-off on to a dirt road that can be very difficult in sections during the rainy season. The road winds through plantain plantations, past a miniature church, down a steep paved section and across a tiny bridge where women do laundry in the creek. The water is very clean upstream from here and great for swimming at its source (hotels in Santo Domingo offer a cheap excursions to swim in the spring's crystalline waters). The road rises over a pass that allows a view of both cones and then dips into beautiful (and cooler) tropical dry forest and Santo Domingo.

Playa Santo Domingo

This long sandy coastline is one of the prettiest freshwater beaches in Nicaragua and, with the forest-covered Volcán Maderas looming at the beach's end, it is truly exotic. The warm water, gentle waves and gradual shelf make it a great swimming beach. If you wade out you'll be able to see the cone of Concepción over the forest; a dual volcano swimming experience. The lake here is very reminiscent of a sea. In fact, many visitors, forgetting that it is fresh water, have been startled to see horses going down to drink from its shores. On this side of the island the trade winds blow nearly all year round and keep the heat and insects to a minimum. The width of the beach depends on the time of year: at the end of the dry season there's a broad swath of sand and at the end of the rainy season bathers are pushed up to the edge of the small drop-off that backs the beach. It is not unusual to see a school of freshwater sardines bubbling out of the water being chased by a predator. And around the beach there are many magpie jays, parrots, vultures and hawks. Santo Domingo can be used as a jumping-off point for the ultra-tranquil Maderas side of the island or for climbing either volcano. Services in Santo Domingo are limited to the hotels, one micro-store and one bar; there is no town. Stock up on water (cheaper than in the hotel) or cookies at the small store in front of the parking lot of the *Villa Paraíso*.

Sleeping **B-F** *Villa Paraíso*, beachfront, T453-4675, vparaiso@ibw.com.ni In cabañas with pri-
& eating vate bath and a/c or fan, or in lodge with private bath or shared bath, an Aus-
■ *on map, page 141* trian-Nicaraguan couple run the hotel, German and some English spoken. The cabañas are very cute with river stone baths and lots of wood and brick, clean, some rooms have patio onto a lake view, friendly, peaceful, lovely setting, and best food on the island. Try fried *guapote* or *mojarra*, also vegetarian dishes, excellent fruit and pancake breakfast, good bird-watching. Horses and mountain bikes for rent. Excursions to both volcanoes with responsible guides. Highly recommended. **D** *Hotel Istián*, south of *Villa Paraíso*,

Charco Verde – the legend of Chico Largo

Chico Largo takes care of the island, even today. He watches over the coastal pond called Charco Verde, a mysterious 300 x 200 m body of dark green water. At the bottom of the pond is a magic city called El Encanto. No one goes hungry or even cooks there. At mealtimes, abundant quantities of food appear ready to eat, on a perfectly set table. Admission to the city is easy; just steal something from Charco Verde. Cutting some fruit from a tree or hunting the animals around the pond's waters grants you lifetime membership.

The city is governed by Chico Largo, the ghost of the descendants of one of Nicaragua's most accomplished sorcerers, an Indian shaman, who escaped from Rivas at the arrival of the first Spanish explorer Gil González. Chico Largo was a tall thin, strong man with black eyes, straight hair and a palm hat.

According to the islanders, anyone who is rich has made a pact with Chico Largo in order to enter El Encanto. After you serve duty for Chico Largo you will be converted into an animal and will be granted free admission to El Encanto.

across the road from the beach, reservations through *Ometepetl*. Basic, dirty, friendly, fan, bath, views to both volcanoes. **F** *Finca Hotel Santo Domingo*, just north of *Villa Paraíso*, the backpacker cousin of *Villa Paraíso*. Relaxed, comfy, shared baths, nice terrace. **NB** Scorpions are common on the island and especially along this beach. They prefer wet swimming trunks and soap dishes, but they are not deadly; kill them with a thick-soled shoe.

Entertainment might be too strong a word, but there is a bar just south of the *Villa Paraíso* parking lot that will stay open if someone is interested (don't show up late or it may not open at all). It has a billiard table and table tennis with some very big speakers, the opportunity to dance, and cold beer. **Entertainment**

Transport can be a problem for the budget traveller. There are big, flat-bed trucks that supplement the handful of buses per day. Ask hotel workers when the trucks and buses normally pass. *Villa Paraíso* offers round-trip transfers from Moyogalpa in a nice 4WD with a/c for a whopping US$60. **Transport**

Volcán Maderas

The road towards Maderas is sandy and ends at a fork that leads to Balgues or San Ramón. The road to **Balgües** is rocky and scenic, but the village itself is a little sad in appearance, though the people are warm and friendly, especially if you are travelling with a local. If you get the feeling that everyone knows everybody on Ometepe then it is magnified here as most locals have a relative around every corner. This village is the entrance to the trailhead for the climb to the summit of Maderas. You should allow five hours up and three hours down for the climb, though relatively dry-trail conditions could cut time considerably. Expect to get very muddy in any case. Ropes are necessary if you want to climb down into the Laguna de Maderas after reaching the summit. This climb can be done without a guide, but hikers have been known to get lost and paying a guide helps the very humble local economy. Guides are also useful in pointing out animals and petroglyphs that outsiders may miss. ■ *There is an entrance fee of US$1.75 to climb Maderas*. The trail leads through farms, through fences and gets steeper and rockier with elevation. The forest changes with altitude from tropical dry, to tropical wet and finally cloud

Ometepe Island and Rivas Isthmus

forests with howler monkeys accompanying your journey. Guides can be found for this climb in Moyogalpa, Altagracia and Santo Domingo or at the coffee co-operative in Balgues, *Hacienda Magdalena*.

Sleeping & eating There are 2 places to sleep in Balgues, both very basic and willing to cook very cheap meals. **G** *Hacienda Magdalena*, a working co-operative farm, hammock space US$1, good meals around US$2, friendly, basic, very popular with travellers. You can work in exchange for lodging, 1 month minimum. **G** *Hospedaje Madera*, on main street of village.

San Ramón Cascade

From the fork at Santa Cruz the road goes south past small homes and ranches and through the towering palms of the attractive village of **Mérida**, in an area that was once an expansive farm belonging to the Somoza family. The road drops down to lake level and curves east to the surprisingly affluent **San Ramón**. Some of Managua's wealthy have built vacation homes here and there is a new dock for their boats to come direct. From the village is a path that leads to a 110-m waterfall that is great for bathing after a warm hike. This is a less athletic climb than the hike to the summit and a good way to experience the forest. It is sunny and hotter on this side of the mountain with less advantage from the trade winds that blow from the east. Transportation is very difficult on this side of the island and you may have a long walk back or have to hire hotel transfers. *Villa Paraíso* has packages that are reasonable if you can get together at least two other hikers. There is lodging available at **F** *Punta del Sol*, close to the lake near the path on the way to the waterfall. Swiss owner, very quiet, breakfast US$2.50, dinner US$4.

Rivas to San Juan del Sur

Back on the mainland and south from Rivas, the Carretera Panamericana cuts through some of the most beautiful cattle ranches in the country with rolling green hills giving way to Lake Nicaragua and Ometepe Island as a backdrop.

La Virgen This little windswept village has some less-than-clean beaches and a stunning view of the big lake and Ometepe. If you come early in the morning you may see the curious sight of men fishing in the lake, while floating in the inner tube of a truck. Particular to this small village, the fishermen arrive at the beach in the early morning and blow up the big tyre tubes, tie bait to a thick nylon cord and wade out, seated in the tubes, as far as 3 km from the coast. When they get out of the water, often fully clothed and always drenched with lake water, the cord can have 15 or more fish hanging from it.

In the 19th century the lake steamships of Cornelius Vanderbilt stopped here (after a journey from New York via the Río San Juan) to let passengers off for an overland journey by horse carriage to the bay of San Juan del Sur. The legendary North American novelist and humorist **Mark Twain** came here in 1866, doing the trip from west to east (San Francisco – San Juan del Sur – La Virgen – Lake Nicaragua – San Carlos – Río San Juan – San Juan del Norte – New York). He gazed out at the lake here and waxed poetic about the splendour of Lake Nicaragua and Ometepe from his viewpoint in La Virgen (see box). The dock used by the steamships is no longer visible and there is some debate among the villagers as to where it actually was. Some point out the old pylons in the far north of the village as part of the structure, while others insist it was situated at the current site of the swimming pool at the town's only hotel.

B *Hotel Cibalsa*, Km 123, T453-0021, 15 rooms, a/c, private bath, laundry service, bar, restaurant, murky swimming pool with an unrivalled view of Lake Nicaragua and Isla de Ometepe. Basic and overpriced and without any sign of functioning management, but a delightful spot with a million-dollar view.

There is an exit from the carretera at La Virgen, which leads to the popular Pacific beach town of San Juan del Sur. It is here that the distance between the waters of Lake Nicaragua and the Pacific Ocean is shortest, only 18 km blocking a natural passageway between the Atlantic and Pacific oceans. Incredibly the continental divide lies yet further west, just 3 km from the Pacific; the east face of this low coastal mountain ridge drains all the way to the Caribbean sea via the lake and Río San Juan. The road is paved to San Juan de Sur and follows to a great extent the path used in the 1800s by horse carriages (and ox carts with luggage) of the inter-oceanic gold rush route of Vanderbilt. What had been a full-day's journey through rough terrain was made into one of just under four hours by the construction of this road in earthen form in 1852 by Vanderbilt's company. Just before the limits of San Juan town, a dirt road branches south to beautiful undeveloped beaches and the La Flor wildlife refuge (see below).

La Virgen – San Juan del Sur

San Juan del Sur

In recent years this little town on a big bay has become a popular escape from the built-up beaches across the international border to the south. In 1999 cruise ships began to anchor in its deeper waters and tourists have begun to arrive in quantity, although most use their one day in Nicaragua to visit Granada and Masaya. The rest of the year San Juan resembles other Nicaraguan beaches, crowded on Sundays in the dry season and at Christmas and Holy Week, and nearly empty the rest of the year.

Colour map 3, grid C4
Population: 14,621
Altitude: 4 m

Ometepe Island and Rivas Isthmus

History

Andrés Niño, the first European to navigate the Pacific Coast of Nicaragua, entered the bay of San Juan del Sur in 1523 while looking for a possible passage to Lake Nicaragua or the Caribbean, but San Juan del Sur remained a sleepy fishing village until after Nicaragua's Independence from Spain. It began working as a commercial port in 1827 and in 1830 took the name Puerto Independencia. Its claim to fame came during the **California Gold Rush** when thousands of North Americans, anxious to reach California (before the North American railroad was finished), found the shortest route to be through Nicaragua. It is estimated that some 84,880 passengers passed through San Juan en route to California, and some 75,000 on their way to New York. In 1854 the local lodge, *El United States Hotel*, charged a whopping US$14 per day for one night's lodging and food of bread, rice, oranges and coffee made from purified water. But as soon as the railway in the USA was completed, the trip through Central America was no longer necessary. The final crossing was made on 8 May 1868 with 541 passengers en route to San Francisco.

The steamship was taken over for a while by William Walker to re-supply his invasion forces in the mid 1850s. Later, in 1857, Walker escaped to Panamá and later New Orleans via San Juan. Walker was believed to be attempting another attack on Nicaragua via San Juan del Sur in 1858, but was blocked by the British Navy ship *Vixen*.

There was some tough fighting during the 1978-79 Revolution in the hills behind San Juan. A ragged group of Somoza's National Guard managed to escape out of San Juan (threatening to burn it down), just as the south of the country was being taken by Edén Pastora-led Sandinista rebels. San Juan saw an influx of wealth in the 20th century with many expensive homes being built along the low ridge that backs the beach and in the northern part of the bay.

Sights

Mark Twain described San Juan as "a few tumble-down frame shanties" in 1866, and said the town was "crowded with horses, mules and ambulances (horse carriages) and half-clad yellow natives". Today there are plenty of half-clad people, though few are natives and most are enjoying the sun and sea. Most of the horses and all of the mules have been replaced by bicycles, which are the preferred form of transport in town.

What makes San Juan del Sur different from other Nicaraguan beach towns is the growing ex-patriot crowd that has migrated north from the highrise-blighted beaches of Costa Rica or came on an international mission to Nicaragua and fell in love with what most consider its most beautiful beach with infrastructure. There are many Austrians, French, North Americans (and even a Norwegian) who have found it too beautiful to leave. San Juan is a natural bay of light brown sand, clear waters and 200 m cliffs that mark its borders. The sunsets here are placed perfectly out over the Pacific, framed by the boats bobbing in the bay. The beach is lined by numerous small restaurants that offer the fresh catch of the day, along with lobster and shrimp. San Juan is a good base to visit some of the many deserted beaches that line the coast to the north and south and surfers can find easy access to very good breaks along the same coastline, one that has a year round offshore breeze. Swimming is best at the north end of the beach.

Essentials

Sleeping L *Piedras y Olas*, 2 c west of church, T458-2110, pelican@ibw.com.ni 20 rooms, a/c,

Note that hotel prices in San Juan del Sur double for Semana Santa and between Christmas and New Year

TV, private bath, kitchenette, ocean view, restaurant, bar, swimming pool, suites, owner of *Pelican Eyes* boat, packages available.

A *Hotel Casablanca*, opposite *Bar Timón*, T/F458-2135, F458-2307, casablanca@ibw.com.ni A/c, cable TV, private bath, restored house, clean, friendly, small swimming pool, laundry service, secure parking, transfers to San Jorge or Peñas Blancas US$25 per person, in front of beach. Recommended. **A** *Hotel Villa Isabella*, behind the church to the left, T458-2568, www.sanjuandelsur.org.ni 5 rooms, includes breakfast and coffee or tea, a/c, and fan, private bath, very clean, lovely wooden house with hardwood floors, well decorated with ample windows and light, video library, disabled access, English spoken, very helpful, 4 blocks from beach, transfer to San Jorge US$25, to aiport US$70. **B** *Aramara Lodge*, de La Cabañita, 1 block north, T458-2259, aguzman@uam.edu.ni **A** at weekends. Includes breakfast, a/c, cable TV, pool, traditional house, very cute with balconies and living room, friendly, 1 block from beach. Recommended. **B** *Colonial*, T458-2539, www.hotel-nicaragua. com Includes continental breakfast, private bath, hot water, cable TV, a/c, 3 blocks from beach. **B** *Royal Chateau*, from the church 2 blocks north. A/c (cheaper with fan), cable TV, clean, secure parking, pool, bar and restaurant, breakfast US$2.50, other meals to order, 4 blocks from beach.

Apartamentos San Juan del Sur, *Restaurante Las Lugo*, 50 m north, T458-2594. 2 apartments with room for 6 in each, a/c, kitchen, refrigerator, private bath, TV.

C *Hotel Joxi*, T458-2348. Friendly, clean, a/c, bath, bunk beds, Norwegian run, restaurant, bar, internet rental, sailing trips on the boat *Pelican Eyes* can be arranged here, windsurf boards for rent. **E** *Hospedaje Casa No 28*, 40 m from beach, near minibus stop for Rivas. Shared showers, mosquitoes (ask owner for coils), kitchen and laundry facilities, clean, friendly owners, good. On same street as *Joxi* is **E** *Hotel Estrella*, on Pacific, T458-2210. With meals, balconies overlooking the sea, partitioned walls, shower, take mosquito net and towel, clean, nice looking house, the oldest hotel in town, popular. **E** *Guest House Elizabeth*, opposite bus terminal, T458-2270. Clean, fan, friendly and helpful owner, with tied-up monkey.

F *Hospedaje Juliet*, from the church 1 block north, T458-2333. Dark clean rooms, ask for fan, some with bath, others without, basic, soft beds, breakfast US$1.50, family-run, 4 blocks from beach. **G** *Hospedaje La Fogata*, south side of market, T458-2271. Some with private bath, clean, friendly, family-run, good food, keep an eye on your things. **G** *Beach Fun Hotel*, market, ½ c south, T458-2441, portasol@ibw.com.ni 14 rooms, private bath and fan.

Eating

Las Lugo, from Correos 1 block east. Expensive seafood, fresh fish, despite being by the sea not as good as its sister restaurant in Managua. *La Cabañita*, Texaco, 200 varas east, T458-2203. Ceviche, fish soup, 0900-2200 daily. *O Sole Mio*, from *Hotel Casablanca* 500 m north, T458-2101. Best and only Italian, mid-range, pizza and pasta. Recommended. *Iguana Beach*, next to *Timón Bar*, Euro and Nica food as at *Marie Bar* (sadly no iguana on menu). *Soya*, across from *La Cabañita*, T458-2572. Daily 0700-2200, vegetarian and meat dishes, fruit, *refrescos*, *chorizo de soya*, good, cheap and friendly, also has a room to rent. *El Globo* and *Eskimo* share the same space, 75 varas south of *Hotel Estrella*, T458-2282, both are very popular with locals, cheap sandwiches, ice cream. *Buengusto*, across from *Hotel Estrella*, T458-2304. Good seafood, moderate prices, try *sopa marinera* or *camarones a la plancha*, daily 0700-2000. *Panadería* (bakery), 1 block from beach. Good cafés along the beach for breakfast and drinks. *El Timón Bar*, shrimp, lobster (US$9), most popular place in town, good *pargo rojo* or *negro* (red or black snapper) cooked whole, US$5. *Lago Azul*, *Hotel Estrella*, ½ c south, T458-2325. Good cheap food, as well as shrimp in garlic butter, daily 0800-2300. *Marie Bar*, opposite, OK food with an attitude, English and German spoken. *Ricardo's Bar*, north of *Bar Timón* on beach, popular with foreigners, cybercafe, good chicken salad. *Coquismar*, on beachfront, T458-2569. Try boneless sea bass. Breakfast and lunch in market, eg *Comedor Zapata*, *Comedor Angelita*, serve very good fish dishes.

San Juan has power rationing in high season, which means the restaurants trade off time without electricity; the ones with the lights just going out have the coldest beers

Festivals

The patron saint is *San Juan* and his celebration is every **24 Jun**.

Transport

Bus San Juan del Sur-Managua, every hour, 0500-1600, US$2.25, 3½ hrs. San Juan del Sur-Rivas, every ½ hour, 0630-1700, US$0.70, 40 mins.

4WD You can usually find a 4WD pick-up to make trips to outlying beaches or to go surfing. You should plan a day in advance and ask for some help from your hotel. Prices range from US$20-75 depending on the trip and time. **Van** Some hotels offer transfers to San Jorge for visits to Isla de Ometepe, the border or Managua (see *Casablanca* and *Villa Isabella* above for sample costs).

Motorboat Small boats with outboards can be rented to explore and will cost about US$25 per hour, plus gasoline. You will have to ask your hotel to recommend one of the fishermen to take you around. This is a great way to explore deserted beaches. Prices depend on how good the fishing is and how much they want to go out again, bring all supplies with you and ask the boatman to bring a cool box. **Yacht** *Pelican Eyes'* owner Chris Berry knows how to take care of his customers; you will have to rent the whole boat, however, which is US$240 for the day and includes a good meal and open bar, T458-2110, pelican@ibw.com.ni

Directory   **Banks** There is no bank. Hotels *Casablanca* and *Joxi* and some shops, like *Pulpería Sánchez*, will change money. **Communications** Internet: *Casa Joxi* has internet services, US$12 per hour, also at *Ricardo's Bar*. **Post Office** is 150 m south along the seafront from the main junction, T458-2160. **Telephone** *Entel* is located along the beachfront heading towards the dock, T458-2290. **Laundry** Most of the mid- to upper-priced hotels will do laundry for their guests on request. Hand wash, line dry near *Soya Restaurant* (ask there). **Medical services** The dispensary, where you have to pay for medicines, has good service.

Excursions from San Juan del Sur

A well-kept earth and rock road runs south from the bridge at the entrance to San Juan del Sur. Signs mark the way to a housing and apartment development in Playa El Coco called **Parque Marítimo El Coco** and also serve as directions to the superb beach and turtle nesting site of La Flor. You will have to cross three rivers that are small during the dry season, but will require high- clearance and four-wheel drive vehicles most of the year. The drive is over a beautifully scenic country road with many elevation changes and vistas of the ocean and the northern coast of Costa Rica. If followed to its end it arrives at **Playa Ostional**, the site of an important pre-Columbian settlement and excavations, but not as nice as the beaches of El Coco and La Flor. A lone hilltop home marks the entrance to El Coco.

Playa El Coco   This is a long copper-coloured beach with strong surf most of the year. Much of it is backed by forest and there are several families of howler monkeys that live between here and La Flor beach two beaches to the south. There is a growing development at the north end of the beach with a mixture of condos, bungalows and homes for rent. This is by far the closest lodging to La Flor without camping. Prices for rental range from one night in a one-room apartment for US$60 to a week in a house with capacity for 10 at US$1,900 during high season. The Austrian owner, Sigmund Kripp, has an office in Managua at: *Cine Rex*, 1 carriba, ½ c al lago No G88, T249-1192, www.playaelcoco.com.ni There is a restaurant on the beach, *Puesta del Sol*, which has moderately priced dishes with some good fruit juices and shakes.

Refugio de   Just past Playa El Coco and 18 km from the highway at San Juan del Sur, the
Vida Silvestre   Playa La Flor Wildlife Refuge protects tropical dry forest, mangroves, estuary
La Flor   and 800 m of beachfront. This beautiful, sweeping cove with light tan sand and
Colour map 3, grid C4   many trees is an important site for nesting sea turtles. The best time to come is
Altitude: 0-80 m   between August and November. Rangers protect the multitudinous arrivals of
Area: 800 ha   the turtles during high season and are very happy to explain, in Spanish, the ani-
mals' reproductive habits. Sometimes turtles arrive in their thousands usually over a period of three days. Even if you don't manage to see the turtles, there is plenty of other wildlife. Many birds live in small, protected mangroves at the south end of the beach and you may witness a sunset migration of hundreds of hermit crabs at the north end, all hobbling back to the beach in their infinitely

Mark Twain – "The Nicaragua route forever!"

Samuel Clemens, better known by his pen name Mark Twain, first saw the Pacific Coast of Nicaragua on 29 December 1866, after a long boat journey from San Francisco. He described the approach to the Bay of San Juan del Sur: "... bright green hills never looked so welcome, so enchanting, so altogether lovely, as these do that lie here within a pistol-shot of us." Twain was writing a series of letters to a San Francisco newspaper Alta California, *letters that would be published in book form more than 60 years later, in 1940, in a collection called* Travels with Mr Brown. *Twain's sharp eye has left us some interesting notes on his journey from Pacific to Caribbean, travelling on the inter-oceanic steamship line of Cornelius Vanderbilt.*

Twain crossed Nicaragua in three days. The first was spent overland in horse-carriage from San Juan del Sur to the Lake Nicaragua port of La Virgen. During the only land part of his journey from San Francisco to New York he was amazed at the beauty of the Nicaraguan people and their land. He and his fellow passengers gleefully exclaimed, "the Nicaragua route forever!" It was at the end of that 3½-hour carriage ride that he first saw the great lake and Island of Ometepe. "Out of the midst of the beautiful Lake Nicaragua sprint two magnificent pyramids, clad in the softest and richest green, all flecked with shadow and sunshine, whose summits pierce the billowy clouds. They look so isolated from the world and its turmoil – so tranquil, so dreamy, so steeped in slumber and eternal repose." He crossed the lake in a steamship to San Carlos and boarded

another that would take him down the Río San Juan to El Castillo, where passengers had to walk past the old fort to change boats beyond the rapids there. "About noon we swept gaily around a bend in the beautiful river, and a stately old adobe castle came into view – a relic of the olden time – of the old buccaneering days of Morgan and his merry men. It stands upon a grassy dome-like hill and the forests loom up beyond."

Back on the river Mark Twain was immersed in the beauty that today is the Indio-Maíz Biological Reserve: "As we got under way and sped down the narrowing river, all the enchanting beauty of its surroundings came out. All gazed in rapt silent admiration for a long time as the exquisite panorama unfolded itself. The character of the vegetation on the banks had changed from a rank jungle to dense, lofty, majestic forests. There were hills, but the thick drapery of the vines spread upwards, terrace upon terrace, and concealed them like a veil. Now and then a rollicking monkey scampered into view or a bird of splendid plumage floated through the sultry air, or the music of some invisible songster welled up out of the forest depths. The changing vistas of the river ever renewed the intoxicating picture; corners and points folding backward revealed new wonders beyond." Twain wrote that he would like to return to Nicaragua, but he never did. He would soon achieve international fame with his humorist writings, political commentaries and now classic novels, the first of which, Tom Sawyer, *was published 10 years after his trip across Nicaragua.*

Ometepe Island and Rivas Isthmus

diverse shells. Camping can be provided (one tent only) during the turtle arrivals, US$10 per night. Bring hammock and mosquito netting, as insects are vicious at dusk. Ranger station sells soft drinks and will let you use their outhouse; improved facilities are planned by the *Cocibolca Foundation*, T458-2514, which also manages Volcán Mombacho's cloud forest reserve. You can contact their local office for information on possible turtle arrivals. ∎ *US$5, US$2.50 student discount, 4WD or on foot.*

La Virgen to Peñas Blancas

The Carretera Panamericana continues south from La Virgen to the coastal town of Sapoá and Peñas Blancas, which is the one land crossing between Nicaragua and Costa Rica. The landscape changes dramatically as the rainforest ecosystem of the southern shores of Lake Nicaragua meets the tropical dry forest ecosystem of the Pacific Basin. It is possible to follow a basic, dirt, four-wheel drive-only track from **Sapoá** all the way to the town of **Cárdenas**, 17 km away on the shores of Lake Nicaragua and close to the western border of Los Guatuzos Wildlife Refuge (see page 152). From here you could try to hire a private boat to Solentiname, Río Papaturro or San Carlos (see page 152).

Peñas Blancas: border with Costa Rica

Crossing by bus or on foot

There are two duty-free shops, a hotel and several comedores on the Nicaraguan side

When **entering** Nicaragua (immigration open 0600-2000) show your passport at the border completing Costa Rican exit formalities and then walk the 500 m to the new Nicaraguan border controls. International bus passengers have to disembark and queue for immigration to stamp passport. Then you must unload your baggage and wait in a line for the customs official to arrive. You will be asked to open your bags, the official will give them a cursory glance and then you reload. Passports and tickets will be checked again back on the bus. For travellers not on a bus, there are plenty of small helpers on hand. Allow 45 minutes to complete the formalities. You will have to pay US$7 to enter Nicaragua plus a US$1 *aclaldía* charge. If you come before 0800 or after 1700 Mon-Fri at any time at the weekend you will have to pay US$12 plus the US$1 mayor's charge.

Leaving Nicaragua pay US$1 mayor's fee to enter the customs area at the border and then complete formalities in the new customs building where you pay US$2 to have your passport checked between 0800-1700 or US$4 0600-0800 and after 1700 Mon-Fri or any time on Sat and Sun. Then walk the 500 m to the Costa Rican border and simply have your passport stamped. Buses and taxis are available from the border – hitching is difficult.

Crossing by private vehicle

There is no fuel going into Nicaragua until Rivas (37 km)

When **entering** Nicaragua, go through Migración then find an inspector who will fill out the preliminary form to be taken to Aduana. At the *Vehículo Entrando* window, the vehicle permit is typed up and the vehicle stamp is put in your passport. Next, go to Tránsito to pay for the car permit. Finally, ask the inspector again to give the final check. Fumigation is US$1 and mandatory.

When **leaving** the country, first pay your exit tax at an office at the end of the control station, receipt given. Then come back for your exit stamp, and complete the Tarjeta de Control Migratorio. Motorists must then go to Aduana to cancel vehicle paper; exit details are typed on to the vehicle permit and the stamp in your passport is cancelled. Find the inspector in Aduana who has to check the details and stamp your permit. If you fail to do this you will not be allowed to leave the country – you will be sent back to Sapoá by the officials at the final Nicaraguan checkpoint. Fumigation is US$0.50 and mandatory.

Transport **Peñas Blancas-Rivas**, every ½ hr, 0600-1800, US$0.60, 1 hr. **Rivas-Managua**, every ½ hr, 0330-1800, US$1.50, 2 hrs 45 mins. **Rivas-Granada**, every 45 mins, 0530-1625, US$1, 1 hr 45 mins. **NB** There can be long waits when the international buses are passing through. A good time to cross, if you are going independently, is around 0900, before the buses arrive.

Directory **Exchange** Same rates on either side, so try to find out the rate before arriving at the border to avoid being stung. This is the last chance to change colones if leaving Costa Rica or *córdabas* if leaving Nicaragua.

Río San Juan

7

Río San Juan

This is the best place in Nicaragua to view wildlife, to travel into a world of towering jungle canopies, howling monkeys and exotic birds and still bed down each night in a decent hotel room. Travel is either on foot or by boat, as the entire region only supports two roads, neither paved and both in the extreme west of the department.

The immense commercial importance of the Río San Juan, the second longest river in Central America, has diminished over the centuries. After the Europeans first arrived it was the natural inter-oceanic canal of the Americas, the key, they believed, to domination of the two seas. But the massive commercial failure in recent centuries has been the key to its resounding ecological success. The Río San Juan with its pristine tributaries and the magnificent Reserva Biológica Indio-Maíz together make this region a mini-Amazonas; they are the lungs of Central America, one of the last of the great forests on the Central American isthmus. In this sparsely populated region of Nicaragua, nature truly dominates. Among the inhabitants of the Solentiname Archipelago in Lake Nicaragua is the internationally known community of rural artists, whose primitive-style paintings and wood carvings of tropical birds and fish, reflect the natural wealth and diversity of their world.

San Carlos

History

Since the so-called 'discovery' of the Río San Juan by the Spanish **Captain Ruy Díaz** in 1525, San Carlos has had strategic importance for the successive governments of Nicaragua. Its location at the entrance to the Río San Juan from Lake Nicaragua and at the end of the Río Frío, which originates in Costa Rica, has meant that controlling San Carlos means controlling the water passages from north to south and east to west. The town was first founded in 1526, with the name **Nueva Jaén**, under the orders of King Carlos V of Spain but it was not officially a port until 1542. The town and a fortress that has not survived were abandoned for an unknown length of time and were refounded as San Carlos during the 17th century. A new fortress was built but was sacked by pirates in 1670; part of it survives today around the *El Mirador* restaurant. The fort was used for supply backup and troop fallbacks during attacks on the frontline fortress of El Castillo by Dutch and British pirates in the 17th century and British forces in the 18th century. San Carlos was embroiled in the post-Independence struggles between León and Granada, and William Walker's forces also occupied the fort briefly.

When **Mark Twain** arrived in 1866 he described it simply as Fort San Carlos, making no mention of any town. In 1870 the English naturalist **Thomas Belt** arrived after the long journey up the Río San Juan when rubber tappers were working in the nearby forests. He spent the night on one of the docked steamships and wrote of skirmishes between the **Guatuzo Indians** and the locals of San Carlos, who had just kidnapped a Guatuza woman. During the Revolution of the late 1970s, rebels from San Carlos and Solentiname took the government military base in San Carlos after a four-day trek through jungle in Costa Rica, but were forced to flee back into Costa Rica after other attacks failed around Nicaragua. It was the **first military victory** of the Revolution and after the war's final victory in 1979 the Sandinista administration set up a base in San Carlos that was used to fight off Contra insurgents in the 1980s. The city's waterfront was burnt down in 1984 and was rebuilt in the ramshackle manner that can be seen today. The town is used as a jumping-off point for Nicaraguan migrant workers en route to Costa

San Carlos

Sleeping
1 Cabinas Leyka
2 Hospedaje Peña
3 Hospedaje Yure
4 San Carlos

Eating
El Mirador
2 Granadino
3 Kaoma

Rica and for a small but growing number of tourists to the river, southern lake islands and nature reserves.

Sights

San Carlos stands in sharp contrast to the immense natural beauty that encircles it. It is gritty, even ugly. Most people's initial reaction is "How can I get the hell out of here?" Few would imagine that the city hides a historic fortress and that elegant wooden colonial homes once lined cobblestone streets here. Recent history and local mayors have been very unkind to the appearance and cleanliness of the city, the capital of the Río San Juan department, where the only bank and hospital in the entire region are found. Plans have been made (once again) to improve this gateway to the Río San Juan and Lake Nicaragua, and with a new mayor in office in 2001, hope reigns supreme for the very friendly and welcoming people of the city. Thanks to San Carlos' last-outpost status, it has some shifty folks passing through on the way to Costa Rica or more distant destinations. It is here that the last buses arrive from the outside world via a tedious, 9½-hour plus journey. The big boat from Granada docks here after 15 or more hours on the lake. The daily single-prop Cessna arrives from Managua on a dirt and gravel landing strip, waits for 10 minutes and takes off again. And the long, narrow river and lake boats arrive from the surrounding settlements and wilderness. If you get your timing right you'll be able to enjoy lunch in the remains of a colonial fort, chat with the friendly locals and get on with your journey.

Colour map 3, grid C6
Population: 39,536
Altitude: 39 m

Essentials

C *Cabinas Leyka*, Policia Nacional, 2 c west, T283-0354. With private bath, a/c, **E** with fan, balcony with view of the lake, serves breakfast. **F** *Hospedaje Yure*, across from *Ferrertería Chaflama*, T283-0348. 10 rooms, private bath and fans, nice rooms, friendly, **G** with shared bath, laundry, breakfast. **G** *Hospedaje Peña*, opposite *Billares Ochomogo*, T283-0298. 12 rooms with shared bath, unhelpful. **F** *Karely*, Catholic church, ½ c north, T283-0389. Private bath, fan, clean, nets. **F-G** *Hotelito San Carlos*, next to *BDF*, T283-0265. Shared bath, with fan, basic, breakfast US$1.25. **H** *El Madroño*, on waterfront, T283-0282. Shared baths, the dream hotel of the broke, at US$1.25 per night this one opens a new category.

Sleeping
There is a lack of clean, good quality lodging in San Carlos. Hotel rats and insects will not make the endangered species list any time soon. Pull your bed away from the wall

There are many *comedores* along the main street, floating dock and market, including *Félix Dining Room*, 2 plastic tables on the main street, good meal for US$1.50. The legitimate restaurants are marginally cleaner and not much more expensive. The best place for its view and historical value is *El Mirador*, Catholic church, 1 ½ c south, inside the ruins of the old **Fort San Carlos**, T283-0377, 0700-2000 daily. Superb view from patio of Lake Nicaragua, Solentiname, Río Frío and Río San Juan and the jumbled roofs of the city. Decent chicken, fish and beef dishes starting at US$3 with friendly service. Highly recommended. *Bar y Restaurante Kaoma*, in front of market, difficult to find, ask, T283-0293. Daily from 0900 until the last customer collapses. This is a funky place, decorated with dozens of *oropéndula* nests. Moderate prices, hard-drinking, friendly clientele, fresh fish caught by the owner. Good *camarones de río* (freshwater prawns), dancing on good nights. Recommended. *Bar Miralago*, by the lake, painted pink and purple, good grilled meat and salad, but fearsome mosquitoes in the evening. *Granadino*, opposite the sports field, T283-0386. *Camarones en salsa*, steaks, fried fish, 0900-0200 daily.

Eating
Thankfully, eating in San Carlos is much less traumatic than checking into a hotel room

The patron saint is none other than *San Carlos*, whose day is **13 Oct**.

Festival

Transport

Air   *La Costeña* has daily flights from San Carlos to Managua, US$76 round-trip, US$38 one-way. Fights depart at 1000 daily, except Sun and Fri when they depart at 1300. The single-prop *Cessna Caravan* touches down, unloads and takes off, so you must be there on time. Arrive 0900 for morning flights and 1200 for afternoon flights. If flights are overbooked they will send another *Cessna* in 20 mins or 2 hrs. There are no reserved seats and only 5 seats with a good view for San Carlos-Managua, all on the left. The seat behind the pilot or in the back bench are best for photography . All heavy passengers (which normally means all foreigners due to height) are pushed to the front of the aeroplane for balance reasons. You will be asked your body weight (don't be proud, or you could put flight in danger) as there's a maximum acceptable for flight. Keep an eye on your checked bag to make sure it is not forgotten on the landing strip. Take out film and camera for arrival in Managua where all bags are X-rayed. Do not lose little cardboard stub or you will not be able to recover your checked bag in Managua. Tickets can be bought at *La Costeña* office one block from main dock. The only way to the strip (*la pista*) is walking or a taxi up the hill from *Enitel*. Do not photograph little military instalment at landing strip.

Taxi   Old Russian jeeps are the taxis. They wait for arriving flights at the landing strip and once they leave you will have to walk to town (30 mins). To get to the landing strip they can be found in town between the market and the *BDF*. All fares are US$1, exact change is essential. Drivers are very helpful.

Bus   Managua-San Carlos is a brutal ride, but the locals prefer it to the Granada ferry boat trip. There are some lovely mountain ranges and formations during the early part of the trip and just pure pain in the kidneys during the final sections. **San Carlos-Managua**, daily, 0200, 0600, 0800, 1100, US$7, 9½ hrs. **Managua-San Carlos**, daily, 0500, 0600, 0700, 1300, US$7, 9½ hrs.

Motorboat   Small motor boats are *pangas*, long, narrow ones are *botes* and big broad ones are *planos*.

Solentiname Archipelago, stopping at islands La Venada, San Fernando, Mancarrón from San Carlos, and in reverse en route to San Carlos: **San Carlos-Solentiname**, Tue, Fri 1300, US$4, 2½ hrs. **Solentiname-San Carlos**, Tue, Fri 0400, US$4, 2½ hrs.

Los Guatuzos Wildlife Refuge, stopping at village of Papaturro, **San Carlos-Río Pappaturro**, Tue, Fri 0800, US$5 5½ hrs. **Río Pappaturro-San Carlos**, Mon, Thu 0500, US$5, 5½ hrs.

Border with Costa Rica, from **San Carlos-Los Chiles**, daily 1000, US$4, 2 hrs. **Los Chiles-San Carlos**, daily 1600, US$4, 2 hrs.

San Carlos-El Castillo, 0800 daily except Sun and daily at 1400, US$5, 3-4 hrs. **El Castillo-San Carlos**, daily 0430, 0500, 0600, US$5, 3-4 hrs.

San Carlos-San Juan del Norte, Thu 0800, US$15, 12-14 hrs. **San Juan del Norte-San Carlos**, Sun 0330, US$15, 13-15 hrs.

These are public boat schedules. Private boats are available and expensive, but afford freedom to stop and view wildlife; they are also faster and leave when you want. Ask at docks, restaurants, taxi drivers or at tourism office. Average round-trip rates: **El Castillo** US$190-250, **Solentiname** US$75-100. Packages are available from tour operators in Managua (see page 74) with private transfers and tours of wildlife reserves, but unless there are at least 4 travellers it will be prohibitively expensive.

Ferry   **San Carlos-Granada** leaves from main dock, Tue and Thu at 1400, US$4, 15 hrs or more.

Things to do in Río San Juan

- Make an early start at the wildlife refuge of Los Guatuzos for the unforgettable symphony of tropical birds and glassy reflections of gallery forest.
- Visit the house of one of Solentiname's many rural artists.
- Stop off to visit the 17th-century fortress at El Castillo; the excellent museum inside provides a very complete history of the river and is one of the best in the country.
- Try the *camarones del río* (freshwater lobster) grilled in garlic butter sauce at the *Albergue El Castillo* next to the fortress.
- A dawn walk in the Reserva Biológica Indio-Maíz is sure to uncover some of the secrets of Central America's largest primary rainforest reserve.
- From San Juan del Norte, continue downstream along the Río Indio for a wilderness experience that exists in very few places in the world.

Airline office *La Costeña* is 1 block west of the public toilets, T283-0271. **Bank** *BDF*, T283-0144, is the only bank, they are on the main street, next to the market and floating dock. They should change American Express (only) travellers' cheques and US dollars. Queues can be tremendous on, or near, the 15th or 31st of each month, as this is the only bank on the river. You can also change with the *coyotes* at the entrance to immigration and customs, dollars, córdobas or colones, with fair to poor rates. **Communications** Post office: *Correos de Nicaragua* is across from Los Juzgados de Distritos, T283-0000. **Telephone**: *Enitel* office is on road from landing strip to town, T283-0001. **Shopping** Stock up on purified water and the food you may need for a long journey. The market is a cramped nightmare, but in front of immigration there are stalls to buy hard goods. High-top rubber boots (Wellingtons) are standard equipment in these parts, perfect for jungle treks and cost US$5-8, though large sizes are rarely found. You can hose them down rather than ruin your high-tech US$100 hiking shoes in 2 hrs. **Tourist office** *INTUR* has a branch office in front of the Clínica San Lucas, T283-0301 or 283-0363. The delegate is the very helpful and charming Sra Julieta Centeno de Pilarte. **Useful numbers** Fire: T283-2149. **Hospital**: T283-0238. **Police**: T283-0350.

Directory

Río San Juan (vertical, right margin)

Río Frío

This is the river that connects northern Costa Rica with Lake Nicaragua and the Río San Juan. Passengers from Costa Rica pass through customs at San Carlos and then continue to Managua (by bus or plane), or down the Río San Juan towards the Caribbean. The river enters a reserve once you pass into Nicaragua territory, marked by a little green guard house. The reserve is the superb Refugio de Vida Silvestre Los Guatuzos (see page 160). The east bank is also home to a small project within the reserve called **Esperanza Verde**, a nature reserve with an investigative centre and some basic lodging. **F** *La Esperanza*, 15 minutes from San Carlos, T283-0354, shared baths, restaurant, nature trails for bird-watching. Although the river is used mainly as a commuter route, there is some beautiful flora and fauna and it is rare not to see at least one clan of howler monkeys along the banks or even swimming across the river. Although they tend to avoid swimming at all costs and rarely even come down to the forest floor, they manage a very methodical doggy paddle with their little black heads sticking out of the water.

It is not really a 'cold river' when it reaches Nicaragua, but its source is in the northern mountains of Costa Rica

As late as the 1870s the **Guatuzo Indians** (Maleku Indians) inhabited the riverbanks of this area. The Guatuzos were the same Indians that are called Rama today and populate the Rama Cay in Bluefields Bay (see page 84). The

The indigenous name for the river was Ucubriú

Spanish were unable to subjugate the Guatuzos and the naturalist Thomas Belt recounted battles that were going on between the rubber tappers and the Guatuzo people who were fighting to stop the invasion of their land. It seems that the original explorers of the Río Frío were attacked and killed by the Guatuzos with arrows. This gave the area a name for being hostile and the Guatuzos were left alone for years. However, when the india-rubber trade grew and the supply of trees along the Río San Juan was exhausted, the rubbermen were forced to explore the Río Frío. This time they came heavily armed, killing anyone in their path. By 1870, just the sight of a white man's boat along the river sent the Indians fleeing into the forest in desperate fear. After that the end of the culture was quickly accomplished thanks to illegal kidnapping and slave trading with the mines and farms of Chontales.

Today you can see many white plastic jugs, 2-litre Pepsi and Coca-Cola bottles floating in the river. These are not garbage, but rather markers for lobster traps, as the river is very rich in *camarones del río* (freshwater lobster). See San Carlos, page 122, for boat schedules.

Border with Costa Rica at Los Chiles

Immigration & customs This is a frequented crossing point between Nicaragua and Costa Rica and is relatively quick and hassle free on the Nicaraguan side. In fact the ease of the operation makes this more pleasant than the land crossings, though queues may be long depending on the numbers of local migrant workers. If you are **leaving Nicaragua** you must go to immigration, located on its own dock just upriver from the main concrete one. It is open seven days a week 0800-1600. Exit stamps must be obtained in San Carlos and cost US$2. If leaving Nicaragua via a different river than Río Frío you still must officially check out in San Carlos.

On the Río Frío there are two **military checkpoints** where all passports are viewed, although the Costa Rican post is often unmanned. Once in Los Chiles, Costa Rica immigration and customs are east from the dock. Buses run between Los Chiles and La Fortuna.

If you are **entering Nicaragua** be sure to have your documents properly stamped in Los Chiles or you will have to return. Entrance fee in San Carlos is US$8 and if arriving at the weekend you will have to pay a US$1.20 customs charge.

Boats from **San Carlos-Los Chiles**, daily 1000, US$4, two hours. **Los Chiles-San Carlos**, daily 1600, US$4, two hours. You may be able to hitch a ride in either direction, though this can bring you problems with the owners of the boats who have purchased route rights.

Refugio de Vida Silvestre Los Guatuzos

History

The original inhabitants of the area that included the Solentiname Archipelago were fishermen, hunters and skilled planters with crops of corn, squash, cacao and plantains. They called themselves the **Maleku**. The Maleku language had sprinklings of the *Náhuat* spoken by the Nicaraguas (a root of the Aztec Náhuatl), but was basically Chibcha (the language root of the Miskitos, Ramas and Sumus). Their name for Lake Nicaragua was **Ucurriquitúkara**, which means 'where the rivers converge'. The Spanish named these people

Guatuzo Indians for they painted their faces red, in a colour reminiscent of the large tropical rodent the *guatuza* (agouti), once very common to the region and now almost extinct thanks to its very delicious meat. It was the extraction of rubber, which began in 1860, that spelled the beginning of the end for their culture. Most of the natives were (illegally) sold as labourers by the rubber tappers to go to work on farms or mines in Chontales. In the 1930s and 1940s the current residents began to move in. You can see traces of the original Maleku or Guatuzo people in a few of the residents of Solentiname. The reserve administrators allow them to practise small-scale agriculture and ranching. Other local residents have become involved in the research and protection of the reserve at the **Centro Ecológico de Los Guatuzos**, run by the non-profit **Amigos de la Tierra** (Friends of the Earth). The ecological centre has 90 species of orchid on display, a butterfly farm (which is being broken into and robbed constantly by local forest animals) and a freshwater turtle hatchery. ■ *US$5 per person. The best guide is Armando (Spanish only) who is a native of the river and expert on orchids.*

Sights

The Los Guatuzos Wildlife Refuge occupies the southern shores of Lake Nicaragua and the southern banks of the first few kilometres of the Río San Juan. Nicaraguan biologists consider it the cradle of life for the lake, because of its importance as a bird-nesting site and other infinite links in the area's complex ecological chain. More than 12 rivers run through the reserve, the most popular for wildlife viewing being the Río Papaturro. The ecosystems are diverse with tropical dry forest, tropical wet forest, rainforest and extensive wetlands. Best of all are the many narrow rivers lined with gallery forest, the ideal situation for viewing wildlife. The flora is stunningly beautiful. There are over 315 species of plants here, including some primary forest trees over 35 m in height and some 130 species of orchid. The reason most visitors come is to see the quality and sheer quantity of wildlife; it is astonishing. This little park is brimming with life, especially at sunrise. There are places in Nicaragua and Central America with a longer species list, but you will see as much wildlife in a four-hour period in Los Guatuzos as you will in a week elsewhere. Eighty-one amphibious species have been documented so far, along with 136 species of reptile, 42 species of mammal and **364 species of bird**. The most noticeable residents of the gallery forest are the howler monkeys, named for the loud growl of the male monkey that can be heard up to 3 km away. The reserve is loaded with howlers (*mono congo*), particularly along the **Río Papaturro**, where you can see 50-60 monkeys in a four-hour period. More difficult to spot, but also present, are white-faced and spider monkeys. Of the reptiles, the easiest to spot are the caimans, iguanas and turtles, especially if it is sunny. Well up-river there is a good chance to see the infamous 'Jesus Christ lizard', famed for its hind-leg dashes across the top of the water. There are also sloths, anteaters and jaguars. The most impressive aspect of the reserve is the density of its bird life. As well as the many elegant egrets and herons, there are five species of kingfishers, countless jacanas, the pretty purple gallinule, wood storks, the roseate spoonbill, jabiru, osprey, laughing falcon, scarlet-rumped tanagers, trogons, bellbirds and six species of parrot.

Colour map 3, grid C6
Population: 706
Area: 43,750 ha

A North American environmental writer recently called this reserve "one of the most beautiful places on earth"

Río San Juan

F *Centro Ecológico de Los Guatuzos*, in the *pueblo* of Río Papaturro, Managua, T270-5434, 270-3561, amigost@ibw.con.ni 2 rooms with 8 bunk beds in each,

Sleeping & eating

shared baths. This is an attractive wooden research station on the riverfront. Meals are served in a local home for customers, US$2-3 per meal. Guided visits to forest trails, excursions to others rivers in the reserve. Night tours in boats to tag caimans. Private boat to and from San Carlos can be arranged. All tours in Spanish only, some Managua tour operators arrange programmes with English-speaking guide (see page 74).

Transport San Carlos-Río Papaturro, Tue, Fri 0800, US$5, 5½ hrs. Río Papaturro-San Carlos, Mon, Thu 0500, US$5, 5½ hrs.

Archipiélago Solentiname

Colour map 3, grid C6
Population: 850
Area: 18,930 ha
Altitude: 30-250 m

This is a protected area, declared a Monumento Nacional and one of the most beautiful parts of scenic Lake Nicaragua. Despite being only one hour in a fast boat from San Carlos, the Solentiname islands are remote. Solentiname is made up of 36 islands in the southeastern corner of Lake Nicaragua. Sparsely populated and without roads, telephones, electricity or running water, this part of Nicaragua is as it was two centuries ago, with only the outboard motorboat as a reminder of the modern world. The islands are home to some of the most industrious, talented artisans in the country and also to some very interesting bird life. The ecosystem is transitional from tropical dry to rainforest and much of the islands' interiors are pasture and agricultural land. About 46 species of fish inhabit the waters around the islands.

History

The islands are products of ancient volcanic activity

Solentiname has been populated since at least AD 500 and is thought to have been populated up until AD 1000, when historians believe it became strictly a ceremonial site.

Today the islanders survive from subsistance farming and artistic production. In the early 1960s, 12 local farmers where given painting classes at the initiative of the resident Catholic priest **Ernesto Cardenal**. In addition, the local inhabitants were trained in balsa woodcarving. This small amount of training was passed from family to family; mother to son and father to daughter and soon the entire archipelago was involved in sculpting or painting. The style is primitivist and many of the painters have become internationally known, and have been invited to study and exhibit as far away as Finland and Japan. The balsa woodcarvings can be found around Central America and the artisans have expanded their themes in recent years. Both the wood and oil arts represent local ecology and legends, with the paintings normally depicting dense tropical landscape and the balsa works recreating individual species of the region. Ernesto Cardenal also helped to organize opposition to the Somoza government in the 1970s and, with help from islanders, the first successful rebel attack on a military base at San Carlos. Cardenal, who writes poetry and sculpts, went on to be the Sandinista Minister of Culture and an international celebrity.

Sights

There is much to do on the islands in the way of visits to local artists, boating, swimming and nature walks. The main problem is the lack of public boats. This means you will have to hire a boat or use a tour operator to organize your

Río San Juan

trip. Bird-watching is great everywhere, with many parrots, oropendulas and ospreys. At night you can see the fishing bat, a spectacular and eerie hunter. The archipelago has four main islands from east to west: **La Venada**, **San Fernando**, **Mancarrón** and **Mancarroncito**, which are detailed below. There are many other beautiful islands that can be visited for the day by boat or for camping, with permission of the locals and some sort of prearranged transport. **Isla de Zapote**, which is in front of the Los Guatuzos river of the same name, is home to over 10,000 birds' nests, perhaps the richest bird-nesting site in Nicaragua. Most of the nests belong to cormorants, white egrets, and there are some roseate spoonbills and heron too. In between San Fernando and Mancarrón is the small forest-covered island of **El Padre**, named after a priest who once lived there; it is the only island with monkeys (howlers), which are said to have been introduced. With a few circles of the island by boat you should be able to find some of them. On the north side of Mancarrón there is a tiny island with an inlet that holds the wreck of a sunken steam ship from the inter-oceanic route. Just the chimney rises above the water and holds a bouquet of tropical vegetation.

On the far west end of the archipelago is another bird-nesting site, on a little rock pile island, just off the west coast of Mancarroncito, with hundreds of egret and cormorant nests. **Mancarroncito** is a big, mountainous island with primary forest. It is possible to do some good hikes in the forest there although the terrain is steep. You should ask for help from the people of the island you are staying on to find the local guide on Mancarroncito.

Named for its plentiful population of deer, La Venada is a long narrow island. La Venada is also home to artists, in particular the house of **Rodolfo Arellano** who lives on the southwestern side of the island. He is one of the islands' original 12 painters, and his wife, daughters and grandson all paint tropical scenes and welcome visitors to see and purchase their works. You can also rent a bed in his house, if you don't mind bathing in the lake. On the north side of the island is a series of semi-submerged caves with some of the best examples of petroglyphs attributed to the Guatuzo people. This cave communicates with the opposite side of the island and was probably used during normal cycles of low lake levels. On the south side of the island, east of Rodolfo's house, there is also a thatched roof patio that has cold beer and food at times.

Isla La Venada

This is one of the two most famous islands for artisan work and painting. It has some of the prettiest houses in the archipelago and is home to the famous artist family of the Pinedas. Rosa Pineda is very friendly and will show you her work. Nearby, on a beautiful hill, is a new museum, **Museo Archipiélago Solentiname**. The museum has a small pre-Columbian collection, with some interesting explanations of local culture and ecology. There is also mural painted by the Arellano family from La Venada. The museum has a fabulous view of the islands and is not to be missed at sunset. If it is closed, ask around, just west of Rosa Pineda's house, to find out who has the key. ■ *US$1, telephone in San Carlos, T283-0095.*

Isla San Fernando

Sleeping   C *Isla Solentiname*, with meals, pretty grounds, acceptable but basic (you wash in the lake). Alternatively, you can stay in private homes, which are basic but very clean.

This is the biggest island in the chain and has the highest elevation at 250 m. The famous revolutionary/poet/sculptor/Catholic priest/Minister of Culture,

Isla Mancarrón

Río San Juan

Ernesto Cardenal, made his name here by founding a primitivist school of painting, poetry and sculpture, and even decorating the local parish church in naïve art. The church is being remodelled and should be open in 2002. There is a monument to the Sandinistas and the tomb of the deceased rebel commander **Alejandro Guevara** who was from this island; his widow now runs the *Hotel Mancarrón*. Hiking is possible on the island where many parrots and Moctezuma oropendulas make their home, ask in the village for a guide to show you the way to the '*mirador*', which has super views of the archipelago. Also at the mirador you can see a *coyol* palm tree which is used to make a sweet palm wine. The indigenous name for the palm is Mancarrón. The village has two small stores and cold drinks, bottled water, crackers and snacks. You can visit the homes of the talented artisans of Mancarrón. There are two places to sleep on the island, both with running water and generated power. **L** *Hotel Mancarrón*, up the hill from the dock and church, T265-2716 (Managua), T552-2059, szerger@ibw.com.ni, includes 3 meals per day, airy rooms with screened windows, rocky beach. Meals (not included are traditional Nicaraguan fare with fruit juices, bar and coffee), purified water, tours in Spanish only, water supply problems, some rooms dirty, ask to see room first, becoming run-down.

Sleeping and eating   C *Hospedaje Solentiname*, turn right before church and yell at gate '*¡Buenas!*', T283-0095, very rustic cabins with full board included, some with private bath, some shared, owned by the famed priest Ernesto Cardenal, beautiful spot.

Transport   The boat stops at islands La Venada, San Fernando, Mancarrón from San Carlos and in reverse en route to San Carlos: **San Carlos-Solentiname**, Tue, Fri 1300, US$4, 2½ hrs. **Solentiname-San Carlos**, Tue, Fri 0400, US$4, 2½ hrs.

Río San Juan

Colour maps 3, grid C6; and 4, grid C1-3
Length: 190 km

The river drops an average of 18 cm per km on its long journey from Lake Nicaragua to the Caribbean

The vast and extraordinarily beautiful Río San Juan is Lake Nicaragua's outlet to the sea. Three major rivers that originate in Costa Rica and more than 17 smaller tributaries also feed this mighty river, which is up to 350 m wide at points. It is an opportunity to experience rainforest flora and fauna and journey from Central America's biggest lake all the way to the thundering surf of Nicaragua's eastern seaboard. From San Carlos, the river passes the easternmost sector of Los Guatuzos Wildlife Refuge before entering a long stretch of cattle ranches that lead to the historic town and fort of El Castillo. Past El Castillo the Indio-Maíz Biological Reserve runs the remaining length of the river's north bank to the scenic coastal estuaries of the Caribbean Sea.

Ins and outs

Getting around   Travel is only possible by boat with one journey per week being undertaken by public transport; private boat hire is nearly the only option to explore this region. All travel times are based on a private boat with capacity for 6-8 passengers and a 65 hp motor or better, travelling down stream, add 20-35% for upstream travel and heavy boats or smaller motors will add much more time, around 150-200%.

History

In 1502 **Christopher Columbus** explored the Caribbean coast of Nicaragua in search of an inter-oceanic passage. He sailed right past the Río San Juan. The river was populated by Rama Indians, the same people that can be found today in the Bay of Bluefields on a small island. In the 17th century the biggest Rama settlement was estimated at more than 30,000 in the Boca de Sábalos (at this time the capital of Nicaragua had some 40,000 residents). Today the Ramas are making a return to the southern forests of Nicaragua, though only in the Río Indio area along the Caribbean coast.

When Francisco Hernández de Córdoba established the cities of Granada and León he sent Spanish **Captain Ruy Díaz** in search of the lake's drainage. Díaz explored the entire lake, reaching the mouth of the river in 1525. He was able to enter the river partially, as far as the first principle northern tributary, Río Sábalo, but was forced to turn back. Córdoba was unfazed and sent a second expedition led by **Captain Hernando de Soto** (who later was the first European to navigate the Mississippi river). Soto managed to navigate only as far as Díaz and was forced to turn back due to the rapids there.

Explorers being preoccupied with gold in Nicaragua's northern mountains, the river was ignored until 1539 when a very serious expedition was put together by the Spanish governor of Nicaragua, **Rodrigo de Contreras**. This brutally difficult journey was undertaken by foot troops, expert sailors and two brave captains **Alonso Calero**, and **Diego Machuca**. Having passed the first set of rapids they encountered more rapids at El Castillo, and Machuca divided the expedition and marched deep into the forest (in theory for the outlet of the river, but more likely looking for gold). Calero continued the length of the river and reached its end at the Caribbean sea on **24 June 1539**, the day of Saint John the Baptist, thus the name of Río San Juan (Saint John). He then sailed north in search of Machuca as far as the outlet of the Río Coco. However, Machuca had left, on foot, with his troops and returned all the way to Granada without knowledge of what had happened to the Calero party.

The newly discovered passage was exactly what the Spanish had been hoping for. It was quickly put into service for the transport of gold, indigo and other goods from their Pacific holdings to Hispañola (Dominican Republic today) and then to Spain. The river was part of the inter-oceanic steam ship service of Cornelius Vanderbilt in the mid-1800s and was used by William Walker for his brief rule in Granada. During the Contra conflict parts of the river were contested by Edén Pastora's southern front troops in attacks against the Sandinista government army.

The dream of the Río San Juan as part of an **inter-oceanic canal** was born as early as 1567, when King Phillip II of Spain ordered a feasibility study. Soon after, a Spanish Jesuit priest warned that opening a passage between the two oceans could lead to the draining of one ocean into the other, creating a massive desert on one side and biblical flooding on the other. By the mid-17th century England had moved in on Spanish holdings, wresting the island of Jamaica from Spain and creating a base for attacks on Central America. Their goal was to conquer the Río San Juan and "divide the Spanish Empire in half". From then on renowned scientists, engineers, business people and public figures would advocate the idea and become directly or indirectly involved in its promotion. The canal dream lived on with none other than **Napoleon Bonaparte III** who legally registered a new business venture in London, under the name of the **Nicaraguan Canal Company** in 1869 (the same year

Río San Juan

the Suez Canal was inaugurated), after obtaining the canal concession from the Nicaraguan government. He proclaimed that to control the Río San Juan was to control the Gibraltar of the Americas and a guarantee of domination of the new world order. He fell from power the following year and nothing was done. The 19th century also saw aborted projects by the Dutch, Belgians and the US. The US **President Ulysses Grant** and Ferdinand de Lesseps carried out parallel studies to find the best option for a Central American inter-oceanic canal. Both concluded that the Nicaraguan route was more feasible than Panama or Tehuantepec, Mexico. In 1885, Aniceto Menocal, an engineer working under the auspices of the US government, estimated that the construction was feasible, could be realized in six years, and would cost around 75 million dollars. The first dredgers arrived in San Juan del Norte at the mouth of the San Juan river on the Atlantic Coast of Nicaragua in 1891. However, in 1893 the project started by the privately owned **US Maritime Canal Company** went bankrupt with only 1 km dredged. The dredge remains in the Bay of San Juan del Norte, a rusting monument to broken canal dreams. In 1901 the US House of Representatives passed a bill in favour of the US government building the canal in Nicaragua, but just as the Senate hearings on the proposal were about to begin a Caribbean volcano erupted killing thousands. A sharp lobbyist for the Panama Canal project distributed to all the senators a Nicaraguan **postage stamp** depicting **Volcán Concepción** in eruption, with the footnote that a Nicaragua canal would have to pass by that very same active volcano, on the Island of Ometepe. The canal project was awarded to Panama. Several projects are still looking for funding for a canal which would surely destroy the natural splendour of the Río San Juan, a river that has survived so many invasions, attacks and close calls.

Along the river

San Carlos-Río Sábalo-El Castillo
Travel time about 2 hrs

Bird-watching is good just outside the limits of San Carlos and continues to be so for some distance down the river as one or both banks are lined with wetlands. Deforestation in this section to El Castillo is increasingly getting worse and, though there are several reforestation projects in progress, barges can be seen on this part of the river with giant trunks of cedar. The Río Sábalo is an important tributary named after the big fish of this region, the **sábalo**, or tarpon. The town of **Boca de Sábalos** is melancholy, muddy and friendly. There is an earth path that leads to a spooky looking African palm plantation and factory, where palm oil is made. From the road it is possible to connect with the **Río Santa Cruz** and navigate that small and beautiful river (great bird-watching) to El Castillo. The road in the dry season goes deep into the backcountry and wildlife viewing at the forest edge is very good with spider, howler and white-faced monkeys, flocks of parrots and many birds of prey. There is one very rustic, tarantula-filled *hospedaje* next to the dock in town with toilets outside and a restaurant for US$4 per night. The people of Sábalo seem happy to see outsiders. There are some small rapids just past the river's drainage into the Río San Juan. The fishing is quite good here for **sábalo real** (tarpon) which can reach up to 2½ m and weigh in at 150 kg. *Robalo* (snook) is also a popular sport fish and much better to eat than the tarpon. Just before El Castillo there is an upscale fishing lodge that also offers river trips. *Monte Cristo River Resort*, in front of the Isla Sombrero de Cuero, T0883-6829, with private bath, a/c, swimming pool and cute cabins, has a dock that is prone to flooding, but the whole construction is attractive and the most ambitious on the river. Just down from *Monte Cristo* is the cute, clean and friendly town of El Castillo, located 60 km from San Carlos and home to a famous 17th-century fortress.

El Castillo

Located in front of the El Diablo Rapids, El Castillo is a sight to behold: tiny riverfront homes with red tin roofs, sitting on stilts above the fast-moving river. Behind, on a grassy green, round hill, a big, black-stone, 325-year-old Spanish fort dominates the view of the town. The peaceful little village of El Castillo could be the most attractive riverfront settlement in Nicaragua. Most people come to see the fort, but the simple, quiet village makes a longer stay worthwhile.

Colour map 4, grid C1
Population: 2,300
Altitude: 40 m

When British pirate **Henry Morgan** made off down the Río San Juan with £500,000 sterling after sacking Granada, the Spanish said ¡*Basta!* (enough!). Construction began in 1673 on the top of a hill that affords long views to the east (the route of attacks) and in front of one of the river's most dangerous rapids. In 1674 French pirates encountered a half-finished fortress, but were repelled. Work was complete in **1675** and today the fort is Nicaragua's oldest standing colonial building (in its original state). Soon to become Nicaragua's second **UNESCO World Heritage Site**, this was the biggest fortress on the Central American isthmus when it was finished.

Fortaleza de la Inmaculada Concepción

In the 18th century the fort came under siege from the British several times. In 1762 the **British Navy** came up the Río San Juan to take the fort and control the river. A new national hero was born in El Castillo, a teenage girl called **Rafaela Herrera**, the daughter of a decorated captain of the Spanish forces who had recently died. The soldiers of the fort were ready to concede defeat, but Rafaela, who had received training in armament, took command of the fortress and troops and fired the first rounds of cannon herself against the British. She is said to have killed a British commander with her third shot. The battle lasted five days. One night, under heavy attack from the boats covered by darkness, Rafaela ordered sheets to be soaked in alcohol, placed on big branches and set alight up river. The flaming torches illuminated the enemy for counter fire and the river carried the burning debris downstream toward the enemy's wooden boats. The British were forced to retreat.

In 1779 English chancellor Lord George Germain devised a serious attack on the Río San Juan that was aimed at securing British domination of Lake Nicaragua and control of the province. Seven warships were brought to the end of the Río San Juan with **a force of 600 British soldiers and 400 Miskito Indian warriors**. Along on the mission was a young Captain Nelson, later to be known as **Lord Nelson** after

Río San Juan

El Castillo

N

Not to scale

Sleeping
1 Albergue El Castillo
2 Hospedaje Aurora
3 Hospedaje Manantial

Eating
1 Bar Cofalito
2 Naranjano

becoming one the British Navy's greatest heroes. In his early 20s, Nelson brought the troops ashore well before the fort and travelled overland through forest to attack the fortress from a hill behind (today the hill is called Lomas de Nelson). The British won the battle and took control of the fort, but Matías de Galvez, the Captain General of Central America, was every bit as capable as the British generals who masterminded the invasion. Galvez decided to let the jungle do his work for him, and using massive troop reinforcements in San Carlos, kept the British forces bottled up in the fort. Soon the Miskito Indians got tired of waiting and left. Jungle diseases, especially dysentery and malaria set in and in less than a year the great majority of the invasion forces had died. The British decided to abandon the fort. Lord Nelson is said to have lost an eye in battles at the fort, others say he lost the use of an arm. It is doubtful that either occurred here, yet the loss of Nelson's eye at San Carlos is an integral part of Nicaraguan folklore.

A museum and library were built inside the fortress in the 1990s. The museum is one of the country's finest with a very complete history of the region (all in Spanish). ■ *0900-1200, 1400-1700. US$1. The views from the fort are lovely and worth the price of admission.*

There is an educative museum behind the fortress, **Centro de Interpretación de la Naturaleza**, with displays and explanations of local flora and fauna. Lunch is recommended here as freshwater lobster (*camarones del río*) and snook (*robalo*) are both excellent.

Sleeping C *Albergue El Castillo,* next to fortress above city dock, T249-2508. Shared bath, fan, shared balcony overlooking river. Beautiful wooden building and rooms with a good restaurant downstairs, friendly service. Recommended. **F** *Hospedaje Manantial*, on left of main street as you leave the boat, none too clean, no view, basic, breakfast US$1.50, lunch US$2. **F** *Hospedaje Aurora*, basic, but kindly owners, veranda with rocking chair overlooking river, serves food.

■ *on map, page 167*
For price codes,
see inside front cover

Eating *Bar Cofalito*, on the jetty, crayfish on menu, good view but poor quality. Better value is *on map, page 167* the *soda* facing the quay. *Doña Amelia*, good meals also on the wharf, very clean, cheap. *Naranjano*, good food.

Transport **Boats** El Castillo, from San Carlos-El Castillo, 0800 daily except Sun and daily at 1400, US$5, 3-4 hrs. El Castillo-San Carlos, daily 0430, 0500, 0600, US$5, 3-4 hrs.
Transfers to Refugio Bartola from El Castillo are normally US$50-70 round-trip. If planning to continue down the Río San Juan past Refugio Bartola from El Castillo, it can only be done by prior arrangement in San Carlos or Managua, or with lots of patience (and cash). You may be able to hitch a ride downstream on a barge, but don't plan on it; ask at the dock when the next one could be passing.

Directory **Telephone** *Enitel*, T552-6124. **Shopping** Just east of the dock is a general store that sells purified water and other basic supplies. If travelling far on the river it may be wise to buy some of the heavy-duty yellow (or orange) plastic bags sold there. Double bag all luggage against the rain. **Tourist office** Right in front of the town dock is a little office for *INTUR*, often unmanned, but good for advice on hiring boats if open.

Travelling downstream from the fortress means running the small, but tricky rapids in front of the town. Locals fish along the rapids and Nicaraguan boat drivers have no problems zigzagging through them. Just 2 km down river, a narrow cut through the forest and a flag marks the border with Costa Rica, which reaches the southern banks of the river here and follows most of the river to the Caribbean sea. The confluence of the Río San Juan and Río Bartola marks the beginning of the splendid Indio-Maíz Biological Reserve.

**El Castillo –
Río Bartola**
*Travel time about
20 mins*

Reserva Biológica Indio-Maíz

This is Central America and Nicaragua's second largest nature reserve and perhaps its most pristine. Several square kilometres here house more species of birds, trees or insects than the entire European continent. The reserve protects what biologists have called "the largest extent of primary rainforest in Central America", with trees reaching up to 50 m in height. Indio-Maíz also has numerous wetland areas and rivers. Its westernmost border is marked by the Río Bartola; at the east is the Caribbean Sea; and northern and southern limits are marked by the Río Punta Gorda and Río San Juan respectively.

Colour map 4, grid C2
Area: 361,875 ha

Inside the reserve's pristine forest are several ancient extinct volcanoes, the highest being Cerro La Guinea at 648 m. The reserve is also home to over 600 species of bird, 300 species of reptile and amphibian, and 200 species of mammal, including many big cats and howler, white-face and spider monkeys. Rainfall in the park ranges from just under 3,000 mm a year in Bartola to 5,000 mm in San Juan del Norte. Sadly little research has been done in the reserve and most of its flora and fauna remain a mystery. In the past decade UCLA (University of California at Los Angeles) biologists have been bringing students to aid in research trips. They report that the density and diversity of the wildlife at the field site (the forest behind Bartola and the MARENA station) is impressive, even by neotropical standards. As well as the three primate species, the students discovered two bird species previously undocumented in Nicaragua and made a list of birds that included 11 species of heron, two of ibis and stork, 12 species of hawk, kite and falcon, and eight species of parrot and macaw. They also documented 11 species of hummingbird, six kingfisher, three toucan, seven woodpecker, 19 antbird and no less than 27 species of flycatcher, amongst many others. The biologists also encountered 28 species of reptile and 16 species of mammal including three-toed sloth, jaguarundi, river otter, tapir, deer, agouti, paca, white-faced, spider and howler monkey. The sheer beauty of the reserve means that non-enthusiasts will also enjoy the enchantment of a virgin rainforest.

Río San Juan

A *Refugio Bartola*, at the confluence of the Río San Juan and the Río Bartola, Apartado Postal 2715, Managua, Nicaragua, T289-4167, F289-4154, bartola@guises.org Including 3 meals, juice and coffee, private bath, night-time generator for electricity, simple wooden rooms with solid beds and high ceilings, very clean. Frogs in toilets at no extra charge. The windows have no screens, ask for mosquito netting, excellent meals, on a set menu, but suggestions for dinner accepted, very good freshwater lobster (*camarones del río*), grilled pork (*cerdo a la plancha*), good coffee and purified water. Pet spider monkey at lodge, Daniela, loves men and bites women (she's very jealous), she was abandoned by her parents and is kept under control when customers are in the lodge or she raises havoc. *Refugio Bartola* is a research station and income from visitors helps keep it open. One of the 2 lodge owners (both are scientists), Daniel Querol, with

Sleeping
*Indio-Maíz can also
be visited via the Río
Indio although there
are no hiking trails*

Costa Rica and Nicaragua – a bridge too far

They appear on the world image map as perfect opposites. The nature- and peace-loving Costa Ricans living happily in their tourist Mecca, the self-proclaimed Switzerland of Central America, the darling of international ecotourism. Across the Río San Juan lie the bad-boy Nicaraguans, always fighting amongst themselves, the country that tried to defy the United States, driving its own economy into poverty, a country synonymous with war and natural disasters.

It was not always this way, but the tables have been turned over the years, creating bitterness on both sides. During the war against William Walker in 1856, Costa Rica rushed to occupy southern Lake Nicaragua, the Río San Juan and the then lucrative inter-oceanic route. Twenty-five years earlier they had occupied and annexed Guanacaste, the Nicoya Peninsula and the southern banks of the Río San Juan. The seeds of an animosity that lives on today were sown. The Río San Juan remained the property of Nicaragua, but the Costa Ricans now have rights to its southern shores east of El Castillo. A treaty was agreed upon by the two countries,

allowing Costa Rica limited navigational rights on the Río San Juan, for commercial traffic only.

During the mid-20th century Nicaragua was a strong, vibrant economy and Costa Rican white-collar workers came to Managua to find quality employment. Then the Nicaraguans, fed up with a government that was great for business and lousy for personal freedom, rebelled. Arms were shipped via South America and Cuba to Costa Rica where the Sandinista southern front made attacks across the border against the Somoza regime. After the Sandinista victory, disillusioned Nicaraguans funded by the CIA mounted Contra attacks against the Sandinista regime, again from Costa Rica. All the while the Costa Ricans were getting a bit tired of being used as a base for rebel operations.

Freedom was finally won after years of war, but Nicaragua's economy was destroyed. With the economy in ruins, much of Nicaragua's work force went in an exodus of undocumented workers to Costa Rica. Social problems in Costa Rica were blamed on immigrants from

---

the aid of numerous local forest experts like the amiable Mercedes Díaz, has published an excellent book (in Spanish) on the many practical uses of the rainforest plants. *Especies útiles de un bosque húmedo tropical* is well illustrated and available at the hotel. The hotel/research station is also a training ground for young Nicaraguan biologists. The lodge's private reserve has a labyrinth of well-mapped trails that lead from the rooms into the reserve. The hotel guides are very knowledgeable (Spanish only); and they will also take you down the glorious Río Bartola by canoe for great wildlife viewing and bird-watching. **NB** Ask as many questions as possible of the guides or they may just walk you through the forest. Snakes are a legitimate danger and the benefits of a night hike must be weighed against the very real dangers of snakebites. Hiking in the reserve without a guide is not recommended as getting lost could mean serious injury or death. Best time to start a hike is 0500-0530; convince the guide that you are serious about leaving early and he will rise in time. Guides expect a tip and hotel charges US$5 per person for hike. **Camping** is also possible in the park. The *MARENA* (the Nicaraguan environmental agency) park rangers at Bartola are very strict, but should let you camp at guardhouse clearing. Their station is across the Río Bartola from the *Refugio Bartola* hotel.

Nicaragua. Several human rights watch groups documented abuses by the Costa Rican military against Nicaraguan immigrant farm workers. Nicaraguans found little humour in the claim that Costa Rica had no military, a feat achieved by calling their large (larger than the entire Nicaraguan military and police force combined), well-trained combat troops a 'Civil Guard'.

It was the same non-existent Costa Rican military that was caught dressed in battle fatigues patrolling the Río San Juan in a camouflage boat in 1998, with automatic rifles at the ready. The news sent Nicaraguans into outrage. While environmental groups demonstrated the pollution of Lake Nicaragua tributaries by Costa Rican banana plantations, Nicaraguans called for a total ban of Costa Rican boat travel inside its borders. Costa Rica threatened to expel all Nicaraguan immigrant workers and both countries lapsed into uncomfortable diplomatic attempts at repair. As of 2001 it appears that Costa Ricans will be allowed to navigate the river once again for commercial purposes, but bumper

stickers can be seen in Managua proclaiming ¡El Río San Juan es Nica! (The San Juan River is Nicaraguan!), with some even proclaiming that it is time for Nicaragua to take back Guanacaste and other land lost to the Costa Ricans in the 19th century. Though the actual ownership of the river has never been in doubt, Nicaragua has long been suspicious of Costa Rica's desires to incorporate it. To add fuel to the fire, an old tourist map published by the Costa Rican government was brought out to show the Nicaraguan river marked as being in Costa Rica.

Most people on the Río San Juan in both countries find all this bickering to be counterproductive. They need one another to do business.

I was last on the Costa Rican bank of the Río San Juan in early 2001, in a Nicaraguan-owned and operated hotel located at the mouth of the Río Sarapiquí. The little hotel has a billiards table. Crowding around the table, Nicaraguan and Costa Rican border guards were playing pool, drinking beer and laughing. I never did find out who won.

Río San Juan

This is one of the most scenic sections of the river, in particular the area around the rapids of Machuca and at the mouth of Río San Carlos, which originates in Costa Rica. Travel is by chartered boat or the once-a-week slow boat to San Juan del Norte (see San Carlos). At the mouth of the pristine Río Sarnoso is a shipwreck from the 19th-century inter-oceanic steam ship service, though the locals like to claim it as a Spanish galleon wreck. A jaguar was spotted on the banks here recently, one of the most difficult jungle animals to see thanks to their preference for night hunting and large territories (up to 11 sq km). To enter the Río Sarnoso you will need to receive advance permission from MARENA in Managua and show the letter to the guards east or west of the river. At the confluence of the **Río San Carlos** there is a checkpoint for the Nicaraguan military and MARENA, where passports must be presented; you can ask to use their outhouse. Across the banks in Costa Rica there is a general store and a basic eatery. Permission can be obtained from the Costa Rican military to make a quick supply or food stop (córdobas are difficult to use on the Costa Rican side, so dollars or colones are recommended as a backup).

Past the Río San Carlos the stunning beauty of the Indio-Maíz reserve on the north bank continues, while the south bank is a mixture of forest and ranch settlements, with some clear cutting. There are sandbars, and slow navigation will allow opportunities to spot sunning crocodiles and turtles, as well

Río Bartola – Río Sarapiquí

Travel time about 2 hrs

El Sarnoso is one of the most beautiful of all navigable rivers in the country

Strange bedfellows – leaf-cutter ants and poison dart frogs

The rainforest reserve of Indio-Maiz is home to one of the most industrious of the ant family and most beautiful of the frog species. The leaf-cutter ant, at 7-10 mm in length, is always at work cutting off little pieces of fresh leaves to carry on his wobbling little body to his colony's underground chamber. The plant matter then grows fungus that is the diet for subterranean community. Their nests are big, well-protected caverns. Leaf-cutter ants defend their nest with zeal and have been documented chasing off animals as large as armadillos.

Coexisting with these ferocious little workaholics is the beautiful and deadly Dendrobates auratus, a bright green and black spotted poison dart frog. The name 'poison dart frog' comes from the toxic solution secreted by the frog and used by the indigenous people of the region to coat their darts and subdue their prey. While researching in the forest reserve behind the Refugio Bartola UCLA biologist Michael La Plante observed that wherever there was a leaf-cutter ant nest there appeared to be a significantly higher population of the bright green and black spotted poison dart frog.

Several theories were put to the test to discover why they were there. Hunger would be the most obvious reason for these frogs to be at the nest sites as 70% of their diet is made up of ants. The frogs must consume ants in order to maintain their toxicity. Test frogs in a bucket with the leaf-cutter ants died of starvation and were actually attacked by the ants. Another possibility is that the frogs use the ant trails as a navigational tool to care for their young. It seems that the male poison dart frog carries the tadpoles to a pool of water, usually in tree holes and returns daily to feed them. Another theory is that the aggressive nature of the ant nest soldiers may help protect the frogs from predators.

After several lengthy experiments La Plante concluded that the frogs stay close to the ants' nests because their skin resembles a large group of leaf-cutter ants or vice versa. These two little characters are part of an intricate forest orchestra that plays a jungle symphony thousands of years old; one of interaction and co-dependence, the song of the chain of life.

as monkeys and toucans in the canopy. The muddy, debris-filled Río Sarapiquí drains into the Río San Juan at the second river checkpoint for the military and MARENA. The Sarapiquí is inside Costa Rica and there is a small village where basic boat and motor repairs can be made. This was the scene of several significant battles between the Edén Pastora-led southern-front Contra forces and the Nicaraguan Sandinista military in the 1980s. At the confluence of the two rivers on the Costa Rican side is a small lodge, the last chance for a bed before the end of the river.

Sleeping, eating & shopping   **F** *Paraíso de la Frontera* or *Doña Adilia's place*, private bath, fan, not terribly clean, bring mosquito net, nice garden with comical parrot. Billiards table next to store popular for games between Nicaraguan and Costa Rican military, restaurant with set meals, US$3. Doña Adilia also has a small store to buy supplies and will accept córdobas. You need to check in with the Costa Rican guard station across from the lodge on the Río Sarapiquí to spend the night, or if you just want to pick up something at the store. If continuing down the river without stopping you only need to check in at the Nicaraguan station on the Río San Juan. Their toilet can be used with permission and the MARENA guard is happy to talk about the nature he protects.

Past the drainage of the Sarapiquí, the Río San Juan travels northeast passing some of the river's 300+ islands including the Isla Nelson. Petrol is available on the Costa Rican side, which is dotted with sprawling ranches. The Nicaraguan side (which includes the river and its islands) is pristine rainforest mixed with some secondary growth where land was reclaimed for the biological reserve. At one of the widest parts of the river it branches southeast and northeast. To the southeast is the mighty Río Colorado in Costa Rica with the San Juan continuing to the northeast. Thanks to sediment build-up in the Bay of San Juan, since the mid-to-late 1800s, the majority of the water now drains out of the Río Colorado. There is another checkpoint here and past the intersection of the two rivers the Río San Juan becomes narrow and travels almost due north. The section is normally quite good for viewing monkeys and toucans. Near edge of the continent the Río San Juan begins to snake wildly. It switchbacks past wetlands and the broad, handsome swamp palms that are common to this area, until it meets the sea at a dark sandbar called simply **La Barra** (the bar). The sandbar has fooled navigators for hundreds of years and has been responsible for many a sailor's death. After hours of dense jungle, the sight of the windswept beach is exhilarating. Here the Caribbean is muddy, filled with sediments from the river and literally teeming with sharks that are feeding on the many fish in this rich combination of fresh and salt water. Swimming is to be done with trepidation and there are normally strong surf and currents to aid the sharks in their game of seek and eat.

Río Sarapiquí – Río Colorado – Caribbean Sea
Travel time about 3 hrs

North of the sandbank is a series of connected coastal estuaries known collectively as the Bahía de San Juan. If sunny the bay is brilliant, glorious with deep blue water reflecting dense green rainforest and shores lined with flowering water grass. This is the end of the earth: complete paradise. It is also one of the wettest places in the Americas, with an average annual rainfall of 5,000 mm. Standing sadly in the bay is the more than 100-year-old dredge that was to begin the canal project to connect the two seas. Today it acts as a giant planter with varied vegetation spurting from its rusted body. At the edge of one of the lagoons is a small, decaying wooden dock and a Nicaraguan flag marking the entrance to the historic and now-deserted frontier town of Greytown.

La Barra – Bahía de San Juan – Greytown

Río San Juan

Greytown

This is all that remains of the original San Juan del Norte, known to most as Greytown (its 19th-century label), a British governor of Jamaica. Its claim to international fame was during the gold rush years of the mid-1800s, when the shores of the town were filled with steam ships making the journey up and down the Río San Juan. Mark Twain slept here on his 1866 journey and described the town as a "peopled paradise...composed of 200 old frame houses and some nice vacant lots, and its comeliness is greatly enhanced, I may say is rendered gorgeous, by the cluster of stern-wheel steamboats at the water front. The population is 800 and is mixed – made up of natives (Nicaraguans), Americans, Spaniards, Germans, English and Jamaicans." He added that "the transit business has made every other house a lodging camp and you can get a good bed anywhere for a dollar." Today the only beds are in the town's cemeteries, which are preserved as a national monument. The city was the site of fighting between Contra guerrillas and the Sandinista military, when it was evacuated then burned. But its demise had come much earlier when the inter-oceanic service was finally retired. It was brought back to life by canal projects, then relegated to obscurity for the 20th century and reduced to 300 inhabitants. After the burning, the village did not exist at all for six years, until, in 1990, it was re-founded nearby. There is a nice quiet trail that leads through Catholic, American, Masonic and Anglican cemeteries. They are all divided, with faded tombstones wrapped in rainforest greenness. The jungle has taken over the place and has now erased any sign of a town apart from the graves, the bell from the town church and the front steps of the Pellas family house. Draining into the bay is one of the region's principal rivers, the Río Indio. Just upriver, is the new location of San Juan del Norte.

San Juan del Norte

Colour map 4, grid C2
Population: 275
Altitude: 5 m

San Juan is a good base for visiting the reserve via the Río Indio and some of its secret tributaries

The end-of-the-world feeling is not lost in this little village of winding paths, homes on stilts and flooded yards. Fishing (particularly lobster) is the main source of income The residents of San Juan del Norte are very friendly and a mix of Afro-Caribbeans from Bluefields, Hispanics from the Pacific and Rama Indians from Bluefields Bay. The village lines the west bank of the Río Indio, one of Nicaragua's most beautiful rivers, 200 m wide at this point. Across the river is a 400-m wide strip of land full of coconut palms, dense forest and beach that separates the copper-coloured Río Indio from the crashing Caribbean sea. It is a delightfully surreal experience to watch the sun set over the bright green rainforest that separates the two bodies of water, and the jungle river flow south, while being serenaded by the muffled roar of the sea.

Sleeping **E** *Hotel Lost Paradise* or *Melvin's Place*, on the river at the south end of town. Ceiling fan, private bath, screened windows but bring coils or mosquito netting. Owner Melvin speaks Creole English and is very helpful, bar, restaurant, night-time generated power, fabulous gazebo on the river with TV, bottled water is sometimes for sale. Recommended. **NB** You will need to inform the kitchen at least 2 hrs in advance if you want to eat.

Eating The food in San Juan del Norte is simple, fresh lobster if in season, if not, the fried *robalo* (snook) is recommended. Any seafood is fresh, otherwise chicken is probably the only other option. *Doña Ester's Place*, just upriver from *Melvin's Place*, is the town's restaurant, average dish costs US$3. Drinks in town consist of Costa Rican beer, Nicaraguan rum and Coca-Cola. There is a pleasant bar just upriver from *Ester's Place* with a big palm ranch and somewhat cold beer, card-playing locals and friendly Rama Indians; they might also have some food to offer. At times it can be difficult to find someone in San Juan to cook a meal, so bring snack supplies and arrange meals at *Dona Ester's* or *Melvin's Place* in advance. **NB** If you try to buy direct from the fishermen prices tend to be double what the locals pay.

Entertainment There is 1 disco functioning at the moment. It is full of festive locals at weekends. Dancing is to reggae as well as salsa, rap and merengue and music is loud. If staying at *Melvin's Place* (and Melvin is in town) he will take you to the disco at night to make sure you have a good time and make it back home. **NB** There are no police in San Juan and the locals are very honest, but this is frontier country, there are some transient characters and care should be taken if out at night. The best idea is to take a local with you if you go out at night or you could turn in early.

Shopping There is something that resembles a central avenue with little palms and brightly painted benches and 2 footpaths. This runs parallel to the river about 50 m inside the village. Near the school sports field are a couple of good shops, one of which has a great variety of supplies including rubber boots or Wellingtons (*botas de hule*) in big sizes (not found elsewhere in Nicaragua).

There are no roads, but an airstrip is being built, slowly. Boats are all private except for **Transport** the once-a-week arrival and departure to and from San Carlos.

San Carlos-San Juan del Norte, Thu 0800, US$15, 12-14 hrs. **San Juan del Norte-San Carlos**, Sun 0330, US$15, 13-15 hrs. You may be able to hitch a ride to Limón, Costa Rica or Bluefields from here, though you will probably be asked for a considerable contribution.

There now appears to be Nicaraguan customs and immigration at San Juan del Norte, **Nicaraguan** but it is not clear if entrance and exit stamps can be obtained. **Limón**, Costa Rica is **immigration** the nearest official point of entry and exit for Costa Rica. If coming from Costa Rica to Nicaragua ask in San Juan about entrance stamps. If you are planning to leave Nicaragua via San Juan it is advisable to check in depth with the immigration officials in San Carlos to see if an exit stamp can be obtained in San Juan or would be better obtained in advance in San Carlos.

Banks There are no banks and the most common currency is Costa Rican colones **Directory** thanks to the (relatively) easy access to Limón, Costa Rica. You can pay in córdobas or dollars, but expect change in colones. Several people in the village may be willing to change money at wilderness rates, options are few, but ask around. **Telephone** There are two shops that offer the use of a telephone when it is working, which is a cellular phone that calls via Costa Rica to Nicaragua.

Excursions from San Juan del Norte

If coming in your own boat (chartered), a trip further down the Río Indio is **Río Indio** recommended, with lots of wildlife, virgin forest and occasional encounters with Rama Indians (please respect their culture and right to privacy) who are returning to the region after centuries of exile. If coming by public boat, Melvin can arrange a tour down the river in one of his *super-panga* boats. Upriver is truly spectacular, like a miniature Amazon with kilometre after kilometre of virgin forest. It is important to leave early to see wildlife, and bring plenty of petrol, water, etc. You will need permission from the military and MARENA checkpoint at the north end of town on the riverfront. The possibility for serious adventure exists on this river, but your budget must be healthy, as there is no public transport. Rama Indians navigate the river in canoes to buy supplies every week or so but could only offer a one-way ride to the jungle. The river goes into the heart of the Indio-Maíz reserve. Tour companies in Managua can offer excursions of the Río San Juan complete with visits down the Río Indio.

Locals swim in the Blue Lagoon, just past the military checkpoint on the bar **Blue Lagoon** that separates the river from the sea. There can quite a bit of rubbish on the banks of the lagoon, but the water is clean and there are no sharks or crocodiles. The sea beach is not only full of sharks and very rough, but it has never been cleaned, so debris from boats at sea litters the beach.

León and El Occidente

8

León, the colonial capital of Nicaragua, is a vibrant, young and active city full of well-worn Spanish colonial homes and more than a dozen colonial churches. It is also the artistic and intellectual capital of Nicaragua, and former home of its three greatest poets, including the undisputed national hero Rubén Darío.

Beyond León, the Maribios volcanoes dominate northwestern Nicaragua. The region is bordered in the north by the lowland estuaries east of the extinct Volcán Cosigüina and the scenic and steamy Golfo de Fonseca. The lake-filled crater of Cosigüina also marks the westernmost point in Nicaragua and the end of Cordillera Los Maribios, one of the most densely active volcanic chains in the world. Volcán Momotombo on the northern shores of Lake Managua is the southern bookend of this spectacular volcanic chain and it shadows the UNESCO World Heritage site of León Viejo.

The departments of León and Chinandega enjoy miles of Pacific coastline that are accented by barrier islands and coastal lagoons housing important commercial shrimp farms. Thanks to the ultra-fertile volcanic soil of the Maribios' western slopes, this is rich arable land with sprawling crops of sugar cane, bananas, peanuts and basic grains.

North from Managua

There are two routes from western Managua that lead to the city of León, **Carretera Vieja a León** and **Carretera Nueva a León** (the old and new highways). Neither road appears remotely new, and plans exist to repave both, but the older one is in terrible condition and all through traffic uses the bumpy patchwork pavement of the Carretera Nueva, the only decent choice. The new highway also has some fine views of the most beautiful and cleanest parts of Lake Managua. From the Pan-American Highway in western Managua (Carretera Sur) the Carretera Nueva a León heads north and, at Km 14, passes the entrance to Xiloá Crater Lake (see page 80) and the Chiltepe Peninsula with its 1,800 ha of tropical dry forest reserve. The peninsula is very active seismically and there are dozens of minor tremors every day. Most of the land is used for cattle ranching, although low-cost, tax-free clothing factories have been opened along the highway at Km 15.

Mateare

Colour map 3, grid B3
Population: 25,172
Altitude: 50 m

At Km 25, the highway comes to the pleasant, clean fishing and agricultural town of Mateare, which has the finest fish from Lake Managua. Although this part of Lake Managua is still not as clean as Lake Nicaragua, it is dramatically cleaner than along the shores of Managua and the fish here is safe to eat. The locals say once you eat their enchanting *guapote* (lake perch) you will always return to visit or live in Mateare. Most of the locals who do not fish have small farms in the hills across the highway.

Eating *Bar El Ranchito*, on Parque Central, serves fried chicken, fish and cold beer and offers an up-close glimpse of village personalities (and drinking capacities) along the rural northern lakefront.

Buses pass through Mateare every 15 mins between León and Managua.

Isla Momotombito It is not easy to arrange but, with some asking around (try at the *Araica* residence on the east side of Parque Central), the fishermen can take you to the small volcanic island of **Isla Momotombito**. The best time of year to visit is during the rainy season, when the island is green and the swell on the lake small. Dry (windy) season trips mean a white-knuckle ride and a lot of water in your face. Boats have turned over on occasions during a big swell. Price about US$60-70 for the day and you may need to drive out of town to fill up the fisherman's gasoline jug in Los Brasiles. The ride is 30-60 minutes depending on the lake swell. Situated in the northwest of Lake Managua in the shadow of the active **Volcán Momotombo**, Momotombito (little Momotombo) has much bird and reptile life and a remarkable family of albino crocodiles. There is a small military outpost on the calm side of the island. Stop there to check in if you wish to hike on the islands. Bring drinks or food as gifts for the (non-uniformed) guards, who are very friendly, usually quite bored and thrilled to see visitors. They might take you hiking for a small fee to see what is left of the island's many pre-Columbian statues. Momotombito, like the islands of Lake Nicaragua, is believed to have been a religious ceremonial site for the Chorotega Indians who lived on the lake shore. Most of the basalt idols have been either looted or taken to museums. Some can be seen at the Museo Nacional in Managua (see page 99). The guards claim to know of others still on the island, but if digging is involved it is best to leave them alone; the absence of a qualified archaeologist will mean that valuable reference information will be lost forever once removed from the ground. **NB** Beware of snakes; there are literally hundreds on the island and the guards claim to kill more than 20 a day just to keep their hut snake-free. A few kilometres north of Momotombito are several small rock islands where you can see some lake-level petroglyphs and sublime views of the steaming Volcán Momotombo.

Back on the highway north to León there are more stunning views of Lake Managua, Momotombito and Momotombo. At Km 31 is a charming out-door restaurant, **Mirador Momotombo**, with typical beef, pork and chicken dishes at cheap to mid-range prices. The grounds of the restaurant are great for photography and if you don't wish to eat or drink there you can pay US$1.50 to use the grounds to take photographs. Tables are spread out under little palm-roofed huts and it is worth stopping for a drink at least, though a day with no lake breeze will mean lots of insects. Camping is also possible next to the restaurant on an adjacent lakefront field for a small fee, enquire at the restaurant. At Km 41 is the entrance to Nagarote.

Nagarote

Rising out of the intense heat that cooks the lakeshore plains, Nagarote is a rustic and scenic ranching town and birthplace of a famous dish, **quesillo con tiste**, one of Nicaragua's best-loved traditional meals. *Quesillo* is a local version of braided Mozzarella cheese, served wrapped in a warm tortilla and bathed in onions and cream. *Tiste* is a traditional Indian drink of corn and cacao (raw chocolate) served, as it has been for over 1,000 years, in the dried and gutted shell of the oval *jícara* fruit. The nearby village of La Paz Centro (see below) competes for title of the country's best *quesillo,* and the highway passing through both towns is lined with numerous *quesillo* eateries. The most famous place in Nagarote for a good *quesillo con tiste* is the *Quesillos Acacia*, located at the southern highway entrance to Nagarote. It's a sit-down restaurant, with a waitress, but the only thing on the menu is *quesillo*. Here you can eat them off of a plate with knife and fork (a rare luxury) or you can grab one 'to go' (*para llevar*) in a tiny plastic bag. The eatery can be distinguished from the others by its thatched palm roof; *quesillos* cost US$1 each.

Colour map 3, grid B2
Population: 33,988
Altitude: 76 m

León and El Occidente

The centre of Nagarote lies well west of the highway. During the morning oxcarts arrive from surrounding farms full of metal milk cans, and boys ride into town on bicycles with live chickens dangling from their handlebars. There are many rustic and charming colonial homes and the people of Nagarote are helpful and laid back. Parque Central is sleepy and there's a pretty adobe church with red-tile roof; inside, the dining room chandeliers and green curtains give it a homey feel. One block north is the original home of Silvio Mayorga, one of the Sandinista party founders who was killed during the Revolution of 1978-79. One block north and four blocks east of Parque Central is a small unassuming park with what is believed to be Nicaragua's oldest living tree. This wide, ancient trunk with several surviving branches is the more than 950-year-old **Genízaro** tree (*Pithecellobium saman*). It could tell a tale or two. In pre-Columbian times this same tree gave shade to a Chorotegan outdoor market. At the corner of the park is a beautiful carved wood sculpture depicting a Chorotega chief on the front side and an Indian woman at the back. The broad hardwood monument was carved in 1999 out of a single branch of the ancient tree that watches over it.

Buses pass on the route between León and Managua every 15 mins and direct buses from Nagarote to Managua leave every 30 mins, US$0.60. Buses from Managua to La Paz Centro leave from Mercado Israel Lewites (also called Mercado Boer) every 30 mins.

La Paz Centro

Colour map 3, grid B2
Population: 31,233
Altitude: 67 m

At Km 54 is the exit for the mostly paved road that leads 12 km to the lakefront village of Puerto Momotombo and León Viejo (see below). Just beyond the exit is the friendly, dusty and sad-looking town of La Paz Centro. A few people from León Viejo settled here in the early 17th century. The area has a long history of ceramic production as well as many artisan brick and tile factories. The beautiful clay tiles used on the roofs and floors of the colonial homes of León and surrounding villages are made here in big wood-burning ovens utilizing the local soil. To see this centuries-old way of making bricks and tiles it is best to visit before 0900 or after 1700 when the small factories take advantage of relatively cool temperatures to put their ovens to work. The palms used for making the traditional thatched roofs (*ranchos*) are also prevalent in the surrounding countryside.

Sleeping and eating There are a couple of very basic hotels **F** *Hospedaje El Caminante*, close to highway, basic, friendly, cheap, and **F** *Hospedaje El Buen Gusto*, friendly, fairly clean, basic. The battle of La Paz Centro and Nagarote for Nicaragua's best *quesillo* is won by La Paz (personal opinion). The perpetually crowded **Quesillos Guilliguiste** is the **country's best** *quesillo* eatery for its fast cafeteria-style service, super-fresh ingredients and generous servings. It is located in the centre of the long line of *quesillo* eateries on the *carretera*. *Quesillos* are US$1, you order at the counter and watch it wrapped and filled on the spot. They are served in tiny open-ended plastic bags, which should keep at least some of the cream off your shirt.

Buses pass every 15 mins between León and Managua and some stop at Quesillos Guilliguiste for a collective feast. Direct buses from La Paz Centro to Managua leave every 30 mins, US$0.60. Buses from Managua to La Paz Centro leave from Mercado Israel Lewites (also called Mercado Boer) every 30 mins. For León Viejo (Puerto Momotombo) times see below.

León Viejo and Puerto Momotombo

Colour map 3, grid A2

Located inside the very poor, seemingly forgotten coastal village of Puerto Momotombo, León Viejo or Sitio Histórico Colonial Ruinas de León Viejo, as it is officially known, is a must for anyone interested in colonial history and archaeology. Confirming its historical significance, not just for Nicaragua but for the world, León Viejo was declared a UNESCO World Heritage Site in December 2000, the first to receive such status in Nicaragua. It is a very hot place, with lake breezes rare and humidity high.

History

León Viejo was Nicaragua's first capital, founded in the same year as Granada (1524) by **Francisco Hernández de Córdoba**. The site was selected thanks to it lakefront location and the existence there of an important Chorotega Indian settlement called **Imabite**. The town was laid out in classic colonial fashion with the cathedral facing west to a central plaza and principal avenues running

Things to do in León and El Occidente

- Climb one of the Maribios' five active volcanoes. The easiest, Cerro Negro, is also the most dangerous of the chain as it throws out rocks and lava.
- Explore the UNESCO World Heritage site of León Viejo with a guide and find out about its brutally tragic history (don't miss the view of Volcán Momotombo and Lago de Managua from the ancient fortress).
- Parque Central in León cools off in the late afternoon. Soak up the atmosphere with a large fruit juice on the terrace of the restaurant *El Sesteo*.
- Make an early start for a walking tour of León's many colonial churches before the sun chases the locals inside and the church doors close until late afternoon.
- Enjoy the crashing waves of the Nicaraguan Pacific from the beach-front patio and pool of the *Pacific Suyapa Beach Hotel* (you'll need to buy a drink or some food from the hotel restaurant).

from the park east-west and north-south. León Viejo was the kind of town where, if you had money or power, you slept with your horse saddled. The original ruler, **Pedrarias Dávila**, was by all accounts a brutal old man who came to Nicaragua when he was already in his mid-80s and proceeded to execute the country's founder Captain Hernández de Córdoba and establish the rule of force. He was to set the stage for a long history of unjust rulers, a tradition that would haunt the country almost unbroken for the next 450 years.

Sights

At first sight León Viejo is nothing more than a few old foundations, surrounded by pleasant greenery in the shadow of the imposing Volcán Momotombo. In reality, this still-unfinished excavation site is the remains of one of the most tragic and brutal European settlements, an absurd, cruel stage for one of the uglier scenes of the multi-act play of the Spanish conquest of the Americas. The city of León Viejo was destroyed in a series of earthquakes and volcanic eruptions between 1580 and 1609 and was finally abandoned for León's current site in 1610. Nicaraguans will tell you with no shadow of doubt that León Viejo's destruction was a punishment from God for the crimes committed there. The city was mostly forgotten, though it lived on in legends, including some that claimed it was located underneath Lake Managua. After 357 years of being buried in volcanic ash, excavations began in 1967. In recent years, archaeologists from the Museo Nacional have uncovered homes, a brothel, the country's first mint, the La Merced church and convent, the governor's office and the cathedral. Thanks to hyper-erosion from the 1998 Hurricane Mitch, the **Fortress of León Viejo** was also discovered and the search for funding is on to excavate this potentially most interesting structure. The mound that covers the fort is excellent for photographing the lake, Volcán Momotombo and Isla Momotombito.

In the year 2000 Nicaraguan archaeologist Ramiro García discovered the remains of Nicaragua's founder, Francisco Hernández de Córdoba, in the tomb of the ruins of La Merced church; his bones were resting peacefully next to those of his nemesis Pedrarias Dávila. Córdoba's remains were put in a small glass box and paraded around the country, accompanied by a small guard of honour in the back of a big flat-bed truck. To add to the discovery of the tombs of Córdoba and Dávila, Museo Nacional archaeologists excavated and confirmed the remains of the assassinated Antonio de Valdivieso, Bishop

León and El Occidente

of Nicaragua and defender of the Indians, in the altar tomb of the old cathedral. He lies in a very large and fairly morbid-looking casket in a special roofed exhibit near the park entrance.

■ *0800-1700 daily, entrance US$2, which includes parking and a Spanish-speaking guide, usually a native of Puerto Momotombo. The guide will show the ruins and make comments, but it is essential for the visitor to ask questions to receive the guide's true breadth of information. For more information, contact the park supervisor, Sandra Vallejo, T0886-2087, or Luvy Pichardo, T222-4820, the project director at the Museo Nacional in Managua.*

Museo Arqueológico Imabite, 1½ blocks north of the entrance to the park in a little yellow house is a tiny museum run by a very earnest and charming local woman who gives explanations of local pre-Columbian ceramics. There are also some colonial artefacts and an attempt to reconstruct life before the founding of León Viejo. ■ *Museum hours are irregular and may depend on the caretaker's other commitments.*

Sleeping & eating
F *La Posada de León Viejo*, Centro de Salud, 2 c north, T0882-4434. 3 rooms with shared bath; hotel does not have kitchen, but can arrange meals for customers. This archaeologists' hostel is located just 4 blocks from the excavation site. Across from the little yellow museum outside the park you can buy cold soft drinks in bottles.

Transport
Buses run between Puerto Momotombo and La Paz Centro every 1½ hrs, from 0400-1600, US$0.40.

Volcán Momotombo and Los Maribios volcanic chain

Colour map 3, grid A2
Altitude: 1,297 m
Momotombo translates to mean 'boiling summit' or 'he who watches over the lake', take your choice. It marks the south end of the mighty Maribios volcanic chain that runs to the very extreme northwest of the country at Volcán

León & Los Maribios volcanic chain

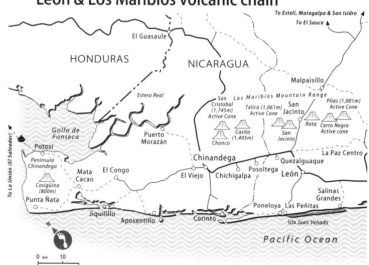

Cosigüina. In many ways a Nicaraguan national symbol, this volcano can be seen as far south as Volcán Masaya and its pleasing shape has been the inspiration for local poets and visitors for centuries. Only 500 ha of the cone is a forest reserve, but there is much nature to see in the lower elevations of the mountain and its seldom-explored lagoons. The volcano is still active, though it has only produced a lot of fumarolic steam since its last big eruption in 1905, from which a big lava flow can be seen on its eastern face. At the western base of the cone is a geothermal plant, recently sold by the government to an Israeli company which promises to increase its power output. There are two principal routes to climb the mountain, the easier of which requires permission from the power company. Check with the police in Puerto Momotombo for procedures. The northern ascent is longer and more difficult, but affords a visit to the lagoons. The forest is full of parrots, iguanas and butterflies. Above the tree line there is a two-hour climb through loose rock that must be done carefully to reach the crater. The view from the smoking summit is breathtaking, one of the most spectacular in Nicaragua. A local guide is strongly recommended and can be found in Puerto Momotombo. Camping is possible and often done just at the edge of the tree line. Puerto Momotombo also offers opportunities to hike more of the Los Maribios volcanic chain than just Volcán Momotombo. There are some beautiful 1,000-m cones northwest of Volcán Momotombo, such as **Volcán El Hoyo** and **Volcán Las Pilas**, which are protected by a 7,422-ha nature reserve of tropical dry forest. El Hoyo has a perfectly round hole in its western face that is a bit of a mystery. One of the country's most beautiful and untouched crater lakes is nearby in **Laguna de Asososca**. Camping is possible on the lakeshore. All of these hikes should be made with a local guide as many private ranches will be traversed and snakes are prevalent.

La Paz Centro to León

The *carretera* opens up after La Paz with sweeping vistas of Volcán Momotombo and cattle ranches. At Km 65 is the meeting of Carretera Nueva and Vieja, which join in a newly paved road that leads to León. The road here was washed away at every bridge by Hurricane Mitch in 1998; now all the crossings are new and the road is in excellent shape. At Km 74 is a scenic dirt track that leads through pleasant pastures to the Nicaraguan Pacific and the long wave-swept beach of **Salinas Grandes**. Past a small settlement the track drops down to pass lobster and shrimp farms before arriving at the simple beachfront with fishermen's homes. Just south of where the main road finishes is where the fisherman roll their boats out of the sea and on to the beach over logs pushed by half the village. Their catch is normally *pargo rojo* or *negro* (red or black snapper) and you can ask at the centre for someone to cook you a fresh *pargo*

If driving, note that there are often radar-enforced police speed traps on the section between the joining of the two carreteras and the city of León

León and El Occidente

for US$3. The beach is fairly littered here but is much cleaner to the north and south. About 1 km north is the mouth of a river where the locals like to swim. North of the river outlet is the clean sand of the long barrier **Isla Juan Venado**, a protected nature reserve that runs all the way to Las Peñitas (see page 198). Bus Salinas Grandes-León, 0900, 1500; León-Salinas Grandes, 0600,1200, US$0.40, 1½ hours.

The road to León ends at the city entrance marked by a sign that reads 'Centro Histórico'. To the right at the petrol station the highway bypasses León and continues to Chinandega.

León

Colour map 3, grid A2
Population: 184,792
Altitude: 109 m

A beautiful city full of intellectual vitality and artistic tradition, León is the finest example of classic colonial Spanish architecture in the country. Erstwhile capital of Nicaragua, León is full to the brim with students who come from all over the country to study in its secondary schools and universities. With more than a dozen colonial churches and Central America's largest cathedral, this fervently Catholic city stages some of Nicaragua's most beautiful religious celebrations and traditions. Despite the persistent heat of the León valley, the setting of the city is fascinating, with the ruggedly majestic Maribios volcanoes just to the east and the crashing surf of the warm Pacific Ocean not far west.

Ins and outs

Getting there
See Transport, page 197, for schedules and costs

León can be reached by regular bus service from Managua, Chinandega and less frequent routes from Estelí and Matagalpa. If arriving from Guatemala, Honduras or El Salvador via international bus, getting off at León is not a problem. Most northbound international buses will stop in León if you have reservations. *Ticabus*, T331-6153, stops at the Shell Station at the intersection of the entrance to León and the bypass highway. See Managua Transport, page 75 for routes and times and add 1½ hrs to departure time from Managua.

Getting around

León's main attractions are all within 5 blocks of the city centre with the exception of the Subtiava barrio. Parque Central in front of the massive cathedral is the main reference point. Taxis pass both the bus station and Parque Central regularly. The bus station is on the the eastern outskirts of town, a hot 15-20-min walk from the centre or a 5-min taxi ride. City buses are frequent and normally uncrowded.

Tourist office

There are 2 tourist offices. Next to Restaurante El Sesteo, on Parque Central, is a small office run by the tourism students of the **UNAN** university in León. They sell a good map of the city and other miscellaneous items and can arrange a guide for tours of the city or outlying areas, but you should give them one day's notice, US$15-25 plus food, depending on trip. The Nicaraguan Institute of Tourism, **INTUR**, has an office further from the centre, marked by a bright blue awning, Parque los Poetas, 2½ c north, T311-3682. They can give advice or brochures and have some interesting books on León and the country.

Best time to visit

León is famously hot. It is slightly drier than Managua and the rest of the Pacific Basin and daytime temperatures are normally 31-33°C with nights dipping down to 24-26°C. The exception is November-January when the sun is lower in the sky and it's slightly

León and El Occidente

cooler (April is the hottest month). The beauty of León's *Semana Santa* celebrations make the week leading up to Easter one of the best times to visit. There are endless processions and extraordinary street paintings in the barrio of Subtiava on Good Friday. During school and university holidays (July, and December until early February) the city is comparatively quiet.

History

León was founded in 1610 after its cursed original location at León Viejo had been abandoned (see page 182). A large settlement already existed in Subtiava probably of **Maribios Indians**, a distinct group from the Nicaraguas and Chorotegas who populated the rest of the Pacific Basin at the arrival of the Spaniards. The Maribios are thought to be related to the native inhabitants of California, with whom they share strong linguistic similarities. They are most famous in Nicaraguan history books for scaring the living daylights out of the Spanish and their horses by dressing in the inside-out human skin of a ceremonial victim. For 240 years León was the capital of Nicaragua until, in 1852, the Nicaraguan congress moved the capital to Managua. Unlike Granada, León was not a regular target for pirates. However, on 9 April 1685, a makeshift army of 520 British and French pirates entered what is today the port of Corinto, marched overland and descended upon the city. The French pirate **William Dampier** described the city: "the homes of León are not tall, but big and solid yes, and with gardens. They have walls of stone and tile roofs. The city has three churches and a cathedral. Our compatriot, Mr Thomas Gage, says that this place is the most pleasant in all of the Americas and so much so that he used the term, 'paradise'. The truth is it exceeds the majority of other places in the Americas in both healthiness and attractiveness." Nevertheless, the pirates set fire to the city on 14 April 1685 and retreated to the Pacific.

León produced one of the heroes of the fight for liberation from Spain, **Miguel Larreynaga**, who helped draft the original Central America constitution and can be seen on the 10 córdoba note today. In 1844 the city was invaded and conquered by the Salvadoran General Malespin, with the help of the conservative army of Granada, in a war that severely damaged the town centre. Fighting between Liberals and Conservatives was fierce in León throughout the 19th and much of the 20th century and much damage was done to the city (some of which can still be seen today). The city is still very pro Sandinista and a line of local mayoral candidates from the Sandinista party has been installed in office since the Revolution.

Sights

The Spanish government's foreign aid project has invested heavily in restoring the city and, though not as thoroughly painted and restored as Granada, León is regaining its visual glory. The simplest and richest pleasure is walking the historic streets noting the infinite variety of colonial doors, ceiling work and window irons, as well as peeping inside the big homes to see their lush interior gardens. Though damaged in 1685, 1844 and 1979, León has retained its colonial Spanish structural and design flavour much more than Granada.

The morning or late afternoon is the best time to beat the heat and find churches open

Reason enough to visit León are its many curious and beautiful churches. The city has more than a dozen, including the cathedral, Central America's

Catedral de León

León and El Occidente

1978-79 Revolution: a commemorative walk

Many people come to León after reading the funny and tragic account of the city's fight against the Somoza régime in the book Fire from the Mountain: The Making of a Sandinista by **Omar Cabezas**. There are still some signs of what happened during the war when León was the centre of heavy fighting with brutal attempts at repression by Somoza's National Guard, including bombing from the air. Revenge was taken on the Guard members after the victory.

You can visit **El Fortín**, the old fort, which was attacked by Somoza García in 1936 and then defended desperately by his son, Somoza Debayle, 43 years later at the end of the Revolution. A commemorative Sandinista march goes there each July. From the cathedral, go west about 10 blocks, then south. The fort is next to the León city garbage dump; ask the men in hammocks for permission to enter (best in early morning). There are great views of León and the Maribios volcano range from the fort.

El Veinte y Uno, the National Guard's 21st garrison, also ruined, was the scene of an important battle in April 1979. The jail around the corner has been converted into a garden with a statue to El Combatiente Desconocido (the unknown warrior), which is three blocks south of the cathedral. A statue of **Luisa Amanda Espinoza**, in Barrio San Felipe, seven to eight blocks north of the market behind the cathedral, remembers the first woman member of the Frente Sandinista de Liberación Nacional (FSLN) to die, in 1970. The women's organization AMNLAE is named after her. Across the street from the north side of the cathedral is an interesting mural covering the history from pre-Columbian times to the Sandinista Revolution, completed in 1990. It surrounds a commemorative park, the **Mausoleo Héroes y Mártires**. There are other murals scattered around León that are visible to the attentive walker.

grandest church. The Catedral of León, officially the Basílica de la Asunción, is the pride of the city and of Nicaragua. This impressive structure is the fruit of 113 years' labour, though it is not the first cathedral to stand in front of León's Parque Central. Five years after the city's founding, a simple cathedral, made of clay bricks and tiles, was consecrated by the first bishop of new León in 1615. The temple was improved by the next bishop of Nicaragua, with funds from Spain, but was burned by the pirate invasion of 1685. Another construction was built bigger still than the first two, with three altars and five chapels. This one would survive for 60 years before the construction of the current cathedral began in 1747. The size of the task and constant shortage of funds meant that the new cathedral was not not completed until 1860. The cathedral had no pews until 1877 and all masses before that date were celebrated on foot or sitting and kneeling on the floor. The Atlas figures in the central bell-tower were added in 1905.

Legend has it that the plans for the cathedrals of Lima, Peru and León were switched by mistake, but there appears to be no evidence to support that charming excuse for such a big church in such a little country. The plans were drawn by Guatemalan architect Diego de Porres, and were added to by two Franciscan friars, also Guatemalan. The style, with its squat towers and super-thick walls, has been described as Central American Baroque, but there are also Gothic and neoclassical elements. Because it was built from back (the side of the market) to front (on the plaza) over more than a century, the structure combines a variety of design influences. It is said that when the builders ran out of mortar they were forced to use turtle eggs from the nearby coast and locals will tell you that this is the reason it has survived so many earthquakes and tremors.

Inside the cathedral are many treasures of colonial art, including 18th-century paintings in gradual ruin from the accumulated years of tropical climate. A famous **shrine**, 145 cm high and covered by white topazes from India, a gift from Philip II of Spain, is kept under lock and key. The cathedral also houses a very fine **ivory Christ**, the consecrated **Altar of Sacrifices** and the **Choir of Córdoba**. The most famous image is called the *Cristo de Pedrarias*. This Gothic work representing Christ on the cross comes from the old cathedral of León Viejo and shows signs of the pirate attack of 1685 on his right foot; he is celebrated with fireworks every 2 July. Most controversial and least admired are the column statues of the **12 Apostles**. At the foot of the Apostle Paul column and guarded by a sorrowing lion is the **tomb of Rubén Darío**, Nicaragua's greatest poet and one of the greats of the Spanish language. Two of Nicaragua's other great poets are also buried in the church, **Salomón de la Selva** and **Alfonso Cortés**, whose starkly beautiful words appear above his tomb.

Other churches & notable buildings

One block west and south of Parque Central is the beautifully restored **Teatro Municipal José de la Cruz Mena**. The theatre was built in the 19th century and was the setting for many important concerts of touring groups from Europe during the early 20th century. Later it fell into oblivion and to add injury to insult was badly damaged by fire in 1956. It has now been reopened after more than 40 years of sitting in ruins. The theatre is named after León's greatest classical composer, José de la Cruz Mena (you can see a portrait of him in the *Restaurante El Sesteo*). Maestro Mena, who suffered from leprosy, was not allowed to be present at the premier of his award-winning composition *Ruinas*. Witnesses say that he sat outside on the steps of the theatre, crying with joy while listening to the interpretation of his work being played inside; leprosy would soon take his life. ∎ *Mon-Fri 0800-1230 and 1400-1700, Entrance to tour the theatre is US$0.40, also plays and dance performances from US$1-15.*

On Calle Central east of the cathedral is the **Iglesia El Calvario**, built in the mid-1700s. It was restored in 2000 and sits directly in front of a towering Momotombo Volcán backdrop. Inside are life-size sculptures of Jesus and the two men he was crucified with; the sculptures are unusual for their stark realism, a rare quality in colonial religious art. Both interior and exterior of the neoclassical church are attractive and the façade is said to show the stylistic influence of France in Spanish architecture of the 18th century.

Two blocks north of the cathedral's lions on Avenida Central is the Mexican-baroque beauty of **Iglesia La Recolección**, with a beautiful façade that tells the entire story of the passion of Christ. It was built in 1786 and has a neoclassical interior with lovely mahogany woodwork. Two blocks north and one block east of La Recolección is the simple yet handsome **Iglesia San Juan Bautista**, which sits on the east side of the Parque San Juan, otherwise known as the *parquecito*. The church dates from 1739 although it was remodelled in the following century. Three blocks west and two blocks north, the **Iglesia San Felipe** was built at the end of the 16th century for the religious services of the black and mulatto population of the city. It was rebuilt in the 18th century in a manner true to its original form, a mixture of baroque and neoclassical.

Two blocks north of Parque Central is the lovely **Iglesia La Merced**. This is León's second most important temple and it holds the patron saint of León, the **Virgen de las Mercedes**. The first La Merced church was founded in León Viejo in 1528 and was recently excavated and found to contain the remains of the country's founder and also its first governor (see León Viejo above). The replacement church in León was founded in 1615 before being burnt down

León and El Occidente

during the pirate raid of 1685. It was rebuilt on two occasions, having suffered earthquake damage, and then, in the early 19th century, there was a fire in the main altar that holds the patron saint of León. Legend has it that the Virgin was saved by a black slave who rushed into the flames, broke the glass case with his bare hands, and ran out of the church with the Virgen in his bloody arms; in gratitude he was granted his freedom. The burnt altar was replaced by the marble one that is seen today. The interior, perhaps the most ornately beautiful in Nicaragua, has much fine woodwork and delicately sculpted altars. It is said to be the most representative of León's 18th-century churches. The exterior was restored in 1999, but funds ran short of a paint job. Next door is Nicaragua's first university, the **Universidad Nacional Autónoma de Nicaragua**

León

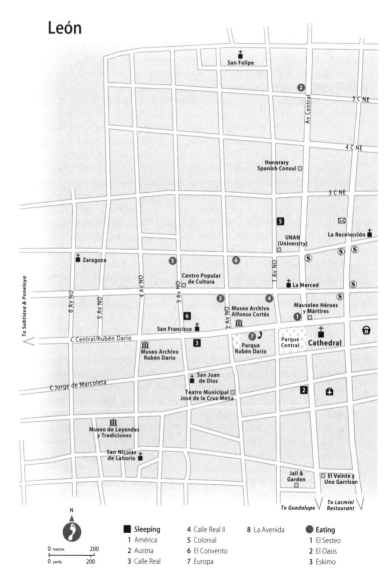

León and El Occidente

Sleeping			Eating
1 América	4 Calle Real II	8 La Avenida	1 El Sesteo
2 Austria	5 Colonial		2 El Oasis
3 Calle Real	6 El Convento		3 Eskimo
	7 Europa		

N

0 metres   200
0 yards   200

(**UNAN**). This fine yellow and white building holds the library and dean's office although there are many less attractive buildings nearby and on the out-skirts of the city.

One-and-a-half blocks north from the little park next to La Merced is the **Centro Popular de Cultura**, which has frequent exhibitions and events, and is the only place in León to see live folk concerts (see schedule on bulletin board in front lobby). Two blocks west of Parque Central is the **Convento y Iglesia San Francisco**. The church was damaged in 1979 during fighting in the Revolution but maintains much of its ancient charm. It was the city's first convent when founded in 1639. The pillars of the temple and two of its altars (the Sangre de Cristo and San Antonio de Padua) remain from the original

building. The façade has been modified greatly over the years, but on the south face of the church you can see the original structure. Many little model wooden homes were attached to one of the Virgin Mary altars to ask for protection from the destructive Hurricane Mitch in 1998. In 1830, after the expulsion of the Franciscans from Nicaragua, the **Convent** was used by various civic organizations; part of it is now a gallery while the rest has been converted into a new hotel called *El Convento* (see Sleeping below). Three streets west and two north is the stone-block **Iglesia de Zaragoza**, which was built between 1884 and 1934 and has two unusual octagonal turrets and an arched door-way with tower above. It resembles a fortress more than a church and is unattractive inside. Three blocks south and one west from the Iglesia San Francisco, the **Iglesia de San Nicolás de Laborio**, founded in 1618 for the local Indian population, is the most modest of the churches in León. It is constructed of wood and tiles over adobe walls with a simple façade and a simple altar, 10 m high. The interior is dark, cool and charming, with the feel of a countryside village parish more than a city church. The local padre is friendly and willing to chat. If the church is closed you can knock on the little door at the back of the north side. The celebration for San Nicolás is 10 September.

The beautiful **Iglesia Parroquial de San Juan Bautista** in **Subtiava** was built on top of the first church founded by missionaries in 1530.

4 Hong Kong
5 La Casa Vieja
6 Rinconcito Flor
   de Sacuanjoche

● **Bars & clubs**
7 Ruinas

León and El Occidente

Rubén Darío – the Prince of Spanish letters

The great Chilean poet Pablo Neruda called him "one of the most creative poets in the Spanish language" and, together with the immortal Spanish poet Federico García Lorca, he paid tribute to Rubén Darío in Buenos Aires in 1933. In front of more than 100 Argentinian writers, Lorca and Neruda delivered the tribute to the poet "then and forever unequalled".

Darío is without a doubt the most famous Nicaraguan, he is one of the greatest poets in the history of the Spanish language and the country's supreme hero. Born Felix Rubén García Sarmiento, in Metapa, Nicaragua, in 1867, Rubén Darío was raised in León and had learnt to read by the age of four. By the time he was 10, little Rubén had read Don Quixote, the Bible, 1001 Arabian Nights *and the works of Cicero. When he was 11 he studied in depth the Latin classics with Jesuits at the school of La Iglesia de La Recolección, and*

in 1879, at the age of 12, his first verses were published in the León daily newspaper El Termómetro. *Two years later he was preparing his first book. Later, he became the founder of the Modernist Movement in poetry, which later crossed the Atlantic and became popular in Spain. His most noted work,* Azul, *revolutionized American literature, establishing a new mode of poetic expression with innovations in form and content.*

As well as a poet, Darío was a diplomat and a journalist. He wrote for numerous publications from Argentina, the United States, Spain and France. In 1916 he returned to the city of León, Nicaragua, and, despite several attempts at surgery, he died of cirrhosis on the night of 6 February. After seven days of tributes he was buried in the Cathedral of León. Darío gave Nicaraguan poetry a worldwide projection and solidified it in Nicaragua as a national passion.

The new church was finished in 1703. Bartolomé de las Casas, the Apostle of the Indians, preached here on several occasions and the featureless plaza in front of the church was baptized in his name in 1923. The church is one of the most authentic representations of Nicaraguan baroque and is famous, among other things, for the Indian influences of its ceiling; thankfully it has survived the battles of the years intact. The colonial altar was donated by the king of Spain and brought to Subtiava in pieces. There is an interesting representation of the sun carved in wood on the ceiling of the central nave. San Juan Bautista de Subtiava was declared a national monument in 1944 and the church was restored in 1992, without intentional irony, for the 500-year anniversary of the first arrival of Columbus to the Americas. On the west side of the **Plaza de Bartolomé de las Casas** are the traces of what was the palace of the great leader of the people of Subtiava, **Chief Adiac**, who, according to local lore, was hanged on the nearby tamarind tree by a Spanish captain (the tree is still growing there today; ask a local to show you). Inside the **Parroquial de San Juan** you can see the **Cristo de la Iglesia de Veracruz**, which was rescued from the ruins of the church of the same name, destroyed in the Salvadoran attack of 1845. The ruins of the church lie behind a chain-link fence just west of the plaza. Three blocks east of the Parroquial de San Juan is the **Ermita de San Pedro**. Built in 1706 on top of an older structure, this is a fine example of primitive baroque design popular in the 17th century. The adobe and red tile roof temple was refurbished in 1986.

Alfonso Cortés – the insanity of genius

None of Nicaragua's great poets can match the striking simplicity of the great metaphysical poet Alfonso Cortés, who spent most of his life in chains, but who, in an impossibly microscopic script, wrote some of the most beautiful poems the Spanish language has ever seen.

Alfonso Cortés was born in León in 1893. He lived in the very same house that had belonged to Rubén Darío and today is the Museo-Archivo Rubén Darío. It was in this house that Cortés went mad one February night in 1927. He spent the next 42 years in captivity, tormented most of the time but, for the good fortune of Nicaragua, with lucid moments of brilliant productivity. Cortés was kept chained to one of the house's colonial window grilles and it was from that vantage point that he composed what poet-priest Ernesto Cardenal called the most beautiful poem in the Spanish language, La Ventana *(The Window).*

Later, at the age of 34, Alfonso Cortés was committed to a mental institution in Managua, where he was to live out the rest of his life. In these incredibly adverse conditions, Cortés produced a number of great poetic works, most of which were published with the help of his father. When he was not writing he was tied to his bed, accompanied only by his guitar hung on the wall and a small north-facing window.

According to Cardenal, the poet spoke slowly while shaking and stuttering, his face changing from thrilled to horrified then falling totally expressionless. He used to say "I am less important than Rubén Darío, but I am more profound". Like Darío, Alfonso Cortés died in the month of February, but 53 years later, in 1969. Today, just a couple of metres separates these two great Nicaraguan poets who are both buried in the Cathedral of León.

The most widely visited museum is the former house of national hero Rubén Darío. Founded in 1964, the **Museo Archivo Rubén Darío** is located one block west of the Iglesia San Francisco on the Calle Central. It has an interesting collection of personal possessions, photographs, portraits and a library with a wide range of books of poetry in Spanish, English and French. Alfonso Cortés, the great metaphysical poet, lost his mind in this house and was said to have been chained to the bars that are next to Darío's bed. Cortés died here in 1969 and was buried near to Darío's tomb in the cathedral. ■ *Tue-Sat 0900-1200, 1400-1700, Sun 0900-1200, entry and guided tour free but donations appreciated.*

Museums
All information in the museums is in Spanish

Cortés has his own museum across from the small Parque Rubén Darío on Calle Central. The **Museo Archivo Alfonso Cortés** has dusty little displays containing the great poet's manuscripts, photographs and other personal objects. ■ *Mon-Sat 0800-1200 and 1400-1700, donations appreciated.* Three blocks south and ½ block west of Parque Central on Avenida Central is the **Museo de Leyendas y Tradiciones**. This project of Doña Carmen Toruño is a physical demonstration of some of the many legends that populate the bedtime stories of Nicaraguan children. León is particularly rich in legends and Doña Carmen has handcrafted life-size models of the characters of these stories to help bring them to life. Most impressive of the displays is the *Carreta Nahua* or *Nagua* ('haunted oxcart'), a story that has kept many a child shivering in his sheets. One block north of the Parroquial de San Juan Bautista de Subtiava is the little **Museo Adiac**, which is marked by a colourful mural on Calle Central. This is the indigenous community's own museum and the only example of its kind in Nicaragua of the indigenous people protecting their patrimony in their own museum. The tiny rooms are packed full of statues and ceramics from the surrounding area and the museum is named after the great Indian chief who was said to have been hanged after challenging the local Spanish authority. ■ *Mon-Fri 0800-1200 and 1400-1700, Sat 0800-1200, donation greatly appreciated. T311-5371.*

Museo de Arte Fundación Ortiz-Gurdián, across from the Iglesia San Francisco, is a lovely colonial home that doubles as an art museum with works from Europe, Nicaragua and the rest of Latin America. The visit is worthwhile for the building alone. Most of the European works are of little consequence but there are some interesting Latin American and Nicaraguan pieces. ■ *Mon-Fri 1100-1900, US$1.*

The foremost expert on Nicaragua's insect life and in particular its amazing array of butterflies shares his collection with the public at the **Museo Entomológico**, across from the *Farmacia Fraternidad.* ■ *T311-6586, by appointment only.*

Essentials

Sleeping

■ on map, page 190
for price codes see
inside front cover

L-AL *Hotel El Convento*, connected to Iglesia San Francisco, T311-7053, F311-7067, www.hotelconvento.com.ni A/c, private bath with hot water, cable TV, beautiful colonial design, decorated by antiques with a lovely interior garden, moderate priced restaurant, peaceful and elegant, Nicaragua's most charming colonial hotel and León's best. Recommended.

B *Hotel Austria*, from cathedral, 1 c south, ½ west, T311-1206, F311-1368, www.hotelaustira.com.ni Central, often fully booked, hot water, a/c, cable TV, ultra-clean, secure parking, internet rental, breakfast US$3. Recommended. **B** *Hotel Colonial*, 2½ blocks north of Parque Central, T311-2279, F311-3125. Pleasant, fine old building and patio, small, very dark rooms and in need of refurbishment, a/c, **C** with fan, bath (**D** with shared bath). Good views from upstairs, front rooms with balcony can be noisy from disco opposite at weekends, not good value, restaurant, breakfast US$3, other meals US$4. **B** *Hotel Europa*, 3 c NE, 4 Av, 2 blocks south of railway station, T3116040, F3112577. With bath and a/c, **D** with fan, cold water, brusque service, comfortable patios with bar and shade, coffee available, restaurant expensive, limited parking inside, guard will watch vehicles parked on street. **B** *Grand Hotel*, from bus terminal ½ block south, T311-1327. With bath, a/c, clean, safe parking, breakfast US$4, other meals US$5, book ahead, often full.

D *Hotel América*, Av Santiago Argüello, 2 blocks east of cathedral. With bath and fan, clean, good value, nice patio, a bit run down, friendly, nice garden, breakfast US$2, other meals US$3, cold drinks, convenient location, secure garage nearby. **D** *La Avenida*, near Mercado San Juan, T311-2068, **F** without bath, family run, fan, cable TV, good food US$1-2, friendly, laundry facilities, popular. **D** *La Primavera*, on exit road to Chinandega, T311-4216. With bath and a/c, **E** with fan, helpful and friendly, secure parking, breakfast US$1.50, other meals US$3. **E** *California*, with bath, across from the bus station and new market, friendly, family run, with nice patio, purified water and TV. Recommended.

F *La Posada del Doctor*, 20 m west of Parque San Juan, T311-4343, F311-5986. Shared bath, fan, clean, some rooms with bunks, good value, very nice. **F** *Hotelito Calle Real*, Parque Rubén Darío 25 m west, T311-1120. With bath and fan, has comedor. **F** *Hotelito Calle Real II*, 2 Av SE, ½ block north of C Rubén Darío, T311-2510. Is a response to the

Festivals in León

León has is famous across the country for its religious festivals, particularly **Semana Santa**, which starts a week before Easter on **Domingo de Ramos** (Palm Sunday). The cathedral has a procession every day of the week and the parish church of Subtiava has many events. A programme of processions and events can be obtained from the Nicaraguan Institute of Tourism, INTUR. The most spectacular of all are the sawdust street paintings made on **Viernes Santo** (Good Friday) in Subtiava. A couple of blocks of Subtiava are closed off for the day. Around 1100 you can see the artists framing their sawdust canvas and soaking it in water. Later in the afternoon, damp, dyed sawdust is used to make religious paintings, which serve as carpets for the **Santo Entierro** (the funeral procession of the crucified Christ). These short-lived masterpieces are then trampled and totally destroyed by the procession. Unlike the more famous street paintings of Antigua, Guatemala, no moulds are used in Subtiava; they are created completely freehand (some are mediocre, but others are astounding in their detail and scope). After 1600 many of the paintings are complete and a walk up and down these neighbourhood streets is unforgettable. (Miniature solidified wall paintings of the sawdust art can be found year-round in a gallery along the same street. **La Ronda Small Gallery**, Texaco Guido, 2 c south, ½ east, T311-2980, fquesadamoran@latinmail.com) Including Subtiava, there are 15 different churches, each having its own Good Friday processions.

The other most famous religious ceremonies are on 7 December for **La Purísima** (the Virgin Mary's conception of Jesus). Like Semana Santa, these are celebrated throughout the country, but once again León's ceremonies are the country's most famous. Altars are built in front of private residences and outside churches during 7 December, and that afternoon at 1800 a massive outburst of fireworks opens the **Gritería**, a roaming mass of mostly women and children who visit every makeshift altar to sing songs to the Virgin. In return, they receive small gifts like sugarcane, oranges or more modern snacks. The next day is a holiday and everything is closed. There is also a **Gritería Chiquita** (14 August) that was instituted in 1947 to protect León during a violent eruption of the nearby Volcán Cerro Negro.

In February there are celebrations for the birthday of **Rubén Darío** and the patron saint of León, **La Virgen de las Mercedes**, is celebrated on 24 September. **Santa Lucía** is celebrated most of December in Subtiava with the focal point being 13 December on the plaza in front of the parish church.

Fireworks are an important part of all celebrations in Nicaragua, which are invariably fun and often life-threatening, with rocket launchers flying horizontally into thick crowds and firecrackers set off left and right on the streets.

The **Nicaraguan Institute of Tourism (INTUR)** also sponsors a plaza party every Saturday night which can be fun. As with the INTUR parties in Masaya (Thursday) and Granada (Friday), quality of the performers varies greatly, but it is a good time to find the park full of life.

León and El Occidente

shortage of beds, basic rooms without fan and shared bathroom. **F Yenín**, Av Cdte Pedro Aráuz. Pleasant, garden, good value.

Eating

El Sesteo, next to cathedral, on Parque Central. Renovated, mid-range, excellent food and service. This is the best place to watch León walk by. Try the cerdo asado (grilled pork), also with good fruit juices and a great cacao con leche. **Pizza Caliente**, from Parque Central 1 c east, open 1300-2200 daily, has reasonably good pizza if you order a

● on map, page 190

new one, but not very fresh by the slice, slow service. *Café Taquezal*, across from the Museo Rubén Darío, serves salads, vegetarian dishes, bohemian décor, one of the few places serving cappuccinos to be found in León. Recommended. *Pollos Brosteados*, south side of Iglesia La Recolección, T311-4482, daily 0900-2100, good chicken. *La Casa Vieja*, 1½ blocks north of Iglesia San Francisco. Pleasant bar, good-quality snacks, good value. Highly recommended. *Payita's*, across from Parque La Merced, T311-5857. Daily 1000-0200, fast food, cheap and mediocre, fun crowd. *El Barcito*, northwest of Parque Central. Popular, soft drinks, milk shakes, slow service. *El Oasis*, Calle 5 and Av Central. Good value, limited menu, popular. *Central*, Calle 4 Norte. Good *comida corriente*. *Comedor Las Paiz*, behind the market. Good lunch buffet, includes 1 litre of fruit juice for 20 córdobas. *Rinconcito Flor de Sacuanjoche*, Calle 2 Norte near Central University. Vegetarian meals, meat dishes, lunch and breakfast, good. *Lacmiel*, 5 blocks south of cathedral, T311-4992. Daily 1000-2400, good food, live music, open air. Recommended. *El Rincón Azul*, C Central Rubén Darío, about 1½ blocks west of Parque Central. An excellent bar, very cheap, also a local art gallery, open 1500-2400. Recommended. *Casa Popular de Cultura*, 1 block north of Plaza Central, 2½ blocks west. Sandwiches and burgers, nice atmosphere, find out what's going on. *Hong Kong*, Calle 1 Norte, ½ block north of Parque, T311-6572. Popular with locals, but pretty bad. *Eskimo*, good ice cream parlour, C Rubén Darío at the back of San Francisco. *Los Pescaditos*, Subtiava parish church, 1 c south, 1 c west, T311-2684. Daily 1130-2230, excellent for fish at reasonable prices. Recommended. Also in Subtiava, *Las Caperas,* Colegio Calazans, 2 c south, T311-4163. Daily 100-2200, good Nicaraguan food, try shrimp soup or fish, inexpensive. On the bypass road *Caña Brava*, T311-5666. Daily 1100-2200, for many, the best food in León, *pollo deshuesado* (boneless chicken) with many excellent beef dishes. *Montezerino*, Km 92 on the bypass highway, T311-2638. Outdoor, good meat and fish, try sea bass (*curvina*), pleasant setting.

Bars & clubs

Don Señor, across from Parque La Merced, T311-1212. Wed-Sun after 2000, snacks and drinks, karaoke Wed and Fri (silly and good fun). *Luna*, La Merced, 1 c north, T311-5717. Varied music, dancing, Sat and Sun only from 2000. *Las Ruinas*, next to Parque Rubén Darío, T311-4767. Dinner and dancing in half-ruined building, very loud and fun, Thu-Sun after 1900. *El Balcón Sports Bar*, in front of Iglesia El Calvario, T0885-4634. Daily 1200-1300, cool place in a great setting, draft beer and cocktails, with buffalo wings, sandwiches.

Discoteca Dilectus, at south entrance to city, T311-5439. Elegant crowd, a/c, parking, US$5 entrance, drinks and food expensive, Mon-Sat 2000-0200, Thu *mariachis*, Fri youth night. *Discoteca Nueva Túnel*, at exit to Carretera a Chinandega, T311-2515. Wed-Sun 2000-0200, US$2 cover.

Cinemas

There are 2 cinemas in León. One is tired, but charming and spacious at the southwestern corner of Parque Central. The other, a new complex next to the *La Unión* supermarket, has more compact theatres. All show North American movies with Spanish subtitles. Entrance US$2.50.

Shopping

The best market is in the pale green building behind the cathedral which sells meat, fruit and veg inside, and all the shoes, fans and stereos in the street stalls outside. The inside market is very clean and a good place to find out what tropical fruits are in season. There are other markets near the Iglesia San Juan, and at the bus terminal, which are dirtier and hotter, the way some people prefer it. León is not a very good place to look for crafts. The INTUR party every Saturday night has some stalls with jewellery and other crafts, or you can try *Casa de Cultura Antenor Sandino Hernández*, Parque La Merced, 1½ c west, T311-2116, open daily from 0800.

The best thing to shop for is León's **traditional foods**. The simply named *cosa de horno* (oven thing) is a tasty kind of cornbread with cheese. You can try a fresh baked *cosa de horno* of *Teresa Sánchez*, Texaco Guido, 1½ c south. *Picos* are another special-ity. These triangular pastries filled with bitter cheese, sugar and cinnamon are a very good (and addictive) road food; to get a *pico* hot off the press, try the *Las Salamancas* bakery, Iglesia San Juan 1½ c south. For some traditional León cookies the best bet is *Galletas Leonesas*, Texaco Guadalupe, 2 ½ c east. If you are lucky enough to be in León for the Purísima celebrations in December you can buy the *Dulce de Purísima*, a sweet that is made only at this time of year. You only have to go and knock on the door of *Teresa Altamirano*, Iglesia Laborio, 1 c al sur, 30 m east, or at the home of *Rosa Guido*, Texaco Guido, 2 c north. Any time of year you can find a sugar fix at the *Casa Prío*, Teatro González, 1 c west, where they make a mean *leche burra* (donkey milk), which is small black candy, a lethally good mix of dark molasses and milk.

Bookshops *Libro Centro Don Quijote*, next to *Hotelito Calle Real*, has new and sec-ond-hand books, a few bad ones in English and the owner is very helpful and knowl-edgeable about León. **Photography** *Kodak* is across from the Parque Rubén Darío. **Supermarkets** There is a *La Unión* supermarket 1 block north and 2 blocks east of the cathedral that has all you could need and more.

Sports

The León **baseball** team won the national championship in a dramatic series against Managua in 2001. The stadium is in the far northern part of León. There are **basketball** courts just 1 block north from Parque Central. The Nicaraguan **bullfight/rodeo** (see Essentials box, page 41), happens in Dec in the plaza of Subtiava for the Santa Lucía festival.

Transport

León-Managua, every 30 mins, 0425-2000, US$1.50, 1½ hrs **León-Chinandega**, every 11 mins, 0500-1800, US$1, 1 hr 45 mins. **León-Corinto**, every 30 mins, 0500-1800, US$1, 2 hrs. **León-Chichigalpa**, every 11 mins, US$0400-1800, US$0.75, 1 hr. **León-Estelí**, 0500, 1500, US$2.25, 3 hrs. **León-Matagalpa**, 0500,1500, US$2.25, 3 hrs. **León-San Isidro**, every 30 mins, 0420-1730, US$1.50, 2½ hrs. **León-El Sauce**, every hour, 0800-1600, US$1.50, 2½ hrs. **León-El Guasaule**, 0500, US$2, 2½ hrs. **León-Salinas Grandes**, 0600,1200, US$0.40, 1½ hr.

Bus
The bus terminal is in the far eastern part of town, a long walk or short taxi ride from the centre

There are many taxis in the centre, at the bus terminal and on the bypass road. Average fare is between US$0.40-1.30. Taxis can also be hired to visit Poneloya beach and the fumaroles at San Jacinto (see Excursions below). Rates for longer trips vary greatly, with a trip to San Jacinto normally costing US$10-15 plus US$1 for every 15 mins of waiting or a higher flat rate for the taxi to wait as long as you wish. Trips outside must be nego-tiated in advance. If staying in a **C** level or above hotel ask the front desk to help with the price negotiation and it should be less. One expensive and reliable option is the taxi with a/c of Raúl Bermúdez who is on call 24 hrs a day on T0777-7940.

Taxis

Directory

Banks There are many banks on the 2 roads that lead from the front and back of the cathedral to the north. Next to the La Unión Supermarket is *BAC* (*Banco de América Central*) for travellers' cheques of any kind and credit card advances; across from the police station is *BDF* for American Express only. Cash can be changed with the coyotes 1 block north of the back of the cathedral or at any bank.

Communications Internet: *Hotel Austria*, from cathedral, 1 c south, ½ west, T311-1206, US$5 per hour. **Post office**: *Correos de Nicaragua* is across from Iglesia La Recolección, T311-2102, F311-5700. **Telephone**: *Enitel* is on Parque Central at the west side, T311-7377. Also at bus terminal.

Embassies & consulates España, María Mercedes de Escudero, Av Central #405, T311-4376, F311-2042.

Medical services Hospital: 1 block south of the cathedral, T311-6990. **Laboratories**: Clínico Galo, Dr Elia Diuna Galo García, Teatro Municipal, 75 m east, T311-0437.

Useful numbers Fire: T311-2323. **Police**: T311-3137. **Red Cross**: T311-2627.

Excursions from León

Poneloya and Las Peñitas beaches

Colour map 3, grid B1   The crashing surf of the Nicaraguan Pacific lies only 21 km from León down a bumpy country road. A visit during the week means you have most of the beach to yourself with just a few fishermen to chat to. The exception is Semana Santa when the entire coast turns into the biggest party of the year. Poneloya, the more popular of the two beaches, lies to the north of Las Peñitas, which tends to be a little cleaner and less crowded. Las Peñitas also has the best hotel and restaurant on the coast as, well as access to the nature reserve of Isla Juan Venado (see below). Both beach towns are passed by a single road lined with a mixture of local houses and luxury holiday homes for the wealthy of León. The locals are very friendly and helpful. The beaches themselves are attractive, with wide swathes of sand, warm water and pelicans. Swimming at either beach must be done with extreme caution; the currents are deceptively strong and foreigners die here every year. A good rule is to stay within your depth. Both beaches have inlets, which is where most of the locals swim; the one in Poneloya is at the far north of the beach and in Las Peñitas at the far south. Before you reach the towns there is a store called *Licorería Estela de los Mares* where you can rent four-wheel motorbikes for US$10 per hour; you'll need to show a driver's licence, sign a release form and pay a US$10 deposit. Just past the *Estela de los Mares* the road forks: to the left is Las Peñitas and to the right Poneloya. ■ *US$1 entrance fee if you come by car at the weekend or during the holidays.*

Sleeping   At the entrance to **Poneloya** is the beautiful old wooden building of *Restaurante*
& eating   *Pariente Salinas*, best at weekends when the food is fresher. Also near the entrance is the only decent lodging in Poneloya, **C** *La Posada de Poneloya*, T311-4612. 12 rooms, private bath, a/c, laundry, bar and restaurant, not ideal setting. *La Peña del Tigre*, good restaurant down the road, huge portions (great *repochetas*), friendly, open-air, good

views – it is near a tall rock on the beach where bathing is dangerous and prohibited.

A nice location and building located on the beach side are the trade off at **E** *Hotel Lacayo*, dirty rooms, very basic, meals, bats in the roof and fleas in the beds. At the far north part of Poneloya you can rent a shaded spot above the inlet or eat the fish cooked by women in the little *casitas* there. Otherwise, head for one of the many cheap restaurants there such as **Comedor Margarita** or **Bar y Restuarante Bella Vista**. All of them serve fresh *pargo* or *curvina* (snapper or sea bass) or chicken.

Nicer, though with fewer people to watch is sleeping and eating in **Las Peñitas**. More popular every year is the lovely thatched roof restaurant at the **C** *Suyapa Beach Hotel*, T088-5834, F311-6257. The best hotel on the coast here, private bath with a/c, **D** with fan. Ask for room with ocean view and nice breeze upstairs, very clean, swimming pool that is empty, except for Semana Santa, and outdoor beach shower, group discounts. Many come to use the shade of the restaurant as a base for the beach. You will have to eat something, but there is no more beautiful spot in either town and you have a bathroom, shade and a fabulous view. The moderately priced restaurant has very good fried *pargo* and other typical dishes. Great sunsets from the rock jetty in front of the hotel. There are numerous other small eateries before you reach the *Hotel Suyapa* that cost less and allow you to hog the shade. At the end of the road going south is a small inlet and across the bay is the lovely Isla Juan Venado.

Buses and trucks for Poneloya and Las Peñitas leave from the terminal in Subtiava, every 2 hrs, US$0.50, 45 mins. Service can be irregular so check to see when last bus will return. There are more buses on weekends. **Taxi** to beach is US$8-12 to drop off; more if he will wait.   **Transport**

Reserva Natural Isla Juan Venado

This nature reserve is a turtle-nesting site with mangroves, crabs, iguanas and a healthy aquatic bird life. The island is very close to the mainland, is 22 km long and between 25 m and 600 m wide. It is possible to walk the beach and swim across to Salinas Grandes (see page 185) and take a bus out to the Carretera a León. It is also possible to camp on the island but the mosquitoes are vicious. To check out the entire canal that runs behind the island you should allow about four hours in boat, costing US$50-60. A short trip will run at about US$20. Early morning or late afternoon are the best times to see the reserve, but this is when the fishermen are out working and it may be difficult to find a boat. Try the fisherman who goes by the name of *Toño Ñanga* (legal name Antonio González) who lives just 20 m east of the *Bar Comedor El Calamar* in front of an old washed-away pier.   *Colour map 3, grid B1*
Area: 4,600 ha
Altitude: 0-25 m

Volcán Cerro Negro

This fierce little volcano is the newest in the western hemisphere and the most violent of the marvellous Maribios range. In 1850 what was a flat cornfield came to life and in the short period since has grown some 400 m, with persistently violent eruptions shooting magma and ashes up to 8,000 m in the air. Its most recent eruptions in 1968, 1971, 1992, 1995 and in August of 1999 have coated León in black ash and put on a spectacular night-time display of fire. The 1999 eruption created three new baby craters at its southern base that are smoking quietly, otherwise the short, squat mountain sits quiet until its next hail of rocks, lava and ash.   *Colour map 3, grid A2*
Altitude: 450 m

As its name suggests Cerro Negro is jet-black, made up of black gravel, solidified black lava flows and massive black sand dunes. Hiking on the cone is

León and El Occidente

a surreal experience and quite tiring, for the base is nothing but a giant black sandbox. On the northern skirts of the cone is a strange forest growing in the volcano's seemingly sterile black sand that is full of lizards, birds and flowering trees. This is the only volcano of its kind in Nicaragua and, depending on the route taken, you can choose between a very accessible four-wheel drive, arrive, hike and leave, to a hot day-long excursion. With a four-wheel drive it is possible to reach the southwestern face and the micro-craters on a good earth road that begins on the bypass highway and is marked by a sign **La Ceiba**. Follow the main path and stop regularly to make sure you are on the correct route as there are many detours. There is a physically tiring, but rewarding hike from the dusty and sad little village of **Rota** through ranches, farms and the black sand forest to the north side of the cone. From there you can continue across to the access road and to León. A guide is recommended and can be found in Rota or Malpaisillo. Trucks run from the entrance of the dirt road (at the bypass road) to Rota a few times a day, or you can take an early bus towards San Isidro (for schedule, see page 197), get off at Malpaisillo and walk to Rota and the volcano.

North from León

From León the Carretera a Chinandega runs north along the western slope of the Maribios range. There is a paved highway that connects the Pacific Basin with the northern mountains at Km 101. This scenic road slices in between the range and up to the Carretera Panamericana at San Isidro. After passing the small volcanic cone of the dormant **San Jacinto** (also called **Santa Clara**) is the settlement built in front of active fumarolic fields at Km 115.

San Jacinto

Colour map 3, grid A2

Please respect the privacy of the people who live next to the fumaroles

An interesting place for volcano lovers, this small village lives with amazing volcanic activity in its own backyard. There is one semi-paved entrance to the town at the Pepsi sign. From there you head due north to an arch that marks the entrance to the fumaroles. Known popularly as **Los Hervideros de San Jacinto**, they are the result of the water table leaking onto a magma vein of the nearby Volcán Telica. The water is heated and rushes to the surface with a heavy dose of sulphuric gases; dry gases escape too in what is an ever-changing landscape. Local children greet visitors and offer to act as guide. Choose one and heed instructions as to where it is safe to walk. As a rule it is best to avoid walking on the crystallized white sulphur and to listen for hissing. Increased caution is required after rains, when the ground is particularly soft and prone to collapse. According to a local legend, a horse once fell into one of the boiling mud pools and was melted at once. Dogs can sometimes be seen floating the pools, intact, but burnt to death. Several new micro-craters have opened up in 2001 and are miniature models for the big volcanoes of the range. There are women at the site who sell imitation pre-Columbian ceramic. Buying one of these pieces will help feed local families. A new, very cute, red brick and clay tile lookout restaurant has been built just south of the fumaroles by the mayor's office and should be open soon. It is possible to climb Volcán San Jacinto from here; it is about two hours up and 1½ hours down. Ask the local women to recommend a guide; there are many who can make the climb. At the entrance is the *Restaurante El Rancho*, pretty bad, greasy food, but very cheap and with cold fruit juices and beer.

The **León-San Isidro** buses run every 30 minutes, 0420-1730 or take any **Malpaisillo** or El Sauce bus.

El Sauce

The Carretera a San Isidro continues into the rocky savannah of Malpaisillo. At Km 150 is the partially paved road to the charming highland village of El Sauce. The road is being laid with interlocking pavers taken from Managua's University Avenue. Every year in Managua the students demonstrate to make sure their institutions receive the legally allotted 6% of the national budget. All during the 1990s they ripped up the interlocking pavers to use as barricades, imitating the revolutionary practice of the Sandinista rebels. The University Avenue pavers have now been exiled to this rural highway. The highway passes through pleasant scenery for 28 km to El Sauce, a classic colonial Nicaraguan ranching village, set in a small highland valley. Most of the year not one outsider passes through El Sauce, but every January it comes alive to celebrate **El Señor de Esquipulas**, the black Christ image that was responsible for numerous miracles. One of many is the story of the 18-year-old bride who was being wed in the church of El Sauce around 100 years ago. As she was about to finish her vows she looked above the altar to the Señor de Esquipulas and asked him for the truth. Should she marry, give up her virginity and live a carnal life? Or should she serve God in heaven? She prayed to the Black Christ, asking him for a sign. As the church sat silent waiting for her to say 'I do', she fell to the ground, dying on the steps of the altar. Her virgin death was a sure sign to the people that she was a saint and she is still remembered today with special ceremonies. Celebrations for El Señor de Esquipulas or El Cristo Negro (Black Christ) last over a week, but the principal day is **18 January**, when people congregate in El Sauce on the culmination of a pilgrimage from as far away as Guatemala. Sadly the sublimely beautiful church of El Sauce, built in 1594, was damaged in two fires, the first in 1997 and the second in December of 1999. As local fire fighters battled the 1999 blaze, back-up fire engines were sent for from León, some three hours away, while the church and its colonial relics burned. The walls and façade are still intact, but the search is on for funding to complete the new roof, which currently only covers the back part of the altar. You might sneak into the eerie closed church via an unlocked door next to the aggressive old woman who sells religious souvenirs. The original colonial icon of the Black Christ is being kept in a safe box until the new church roof is complete. There is a small chapel next to the church that houses a poor imitation. There's a donation box for a new church roof in the chapel.

Colour map 3, grid A2
Population: 29,330
Altitude: 163 m

Sleeping & eating

G *Bar y Hospedaje El Viajero*, T319-2325, private bath, fan, clean, friendly, great value. Lunch and dinner on wood tables US$1.50, breakfast US$0.80.

Transport

Bus *El Sauce-León*, every 2 hrs, 0800-1600, US$1.40, 2½ hrs. **El Sauce-Estelí**, 1300, US$1.25, 3 hrs. **El Sauce-Managua**, 0530, US$4, 4 hrs.

Mountain pass highway from El Sauce to Estelí

One of the most beautiful drives in Nicaragua is the dirt and rock highway from El Sauce to Estelí. It can be done slowly and carefully in an ordinary car during the dry season, or year-round in a four-wheel drive. The road passes pretty pastureland, pine trees, tropical dry forest and laid-back mountain cowboys. It climbs and twists up mountains with breathtaking views in all

León and El Occidente

directions. The road, which is alright for the first 20 km (inside the district of El Sauce) becomes a bit rougher over the next 20 km (maintained by Estelí). The entrance to Estelí is via one of its dirtiest and poorest barrios, quite a let-down after the mountain beauty of this great road. This road can also be used as an alternative route to León from Estelí (see page 226).

Highway to Chinandega

From the intersection of the highway to San Isidro and the main route to Chinandega, the road continues north along the western flank of the Maribios volcanoes. The bald west face of **Volcán Telica** (1,110 m) lies to the east. This smoking volcano, which last threw out some serious ash in December 1999, is part of a 9,088-ha tropical dry forest reserve. Telica, one of three cones that erupted in the final weeks before the millennium celebrations, had the doomsdayers singing their last rites. The three towns that lie to the west of the *carretera* were all part of the Maribios culture when the Spanish arrived; now they are agricultural centres. **Quezalguaque** is the smallest and poorest of the three; on 17-18 February solemn processions for its patron saint La Virgen de los Remedios parade through its dusty streets to the melancholy accompaniment of a *chichero* band. Further north is **Posoltega**, a very friendly town that made international news on 30 October 1998. The crater of **Volcán Casita** (1,405 m), saturated with water by the biblical rains of Hurricane Mitch, collapsed a wall that sent a mud slide 20 km from its summit, crossing the highway and killing at least 2,500 people. The settlements of El Porvenir and Rolando Rodríquez were wiped off the map in a horrifying loss of life that had all of Nicaragua in tears for weeks. Today most of the mudslide has been cleaned up and cultivated, although a brown strip of land can still be seen near the volcano's summit. Then US President Bill Clinton came to Posoltega, on a very rare visit by a North American head of state to Nicaragua, to inaugurate a memorial to the victims of the tragedy. The last and most populous of the Maribios towns is Chichigalpa sitting in the shadow of the country's highest cone, the active **Volcán San Cristóbal** (1,745 m) which last erupted in June 2001. San Cristóbal shares 17,950 ha of tropical dry forest reserve with Volcán Casita, with the southernmost occurrence of pine trees in the American continent's northern hemisphere.

Chichigalpa

Colour map 3, grid A1
Population: 46,251
Altitude: 85 m

According to Salman Rushdie, Flor de Caña is the finest rum in the world

Chichigalpa is the rum capital of Nicaragua and possibly of the world. It is a bustling agricultural centre that is best known for having the country's oldest sugar mill, the **Ingenio San Antonio**. The French pirate William Dampier noted the factory's existence on his way to sack León in 1685. It is here that the sugar is processed for Nicaragua's superb rum, **Flor de Caña**. West of the town the road runs along the palm-shaded railroad tracks that connect the village to the sugar mill. This railway line with the Maribios volcanoes as a backdrop is the famous trademark of Flor de Caña and **Cerveza Toña**. There are five trains a day each way May-November, passengers taken, US$0.25; also bus US$0.30. While there are no official tours of the installations, you can apply at Gate (*Portón*) 14 to be shown around (a tip at the gate might facilitate entrance). On the edge of Chichigalpa itself is the Flor de Caña distillery, which produces rum of up to 21 years old and bottled in over 15 flavours.

Buses run between León and Chichigalpa from 0500-1700 with departures every 11 minutes for the 1-hr journey that costs US$0.70. **Transport**

At Km 132 a big roundabout with a statue of the Indian chief Agateyte marks the entrance to Chinandega; the highway to the port of Corinto is to the west and El Viejo is to the east.

Chinandega

Chinandega will not win any beauty contests, for it is grubby and very hot, but the people are welcoming and there are two pretty churches acting as bookends for the city centre. It sits in the middle of the most extensive plain of rich volcanic soil in Nicaragua and is the centre of thousands of hectares of farms that grow sugar cane, bananas and peanuts, amongst many other crops; according to one expert, it is one of the most fertile valleys in all of Central America.

Colour map 3, grid A1
Population: 139,940
Altitude: 70 m

History

When the Spanish first arrived in Chinandega it was a large Nicaraguas Indian settlement with a powerful chief (see El Viejo, page 206). The brutal first governor of Nicaragua, Pedrarias Dávila, found it to be such a wealthy place that he took it for one of his own plantations. It was the site of several failed meetings in the 19th century which attempted to renew a Federation of Central American states. Chinandega used to be known as the 'City of Oranges' for its principal crop at the turn of the 20th century, but cotton replaced the orange trees in the 1940s and the heat of the valley was turned up a few notches. For decades cotton was Nicaragua's main export until a downturn in international market prices, combined with exhausted soil, a war with local insects and greedy middlemen ruined the business. Now the sugarcane and peanut millionaires have moved in and there are profitable shrimp farms in the outlying estuaries.

Sights

At the east end of the centre is the **Iglesia El Calvario**, with its central belltower and white painted wood ceilings with chandeliers that are common in this region. The central avenue runs west from the church past one of three markets. Four blocks west is the avenue of the *Hotel Cosigüina* with its tourist office and just ahead are the *IBW* internet café and the *Hotel Casa Grande*. Six blocks west is the **Parque Central**, unusual for its north orientation to the church. Inside the park are two pools with crocodiles and plenty of turtles, all a bit depressing considering their dirty water and limited living space. (It is not unusual to see a big crocodile sound asleep with locals looking on blankly.) The **Iglesia Santa Ana** is attractive with its typical Nicaraguan baroque design, some gold-leaf altars and faded frescos inside with the same trademark white roof of El Occidente.

Perhaps the most interesting sights in Chinandega are the unusual handmade cameras that are used on the opposite side of the park from the Iglesia Santa Ana. They look like big make-up suitcases and serve to make passport and identity card photographs for the locals at a fraction of the cost of a Polaroid. This extraordinary local invention uses photographic paper to make a negative, then the negative is re-photographed with

León and El Occidente

positive paper and processed by the photographer with a dark glove, all inside the camera. You can have your photo taken by one of these brilliant little box camera-darkrooms for US$1 by Julio César, who makes about 20 portraits per day.

Sleeping
Hotels in Chinandega are overpriced, due to many business visitors and a lack of beds

AL *Los Volcanes*, Km 129 Carretera a Chinandega, at southern entrance to city, T341-1000, F341-1010, hotelosvolcanes@tec.com.ni Private bath with hot water, a/c, cable TV, telephone, bar, restaurant, conference centre, clean, good service. **A** *Hotel Cosigüina*, Esquina de los Bancos, T341-1663, F341-3689, hotelcosiguina@tec.com.ni Private bath with lukewarm water, a/c, telephone, cable TV, bar, restaurant, casino, laundry and internet service. Nicaraguan Institute of Tourism (INTUR) office in reception, very limited information, though owner Orlando Montealegre is a gentleman, very helpful and knowledgeable, if available. Rooms are clean and dark and the service of the hotel is friendly and very professional, overpriced but a very good hotel, central location, recommended. Also offers trips to Cosigüina and fishing excursions in Pacific on owner's 43-ft yacht. **A** *Las Mañanitas*, Texaco Los Encuentros, 75 m north, T341-0522. 9 rooms with private bath and hot water, cable TV, a/c, internet and laundry service, bar and restaurant.

C-D *Hotel Glomar*, Mercado Central, 1 c south, T341-2562. Private bath, bar, safe, may be closed Sun evening, owner will change dollars, good food. **C-D** *Casa Grande*, Banpro, ½ block west, T341-0325. Private bath, some with fan others with a/c, sagging beds in super-hot rooms, central location, poor value, friendly service, cheap meals upon request. **F** *Pensión Cortés*, south of Parque Central, basic. **F** *Chinandega*, basic, fan, shared bath, decent.

Eating
Anthon Che, Casa Pellas, 1 c west, 1 c south, T341-3021. Daily 1000-2400, Sat and Sun until 0300, surf 'n' turf, chicken in curry sauce, *carne a la plancha*. 1½ blocks further south is *Buenos Aires*, T341-3764. Open daily, 1100-2400, beef and fish dishes. *Corona de Oro*, Chinese, 1½ blocks east of Parque Central, T341-2539. Daily 1000-2130, expensive. *Hungaro*, Coipepach, ½ c east, T341-3824. Some Hungarian dishes, moderate priced, also *comida corriente* with generous servings, cheap, nice staff and setting, open 1100-2200 daily. *Hamburlooca*, on avenue north of main street, T341-3264. Cheap combos of burgers and fries, good and not too greasy, also delivery, open daily 0900-2200. *Italian Pizza*, Iglesia San Antonio 175 m east. Good.

Festivals
Chinandega's patron saint is the grandmother of Jesus, *Santa Ana*. Her celebrations begin on 17 July and culminate on 26 July.

Transport
Buses, most buses leave from the new market at southeast edge of town. **Chinandega-Corinto**, every 20 mins, 0600-2100, US$0.30, 30 mins. **Chinandega-Somotillo**, every 3 hrs, 0900-1500, US$2, 2 hrs. **Chinandega-Guasaule**, every 2 hrs, 0600-1600, US$2, 2 hrs. **Chinandega-Managua**, every 30 mins, 0600-1600, US$2.25, 3 hrs. **Chinandega-León**, every 11 mins, 0600-1700, US$1, 1 hr 45 mins. Buses for Potosí, El Viejo and Puerto Morazán leave from the Mercadito at northwest of town. A local bus connects Terminal, Mercado and Mercadito.

Taxis are very cheap around Chinandega, with fares of US$0.35 for short trips while longer trips or night-time service can run to US$1.25. Drivers are very friendly and helpful.

Car hire, there are several: *Avis Rent a Car*, T341-1066, avis@ibw.com.ni; *Toyota Rent a Car*, T341-2303, www.toyotarentacar.com; and *Budget*, T341-3636, www.budget.com.ni

Banks Between the *Hotel Cosigüina* and the Parque Central all the banks are represented. *BDF* is on the Esquina de los Bancos, T341-3015 for cash and American Express cheques only. For cash advance on Visa cards and all travellers' cheques use *BAC*, Texaco Guadalupe, 2 c north, T341-0078. **Communications** Internet: across the street from *Hotel Casa Grande* at IBW or at *Hotel Cosigüina*. **Post office:** *Correos de Nicaragua* is at *BANIC*, 125 m north, T341-0407, F341-3000. **Telephone:** *Enitel* offices are one block east of the central plaza, T341-0002. **Embassies & consulates** *Costa Rica*, Alexa Peters, *BANPRO*, ½ c north, T341-1584, Mon-Fri 0830-1700. *Honduras*, José Alfredo Briceño, across from *Enitel*, T341-0949, Mon-Fri 0830-1630. *El Salvador*, Oscar Rolando Sariles, across from La Curaçao, T341-2049, Mon-Fri 0800-1400. **Tourist office** Located inside the *Hotel Cosigüina*, see above under Sleeping. **Useful numbers** Fire: T341-3651. **Hospital:** T341-4902. **Police:** T341-3456. **Red Cross:** T341-3132.

Puerto de Corinto

From the roundabout at the entrance to Chinandega it is 25 km to the only deepwater port facility in Nicaragua. About 60% of the country's commerce passes through this port and Asian cars seem to flow out of the town year round. The town itself is on what was a sandy island, **Punto Icaco**, now connected with bridges over to the mainland. There are beautiful old wooden buildings with verandas, especially by the port, and the old train station is now a beautiful library. The most popular pastime in Corinto (besides drinking) is riding around Parque Central on bicycles in the evening. There is also an unannounced contest to see how many passengers can fit on one bicycle and still do laps of the park (six appears to be the record). Entry to the port is barred to all except those with a permit and, although immigration and customs are at the port, the only way in or out of here is on a container ship.

Colour map 3, grid A1
Population: 17,414
Altitude: 3 m

There are some nice beaches on the north side of town and on the Corinto-Chinandega road is **Playa Paso Caballo**, named after the Devil who reportedly passes this bridge at night, often on horseback, and is responsible for the many road deaths here; the sea too is treacherous and people drown here every year. There are no facilities in Corinto's barrier islands, but they are beautiful, with crashing surf on one side, and calm and warm swimming water on the other. The longest island (with the lighthouse), **El Cardón**, was a place of inspiration for the poet Rubén Darío. The journey can be negotiated with any fisherman; you can try one called Isidro. Boats can be reserved in advance through Guadalupe Hernández who lives next to the Alcoholics Anonymous building in Corinto, T342-2490. Tell her you want to visit **Castañones**, US$10 each way, pre-arrange departure and pick-up times. Bring anything you might need with you to the island. A *panga* can be rented for the whole day for US$60-75 so you can explore the numerous islands and mangroves. The islands a full of birdlife and sandflies (bring repellent).

León and El Occidente

D *Central*, in front of Portuaria, T342-2380. 10 rooms, clean, a/c. **D-F** *Puerto Plata*, Parque Central, 175 m south, T342-2667. **F** with fan and D with a/c, private bath, good. **F** *Hospedaje Luvy*, fan, dirty bathrooms, 2 blocks from plaza.

Sleeping

Meléndez, on main plaza, good but pricey. *El Imperial*, evenings only, cheapest meals in market, but not recommended. There is also some good seafood in the little eateries

Eating

on the beachfront, ask what the fresh catch is. Most people eat at **Paso Caballo** where *Las Conchitas*, next to the bridge, T342-2309, daily 1000-2000, serves clam cocktails, shrimp and lobster.

El Viejo

Colour map 3, grid A1
Population: 84,628
Altitude: 43 m

When Oviedo, the infamous Spanish chronicler, visited El Viejo in the early 1500s, it was still known by its original name, **Tezoatega**, and was ruled by **Agateyte**, one of the most powerful chiefs of Nicaragua who had his plaza where the basilica stands today. Agateyte ruled at least 20,000 subjects and had a standing army of 6,000 warriors. After much insistence, Oviedo was granted an interview; he learnt from the chief that Nicaraguas leaders must spend one year in solitary prayer before assuming leadership and that during that time they can only be seen by a child who brings a daily ration of food. Oviedo also noted that "The chief wore a thin mantle of white cotton with which he covered himself, and his entire body, arms and legs and neck were painted. He had long hair and a long beard with almost no grey hairs. He was over 70 years old, tall, withered and very serious in speech."

Although they are two separate towns, Chinandega and El Viejo are about to merge into a single sprawl. The somewhat run-down but peaceful town of El Viejo is home to the patron saint of Nicaragua and is the centre of many religious pilgrimages. It is one of the most Catholic places in a very Catholic country. The image in the **Basílica de la Inmaculada Concepción de la Virgen María**, called **La Virgen del Trono**, is 70 cm tall and is one of the most venerated images in all Central America. She first came to Nicaragua from Spain in 1666 and was officially named **Patron Saint of Nicaragua** in May 2000. The church received the title of basilica during Pope John Paul II's visit to El Viejo in February 1996. The original structure dates from 1562 and it was refurbished in 1884. One of the most famous religious events in Nicaragua is the **Lavada de la Plata** (cleaning the silver). This seemingly innocuous activity is an honour for the devout of the Virgen del Trono, who clean all the silver articles that are laid before the ancient icon every 6 December, the day before the huge Purísima celebrations in her name that start the next day all over Nicaragua.

Sleeping & eating
G *Casa de Huéspedes*, Basílica, 3 c north, with shared bath. *Restaurante Tezoatega*, Basílica, 1½ c north, T344-2436. Open daily 1200-2400, a good restaurant with beef and chicken dishes including a tasty *churrasco*.

Transport
Buses run between El Viejo and Chinandega every 10 mins, US$0.25, 20 mins.

The Chinandega Peninsula

Use public bus or 4WD only on the peninsula roads

From El Viejo there is a scenic drive or bumpy bus ride to the Pacific Coast and on to the last of the Maribios volcanoes, **Volcán Cosigüina** (800 m), and the steamy and beautiful **Golfo de Fonseca**. Another interesting trip northeast from El Viejo is to **Puerto Morazán**, which has some simple lodging and some of the friendliest people in Chinandega. The town is on the **Estero Real,** the biggest Pacific Basin nature reserve in Nicaragua at 55,000 ha, an endless labyrinth of estuaries and mangroves. It is the biggest mangrove forest in Central America. You can hire a fisherman's boat in Puerto Morazán to explore.

Hurricane Mitch – a sea of tears

On Saturday 24 October, 1998, tropical storm Mitch reached hurricane status and, sitting off the coast of Honduras for a full week, it brought biblical rains to Nicaragua. The torrential rains poured record precipitation on the region and caused serious damage throughout the northern part of the country. Particularly tragic was the collapse of a wall of the Volcán Casita in western Nicaragua, causing a mudslide that covered an area 20 km long by 3 km wide. More than 2,000 people were killed and many spent several days buried in the mud that came down from the volcano.

Along the Río Coco, Miskito villages were wiped off the map by the river running 15 m above normal. Official statistics can only estimate that 3,000 people died and more than 360,000 had their homes destroyed or partially damaged. A large percentage of the victims were children. In material terms, the damage was calculated at nearly US$1 billion. It was the largest natural disaster in the country's history. International solidarity arrived almost immediately. However, the quantity was insufficient and the process of reconstruction was hampered by accusations of corruption in the government .

El Viejo to Potosí

The first section of the highway is paved and passes gigantic ranches, so big and wealthy that this part of the road is nicknamed **Carretera Millonaria**. Before the paved section ends there are two turn-offs that lead to the beautiful and desolate beaches on the extreme northwest of Nicaragua's Pacific Coast. The first exit leads to Aposentillo and the second to **Jiquilillo** (try saying that that 10 times in a row!). On a sandbar with the black sand Pacific in front and the Estero Padre Ramos behind, **Padre Ramos** is 8,800 ha of protected estuary and mangrove reserve. There are *casitas* that can cook up some fresh fish and G *Hospedaje Los Zorros*, ultra-basic and friendly. Just before the end of the millionaire's highway at **El Congo**, there is a Coca-Cola sign on each side of the road. On the right side you can buy a cold soft drink and make some venison tacos. A plate of grilled venison, rice, beans and tortilla costs US$1.25. Availability depends on how the hunting has been in the hills behind El Congo. The road ahead is in moderate to bad condition, but the scenery is nice and the homes are made in the traditional Indian style of woven thatched palm with wood supports. The feeling of being on a road to the end of the earth is part of the attraction.

Buy purified water and, if driving, top up your petrol tank before leaving El Viejo

León and El Occidente

Just before the intersection that leads to both sides of the Volcán Cosigüina is the tiny settlement of **Mata Cacao**. At the intersection that leads to a shrimp farm (Los Playones) there is a restaurant and a general store. In the house of Nerí Valle you can get a plate of chicken or beef with rice and beans for US$1.25. Next door is *La Caseta*, a little store with everything from cold drinks to children's clothing and petrol. In fact, the 20 litres or so that **José del Carmen Pozo** keeps in the shop may be the only available petrol on the peninsula. José is friendly and will guide climbers on Volcán Cosigüina. He has room in his house for some extra hammocks and suggests a 0600 departure for the climb. The ascent takes between two and four hours, depending on where you start and how fit you are. The path is overgrown, very difficult to follow and full of snakes, so a guide like José with his machete is essential. From the summit you can understand the magnitude of what is said to have been the biggest eruption during recorded history in Latin America. On 23

Volcán Cosigüina

January 1835 Cosigüina blew off most of its cone, reducing it from 3,000 m to its present height of 800 m, and throwing ash as far as Colombia. There are beautiful views of the crater lake, 700 m below, inside the 2,000-m diameter cone. If you want to visit the crater lake you will need climbing gear. The views to the Golfo de Fonseca and its islands are spectacular. The volcano and the surrounding dry tropical forest include a 12,420-ha nature reserve.

Past Mata Cocao the road veers left and right. To the left is access to the very humble Pacific-side village of Punta Ñata accessed by a terrible road. To the right is the earth and rock road that descends to the Gulf of Fonseca port town of Potosí.

Potosí

Colour map 1, grid C1

It is so hot here that even the devil would run for shade (or office)

Though only 60 km from Chinandega, Potosí with its rocky road, searing heat and the chocolate-brown waters of the prehistoric bay of Golfo de Fonseca are other-worldly. If you are looking to relax or warm up even more, there are some thermal baths inland from the rusty hulls of the shipwreck on the east side of the beach. The locals are very friendly here and the ocean is calm and good for swimming, though the dark brown sand gives it a less inviting colour. The Golfo de Fonseca is shared by Nicaragua, El Salvador and Honduras and there is constant bickering over who is fishing in whose waters. From the solitary dock in Potosí it is only 15 minutes by boat to a commercial shipping port in Honduras and 2 hours to La Unión in El Salvador. There are rumours that a ferry boat is being reinstated from La Unión, although it will most likely skip Potosí and go straight to the port of Corinto. At the moment you will have to negotiate a ride with local boats and, to make it worthwhile for the fishermen, it can cost you US$100 or more to go from Potosí to El Salvador. (Reportedly it is a bit easier coming from El Salvador to Potosí.)

Customs & immigration Offices are open from 0800-1700, but close for lunch. Exit is US$2 and entrance is US$7. There is a duty free shop in the old port building.

Sleeping & eating G *Hospedaje Brisas del Golfo* is row of clean, if stark, concrete-block rooms with fan inside, toilet and bath outside. Next to *Hospedaje Brisas* is a nice ranch-style restaurant with *futból* games on Honduran and Salvadoran television channels. *Bar y Restaurante Gilmari*, fried chicken, steak, fish soup. If you order fish the owner will walk down to the dock, buy one and cook it, usually *pargo* (snapper). Most dishes cost US$2-3, jug of beer is US$1.75.

Transport **Buses** leave from **Potosí-Chinandega**, 0230, 0345, 0500, 0620, 0710, 1000, 1500, US$2, 3 hrs.

El Guasaule: land border with Honduras

Traffic on the international border route to El Guasaule and Honduras is much heavier. The road is often in bad condition and the bridge at the border is under constant threat and repair from flooding of the Río Guasaule.

Immigration Immigration hours are 0600-2000. To enter Nicaragua costs are US$7 plus a US$1 Alcaldía charge, to exit it is US$2 plus the US$1 immigration charge.

The distance between the border posts is 500 m. There are no *colectivos*, so you have to walk, hitch or take one of the tricycles with parasol. Vehicles drive across the river; foot passengers are ferried across in small boats when the bridge is down. The international buses use this crossing. When leaving Nicaragua (on *Ticabus*, at least), an official takes all passports from passengers as soon as the bus leaves Chinandega, he fills out all the immigration forms and collects the exit tax. At the border, passengers get off the bus and wait to be called by name to re-embark. This takes about an hour. Once back on the bus, a Honduran official takes your passport and you go through Honduran procedures.

Money changers offer the same rates for córdobas to lempiras as on the Honduran side. *Banco de Crédito Centroamericano*, beside immigration is recommended for good rates and no commission (they will accept photocopy of passport if yours is being checked by immigration). **Money exchange**

From the border **Guasaule-Chinandega**, every 2 hrs, 0600-1600, US$1.90, 2 hrs. **Somotillo-Chinandega**, every 3 hrs, 0200-1600, US$1.90, 2 hrs. **Buses**

Northern Highlands

9

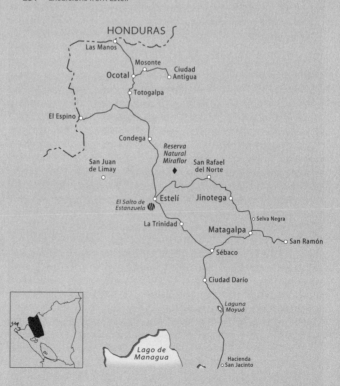

Most of the northern ranges and plains are full of sleepy villages with ancient churches, laid-back cowboys and smiling children. Here, the searing heat, tropical forests and volcanoes of the Pacific Basin have given way to pine trees and granite cliffs. This is where the soil and the adobe-and-tile homes blend into a single red-brown palette. It's a place where horses stand rooted in time, blinking in the shade of tropical highland breezes.

But Nicaragua's ruggedly beautiful northern mountains and valleys have staged most of the historical events that have given the country its plucky reputation. It was here that indigenous groups attacked Spanish mining operations in the 16th century and, in the 19th century, fought confiscation of communal lands that were to go to German immigrants for coffee growing. This is where nationalist Sandino fought the US Marine's occupation of Nicaragua in the 1920s, where the rebel Sandinistas launched their attacks against the Somoza administration in the 1970s and later the Contras against the Sandinista Government in the 1980s. The region was even used by Miami Cubans and the US government for training and to launch the 'Bay of Pigs' invasion of Cuba in the 1960s.

As well as the turbulent history, rustic beauty and kind population, there are cloud forest reserves, pine forests and people actually wearing sweaters. In fact, the cooler climate and higher altitudes make you feel as if you are in a totally different country.

Northern Highlands

Pan-American Highway north from Managua

Just beyond the international airport the Pan-American Highway leaves Managua, heads north into Nicaragua's most beautiful non-volcanic mountains and continues all the way to Honduras. There are two interesting routes, one that leads to border crossings through historic villages, and another that enters the heart of coffee growing country.

On the outskirts of Managua the highway passes the clothing factories of the airport free-trade zone and the sprawling town of **Tipitapa** that lies along the river of the same name. The Río Tipitapa, with the help of a big pond and later an estuary, drains Lake Managua into Lake Nicaragua, though without rain the connection is almost stagnant. Tipitapa suffered extensive flooding during Hurricane Mitch in 1998 and is a crowded and dirty place of more than 50,000 inhabitants, with not much of interest for the visitor and without decent lodging.

Hacienda San Jacinto After Tipitapa, at Km 35 of the Panamericana, is the turn-off for the cattle-ranching departments of Boaco and Chontales (see Managua excursions). At Km 39.5 is the short road that leads to the historic ranch of San Jacinto, where William Walker lost a critical battle against the combined Central American forces in 1856, which is remembered every **14 September** as a national holiday. The ranch is in a pleasant valley and is open as a museum with objects displayed from the celebrated battle. ■ *Tue-Sun, though it may be difficult to find the caretaker on Sun. 0900-1600, US$0.75.*

Laguna Moyuá At Km 57 you'll see the remains of an ancient lake, in the form three lagoons: Las Playitas, Moyuá and Tecomapa, though from the highway they appear to be one calm body of water. During the dry season they are choked with plants, but in the rainy season are a beautiful contrast to the surrounding dry hills and are full of sandpipers, white egrets and ducks. Laguna Moyuá has two islands that show signs of the large pre-Columbian populations that inhabited this area and there are ruins of what could have been a temple. The lagoons are most famous for their delicious *guapote* (native perch), which is sold by children along the roadside. Just north of the waterfront fruit stands is *Comedor Pescafrito*, a cheap restaurant which fries up fresh *guapote* daily.

Ciudad Darío

Colour map 1, grid C4
Population: 11,000
Altitude: 433 m

Near Km 90 is the left turning for the long three-bridge entrance to Ciudad Darío, a sleepy cowboy town set on a hill over the Río Grande de Matagalpa. This is the first of many forgotten towns and villages that dot the northern landscape. What makes this one different is that the country's national hero, Rubén Darío (see page 192), happened to be born here in a small adobe corner house in January of 1867. Living in Honduras, Rubén's mother was fed up with her husband's abusive ways and decided to return to León to have her child. She only made it as far as her sister's house, in the village that was then called **Metapa**; she gave birth, rested for 40 days and continued on to León where Darío was to spend his childhood. Today the **Casa Natal de Rubén Darío**, from city centre, 1 c east, 2 c north, is a museum where you can see the bed he was born on, the china set that was used to wash his mother and a 19th-century

Northern Highlands

kitchen, similar to those still used in much of the country today. The museum staff are very happy to see visitors and Doña Pola will also act as guide to the town. ■ *0900-1630 Tue-Sun, US$0.75.* Ciudad Darío was a big shoe-producing town during the Sandinista years and you can still get a pair of custom-made cowboy boots for US$30 if you can give the craftsman three days. You can pick up smaller sizes ready made in the workshop for $25. Doña Pola or a local taxi can take you to the trailhead for a one-hour hike to the summit of **Cerro de la Cruz** for a panoramic view of the city and surrounding hills and rivers. Legend has it that this mountain was growing out of control, skywards, at an alarming rate, so a local Franciscan monk hiked to the top and planted a cross on the summit; that put an end to the mountain's insolence. No one can agree how many years it has been there, but every 3 May there is a pilgrimage to the cross with a mass held at the summit. 29 July is the celebration of their patron saint, **San Pedro**, is on 29 July and from the 14-18 January there are festivities commemorating the birth of Rubén Darío. The city centre lies up the hill (one block east) from the bus station.

Sleeping G *Casa Agricultor*, 2 blocks north of bus station, T742-2379. Some with private bath, simple, dark rooms with little beds, clean, secured parking, owner Emma López will make coffee in the morning, best in town.

Eating *Restaurante Dariano*, across from bus station. Best seafood in town, mid-range. *Restaurante Metapa*, Plaza Municipal. Good *churrasco* steak and *carne asada*, cheap. *Las Rosquillas*, 1 block from museum. Very good *indio viejo*, cheap.

Transport **Bus** station is at small park just north of the iron bridge on south side of town. Buses leaving from 415-1900 every 15 mins, US$1 north to **Matagalpa**, or US$0.80 south bound to **Managua**.

Directory **Communications** Telephone: *Enitel* is opposite the museum. **Medical services** *Health Clinic* is opposite the church on Parque Central.

Sébaco

Further north along the Pan-American Highway is the dry lake-bed valley and agricultural centre of Sébaco. The Río Grande de Matagalpa was metres above normal here in the hurricane of 1998 and some damage can still be seen when you enter the town via the new bridge. Sébaco is a hot and unattractive town with Nicaragua's most beautiful vegetables in its market and an historic church with a tiny pre-Columbian and colonial museum inside. The town is cut in two by the highway, with the **Vieja Iglesia de Sébaco** located on the right-hand side of the Panamericana heading north. To reach the little temple turn right at the first entrance to the highway after crossing the bridge, go to the back of the new church and head away from the church all the way to the top of the hill and turn right.

Colour map 1, grid C4
Population: 15,000
Altitude: 470 m

The Pan-American Highway forks here with its continuation to Honduras on the left and the road to Matagalpa and Jinotega on the right. Inside the fork in the highway is the market and its luscious vegetables (particularly onions). Sébaco is truly the agricultural crossroads of the northern highlands. There are huge quantities of rice, sorghum and carrots, and some great photo opportunities. Just before market on the east side of the highway is *Banco de Finanzas (BDF)*, T622-0624 for changing cash or American Express travellers' cheques.

Northern Highlands

Sleeping **D** *El Valle*, on the highway 1½ km towards south of town, T622-2209. Private bath, fan, restaurant and bar, quiet, patio with pool, English and Italian spoken.

Eating *Los Gemelos*, next to ENEL, T622-2004. Moderate prices, seafood and good *churrasco* steak, cheap buffet Mon-Fri 1100-1400 (price includes pork, other meats cost extra). *El Sesteo*, Banco de Finanzas, 2 c west, T622-2242. Moderate prices, chicken, shrimp, onion steak, clam cocktail, fried fish. *Restaurante Rosario*, on west side of highway at south entrance to town. Fried chicken or beef dishes, cheap, greasy and happy.

Transport **Buses** pass every 15 mins to/from **Estelí** US$1, **Matagalpa** US$1 and **Managua** US$1.25.

Highway to Matagalpa and Jinotega

From the fork in Sébaco, the highway to the right is the **Carretera a Matagalpa**. Though Matagalpa itself may not be an attraction for many visitors, the area is beautiful and there is plenty to see and enjoy in the vicinity.

The highway rises gradually past the cute village of **Chaguitillo**, at Km 107, home to some important pre-Columbian sites with petroglyphs and a small museum. Ask in the village for the office of *Nuevos Horizontes* to find a local guide to show you around. The *carretera* continues past massive coffee processing plants (*beneficios*) and their extensive, concrete platforms used for drying coffee beans under the sun. Harvest time is November-February when the beans can be seen drying, and the activity of the region as a whole is doubled. The road snakes as it climbs through sparse settlements and yet more coffee *beneficios*, to Km 130 and the highland valley of Matagalpa.

Matagalpa

Colour map 1, grid C5
Population: 62,000
Altitude: 682 m

Set in a broad valley circled by green mountains, including the handsome Cerro de Apante (1,442 m), Matagalpa appears scenic from a distance, though increasingly less so up close. This important and bustling coffee capital of Nicaragua has a vaguely claustrophobic feel to it. The market is dirty and crowded with stray dogs rummaging through street refuse. Parked cars and trucks block the narrow streets, and a circular sprawl of new homes climb the surrounding mountains, threatening to enclose the city in concrete.

History

Matagalpa is the most famous mountain town in Nicaragua. It is in the heart of coffee country, an industry that was started in the 1870s by German immigrants. The government gave them Indian lands, which provoked the Indian War of 1881, when Indians invaded Matagalpa with bows and arrows and killed settlers. The German influence continued until the beginning of the First World War, when the government confiscated all German-held coffee farms. The Germans came back after the war and re-established themselves. The lands were confiscated again in 1941 when Nicaragua declared war on Germany. Most Germans did not return after the end of the Second World War. During the Contra War this was often the front line of battle and many of the residents of this city fought on opposing sides of the battle. There are currently non-profit organizations putting the two sides back together to heal decades-old wounds. Matagalpa has prospered in recent years thanks to

Things to do in the Northern Highlands

- Stop off at the little corner house where poet Rubén Darío first saw the light of day; it's a good excuse to visit the peaceful town of Ciudad Darío.
- Explore the beautiful countryside between the coffee towns of Matagalpa and Jinotega, including the Selva Negra Resort with its ponds, organic coffee farm and cloud forest reserve.
- Visit the town of San Rafael del Norte; it's like a stage-set for a surreal Nicaraguan film, where hooded Franciscan monks and nuns roam the streets alongside rugged mountain cowboys and school children in freshly laundered uniforms.
- Tour one of Estelí's fine cigar factories.
- Discover a world of red-clay homes and earthenware at the ceramic co-operative in Condega.
- Browse the interesting colonial exhibits at the dusty little museum next to the church in the forgotton town of Ciudad Antigua.

increased coffee production, though it is presently suffering economically from the low world prices of coffee.

There are two main streets that run to and from the very attractive cathedral, south to the little **Parque Darío** where it is a bit more peaceful. Along these streets are most of the city's sleeping, dining and entertainment options. The rest of this hilly city is a maze of streets, a mixture of paving and mud. The city's cathedral, the **Catedral de San Pedro de Matagalpa** (1897), is worth a visit and there are two other pleasant city churches: the late 19th-century **Templo de San José de Laborio**, in front of the **Parque Darío** and the primitive Nicaraguan baroque **Iglesia de Molaguina** which is believed to date from 1751. Adjacent to the central plaza is the impressive statue for the (now closed) **Galería de los Héroes y Mártires**. East of Parque Darío is the **Museo Carlos Fonseca**, a memorial to one of the Sandinista's early intellectuals who was murdered in inexplicable circumstances less than three years before the end of the Revolution. ■ *0800-1030, donation requested.* It is possible to visit one of the co-operatives in the city where they make the beautiful **cerámica negra** (black pottery) that the city is famous for. There are unusual indigenous fabric co-operatives making attractive purses, backpacks, etc. **NB** Parque Darío, Parque San José and Plaza Laborio are all names used for the same plaza, located on the south side of the city facing the Templo de San José de Laborio.

Essentials

A *Lomas de Guadalupe*, INAA 500 m east, T612-7505, F612-6390, lomashotel @yahoo.com 26 rooms, private bath with hot water, cable TV, telephone, mini-bar, internet access, new and pretty view, most luxurious in region, not central. **B/C** *Hotel Ideal*, cathedral, 2 c north, 1 c west, T612-2483. Private bath, a/c or fan, TV, restaurant, bar, conference centre. **D** *Hotel Fountain Blue*, cathedral, 3 c north, 2 c west, T612-2733. Private bath with hot water, fan, cable TV, good value.

D *Hotel Wanpani*, Monumento La Virgen, 25 m south, T612-4761, F612-2893. 12 rooms, cafetería, private bath, a/c and fan. **E** *Hotel Caoba*, Colegio Santa Teresita, 1½ c north, T612-3515, private bath and fan. **F** *Bermúdez*, BAMER, 5 c south. Some with bath, fan, poor, run-down, but popular, good car parking, helpful, meals. Half a block west is **E** *Hospedaje Matagalpa*, T612-3834, with bath, **F** without, clean, light and airy. **E** *Hotel Soza del Río*, Av Río Grande, T612-3036. Private bath, fan, nice patio, good

Sleeping
■ *on map, page 218*
for price codes see
inside front cover

Northern Highlands

value, opposite river, basic, meals available. **E** *Hotel Arauz*, Calle Central, T612-7200. Bath, fan, restaurant.

Eating
● *on map below*

Jin shan, BANIC 1 west, T612-3024. Chinese, good. *Comedor Sabita*, 2 blocks south of Laborio on Av José Benito Escobar. Family-run, good breakfasts and lunch. *Rosticería La Casona*, Av José Benito Escobar, T612-3901. Cheap and basic chicken and beef dishes. South on the same street, *El Bambú*, is popular with locals. *Chepi*, northeast corner of Parque Darío. Large portions, excellent value, popular. Also just off Parque Darío is the very fine eatery, *Rosticería La Posada*, T612-2330. Specializes in roast chicken, moderate priced, very good.

White House Pizza, cathedral, 1½ c north, T612-7575. Open daily, will deliver in local area. *Restaurante Pesca Mar*, Cancha del Brigadista 3 c east, T612-3548. Shrimp in garlic butter, red snapper in onions, open daily until 2200. *Cafetería Karla*, in front of Esso station, T612-3666. Seriously cheap, sandwiches, good. *Cafetería Zinica*, across from Casa Pellas, T612-5921. Seriously cheap, tacos and sandwiches. *Cafetería Bar Perfiles*, Alcaldía, 1c west, ½ south, T612-2970. Cheap, popular, try the *caballo bayo* (mixed dishes of traditional meats). Located just south of the entrance to the city is an area of restaurants, bars and clubs called Valle las Tejas. *Restaurante El Pullazo*,

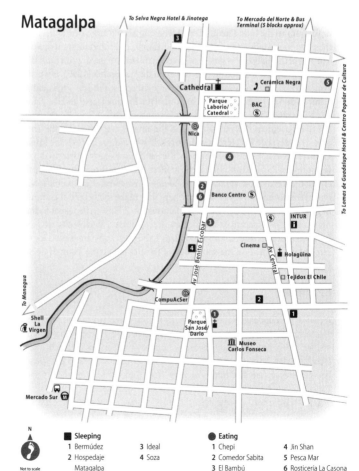

Matagalpa

To Selva Negra Hotel & Jinotega

To Mercado del Norte & Bus Terminal (5 blocks approx)

Cathedral

Cerámica Negra

Parque Laborio/Catedral

BAC

Nica

Banco Centro

INTUR

Cinema

Holagüina

Tejidos El Chile

CompuAcSer

Shell La Virgen

To Managua

Av José Benito Escobar

Av Central

To Lomas de Guadalupe Hotel & Centro Popular de Cultura

Parque San José/Darío

Museo Carlos Fonseca

Mercado Sur

N

Not to scale

Sleeping
1 Bermúdez
2 Hospedaje Matagalpa
3 Ideal
4 Soza

Eating
1 Chepi
2 Comedor Sabita
3 El Bambú
4 Jin Shan
5 Pesca Mar
6 Rosticería La Casona

Nicaraguan coffee – a German brew

Large-scale coffee growing in Nicaragua is directly tied to German immigration, promoted by the governments of Pedro Joaqun Chamorro and Evaristo Carazo. They offered immigrants 500 manzanas (350 ha) of land and 25,000 coffee trees free, as well as 'five cents' for each coffee tree planted on farms with over 500 coffee trees in the north of the country. Much of the land offered at bargain prices was confiscated from Matagalpa Indians' communal lands, helping to spark an Indian uprising in 1881.

The pioneer of German immigration was Ludwing Elster, originally from Hanover, and his wife Katharine Braun, from Baden Baden. They settled in what is today the department of Matagalpa in 1852, in a place called La Lima. Years later, around 1875, Wilhelm Jericho arrived and founded the Hacienda Las Lajas, promising to lure 20 more German families to Nicaragua. More than 200 foreigners arrived, 60 of them Germans. They settled and began growing coffee in Matagalpa and neighbouring Jinotega. At the time, Colombia was yet to become a coffee producer, and the Nicaraguan product was considered among the world's best, along with coffee from Costa Rica and Guatemala. The international coffee price

was around US$8 for a hundredweight of 'green' export coffee. Besides growing quality coffee, the Germans introduced the first vehicle into Nicaragua (1918), the first electric generator with a steam motor (1917), the first movie theatre, the first coffee pulping machine and the technique for washing coffee. Later, Anastasio Somoza García, under the guise of Nicaragua's support for the United States in the Second World War, confiscated the properties of the Germans, even those who had Nicaraguan family and offspring. Many were sent to prison camps in the United States. Most of the coffee haciendas were obtained through rigged auctions, in which Somoza's buyer – with a briefcase and a sub-machine gun – supposedly made the best offer. Today, in the departments of Matagalpa and Jinotega, where the majority of the Germans immigrants had settled, 60% of the nation's coffee is harvested. It is the country's leading export crop, estimated at US$165 mn in the year 2000. A crash in coffee prices in 2001 created economic hardships in Matagalpa, as producers defaulted on loans and farm workers were left without work while prices fell to their lowest level in 30 years.

Northern Highlands

T612-3935, has a famous dish, also called *pullazo*, that is very tasty; it is a very lean cut of beef cooked in a special oven and smothered with tomatoes and onions, served with fresh corn tortillas, *gallo pinto* and a fruit juice, US$4.

Entertainment

Disco Equinoccio, Parque Darío, 8 c south, T612-6223. US$2 entry, salsa and merengue, young crowd. Also with similar crowd and music, *Disco Luz de Luna*, in Valle las Tejas, T612-4774. Most discos do not get going until after 2100, and all Matagalpa discos serve dinner. **NB** A taxi back from any night spot is recommended.

Festival

24 Sep, *Virgen de las Mercedes*.

Shopping

Pottery *Cerámica Negra*, Sociedad Colectiva Lorenza Pineda Rodríguez, next to *Joyería El Zafiro*, T612-4812. A co-operative of 9 women who make black pottery in the northern tradition. This style of pottery is found only in parts of Chile, Nicaragua and Mexico and there is evidence that the tradition dates back to 1500 BC in this region of Nicaragua. Contact: Estela Rodríguez.

Fabrics *Tejidos El Chile*, BANIC, 2½ c south, T612-2290, odesar@nic.gbm.net This is a commercial outlet for a rural fabric co-operative of 7 women, founded in 1984 as part of a cultural rescue programme for the community of El Chile (20 km from Matagalpa). Hand-made backpacks, camera cases, purses and wallets. Visits to the village can be arranged through the shop. Contact: Gloria Gutiérrez.

Transport **Buses** **Terminal Sur**, near Mercado del Sur, is used for all destinations outside of the department of Matagalpa. **Matagalpa-Jinotega**, every ½ hr, 0500-1800, US$0.90, 1½ hrs. **Matagalpa-Managua**, every ½ hr, 0500-1800, US$2.50, 2½ hrs. **Matagalpa-Estelí**, every ½ hr, 0515-1800, US$1, 1½ hrs. **Matagalpa-León**, 0600, 1500, US$2.25, 3 hrs. **Matagalpa-Masaya**, 0700, 1400, 1530, US$2, 4 hrs. **NB** Most buses will charge every piece of luggage for the roof as another full fare; if you have more than one big pack or suitcase this is negotiable.

Terminal Norte, by Mercado del Norte, is for all destinations within the department of Matagalpa: San Ramón, El Tuma, etc. **Taxi** between terminals US$0.75.

Taxi Matagalpa taxis are helpful and cheap. Average fare inside of the city is US$0.50-0.75. Trip to hotel *Lomas de Guadalupe* US$1.50. Fare to *Selva Negra* US$4-5 per person, one-way. There are no radio taxis in Matagalpa, but you can call one of the *cooperativa* offices like *14 de Febrero* T612-4402 or *Oswaldo Martínez* T612-3604. **NB** Always agree on fares over the telephone if calling for a taxi and confirm the fare again with the driver. If travelling long distance ask for their best vehicle.

Directory **Banks** *Banco de América Central* (*BAC* and *Credomatic*) is next to Casa Pellas (Toyota Dealer) just off the central plaza, T612-5905. Changes all travellers' cheques and cash advances on Visa and MC. On Av Central in Centro Comercial Catalina, *Banco de Finanzas*, T612-5444, changes American Express cheques and cash. Other banks on this street change cash only. Money changers near the cathedral. **Car hire** *Budget Rent a Car*, Km 131 at Shell station on entrance to city. T612-3041. **Communications** Internet: *CompuAcSer Internet*, Av José Bento Escobar, 1 block north of Parque Darío. US$7 hr, Mon-Fri 0800-1800. *NicaInternet*, across from police station, T612-4439, US$5 hr. Mon-Fri 0800-1800. **Telephone:** *Enitel*, 1c east of cathedral, daily 0700-1900, T612-4600. **Tourist office** *Instituto Nicaragüense de Turismo (INTUR)*, next to the Iglesia Adventista, T612-7060. Mon-Fri 0800-1700, closed 1300-1400 for lunch. English spoken, very good information on local attractions, history and geography of area available for reading or they will let you make photocopies. Maps of Nicaragua for sale US$1.20. Free printed brochures. There are plans to have tour guides on call in the near future. Jenny Scarleth Pérez, at the tourism office, is available as a local guide at weekends (prior arrangement necessary), she speaks some basic English and is very knowledgeable and helpful. **Useful numbers** Fire: T612-3167. **Hospital**: T612-2081, 612-2082. **Police**: 1c south of Parque Central, T612-2382. **Red Cross**: T612-2059.

Excursions from Matagalpa

San Ramón

Colour map 1, grid C5
Population: 1,900
Altitude: 641 m

East and then south of Matagalpa runs a dirt road to the small town of San Ramón founded by the friar from León, José Ramón de Jesús María in 1800. The small village church is said to be built on a thick vein of gold, which almost caused its demolition until the villagers prevented its destruction. The village can be reached from Matagalpa by buses that leave every hour from the northern terminal, US$1. From San Ramón there is access to **Yucul** and the **Reserva de Recursos Genéticos** (Genetic Resources Reserve). The

4,826-ha reserve was established to protect a pine forest with a rare species (*Pino spatula sp. tecunmumanii*) that reportedly has the finest seeds of its kind on the American continent.

Sleeping, eating & transport

Transport can be arranged by pick-up truck from San Ramón for US$8 with the people of **E** *Esperanza Verde*, Yucul, San Ramón. T612-5003, F612-2004, herma@ibw. com.ni Simple cabins, solar power, shared baths, meals included. The project has a butterfly farm, organic coffee farm, reforestation programmes and paths for exploring the local cloud forest. Guides can be hired from the project.

Selva Negra
Altitude: 1,250 m

The Carretera a Jinotega rises steeply out of Matagalpa giving panoramic views of the city behind and the surrounding deforestation. Seven kilometres from Matagalpa the scenery changes dramatically with pine trees and oaks draped in bromeliads, in a forest that is green all year-round.

At Km 139.5 sits a burnt-out Russian two-person tank that was destroyed by the Contras in the 1980s and which now lives on as an entrance sign to the **LL-B** *Selva Negra Mountain Resort*, T612-5713, F612-3883, www.selvanegra. com Expensive and pretty private cabins, smaller stuffy airless cabins and hotel, private bath, fan, overpriced restaurant (reserve in advance on weekends) located on an artificial pond. The main reason to go is the hotel's private cloud forest reserve, which has excellent trails to be explored either on foot or horse. The 14 paths lead through a 70-year-old secondary cloud forest full of howler monkeys, deer, sloths, pumas, ocelots and agouti. The bird life of the reserve includes the legendary quetzal, toucans, hummingbirds and at least 75 other species. At the end of the trails you can enter primary cloud forest. The coffee plantation is very sustainable and coffee refuse is used as fuel. Horses are also for rent to tour the plantation. Visitors pay US$3 upon entrance to the property for which credit is given in the restaurant. It is possible to come on any Jinotega bus and get off at the entrance. It is then a 3-km walk to the hotel. Otherwise you can hire a taxi in Matagalpa.

Disparte de Potter
Altitude: 1,454 m

Past *Selva Negra* the forest becomes even more beautiful as the road leads past lush forest and highland ranches, coffee and flower farms. At Km 143 is a school and then the *Restaurante El Disparte de Potter*, T612-2553, with a bar and food à la carte. An Englishman, Señor Charles Potter, was the owner of these parts a while back, though no one is sure exactly when. On a clear day the Momotombo and San Cristóbal volcanoes of the Maribios range in the Pacific can be seen from here. The border between the departments of Matagalpa and Jinotega is here and there is access to the small but delightful **Reserva Natural Arenal**. The carretera then passes appetizing local fruit and vegetable stands before looping downward and descending into the broad valley of Jinotega.

Northern Highlands

Jinotega

Nestled in a valley of highland tropical sun, shadowed by green mountains and with a pleasant climate, Jinotega is another important town for the nation's coffee industry, though it is more relaxed and friendly than Matagalpa. In fact the charming and helpful people of Jinotega are one its greatest assets. The town has grown rapidly in recent years to the east of the centre, which has meant that Parque Central is now in the far west of town.

Colour map 1, grid C5
Population: 33,000
Altitude: 1004 m

Arenal Cloud Forest Reserve

Reserva Natural Arenal (575 ha) protects Cerro Picacho (1,650 m) and several kilometres of surrounding forest above 1,400 m. The cloud forest is noted for the abundance of the endangered resplendent quetzal (Pharomachrus mocinno mocinno), considered by ornithologists to be one of the most beautiful birds in the world. A great balsa tree known as Mojagua (Heliocarpus appendiculatus), which is the favoured nesting site for the quetzal, grows here in abundance. The forest is also home to giant emergent oak trees of up to 12 m in circumference and 40 m tall, as well as many strangler figs and tree ferns. For birders, the quetzal shares the forest with 176 species that have been documented up until now, including several species of Amazon parrot, toucans, emerald toucanets, other trogons and numerous colourful hummingbirds such as the violet sawbrewing hummingbird (campylopterus hemileucurus). The three-wattled bellbird's distinctive song can often be heard too. There are 140 documented species of butterfly, here such as the spectacular purple-blue morpho, and the almost-invisible, transparent-winged gossamer. Howler monkeys, agoutis and sloths also inhabit this forest of bromeliads, orchids, mosses, bamboo and even arboreal cacti.

Permission to hike in the forest can be obtained at the government environmental protection agency MARENA, Matagalpa, T612-3926.

History

Jinotega enjoys the highest elevation of any major city in Nicaragua. As a small Indian community in the 17th century it was sacked by a combination of British and Indian forces who attacked from the east. They even stole all the local women. Like Matagalpa, Jinotega is in the centre of coffee-growing country and consequently has suffered the ups and downs of world coffee prices. During the Contra War the hills around Jinotega were the scene of much fighting.

Sights

The area around the main plaza and the very attractive **Templo Parroquial** is criss-crossed with broad streets and has a tranquil, small-town air. Built in 1805, the Gothic cathedral has an interior that reflects the local climate with a lovely, clean and cool, whitewashed simplicity and a large collection of imagery imported from Italy and Spain. The pulpit is dramatic, with a life-sized, suffering Christ encased in glass beneath. The city's symbol is the cross-topped mountain, **Cerro La Peña Cruz**. The cross was put on the mountain by Fray Margil de la Cruz to stop flooding in the city. The population had suffered through several weeks of endless rain and floods and believed the mountain, full of water, was responsible for the inundation. The cross is believed to have saved the city and can be seen best at night to the west of Parque Central. The hike to the summit takes just over an hour and is made every 3 May by more than 5,000 pilgrims from around the region. There's a 0900 mass at the summit. Jinotega is not a city visited by many foreigners apart from those who are working on international projects. The mayor's office is very interested in having more visitors and is now working on a pre-Columbian museum as well as training local guides for a future tourist office.

Northern Highlands

Essentials

C *La Colmena*, Parque Central, 1½ c east, T632-2017. 3 rooms, private bath with hot water, TV with moderately priced restaurant. **C** *Hotel Solentuna Hem*, from pool hall, *El Batazo*, 1½ c north, T632-2334. 23 rooms, private bath with hot water, fan, cable TV, cheap restaurant with set meals and big breakfast, garage, 2 rooms upstairs with windows, pleasant and professional, owner lived in Sweden for 17 years and hotel name means 'green valley home', best in town. Recommended. **D** *Hotel Bolper*, across from Shell station *El Carmen*, T632-2966. Private bath with hot water, TV, parking, restaurant with set meals and à la carte, good value, located far from centre in less attractive area.

E *Hotel Central*, ½ c north of cathedral. 20 rooms with private bath, **G** with shared bath, ask for towel, soap and toilet paper, rooms upstairs with private bath have great mountain view, rooms vary greatly in quality, horrendous electric water pump for rooms upstairs, communal TV and purified-water dispenser downstairs, restaurant with very cheap food, excellent fruit juices, great location, very friendly, rooms with private bath are poor value. **F** *Primavera*, Esso station, 4 c north. 18 rooms, some with private bath and small, dark rooms, **G** with shared bath, family setting with house living room as lobby, good for mixing with locals, breakfast only. **F** *Mendoza*, across from La Casa Cural, T632-2062. Private bath, set meals. **G** *Hotel Tito*, across from Silias Central, T632-9665. Private bath with fan, small rooms in family setting, very helpful and friendly owners, very cheap set meals, great fruit juices, good location, best value. Recommended.

Sleeping
■ *on map*
For price codes see inside front cover. Most hotels and restaurants lock their doors at 2200

Jinotega

To San Rafael del Norte

To Matagalpa

To Hospital Victoria, Bus Station & Tico Restaurant

Parque Central

† Cathedral

□ Alcaldía

Enitel

N

Not to scale

■ **Sleeping**
1 Central
2 La Colmena
3 Solentuna Hem
4 Tito

● **Eating**
1 Pizza Venezia
2 Trochez

Bar y Restaurante La Colmena, Parque Central, 1½ c east, T632-2017. Daily 1130-2130, where the bosses eat, plain décor, attentive service, specialize in beef dishes, mid-range prices with cheap dishes available, also shrimp, chicken, best in town. *Coctelería Faisán Dorado*, across from Kodak, T632-3587. Seafood specialities, mid-range, new. *Restaurante El Tico*, across from La Salle athletic field, T632-2530. Daily 0800-2200, 44-year-old establishment in new, very modern locale, popular with couples, mid-range, try surf 'n' turf (*mar y tierra*) or *pollo a la plancha*, also cheap dishes and sandwiches. Recommended. *Pizza Venezia*, BANIC, 1 c north, 20 m east, T632-3528. Daily 1200-2130, cheap pizza, undercooked crust, bad sauce, only for the desperate pizza fix, also one pasta dish. *Jin Shan*, BANIC, ½ c south, T632-2590. 1100-2200 daily, soups, egg rolls, sweet and sour pork or chicken. Recommended.

Dance Magic, *Banco Caley Dagnall*, 3½ c east, T632-2692. Music from the 1970s, 80s and 90s, Fri-Sun 2000-0200. *El Cafetal*, across from central Esso station, T632-4170. Restaurant open daily from

Eating
● *on map*
Most people eat set meals in hotels, which cost US$1-2 per dish

Entertainment

Northern Highlands

1000 and disco on Fri and Sat, at times with live music. *El Batazo*, *Banco Caley Dagnall*, 2 c east. One of the country's nicest pool halls.

Festival The patron saint of Jinotega is *San Juan* and his festival is **24 Jun**, though there are activities before and after his day.

Shopping A new market is planned for Jinotega, but at the moment the sad, muddy one next to the bus station is the only one. To buy Jinotega coffee, the shop across from *Hotel Central* has local coffee at US$.75 for a half-pound bag.

Transport **Buses** Most destinations will require a change of bus in Matagalpa. **Jinotega-Matagalpa**, every ½ hr, 0500-1800, US$0.90, 1½ hrs. **Jinotega-Managua**, every 1½ hr, 0400-1700, US$3, 3 hrs. **Jinotega-San Rafael de Norte**, every 15 mins, 0600-1700, US$0.70, 1 hr.

Taxis are available for local transport, average fare US$.50.

Directory **Banks** There are many banks within 1 block of the cathedral. For travellers' cheques (American Express only) there is a *Banco de Finanzas* (*BDF*), Rubén Darío school, ½ c south, T632-3314. Also *Western Union*, *Hotel Tito*, ½ c north, ½ c west. **Communications** Post office: Correos de Nicaragua, behind *Banco Popular*, T632-2292. **Internet:** None at the moment, though mid-2002 should see one near Parque Central. **Telephone:** *Enitel*, ½ c south of cathedral, T632-2022. **Tourist office** One is planned soon. Mon-Fri from 0900-1200 and 1400-1700 you can try the Mayor's office (*La Alcaldía*) on the south side of Parque Central. The director of community relations, María Dolores Rodríguez, T632-2058, is working on putting together a museum and a new tourism office. **Useful numbers** Fire: T632-2468. **Hospital Victoria:** T632-2626. **Police:** T632-2215. **Red Cross:** T632-2222.

Excursions from Jinotega

Eight kilometres east of Jinotega is the beautiful **Lago de Apanás**, an artificial lake created by the damming of the Río Tuma. The lake is used to produce energy in a hydroelectric plant and is great for fishing, full of *guapote* (perch) and *tilapia*. Small enterprises that line the lake will fry fish for you. It is possible to rent a small boat and fish on the lake, ask the locals. Buses every hour from Jinotega, 20 minutes, US$0.25.

Continuing north on the paved highway from Jinotega the road rises again passing through cabbage and lettuce fields, rolling terrain with 'bearded' oak trees. The beards are a parasite plant common in this region and used by the locals for scrubbing during bathing. At Km 182, on the right, is the **Sabana Grande** touristic centre, with swimming pools. ■ *US$1 entrance.* The *carretera* veers right past the turn-off for La Concordia to the historic town of San Rafael del Norte, 25 km from Jinotega, and the end of paved roads.

San Rafael del Norte

Colour map 1, grid C4
Population: 3,400
Altitude: 1079 m

A tiny village with a gigantic church, San Rafael was the centre of much fighting from the early 20th century until 1990. The streets are dusty corridors, a study in contrasts where Franciscan nuns walk, smiling, past uniformed school children and grizzled cowboys. The population is relaxed and unassuming, with a faith reported to be as big as their amazing church. First built in 1887 with dirt floors, **La Iglesia Parroquial**, with the help of local Franciscan monks from Italy, was enlarged in 1961, and has grown into a majestic and

Northern Highlands

beautiful structure. The church sits behind a weedy, forgotten Parque Central where horses graze, and next to a Franciscan convent. The brightly coloured interior holds the patron saint of the city, and many other beautiful icons imported from Italy. To the left of the main altar is a gigantic altar to the Virgin Mary that reaches from floor to roof, with a built-in waterfall. The altar is made of volcanic rocks taken from the solidified lava of Volcán Masaya, more than 200 km south. The most famous aspect of the church is a mural next to the entrance on the left depicting the Temptation of Christ. The devil's face was painted in 1977 to resemble the Sandinista leader Daniel Ortega, it is said, by an Austrian painter. The **Museo General Sandino (Casa Museo Ejército Defensor de la Soberanía Nacional)** is where General Sandino used to send telegrams to his troops in different parts of the northern hills. The young woman to whom he dictated his messages became his wife and the town has claimed him as their native son ever since. The museum asks for donations from the visitor and needs them badly. Be very careful walking in the house, as the floor is likely to collapse at any moment. Inside there is an excellent collection of photographs from the years of Sandino's battles and the US Marines' occupation of the country as well as arms and the original telegraph machine. ■ *Donations appreciated.* Across from the museum is the house of the amiable and dynamic mayor of San Rafael, **Dr Alfonso Antonio Valdez Carbajal**. If you are lucky enough to catch him in his office or home he will greet you with an unrivalled enthusiasm and pride for his town and can help find the key to the museum or church if they are closed. If you have a good four-wheel drive, he may also have time to take you to meet one of Sandino's surviving soldiers, Don Clemente Araúz Falcón, who is in his early 90s and fought with Sandino as a 14-year-old. The mayor's office is just before the park and bus stop on the main road. On a steep hill behind the village is the chapel/retreat **Tepeyak**, built as a place for meditation. The **Festival de San Rafael** usually lasts eight days and has traditionally been held on and around 24 October, although the Vatican has now changed his day of celebration to 29 September and no one is sure when the festival will be held (both days, probably).

Sleeping Some 20 m south of the petrol station is the **F** *Hotel Rocío*, T652-2313. Small, intimate and very clean *hospedaje*, with private bath or **G** with shared bath, 3 set meals a day (US$1.50), one of the best in country in this price category.

Eating *Comedor Chepita*, just south of the museum. Offers lunch and dinner dishes of the day. At the exit of town heading south is the dirt road that leads to Yalí and *Bar y Restaurante Los Encuentros*, whose owner Orlando Zelaya speaks some English. The outdoor seating of the eatery overlooks the confluence of hot and cold rivers and is a popular bathing spot. You can eat a whole chicken for US$4 here and beers are US$0.80.

Transport **Buses** San Rafael de Norte-Jinotega, every 15 mins, 0600-1800, US$0.70, 1 hr.

Pan-American Highway: Sébaco to Estelí

The Pan-American Highway branches left in Sébaco and runs northwest all the way to the Honduran border. The highway, repaved in 2001 and in excellent condition, passes large rice fields and, 10 km outside of Sébaco, intersects the windswept brick and stucco village of **San Isidro** and a secondary highway to León. Buses are available here at the stop along the *carretera* (two hours to León, every 30 minutes, US$1). The **San Isidro-León highway** is the only direct, paved connection from the north-central highlands to the Pacific

Northern Highlands

San Isidro-León
Watch out for cows and horses on the San Isidro-León highway, particularly at night

Basin and the changes and contrasts are interesting. The road was built through difficult terrain in 1930 at the cost of many Nicaraguan lives. In 1998 Hurricane Mitch took away its biggest bridges, which are still being rebuilt. The rest of the *carretera* is in good condition and passes through little-seen villages like El Jicaral and Mina La India. La India is an old gold mining town from which the Spanish used to extract riches, as did the Somozas and later the Sandinistas; the local population, as poor as ever, still manages to survive from gold mining. There is some beautiful, rugged river-and-mountain scenery and it is difficult to get further off the beaten path on a paved road in the Pacific. The road continues west, losing altitude and dropping into the rocky savannah landscape of Malpaisillo and the eastern valley of the Maribios volcanic range. The highway reaches the volcanoes and passes between the active Cerro Negro's recent lava flows (to the left) and the always active Telica (to the right, at the back of the small, dormant San Jacinto cone along the highway). The *carretera* then intersects with the León to Chinandega highway to travel south or north respectively.

La Trinidad

Colour map 1, grid C4
Population: 7,500
Altitude: 601 m

Back at San Isidro, the Pan-American Highway continues north, through the little cowboy town of La Trinidad. This, the highland bread capital, has no less than 12 bakeries, some selling their bread as far away as Managua. La Trinidad is set in an impressive, deep canyon surrounded by three mountains: Oyanca, **La Mocuana** and El Hatillo. La Mocuana is the name of a famous Nicaraguan legend about the beautiful daughter of an Indian chief who fell in love with a Spanish priest. The priest, who was only interested in gold and riches, betrayed La Mocuana and left her to die in a mountain cave where she is said to have remained for ever, except when she comes out at night to seek her revenge. Looking at the setting it isn't hard to see how the supernatural could take hold.

About 5 km north of La Trinidad is the interesting restaurant *Antojitos del Desierto*, Comunidad Santa Cruz, T742-2585, grilled rabbit, chicken soup, with a fun table that sits out literally over the *carretera*. The highway continues to climb another 240 m to the departmental capital of Estelí at Km 148.

Estelí

Colour map 1, grid C4
Population: 73,000
Altitude: 844 m

From the highway Estelí appears a jumbled, unattractive place, yet this unpretentious town is one of the most pleasant, lively and industrious in Nicaragua. It is the biggest commercial centre in the north with an endless array of small family shops and countless restaurants along its two main boulevards and many side streets. There are also good schools and universities, which draw students from all over the northern region and, as a result, the population is young and optimistic. The climate too is pleasant with average temperatures of 19°-21°C.

Ins and outs

Getting around The centre of the city lies well to the east of the highway, with the focus of its life and commerce on its two main avenues. The southbound road runs from one block east of Parque Central, 12 blocks south to the south market and bus station. The northbound passes right in front of Parque Central and, two blocks north, reaches the central market. Estelí was founded in 1711 by colonists who abruptly left Nueva Segovia, now Ciudad Antigua, from threats of Indian attacks and British invasions.

Sights

The **cathedral**, first built in 1823 with upgrades in 1889, was the last to be built in the 'Nicaraguan primitive baroque' style, though the façade was altered in 1929 to its current neoclassical look. Inside the church is not inspiring, but it does have a pretty image of the **Virgen del Rosario** for which the cathedral is named. The architecture of the city as a whole is incoherent and unattractive; thanks to heavy damage in the Revolution most of the structures have been replaced in the last 25 years.

There are some buildings in the city centre that remain from the time of the Revolution, their countless bullet holes attest to the intensity of the three major battles that took place here in 1978 and 1979. The **Casa Movimiento Communal**, at the southeast corner of Parque Central, is a good example, as well as the skeleton house across from *Restaurante Las Brasas*. Estelí remains one of the most Sandinista cities in Nicaragua and the party colours of black and red can be seen around the town, along with the revolutionary murals that decorate buildings on Parque Central.

Aside from the city's history during the Revolution, Estelí is known as the **capital of cigars** in Nicaragua. With the finest tobacco in Central America grown in the surrounding mountains, the town is full of cigar factories, some of which produce among the best *puros or habanos* in the world. Most of the factories were founded by exiled Cubans in the 1960s who brought their seeds and expertise with them. Many left during the 1980s, but they returned in force in the following decade. There are some factories that allow visitors, though most ask that you contact them at least two days prior to your arrival (see Shopping below).

B *Alameda*, Shell Esquipulas, 1 c east, 1½ c south, T713-6292, F713-5219. A/c, private bath with hot water, cable TV, pool, restaurant, nice but a little far from centre. **B** *Alpino*, Texaco ½ east, T713-2828, F713-2368. 18 rooms and 4 apartments, private bath, a/c or fan, cable TV. **B** *Moderno*, from the cathedral, 2½ c south, T713-2378, F713-4315. Hot water, clean, friendly, Estelí's most famous hotel. Recommended.

On the *Carretera Panamericana* **C** *Hotel Panorama No 1*, T713-3147. Private bath, hot water, a/c, cable TV, noisy, far from centre, convenient for north station buses. **C** *Hotel Panorama No 2*, from cathedral, 1 c south, ½ c east, T713-5023. Same features as No 1, but much quieter at night, with good access to town centre and restaurants, secured parking, rooms upstairs nicer. Recommended. **D** *El Mesón*, Av Bolívar, 1 c north of central plaza, T713-2655, F713-4029, barlan@ibw.com.ni With shower, fan, clean, restaurant, TV, changes travellers' cheques. Recommended.

E *Mariela*, behind south bus station, T713-2166. Clean, safe, washing facilities, very small rooms, parking inside gates, basic, not best area. **E** *Casa Hotel Nicarao*, 1½ c south of central plaza, T713-2490. With private bath, fan, hot shower. **F** with shared bath, rooms are well worn with tired beds, but with character and they encircle a pleasant, sociable interior courtyard restaurant/café area, very central location, best value. Highly recommended. **E** *Barlop*, Parque Central, 7 c north, T713-2486. 12 rooms, 6 of which are good, 6 basic, the good ones have showers, friendly.

Sleeping
■ *on map, page 228*

Stay in the centre of the city to enjoy the atmosphere, shopping and good dining options

Northern Highlands

Northern Highlands

F *Hospedaje El Chepito*, 4 c north of south bus terminal. Quiet, clean, friendly. **F** *Hospedaje San Francisco*, next to Parque Infantil. Very basic, close to new craft market and south bus terminal. **F** *Hospedaje Ignacio*, near *San Francisco*. With bath, pleasant, nice garden, laundry facilities. **F** *Hotel Miraflor*, Parque Central, ½ c north. Restaurant, private bathroom, hot water, TV in restaurant, basic, but OK if others are full.

Eating
● *on map*

For directions keep in mind that the cathedral faces due west. Directions from Parque Central start at the street that runs on the other side of the park, opposite the church, directions from the church start at the street that passes directly in front of the church

Cafetería El Rincón Pinareño, across from *Panorama No 2*. Cuban and Nicaraguan dishes and pastries, try *vaca frita* (shredded fried beef with onions and bell peppers), *sandwich cubano*, US$2 minimum charge, very good service and food, cheap to mid-range. Recommended. 1200-2100 daily. *China Garden*, on central plaza, good food, friendly waiters, but a bit like a hangar. *Cocina Tía Rose*, Intur, 1½ c north, T713-3315. Cheap lunch menu Tue-Sat 1200-1600, dinner menu Tue-Sat 1800-2100, excellent food and service, many unusual dishes in pleasant home-like setting, try *rollitos a la Vienesa* (stuffed beef rolls), or the *cerdo imperial* (breaded pork in peach sauce), or sea bass in mustard sauce. Highly recommended. *Restaurante Palermo*, next to *BANIC*, T713-2569. Very good Italian dishes, 1200-2200 daily, cheap to mid-range. On the same street, *El Caporal* offers simple meat and fish dishes at good prices. *El Mesero*, *Teatro Estelí*, 2 c east, T713-6539. Good and very big bowls of soup, nice setting, popular and very good, mid-range to cheap, 0900-2200 daily. *Burger King*, across from *Enitel*, T713-2090, the real king of burgers (not the US chain) with 12 types of hamburgers, 1130-2230 daily, seriously cheap. About 3 blocks north of park on Av Bolívar is *Panadería España*, good but pricey. *Las Brasas*, just off northeast corner of Parque Central, T713-4985. Tue-Sun 1130–2400, very good Nicaraguan food, try *cerdo asado*, very popular, liveliest place during the week. Recommended. Next door is *Café Bar Punto de Encuentro*, good cheap food and beer, giant cheap breakfast upon request,

Estelí

To Las Praderas Bar & Restaurant, Somoto & Honduras

To Cigar Factory (Segovia Cigars)

Taksi Disco

Río Estelí

Gran Vía Bolívar

Cyberplace

Crafts

Soluciones Computarizados

Parque Central

Cathedral

Estelí Cigar SA

Galería de los Héroes y Mártires

BDF

C Perú

Casa de Cultura

BANIC

Amnlae Women's Centre

Carretera Panamericana

El Salvador Cooperative

Ministry of Health Information Centre

Cenac Language School

Principal

INTUR Craft

Horizontes Spanish School

Parque Infantil

Pol

Bus Station North

Gran Vía Bolívar

Buses South

To Managua

N

Not to scale

3 Hospedaje
   San Francisco
4 Mariela
5 Miraflor
6 Moderno
7 Nicarao
8 Panorama 2

■ **Sleeping**
1 Barlop
2 El Mesón

● **Eating**
1 Cocina Tía Rose
2 El Caporal
3 El Mesero
4 Las Brasas
5 Panadería
   España

popular. *Soda La Confianza*, ½ c south of Parque Central. Cheap, good greasy food, cheap pitchers of *Victoria* beer.

Pan-American Highway has a good restaurant and several good open ranch-style restaurants that offer dancing on weekend nights. Across from Casa Pellas, still in town, is *Restaurante Los Cubanitos*, T713-6976. Moderately-priced Cuban food with several excellent pork dishes. Heading north from Estelí past the bridge are 2 great places to eat, drink and be merry: the first is *Restaurante Las Praderas*, T713-6516. Large open-air patio with mid-range and cheap food, very nice on weekend nights with dancing to variety of music, happy, young crowd. Recommended. The other, just further north on the *Carretera Panamericana*, is *Restaurante El Rancho de Pancho*, T713-2569. Another open-air patio restaurant with dancing nightly, good beef dishes, mid-range to cheap prices, set right on the edge of a tobacco plantation with good view of the plants during season. Recommended. **NB** If going at night to *Rancho de Pancho* or *Praderas*, you may have trouble finding a taxi back into the city, so ask the driver who takes you to return at a pre-set hour.

There are numerous options for dancing in Estelí from Thu-Sun. Otherwise you can dance at the restaurants mentioned above. *Discotek Traksis*, conveniently located next to the Victoria Brewery, is one of the city's most popular clubs with a wide variety of music on tape, entrance US$1.50 (Thu free admission for women). *Discotek Cyber*, where *Telcor Calvario* used to be. This is the disco used mostly by gay and lesbian night dancers, entrance US$1. *Discotek Flan's Boyan*, next to *Restaurante Anival*. Here you can dance with the local street gang members, check in your knife and chains at the door, entrance is US$1 (Sun is free for women). *Discotek Zodiacal*, 1 c west, 20 m north from Parque Central. This is the most central of the night spots, entrance is US$1.50. **Entertainment**

For American films with Spanish subtitles on the south side of the Parque Central is *Cine Estelí*, entrance US$2. For live music on weekends there is *Villa Vieja*, ½ block north of Parque Central on Av Bolívar, good atmosphere. **NB** If out after 1100 it is recommended to use a taxi, as there are youth gangs who look for trouble after those hours, though the centre seems to be relatively problem-free.

16 Jul there are celebrations dedicated to the *Virgen de la Canderlaria*, there are also processions on **7 Oct** for the *Virgen del Rosario*. **Festivals**

Cedro Real and *Flor de Estelí, Briones Cigar Company*, Shell Estelí, 100 m west, 50 m south, T713-2775, F713-2775. Contact: José Briones, Mon-Fri 0700-1130, 1400-1630, Sat 0800-1130, bricigar@ibw.com.ni Other factories need at least two 2 days' planning (or the help of a Managua tour operator) and include the superb *Padrón* brand made by *Tabacos Cubanica*, SA, de Obispado, 1 c south, T713-2383, F713-2669. Contact: José Orlando Padron, Mon-Fri, 0700-1130, 1400-1630. There is also the *Two Reynas, Dinastía Pintor* cigar maker, *Tabacos Pintor y Pintor*, T713-5636, Mon-Fri 0700-1130, 1400-1630, pintorsaa@ibw.com.ni Contact: Ricardo Pintor. Also *Segovia Cigars*, T713-5903, F713-4074, taonic@ibw.com.ni Contact: Amed Fernández, Mon-Fri 0700-1130, 1400-1630. The best-selling Nicaragua cigar may well be *Joya de Nicaragua*, made by *Tabacos Puros de Nicarag*ua, Km 147 Carretera Panamericana, T713-7133, F713-2757, tpn@ibw.com.ni Mon-Fri 0700-1130, 1400-1630. Contact: Mario Perez. **Shopping**

There are several nice craft stores in Estelí. *La Esquina* is opposite *Hotel Mesón* and 1 south of the cathedral is another. There are 2 principal **markets**: one just 1 block north of Parque Central and the other next to the south bus station. On the Calle Principal there is a good supermarket called *Supermercado Económico*, on the same street closer to the centre is **Kodak** for photography supplies. There are some nice cowboy hats in a small shop **Perfumería Record**, which is ½ block south of Parque Central.

Transport **Buses** enter and leave Estelí via 2 separate terminals. The **south terminal**, next to the southern market, serves all routes to the south including destinations that are accessed via Sébaco (which lies south of the city), such as Matagalpa and Jinotega. The other routes north are served by the new **north terminal**, which has small shops and cheap places to eat and appears to be the nicest bus terminal in Nicaragua.

North station: all buses for northern destinations. **Estelí-Somoto**, every ½ hr, 0530-1800, US$1, 1½ hrs, for border crossing at **El Espino** use this to connect to border bus. **Estelí-Ocotal**, every hr, 0600-1730, US$1, 2 hrs, use this for bus to **Las Manos** crossing. **Estelí-San Juan de Limay**, 0915 and 1215, US$2.25, 4 hrs. **Estelí-Matagalpa**, every hr, 0620-1730, US$1.50, 1½ hrs. **Estelí-Jinotega**, every hr, 0730-1530, US$1.50, 2 hrs. **Estelí-El Sauce**, 0900, US$1.25, 3 hrs.

South station: Estelí-León, 0625 and 1500, 2 hrs, US$1.50. Alternatively, take any bus going south on the Panamericana and change at **San Isidro**, ½ hr, US$0.50; from here wait by the roadside for buses south to León. **Estelí-Managua**, every hr, 0445-1515, US$2.25, 2¾ hrs, also 2 daily **Luxury Express Estelí-Managua**, 0545, 0645, US$3, 2¼ hrs.

Taxi Taxis are common on the Carretera Panamericana in Estelí, the bus stations and the town proper. Fares per person, inside the city centre US$0.50, from the bus stations to centre US$1 per person. Night fares are higher and trips to the dance restaurants on the outskirts like *Rancho Pancho* and *Las Praderas* should cost US$1.50. As always, agree on fare before getting in.

Directory **Banks** Almost every bank in the city is located in one city block. One block south and 1 block east from Parque Central will bring you to the 2 banks that change travellers' cheques, **Banco de América Central, BAC**, T713-7101, which changes all brands of travellers' cheques, and **Banco de Finanzas, BDF**, T713-3101, which changes American Express only. You can change cash in any of the banks including **BANIC**, T713-2947, and **BANPRO**, T713-2633, for cash advances US$3 charge, which are also on this corner. **Agencia de Viajes Tisey**, T713-3099, in Hotel Mesón changes travellers' cheques as well.

Car rental **Budget Rent a Car**, cathedral, 1 c north, T713-4030. **Toyota Rent a Car**, Edif Casa Pellas, Km 148 Carretera Panamericana, T713-2716.

Communications Internet: *Cyberplace*, Parque Central, 2½ c north, T713-2475, 0800-2000, US$4 per hr. *Computer Soluciones*, on northwest corner of plaza, US$5 per hr. Post office: *Correos de Nicaragua*, 75 m east of the banks, T713-2085 F713-2240. Telephone: *Enitel*, cathedral, 1 c south, T713-3280.

Spanish schools *Cenac*, Centro Nicaragüense de Aprendizaje y Cultura, Apdo 40, Estelí, T713-5437, cenac@tmx.com.ni 2 offices: Texaco 5 blocks east, ½ block to south, and from the banks, 1 block south, ½ block east, opposite *Farmacia San Sebastián*, T713-2025: 20 hrs of Spanish classes, living with a family, full board, travelling to countryside, meetings and seminars, opportunities to work on community projects, cost US$120 per week. *Cenac* also teaches English to Nicaraguans and others and welcomes volunteer tutors. *Cenac* is run by women, but is separate from the Movimiento de Mujeres, **Casa Nora Astorga**, Apdo 72, Estelí, which also occupies one of the Cenac buildings and offers classes. Also **Casa de Familias**, Costado Noreste del Hospital, 1 block from Carretera, US$100 per week. **Los Pipitos-Sacuanjoche Spanish School**, de Petronic 1 c south, 2 c east, T713-5511, F713-2240, sacuanjoche@ibw.com.ni, all profits go to disabled children and their families, excursions to local co-operatives, political parties, social projects are part of the course, staying with families, US$120-170 per week, flexible, co-ordinator is German, Katharina Pförtner.

Tourist office *INTUR, Instituto Nicaragüense de Turismo*, Antiguo Hospital Alejandro Dávila Bolaños, T713-6799, 713-6798. The office has information on the city and surrounding attractions, all in Spanish. The building, once a hospital, is being renovated to become a craft market with some cafés and is located in between the south market and city centre.

Useful numbers Fire: T713-2413. **Hospital**: *San Juan de Dios*, Carretera Panamericana, T713-6300. **Immigration**: T713-2086. **Police**: T713-2615. **Red Cross**: T713-2330.

Excursions from Estelí

Nicaragua has few waterfalls that are accessible to the visitor and this is perhaps the most beautiful of those that are reachable without an arduous journey. Just south of the entrance to Estelí and the new hospital, on the *carretera*, is a small sign marking the dirt road that leads west to the site, located 5 km from the highway. Most of the year this road will not be passable except in a four-wheel drive, but it's a pleasant walk over farmland and through a small oak forest. Turn right about 4½ km down the road onto a smaller road (there is only a post where a sign once marked the turn-off). The locals are friendly and will keep you on the right track if you ask them. From the smaller road you pass over two crests and then down into the river valley. It is a cool place with a beautiful 40-m waterfall and the pool beneath it is deep and good for swimming. **NB** The area in front of the waterfall is a popular picnic spot for visitors from Estelí.

El Salto de la Estanzuela

Reserva Natural Miraflor

This is one of Nicaragua's best-kept secrets. Though only 206 sq km, this pristine mountain nature reserve is full of diverse flora and rare fauna. The ecosystem changes with altitude from tropical savannah to tropical dry forest, then to pine forest and finally cloud forest at its highest elevations. The resplendent quetzal lives here, along with trogons, magpie jays, the beautiful turquoise browed mot-mot (the national bird), many birds of prey, howler monkeys, mountain lions, ocelots, jaguars, deer, sloths, river-otter, racoon and tree frogs. The reserve also has some gallery forest, ideal for viewing wildlife, a variety of orchids and a 60-m waterfall that flows during the rainy season. **Laguna de Miraflor** is a 1½-ha body of water at 1,380 m with a magical deep-blue colour and an unknown depth. The reserve is shared by the departments of Estelí and Jinotega, but access is dramatically easier from the Estelí side of the mountains. The entrance to the dirt road (often difficult in rainy season) that leads towards Yalí and passes by the entrance to the reserve is at the Texaco petrol station heading out of Estelí northbound on the Pan-American Highway. The narrow dirt road leads up into the mountains with spectacular views of the valley below. The entrance to the park is after the rocky fields of bearded oaks.

Colour Map 1, grid C4
Altitude: 700-1,484 m

Northern Highlands

D *Cabañas Miraflor*, in El Terrero, T713-2971, miraflor@ibw.com.ni 4 bungalows, each with solar power and a bath. The bungalows have 3-4 rooms each that hold 3-4 people each. The minimum charge per room is US$10 with US$5 per person extra in each room. A 3-meals per day plan is US$9. Reservations should be made at least 3 days in advance if

Sleeping & eating

possible. Contact Erica or Porfirio Zepeda (speaks English), T/F713-2971 (address: contiguo a Talleres del Mingob, Estelí), or Katharina Pförtner (see *Los Pipitos-Sacuanjoche*, above) and Gene Hinz, T713-4041.

Tours   The foundation in charge of the reserve offers guided hikes ranging from US$12 per half-day to US$15-25 per day. Horses can be rented for US$3.50 half-day to US$5 for full day.

Transport   **Buses** leave 3 times per day, 0600, 1200, 1600 from Estelí's north station towards San Sebastián de Yalí, US$1. Return buses pass at 0700, 1100 and 1620. You need to get off at the bus stop which says *'Ecotourismo'* where there is also a sign for the environmental protection agency, *MARENA*. From there you must walk about 15 mins into the reserve to the cabañas.You can also come in 4WD; there are 2 rental agencies in Estelí (see above).

   NB Travelling at night on the dirt roads between Estelí and Yalí is not recommended due to robberies. Police have now opened a station just outside the Miraflor reserve and it is reported to be safer.

San Juan de Limay

Colour map 1, grid C3
Population: 3,700
Altitude: 281 m

North of Estelí there is a very poor dirt road that runs west to the rural village of San Juan de Limay. The journey can take up to two hours but is worth it for those who like crafts. The people of San Juan make soapstone carvings and sculptures, some smaller than a child's hand (usually tropical birds and reptiles), others weighing up to 75 kg (mostly humans). The workmanship is superb and can be found in markets all over Central America. The locals are happy to receive visitors in to their houses, which, as with 99% of Nicaraguan artisans, double as their workshops. The locals also cultivate freshwater lobster (*camarones de río*) and there are iguana farms being planned.

Sleeping & eating   Lodging is not available, but you can ask for someone to rent their bed for the night (or for a place to string up your hammock) and buy some meat and rice to be cooked in their house.

Transport   **Buses** twice a day from north terminal, **Esteli-San Juan de Limay**, 0915 and 1215, US$2.25, 4 hrs. **San Juan de Limay-Estelí**, 0615, 1215, US$2.25, 4 hrs. A 4WD can be rented in Estelí; do not attempt this journey in a passenger car.

Estelí to El Espino   Continuing north on the Panamericana there is a hill with a wrecked aeroplane on its summit that marks the arrival at Condega. The plane was used by the Contra northern forces to air-drop supplies to the rebels and was shot down by the Nicaraguan government forces. The American co-pilot of the plane survived the crash and tried to escape north to Honduras; instead, completely lost, he headed south right into the arms of the Sandinista army. With no shortage of media hoopla, he was taken to Managua and later turned over to the US Embassy.

Condega

Colour map 1, grid C4
Population: 8,000
Altitude: 561 m

On the east side of the highway is the sleepy village of Condega, another vehemently Sandinista town, with a very indigenous population. The name Condega means 'pottery makers' and the town's artisans make very traditional and rustic, red-clay pottery. Condega's Parque Central is a quiet place with an

18th-century church, **Iglesia San Isidro**, that was recently rebuilt. On the southeastern side of the square is the **Casa de Cultura**, which produces plays, runs art classes and has a good little pre-Columbian museum run by Miriam Rugama. ■ *Mon-Fri 0800-1200, 1400-1600, Sat 0800-1200.* Miriam can show you the guitar maker's shop in the back of the cultural centre and, if you have transport, will accompany you to a ceramic co-operative on the west side of the highway. **Taller Cerámica Ducuale**, T752-2418, is located north of the town and about 3 km down a dirt road from the highway. It is possible to walk there, and should take about one hour from the town centre. Founded in 1990 The Ducuale co-op is made up of 13 female artisans. Pottery has been a tradition in this area for thousands of years and its red and rustic colours are lovely. Visiting the workshop gives the opportunity to meet the artists and buy their work, which is not available for sale at most of the markets in the country. ■ *Mon-Fri 0700-1700.*

G *Hospedaje Framar*, on main plaza next to Casa de Cultura, T752-2393. 14 rooms, very clean and pleasant, cold showers, shared facilities, nice garden, very quiet, safe, friendly, owner speaks English, excellent value. Recommended.

Sleeping

About 6 very cheap places including *Comedor Rosa Amelia Peralta*. 1 block north off main plaza and 3 blocks north of Parque Central is *Comedor Herrera*. On the Pan-American, at the south entrance to Condega there is a cute place with a great view south towards the valley of Estelí, *Bar y Restaurante Linda Vista*, with cheap *comida corriente* and cheap to mid-range full menu. They have a few tradional soups and drinks that are very good like *sopa de frijoles* (bean soup) and *leche con banana* (milk and banana drink).

Eating

Buses north and southbound pass through Parque Central in Condega every ½ hour. Bus to **Ocotal** 1 hr or **Somoto** 1 hr is US$0.75 and to **Estelí** 40 mins, US$0.50. From Condega there is a rough dirt road to **Yalí** that crosses the Río Estelí, 2 hrs, US$1.

Transport

There is a telephone in Condega 1 block north of the church at the *Enitel* office, as well as 1 bank, *BanPro*. 3 blocks north of the park is the bar and disco complex *Enamore*, with dancing on Sat night only.

Directory

North of Condega the Carretera Panamericana enters into the department of **Madriz**, the land of *rosquillas*, a traditional biscuit made of egg, cheese, cornmeal and butter. *Rosquillas* are small, hard and dry, yet very tasty and addictive, in particular the *viejita* which has melted cane sugar in the centre. No Nicaraguan would dream of visiting these parts without picking up a few bags, as they are the best in the country. They are the ultimate northern highlands road snack and also great for dunking in coffee or milk, or washed down with a cold *Victoria* beer. Just before Km 204, where the road dips down to run along a smaller river, is one of the best places to buy famous biscuits: *Rosquillas Mata Palo*, small bags are US$0.40 and big ones US$0.80. At **Yalaguina** is the turn-off to the highway to Ocotal and the border crossing Las Manos (see below). The Pan-American Highway continues to the left and has recently been undergoing heavy repairs. The land is rocky and mountainous with a scattered population.

North of Condega

Somoto

Somoto, the most important town in the department, is where everything happens in good time. The peacefulness of the town is overwhelming. The population is as quiet as the town, with a shy smile often breaking their sombre exterior. There is almost no tourism in this part of Nicaragua, only the occasional traveller who is crossing the border and decides to stay for a night. One of the safest towns in the country, Somoto is best known for its superb *rosquillas* and its world-famous sons, the folk music artists **Carlos and Enrique Mejía Godoy**. The Mejía Godoy brothers' mother Elsa has moved back from Managua to the profound peace of the town, and lives across from the INSS office. The church of Somoto was built in 1661 and is an original adobe structure with tile roof, a simple, cool interior and a black Christ above the altar. There are some beautiful walks, or horse rides (horses for rent from Johanna Moncada, *Restaurante Las Delicias*) in the surrounding mountains, as well as some important archaeological sites to visit. The mayor's office is planning to map them and to arrange guides for visitors. Check at the Alcaldía for progress on this project or ask around for a guide at your hotel. The Alcaldía also has a small but important **pre-Columbian museum** which displays ceramics with unusual iconography and evidence of much trading with Honduras. ■ *Mon-Fri 0800-1200, T722-2210.* If arriving on a Sunday between October and May, you may want to check out Nicaraguan division-one football (soccer) at the 2,500-seat **Santiago Stadium**, where the local team *Real Madrid* plays. ■ *Admission US\$1.50.*

Sleeping **D** *Hotel Colonial*, ½ c south of the church, T722-2040. Private bath with hot water, TV, fan, very smart rooms in family-run hotel. **D** *El Bambú*, Policía Nacional, 2 c north, T722-2330. Private bath and a/c, good restaurant with dancing. **F** *Hotel Panamericano*, on north side of Parque Central, T722-2355. Private bath with hot water, fan, TV, mini-fridge, very clean, airy rooms, **G** with shared bath and dark interior rooms, parking, restaurant. Rooms with private bath are one of the best hotel values to be had in Nicaragua, very helpful and friendly staff, great location. Highly recommended. **F** *Baghal*, Centro de Salud, 1½ c south, T722-2358. Enter through house, private bath, small dark rooms with sagging beds and no toilet seats or shower heads, friendly family. **F** *Internacional*, 1 block from central plaza. Clean and basic.

Eating *Restaurante Tepezonate*, Centro de Salud, 2½ c west, T722-2462. Moderately priced menu featuring seafood dishes and mixed grill, cheap daily dishes, country charm, good, open 1000-2300 daily. *La Llanta*, 1 c west of PETRONIC, T722-2291. Good pork dishes, hot pepper steak, mid-range with cheap dish of the day, open Mon-Fri 1000-2200, Sat-Sun 1000-2400. *Restaurante Somoteño*, at north entrance to town on highway, beef grill. *Restaurante Almendro*, ½ c south of church. Moderate, famous for its steaks and subject of a Mejía Godoy song. Recommended. *Cafetería Bambi*, Enitel, 2½ c south, T722-2231. Strangely no deer on the menu, a lot of cheap sandwiches, hamburgers, hot dogs, tacos and fruit juices, open Tue-Sun 0900-2200. *Discoteque El Turco*, Fri-Sat, taped music, US\$1 entrance fee.

Festival 25 Jul there is a festival to celebrate *Santiago* the patron saint of Somoto. There is also the local version of *carnival*, which is really a huge block party in Parque Central, with musical bands coming from all over Central America to perform from 1800-0600 non-stop, on a moving date within the last **15 days of Nov.**

Crafts *Hotel Panamericano* has the most diverse and complete craft shop in the department with ceramic and wood from all over the northern highland region. Especially interesting are the white ceramics of Somoto, along with the red clay of Mosonte and black of Matagalpa; worth a look. **Rosquilla Bakers** *Toña Soza*, PETRONIC, 1 ½ c south, *Betty Espinoza*, *Enitel*, 3 c north, T722-2173, *Guadalupe Espinoza*, PETRONIC, 1 c south, ½ c east, *María Luisa Vilchez*, *Enitel*, 8 c south, 1 c east, T722-2002, *Leticia Corrales*, Cotrán, 2 c south.

Bus Somoto-El Espino and the Honduran border, every ½ hr from 0500-1700, 1 hr, US$1. **Somoto-Managua** twice a day 0715 and 1400, 3½ hrs, US$3. **Somoto-Ocotal**, every 45 mins, 0600-16.15, US$1.50, 2½ hrs.

Banks *Banco de Finanzas (BDF)*, T722-2240, in front of the *Alcaldía*. Changes American Express travellers' cheques and cash. **Communications** Post office: *Correos de Nicaragua*, southeast corner of park, T722-2437, F722-2257. **Telephone**: *Enitel*, behind church, T722-2374. **Useful numbers** Fire: T722-2776. Hospital: *Centro de Salud*, west side of Parque Central, T722-2247. **Police**: T722-2359. **Red Cross**: T722-2285.

El Espino: border with Honduras

Some 20 km west of Somoto on the Carretera Panamericana is El Espino, which is 5 km from the Honduran border at **La Playa**. The El Espino route will take you to Choluteca, in the Gulf of Fonseca lowlands of Honduras. For Tegucigalpa use the crossing at La Manos (see below), which connects with the highway to the Honduran capital. Otherwise, you can use El Espino and head north from Choluteca.

There is a duty-free shop and a food bar on the Nicaraguan side and several cafés on the Honduran side. No money changers on Nicaraguan side but locals will oblige, even with lempiras. There is nowhere to stay in El Espino.

Nicaraguan passport control and customs are in the ruined customs house, 100 m from the Honduran border. The Nicaraguan side is open 0600-1200, 1300-1700. If you're arriving or leaving Nicaragua you'll have to pay US$7 plus a US$1 *Alcaldía* charge.

Crossing by private vehicle Motorists leaving Nicaragua should enquire in Somoto whether an exit permit has to be obtained there or at El Espino. This also applies to cyclists.

Transport Bus El Espino-Honduran border, US$0.40 plus US$0.40 per bag. **El Espino-Somoto**, 0500-1700, US$0.90, 1 hr. **Taxi** El Espino-Somoto, US$6-8.

Carretera a Ocotal

The other route to Honduras uses the highway to Ocotal and Las Manos and also provides access to explore the very historic and mountainous department of Nueva Segovia, Nicaragua's northernmost province. From the Carretera Panamericana the **Carretera a Ocotal** travels north and the landscape changes into jagged hills and pine trees. The bridge just before Ocotal, which crosses Central America's longest river, the Río Coco, is under constant repair, but the road from the Panamerican to the bridge is excellent. Before the Río Coco is the small red-earth village of Totogalpa.

Northern Highlands

Totogalpa

Colour map 1, grid B3
Population: 1,600
Altitude: 661 m

Totogalpa is the first of the historic villages that dot the far north of Nicaragua. Places like Totogalpa are a reminder of how easy it is to feel you have arrived at the very end of the earth in Nicaragua. These seemingly forgotten towns with romantic, pretty colonial churches and a slow-walking, ageing population, have seen their youth move to cities and foreign lands. The bright red clay streets of Totogalpa and its crumbling, yet attractive adobe homes add to the town's rustic otherworldliness. The central plaza is small and its humble colonial-style church, built in 1774, is charming, new roof and all. Totogalpa celebrates its patron saint **Virgen de la Merced** from 8-23 September. There are some interesting hikes in the surrounding area and a chance to explore the most westerly part of the Río Coco that drains all the way to the Caribbean sea.

One kilometre north of Totogalpa is **Cerro de las Rocas** and a trail that leads to a cave inside the mountain, **La Cueva del Duende**. The name, 'Elf's Cave', relates to an interesting legend, one that's very common in northern Nicaragua. It is said that once inside the cave all flashlights fail to function. Danni Altamirano, at the *Hotel El Camino* in Totogalpa, is brave enough to take visitors to the cave. He, or his brother, can also take you up to the **Río Coco** for some balsa wood rafting (prices negotiable).

Further north, along the very smooth highway is the bridge for the Río Coco, a big project by Nicaraguan standards and one that has been rebuilt twice in the last three years. On the north side of the river valley is Ocotal, capital of the historic and scenic Nueva Segovia department where pine trees are the dominant vegetation.

Sleeping **F** *Hotel El Camino*, just off the highway, along the main entrance road to Totogalpa, private bath, fan, parking, clean, light rooms. Recommended. 3 cheap meals a day are available from Danni's mother, in their house.

Transport **Buses** pass the village on the highway, every 15 mins for **Ocotal** (US$0.40) or **Estelí** (US$0.80).

Ocotal

Colour map 1, grid B3
Population: 27,000
Altitude: 606 m

This little city with sprawling suburbs is the financial and trading centre for the region, but has little to offer visitors. The population is more serious and less friendly than in most parts of the country and the city centre is void of any decent lodging or interesting places to eat. Ocotal is a possible jumping-off point to visit some of the beautiful villages in the region, or to rest before or after the border crossing at Las Manos.

The church on the Parque Central is attractive, and worth a look. Founded in 1803, **El Templo Parroquial de Ocotal** was not finished until 1869, and its baroque and neoclassical façade hide a simple and attractive interior with pine columns and comfortable curved pews. There are some very pretty icons inside, which are said to have been imported from La Antigua, Guatemala. Ocotal's one very special attraction is its **Parque Central**, which is like no other in Nicaragua. **Parque Las Madres**, as it is called, is a central plaza turned lush tropical garden. The brainchild of the ex-mayor of Ocotal and tropical plant expert Don Fausto Sánchez, this park is a stunning display of plant diversity, a dense tapestry of greens, reds, oranges, yellows and pinks. It is easy to lose yourself in its well-manicured paradise. Set within the relative ugliness of Ocotal, the park is a leafy refuge, a reminder of the stunning fertility of the

Devilish elves: los duendes

The legend of the duendes is prevalent throughout the country, but seems to be most popular in the northern mountain ranges and in the central departments of Boaco and Chontales. People of all ages believe in the existence of these little people. Duendes are something akin to demonic elves; a race of very small alien people, dressed usually in red, with pointy hats and, more often than not, sporting beards. The duendes make frequent contact and pacts with the Devil in their homes, the country's hillside caves. Their main purpose, or joy, is to steal yet-to-be baptized babies or unwed young women, though they are happy to play with the sanity of any farmer or schoolboy. Duendes enjoy making life difficult for the people of the countryside, putting farm animals in high places where they can't climb down, or dropping roof tiles off the house at night; and all the while they can be heard laughing their contagious duende laugh, in the deep forest.

tropics. If you are fortunate to catch Don Fausto inside the park caring for his garden, he may take you on an impromptu tour, naming the more than 100 species and highlighting each plant's special charm. There are more than eight species of roses, magnolias, gardenias, pearl of the orient, bird of paradise, orchids, jupiters, wild ginger, heliotrope, begonias, etc. There are much more than flowers in the garden, which is framed by the cypress and pine trees that are more than 100 years old. There is also a guard inside the park to keep would-be Romeos from cutting all the flowers.

Sleeping

Ocotal has a healthy mosquito population, even in the dry season; bring netting

B Hotel Frontera, Behind Shell station on highway to Las Manos, T732-2668, F732-2669, hofrosa@ibw.com.ni Private bath with hot water, a/c, TV, telephone, swimming pool, restaurant and bar, big, light rooms, new hotel with moderately priced restaurant, arrogant, stuffy front-desk staff, best hotel in region.

D Hotel B River, from Shell on highway, 1½ c east. Private bath with hot water, TV, fan, parking, popular. **E** Hotel Benmoral, at south entrance to city, across from Enel, T732-2824. Private bath with hot water, TV, fan, dark clean rooms, friendly staff, cheap restaurant, good value. Highly recommended. **E** Hotel Restaurant Mirador, opposite bus station. Private bath, TV, clean, friendly. **F** Hospedaje El Castillo, ½ c south of police station. Shared bath, basic, quiet, close to bus. **G** Hotel El Viajero, Esso station, 3½ c west, T732-2040. Shared bath, fan, best of the cheapies.

Eating

Most restaurants have a mid-range menu and a cheap or seriously cheap comida corriente

On the south side of Parque Central Llamarada del Bosque, T732-2643, has good comida corriente. At south entrance there are several good restaurants with nice atmosphere, such as Restaurante La Cabaña, next to Hotel Benmoral, T732-2415, with good steak dishes like filete a la cabaña or jalapeño steak, moderate prices, shrimp dishes are not recommended, lovely garden setting with banana trees and separate little gazebos for the tables, daily 1000-2300. Also near the south entrance is Restaurante El Paraíso, 1 c east, 1½ c north, T732-3301. Nice open-air setting, steak, chicken and pork dishes, moderate prices sometimes with parties.

Restaurante La Yunta, Centro de Salud, 1 c north, T732-2180. Good sea bass and grilled pork, often recommended, moderate prices, 1100-2400 daily. Restaurante La Quinta, live guitar music on Sat. Doña Pizza, Enitel, ½ c south. Decent pizza. El Deportivo, Esso ½ c east, seafood and soups, mixed reviews, 1000-2200 daily.

Festival

The patron saint of Ocotal is the Virgen de la Asunción whose day of celebration is **15 Aug**, though the festival lasts all week. There is a nice touch here to the proceedings in

Northern Highlands

the form of a parade of 22 brightly decorated ox carts, one of which holds the festival queen. On **11 Aug** is the northern Nicaraguan version of *Carnival*, sort of a mini-Woodstock in Parque Central, with an endless flow of bands.

Transport   Bus The bus station is on the highway, 1 km south of town centre, 15-20 mins' walk from Parque Central. **Ocotal-Las Manos/Honduras Border**, every 30 mins, 0545-1730, US$0.50, 45 mins. **Ocotal-Somoto**, every 45 mins, 0600-1600, US$1.50, 2½ hrs. **Ocotal-Managua**, every hr, 0510-1515, US$3.25, 4 hrs. **Ocotal-Ciudad Antigua**, 1 daily, 1200, US$1, 1 hr. Bus **Ocotal-Estelí**, leaves the city market every hr, 0600-1700, US$1, 2 hrs.

    Taxi Local taxis are cheap, with rides within town costing about US$0.40. A ride to **Las Manos** and the border with Honduras will cost from US$7-9.

Directory   Banks 1 block south of the Parque Central is *BANIC*, T732-2272, also just ½ block south of the market is *BanPro*, T732-2555, and *Banco Caley Dagnall*, T732-2299, is 1½ blocks north of Ferretería Norte Centro. All will change cash. For travellers' cheques (American Express only) you must use *Banco de Finanzas* (BDF), which is next to the store *El Curacao*. The Shell petrol station on the highway may also change dollars. **Communications Post office:** *Correos de Nicaragua*, BANIC, 1 c west, T732-3021, F732-2018. **Telephone:** *Enitel* is on the north side of Parque Central, ½ c north, T732-2321. **Tourist office** 1 block west of the north side of Parque Central, T732-3429. Brochures of general interest in English, very little information on Ocotal at the moment, but some interesting routes around the region are planned. Some English spoken. **Useful numbers Fire:** T732-2390. **Hospital:** T732-2491. **Police:** T732-2333. **Red Cross:** T732-2485.

Mosonte Just north of Ocotal, a paved bridge connects to the dirt highway (no sign) that branches off to the right and connects with the road to Ciudad Antigua. The road winds past wood and coffee processing plants and leads to the sleepy, ancient-looking village of Mosonte, which is known for its local ceramic crafts. You can visit the local artisans if you ask around the village. Mosonte has a humble church built in 1701 and an eerie-looking chapel that sits alone on the summit of the sharp hill in the north of the village, adding to the feeling of an ancient ghost town. The hilltop chapel is reached by a long flight of stairs in the extreme north of the town.

Ciudad Antigua

Colour map 1, grid B4
Population: 1,200
Altitude: 640 m

After the village of Mosonte and its lookout chapel, the highway crosses the Río Kisulí. Here lies more harsh evidence of the scope and force of the damage caused by the rivers in this region during the torrential rains brought on by Hurricane Mitch in late October 1998. Many of these rivers were flowing at 8-15 m above their normal level. After crossing several little bridges the road passes the surprisingly affluent settlement of **Salmaní** and forks: the main highway continues west and later north to the logging and tobacco town of Jalapa; the secondary road to the right travels south to Ciudad Antigua.

    Nestled in a valley of rolling hills, the Ciudad Antigua of today is truly in the middle of nowhere. This was not always the case. Originally called **Nueva Segovia**, it was founded in about 1620 by Spanish colonists who hurriedly abandoned the first settlement, as a result of continued threats from Indian populations. The economy of the second Nueva Segovia was based on pine pitch extraction, which had value as caulking for sailing ships, and also to seal barrels that were used to transport wine from Peru. The church in Ciudad Antigua, is one of the finest example of Mudéjar-Arabic-influenced construction, and is very similar to the churches of nearby Totogalpa and Subtiava. From the 17th century, the town was attacked by English and French pirates, one of whom, Ravenau de Lussan, wrote a description of the church and town that would still be accurate today. The British pirate Charles Morgan also sacked the town and the locals today blame the pirates for their poverty. During the Contra War, 1980-90, Ciudad Antigua was the scene of heavy fighting between Contra and Sandinista troops and the lands around the town were a free fire zone.

Parque Central lies to the left of the road entrance. The park is elegant, inexplicably large and infallibly empty. The lovely church was built in 1654 and many of its original 17th-century doors and walls are intact. The interior of the church is whitewashed adobe, with an ornate gold-leaf altar that bears a famous image of Jesus or **El Señor de los Milagros**, donated by an Austrian queen. The image is said to have been brought into Ciudad Antigua, along with the heavy altar, via a Caribbean port in Honduras and transported here entirely on the backs of men. The locals relate that during the many pirate raids the icon was not willing to be stolen, so he grew too large to be extracted through the massive front doors, despite repeated attempts to take him out. He is celebrated every 20 January with processions in the town.

Museo Religioso de Ciudad Antigua is a small, musty and delightful museum of ancient religious artefacts next to the church. Doña Rosivel (often found in the little crucifix store in front of the church) has the key, and though she claims she does not know much about local history, is the best guide in town. She can take you into the museum to see rare colonial artefacts (and bats!). ■ *Mon-Fri, T732-2227.* The talkative Roque Toledo, the official town guide, is a lot of fun, but if your Spanish is not perfect his long-winded explanations can be exhausting, bewildering or both. Both Roque and Doña Rosivel are very helpful and possess a melancholy pride for their village. Roque will also take you to the southern outskirts of town to see the ruins of the **Iglesia La Merced** and the baseball stadium.

Sleeping & eating There is nowhere to sleep in Ciudad Antigua, although with persuasion, someone may allow you to string up a hammock in their yard. One block north from the westside of the park is the house of Sara Tercero who will cook cheap meals upon request and has some tables inside her house to eat at. One block further west is a small *cantina*, *Doña Natalia*, which serves rum and beer.

Transport There is 1 bus per day that arrives at 1330 from **Ocotal** and leaves at 1400. The journey is 1 hr and costs US$0.75.

Las Manos: border with Honduras

The highway continues north from Ocotal past the turn-off for the highway to the logging and tobacco-growing region of Jalapa, also used to reach the historic Ciudad Antigua (see above). The highway to the border is under repair, as some sections were completely washed away by Hurricane Mitch in 1998. The scenery is very impressive with the jagged granite, pine covered cliffs of Nicaragua's highest mountain range in Dipilto, which includes the **Cerro Mogotón** (2,106 m). The variation of the flora along the highway is impressive with tropical dry forest, cloud forest and pine forest all mixed with the local agriculture. The border between Nicaragua and Honduras is a few little restaurants and a single rope.

The quickest way to Tegucigalpa is through Las Manos; if travelling to El Salvador via Choluteca the El Espino (Somoto) route is best

Northern Highlands

Nicaraguan immigration Offices are open 0800-1200, 1300-1700. When you arrive in Nicaragua you will have to pay US$7 plus a US$1 *Alcaldía* charge; to leave you must pay the US$1 charge as well, with US$2 exit fee. All those arriving must fill in an immigration card, present their luggage to the customs authorities and obtain a receipt, and then present these to the immigration authorities with passport and entry fees. Leaving the country, fill out a card, pay the tax and get your passport stamped.

Crossing by private vehicle After completing immigration procedures, go to *Tránsito* to pay for the vehicle permit, obtain clearance from *Revisión*, and get your vehicle permit from *Aduana* (customs). If it is busy, go first to *Aduana* and get your number in the queue – if necessary shout at the clerks until they give you one. On leaving the country, complete the immigration requirements, then go to *Tránsito* to have the vehicle checked, and to *Aduana* to have the vehicle stamp in the passport cancelled. Surrender the vehicle permit at *Aduana* and take another form back to Tránsito; this will be stamped, signed and finally handed over at the exit gate.

Money exchange Money changers operate on both sides offering *córdobas* (if they have any) at a slightly better rate than the street market rate in Nicaragua. Rates for cash and travellers' cheques are better in Estelí.

Transport **Buses** **Las Manos-Ocotal**, every 30 mins, 0545-1730, US$0.50, 45 mins. **Taxi** As always, agree on fare before entering, Las Manos-Ocotal US$8-10.

Caribbean Coast and Islands

10

Caribbean Coast and Islands

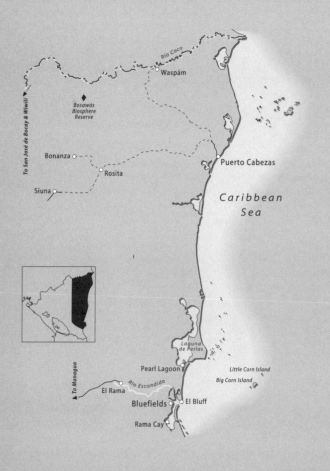

The Nicaraguan Caribbean is a sweeping expanse of deserted coastline, dozens of islands, virgin rainforest and gigantic coastal lagoons. The area's most famous destination is the Corn Islands, two sparkling white-beach gems shining in clear turquoise waters. There are also numerous cays that make up two archipelagos off the coast of Bluefields and Puerto Cabezas. The area is bordered by the biggest rivers in Central America: the Río Coco in the north and Río San Juan in the south.

La Costa, as it is known in most of Nicaragua, is culturally a world apart from the rest of the country; the region's relative isolation has allowed an ancient language and several dialects to survive into the 21st century. The cultures of the Miskito, Sumu and Rama Indians have been fairly homogenized, but their heroic skills as navigators, their languages and their essential identities have remained largely intact. However, the lingua franca of the coast is actually Creole English which was brought by immigrants from islands like Jamaica, thus intensifying the cultural diversity of Nicaragua's Atlantic, which also includes a small group of the Garífuna people who originated from Saint Vincent.

Corn Islands

*Colour map 4,
grid A/B3
Population: 6,370
Altitude: 4 m*

These two islands are a reminder of what the Caribbean used to be like before big business moved in. Relaxing, undeveloped and unpretentious, the Islas de Maíz, or Corn Islands, are the best place in the Nicaraguan Caribbean to snorkel, eat fresh lobster and soak up some rays on sugar-white beaches. The islands are 70 km off the mainland of Nicaragua. The big island is a bit less than 6 sq km and the little one is 3 sq km. About 7 km of Caribbean Sea separates the two. The highest point, at 225 m, is Mount Pleasant on Big Corn.

History

During his fourth and final exploratory voyage, Columbus encountered the islands and named them **Islas Limonares**. At the time, they were inhabited by Kukras Indians of whom little is known today except for a reported tendency to eat human flesh. During the 18th century the islands became a haven for pirates resting in between pillages. Eventually they were settled by ex-slaves from Jamaica who arrived via the neighbouring islands of San Andrés (now occupied by Colombia). The local economy was based on the production of palm oil until the devastating winds of Hurricane Joan in 1988, which reached over 200 kph and destroyed most of the palm trees on the island. Lobster fishing is now the biggest industry. Big Corn's reefs were damaged in both hurricanes Joan of 1988 and César of 1996; somewhat incredibly, Little Corn's reefs suffered only minor damage.

Today the islands' dynamics are changing quickly, thanks to their proximity to the San Andrés Islands, which come under Colombian jurisdiction although they are located inside Nicaragua's ocean platform (the root of a dormant but perpetual state of dispute). The traffic between the islands is natural, but with the cocaine problem in Colombia, the influx of cocaine into the Corn Islands has increased dramatically in the last few years. There are now reports of crack houses on Big Corn, and of Little Corn being used as a drop-off and pick-up point on the northbound smuggling route. There has also been a small-scale Miskito Indian migration from the mainland to the island; this, combined with foreign interests buying up land, means that the little islands are becoming increasingly smaller for the local inhabitants.

Sights

Big Corn Big Corn has a landing strip and a couple of decent hotels. The beaches on the west and southern side of the islands are best for swimming. West of the landing strip is **Brig Bay** and the best hotel on the island. The north end of the bay has a dock, but the southern part is very clean and great for swimming. Around **Waula Point** is **Picnic Centre**, another fine swimming and sunning beach. Both are also the near the main population centre of the island. On the sparsely populated southeastern part of the island is the long and tranquil **Long Beach** in Long Bay. With **Queen Hill** rising above the western part of the bay it is also very scenic. Snorkelling is best on the northern coast of Big Corn, just west of **Sally Peaches**, in front of the sadly neglected *Hotel Bayside*. The eastern side of the island is the most rustic and quietest and is windward with waves and plenty of rocks. There are lagoons and wetlands there and a proposed Italian development that could change the landscape dramatically. The locals on the entire island are very friendly and happy to return a smile and a wave. There are buses that circle the island every hour on its one coastal loop-road that is paved in limited sections, but walking will take you around the entire island in a couple of hours. Climbing to the top of **Mount Pleasant** is worthwhile for the view, though long trousers are recommended as there are numerous ticks.

To visit Little Corn you will have to take the daily water-taxi or hire a private **Little Corn** boat (see below). The small island has the finest coral reefs in Nicaragua, and is a superb place for snorkelling. *National Geographic Explorer* rated the reefs nine on a scale of 1-10. Little Corn is even more lost in time than the big island. A project planned for a giant resort-condo-supermarket complex has fallen through, but a more reasonable dive centre and bungalow project is planned by Italian investors. On Little Corn there are numerous empty white sand beaches and one little dock on its wayward side. The surf can be quite treacherous on the windward side of the island, which should be avoided when the sea is agitated. There is a good, simple hotel on Little Corn overlooking a pleasant beach (though prone to wind swells), that is run by a North American couple.

Essentials

Big Corn A *El Paraíso Club Cabinas*, Brig Bay, T285-5111, F285-5125. With private **Sleeping** bath, fan, screened windows, private porches with hammock, clean. The bar and restaurant service is slow and they have problems keeping track of the customer tabs *For price codes see* (keep careful count of your expenses). Rent of horses, bicycles and snorkelling gear. *inside front cover* This can be a noisy part of the island at night, but is a good beach for swimming. The

■ *on map*

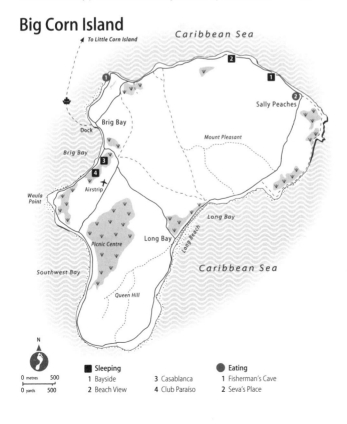

Big Corn Island

To Little Corn Island

Caribbean Sea

Sally Peaches

Brig Bay

Dock

Mount Pleasant

Brig Bay

Airstrip

Waula
Point

Long Bay

Long Bay

Long Beach

Picnic Centre

Caribbean Sea

Southwest Bay

Queen Hill

N

0 metres 500
0 yards 500

■ **Sleeping**
1 Bayside
2 Beach View
3 Casablanca
4 Club Paraíso

● **Eating**
1 Fisherman's Cave
2 Seva's Place

Caribbean Coast and Islands

best on either island and recommended. **B** *Bayside Hotel*, on the north side of the island, west of Sally Peaches, T285-5001, F249-0451. Private bath and a/c, located oceanfront on the best snorkelling reef on the island with a view to Little Corn. Geologically slow service. This was the banner hotel of the island before the hurricane ripped it apart in 1996. The dock restaurant has been rebuilt, but high tide still runs underneath the rooms and the floors have become an impromptu dock. Keep room doors closed to keep confused land crabs out.

D *Beach View Hotel*, east of Catholic church. Great view from 2-storey structure, simple, friendly and rustic, serves meals. **E** *Brisas del Mar*, Playa Coco. Basic, loud disco in same building, good breakfast, restaurant. **E** *Casa Blanca* (actually blue), at Playa Coco, Miss Florence's house. Running water, noisy. Electricity 1400-2400 only, and failures are not uncommon.

Little Corn A-D *Casa Iguana*, on a 3-ha bluff overlooking the sea, www.casaiguana.nu 3 deluxe cabins with private bath and other very simple rooms with shared baths, as well as a central lodge. The hotel is run by a North American couple; Grant is very friendly and helpful and can take visitors fishing or snorkelling in his skiff. Book in advance so they have food. They can also pick up visitors from Big Corn if arranged in advance. **F** *Miss Bridget's*, west of the dock. Shared bath, simple and friendly, good kitchen.

Eating

● *on map, page 245*

Seafood lovers are in heaven, others could go hungry, but chicken and coconut bread should sustain the non-fish eaters

Seva's Place, 500 m east of *Bayside Hotel*, T285-5058. Great seafood, chicken, fine location, mid-range, try breakfast on rooftop overlooking Caribbean in morning sun, best food on the island. Beach in front of Seva's good for swimming. *Fisherman's Cave*, next to dock. Popular, mid-range, average food and slow service. *Comedor Lissie*, good hearty meal US$2. Several bars and reggae clubs. *Dugout de la Tonia* has the cheapest beer and good music. Ask around for where meals are available; the restaurants serve seafood, chicken and chop suey, but in private houses you can find much better fare. Try fresh coconut bread (from family stores – don't miss it), banana porridge and sorrel drink (red and ginger-flavoured). There is occasionally a shortage of bottled water. Main **market** area is near Will Bowers Wharf and is a cheap place to eat.

Festival

To celebrate the abolition of slavery in 1841, Big Corn holds an annual festival, culminating on the anniversary of the decree on **27 Aug** (book accommodation well in advance if coming during this week) with the *Crab Festival*. A Crab Festival Queen is elected and there are other activities and lots of crab soup being served up. Both islands are populated by big, menacing-looking land crabs that aren't good for eating whole, but make a very hearty soup.

Transport

Air *La Costeña* flies from **Managua** and **Bluefields** to the Corn Islands, daily at 0630 and 1400 from Managua, 0700 and 1535 from Corn Islands (0845 and 1535 on Sun), US$105 round-trip. When you arrive check into the little airline office to confirm return seat, T285-5131 (on Corn).

Sea A small motor boat leaves **Big Corn** every morning at 1000 from the dock in Brig Bay for **Little Corn Island** and returns at 1600, US$5 each way. To hire a boat, ask at a hotel or the dock, normal charge US$50 one way, US$100 for the *panga* for a full day.

Passenger-carrying cargo boats leave **Bluefields** for the Corn Islands from the docks of **Copesnica**, north of town, around a small bay and past the ruined church: Wed, Fri, Sun 0700-1000, return Thu, Sun, Tue, US$4.35 one way. The water around Bluefields is muddy brown, soon becoming a clear, sparkling blue. There is usually a boat from Bluefields (the *Lynx Express*), via **El Bluff** on Wed at 0830, 4 hrs, but this is not guaranteed. Boats back to Bluefields leave from Will Bowers Wharf; tickets available in advance from nearby office. You may be able to find a lobster, or other fishing boat that will take you,

Things to do on the Caribbean Coast and Islands

- Snorkel around the coral reefs of Little Corn Island; it's worth the long journey.
- Sample the fresh lobster on the patio of *Seva's Place*, on Big Corn Island, while enjoying the turquoise Caribbean view.
- Pay a weekend visit to the *Four Brothers*, Bluefields, for an un-commercialized roots and dance hall experience.
- Go on a boat tour of Pearl Lagoon to surrounding Miskito, Creole and Garífuna villages: a rich cultural mix under an endless Nicaraguan sky.
- Base yourself in Puerto Cabezas, the centre of the Miskito world, and explore the forgotten settlements and deserted beaches both north and south.
- Visit Waspám on the Río Coco, Central Americas longest river, and arrange a boat trip with the locals to get an authentic view of Miskito river life.

but make sure the boat is properly equipped and seaworthy. Check with the *Capitanía* in Bluefields, or in El Bluff or with anyone on the docks. Trip takes 6-8 hrs.

Directory

Banks The only bank is *Banco Caley Dagnall* in Promar on Big Corn, T285-5107. No credit card advance or travellers' cheques accepted or changed. Dollars are widely used on the islands, take all the cash you need with you. **Communications** Telephone: *Enitel* is T285-5061. **Hospital**: In Brig Bay, T285-5236.

El Rama

Colour map 4, grid B1

From Managua it is a 290-km bus ride to El Rama then a 96-km boat trip down the Río Escondido. The land portion is a horrible test of patience and endurance, and the prospect of spending a night in El Rama is not terribly inviting. Still many use the route to see what exists between the two coasts. The trip can be broken up by sleeping one or two nights in Juigalpa (see page 86). El Rama itself is a sad and dirty town that hasn't recovered from Hurricane Joan in October 1988 when the river rose 16 m above its normal height.

Sleeping & eating G *Ramada Inn*, not to be confused with the slightly larger hotel chain, this is a decent option. **G** *Las Cabinas*, T817-0021, F817-0013. Has a/c and garage parking. *El Viajero* is quite good. **G** *Amy*, *mercado* 1 c west, T817-0034. Fairly clean and quiet, shared bath and food prepared, near main jetty. Good cheap food at *Comedor Torres*, and *Restaurante El Manantial* has lodging and food.

Transport Boat: Express boats Tue, Thu, Sat, Sun at 1700 **El Rama-Bluefields**; 0500 from **Bluefields-El Rama**; ordinary boat Mon, Wed, Fri in the early morning from El Rama, between 1100 and 1300 from Bluefields. Food and soft drinks are sold on the ferry. Fast boats, *pangas*, can be hired for US$12-15 per person El Rama–Bluefields, taking 1½ hrs, or hire the entire boat for US$50.

Bus: From Managua buses leave from the Mercado Mayoreo. **Managua-El Rama**, every hr, 0400-1130, US$5.50, 8-10 hrs. **El Rama-Managua**, every hr, 0400-1130, US$5.50, 8-10 hrs. **El Rama-Juigalpa**, every hr, 0800-1500, US$3.75, 6 hrs. **Juigalpa-El Rama**, every hr, 0800-1500, US$3.75, 6 hrs.

Bluefields

Dirty, chaotic and curiously inviting, Bluefields is the heart and soul of Nicaragua's Caribbean world and the capital of Southern Atlantic Autonomous Region (known by its acronym RAAS). It is located at the mouth of the Río Escondido, which opens into Bluefields Bay in front of the city. The majority

Colour map 4, grid B2
Population: 42,665
Altitude: 20 m

Caribbean Coast and Islands

of the population is Afro-Caribbean, though the other ethnic groups of the region are represented and the main attraction of the town is its ethnic diversity and west Caribbean demeanour. The main church of the city is Moravian, the language is Creole English and the music is calypso and reggae. Bluefields is a good jumping-off point to visit Pearl Lagoon and other less-explored areas of the wide-open region.

Bluefields was named after the Dutch pirate **Henry Bluefeldt** (or Blauvedlt) who hid in the bay's waters in 1610. The native Kukra Indians were hired by Dutch and British pirates to help them with boat repairs and small-time trade also began with the Europeans. The first permanent European settlers arrived near the end of the 18th century and a change in the population began. The 19th century saw a healthy banana business and an influx of Afro-Caribbeans from Jamaica to work in the plantations and administer the Anglican and Moravian churches. The British Government's pact with the Miskito Indians also changed the ethnic mix of the area as Afro-Caribbeans started to marry with Miskitos. During the 20th century, Chinese immigrants also came to Bluefields, creating what was thought to be the largest Chinese community in Central America. The fighting of the Revolution was not felt much here, but the Contras of the 1980s used the eastern coast to harass Sandinista positions and many of the Chinese left during these problem years. Bluefields was damaged heavily, nearly wiped off the map, by Hurricane Joan in October 1988. Some 25,000 residents were evacuated and most of the structures were destroyed. A soldier who arrived the following day said it looked as though it had been trampled by a giant with nothing left of the buildings but wooden footprints. The famous *Bluefields Express* boat that worked the 96-km journey from Rama to Bluefields was found later wrecked in the middle of thick forest, some 4 km from the river banks.

Essentials

Sleeping **A-C** *South Atlantic*, Barrio Central, across from *Enitel*, T822-2242. With private bath, a/c, cable TV, fridge, safe box, clean, friendly, excellent food. In the same price range is **A-C** *South Atlantic II*, Barrio Central, next to petrol station Levy, T822-2265, F822-1219. Private bath, a/c, cable TV, telephone, laundry service, fax, safe box, nicer than the original *South Atlantic* with *Sports Bar* looking across the bay and main street. **A-C** *La Casona*, Barrio Central, across from *Disco Bacchus*, T822-2436. 9 rooms, private bath, a/c or fan, cable TV, breakfast included. Just outside of Bluefields is **A-D** *The Groovy Ant Farm*, T/F822-2838, tiairene@ibw.com.ni Owned by enthusiastic Canadian Carol Bidon, this was formerly an agroforestry demonstration farm, but is now ideal for nature lovers, fishing and bird-watching, basic *cabaña* accommodation, with running water, 15 mins by *panga* from town. Call or write in advance to book and arrange transport, group rates available. **B** *Bluefields Bay Hotel*, Barrio Pointeen, T/F822-2838. A/c, with private bath, clean, owned by the autonomous region's university URACAN. Rooms upstairs better and less damp than downstairs ones. Excursions offered to surrounding areas. Very good value and recommended.

D-E *Caribbean Dreams*, Barrio Punta Fría, opposite market, T822-0107. Private bath, a/c or fan, basic but clean, cable TV, water erratic, owners helpful. **D-G** *Hotel Hollywood*, 4 blocks south of the dock, T822-2282. 12 rooms, private bath with a/c or shared baths with fan, cable TV, laundry service, bar and restaurant, nice old building rebuilt after hurricane.

Nicaragua's British Coast – La Miskitia

Although the modern history of the Pacific Coast of Nicaragua begins early in the 16th century, that of the Caribbean Coast begins much later. Throughout the 16th century, the Spaniards never came close to having a presence on the Caribbean Coast. The first Spanish governor appointed to the Caribbean Coast, Diego de Gutiérrez, was eaten by the Miskito Indians in 1545. By 1610 the Indians had run the Spaniards out of their easternmost town, Nueva Segovia, and forced them to rebuild it 90 km west, at present-day Ciudad Antigua. After that, the Spaniards kept a healthy distance from the Caribbean Coast.

The first successful European interaction with the coast was when the British set up a trading colony on the Caribbean island of Providencia (today occupied by Colombia) to begin trading with the Miskito Indians. After some conflicts with Spaniards on Caribbean islands, the British created the hoax of the Miskito Kingdom and, in order to guard their own interests, crowned the first 'Miskito King' in the middle of the 17th century. British interests on the Miskito Coast were similar to those in many parts of the world: a military alliance with the natives, safe harbours for ship repair and re-supply, and profitable trade with the natives (in the case of Nicaragua, turtle shells, dye woods, sarsaparilla and vanilla extract).

The headquarters of operations for British interests was Bluefields. As a result, whenever Great Britain and Spain were at war, Bluefields was used as base for attacks on Nicaragua. The War of Spanish Succession, 1700-13, The War of Jenkins Ear, The Seven Years' War, 1756-63, and the War Between Great Britain, France, and Spain, 1778-83, all brought British incursions to Spanish Nicaragua from the Caribbean Coast. Finally, the Treaty of Paris of 1783 settled the matter, for the time being, with Great Britain agreeing to remove all colonists from the Caribbean shore, with the exception of Belize. By 1787 this process was complete.

With the collapse of the Spanish Empire in 1821, helped along by British foreign policy, the British sought to take control of the Miskito Coast again. Great Britain simply reinvented the Miskito Kingdom, which asked for British protection as soon as it was resuscitated. In 1850 the United States and Great Britain agreed to divide up control and influence of the Miskito Coast, with neither party having complete control of the area. With the Treaty of Managua of 1860 the British agreed to give up all interests in the Miskito Coast, but they never got around to actually pulling out. Finally, Nicaraguan president José Santos Zelaya sent General Cabezas to take control of the Miskito Coast by military force in 1894. British control over the Caribbean Coast of Nicaragua had finally come to an end.

Caribbean Coast and Islands

F *Marda Maus*, Barrio Central, T822-2429. Shared bath, fan, dark, not too clean, bar and restaurant. **F** *El Dorado*, Barrio Punta Fría, T822-2365. Private bath, TV, quiet spot away from main street, may offer floor space to late arrivals. **F** *Airport*, above *La Costeña* office at airport. Clean, friendly. **F** *Claudia*, clean, comfortable, room on street side best. **G** *Hospedaje Pearl Lagoon*, Barrio Central, across from UNAG, T822-2411. 9 rooms, private baths, laundry and safe boxes, restaurant. **F-G** *Hotel Costa Sur*, Barrio Central, across from Lotería, T822-2452. Shared baths, fans, bar and restaurant.

Arco Iris, Barrio Central, across from the *Casa de las Ofertas*, T822-2436. Daily after 0700, lobster, beef and chicken dishes and salads, nice terrace. ***Bella Vista***, Barrio Punta Fría, T822-2385. Very good seafood dishes, daily 1000-2300. **Eating**

Café Central, good-value meals. *El Flotante*, Barrio Punta Fría, T822-2988. Daily 1000-2200, built over the water at the end of the main street, mid-range prices, good shrimp and lobster, slow service, great view and breeze, also with dancing at weekends. *Cocktails*, international menu, but seafood is excellent, reasonably priced. Highly recommended. *Bay View Restaurant*, next to *Hotel Bluefields Bay*. Beautiful, stylish spot on the water to watch the world go by with a drink, popular. In Barrio **Teodoro Martínez**, there are 3 good restaurants: *Chez Marcel*, from *BANIC*, 3½ c west, T822-2347. Filet mignon, shrimp in garlic butter, grilled lobster. Next door is *Salmar*, T822-2128. Daily 1600-2400, chicken in wine sauce or grilled chicken breast or beef. Across the street is *Tauro's*, T822-2492. Good local soups, fish, daily 1000-2300.

Entertainment *Four Brothers*, Cottontree, from the *Hotel Hollywood*, 2 c south, 2 c west. This is the best reggae spot in Nicaragua and usually open from Tue-Sun, a big ranch full of great dancing. The dance hall is not just for reggae so ask around to see what kind of music is playing, admission is US$1. Another well-known place to dance, and with a younger crowd, is *Bacchus*, Parque Reyes, ½ c south, T822-2628, Thu-Sun from 2000.

Festivals *Bluefields* is best known for its dancing. It is the reggae capital of Nicaragua and many have described the method of dancing as being very sexual. The locals are very friendly so don't be shy to get out on the dance floor. To see the locals dance the *Palo de Mayo* (maypole) celebrations is the highlight if the year. The festival lasts the whole month and there are countless celebrations of dance and dance contests between different neighbourhoods. The only rule is to hang on to the ribbon connected to the maypole and move. There is also local music and poetry in the Palo de Mayo festival, also referred to using its promotional name ¡**Mayo Ya**!

Transport **Sea** Several piers near the market provide access to the port. **Motorboats** (*pangas)* can be rented for trips to all outlying areas. From the main wharf small boats leave irregularly for villages along the coast. There are at least 2 *pangas* per day to **Pearl Lagoon**, which can also take you to Tasbapauni. Cost is US$7. Three times a week a bigger and slower boat full of trade goods leaves for Pearl Lagoon from Bluefields and costs US$3. The locals call it the **Mail Boat**.

Air The airport is 3 km from the city centre, either walk (30 mins) or take a taxi US$1. *La Costeña*, T822-2500, and *Atlantic Airlines*, T822-1299, share the service to and from Bluefields. *La Costeña* flights from Bluefields: **Bluefields-Managua**, 0740, 0840, 1120, 1610, US$45 one-way, US$80 round-trip, 50 mins. **Bluefields- Corn Island**, 0740, 1530, US$36 one-way, US$67 round-trip, 20 mins. **Bluefields-Puerto Cabezas**, 1210, US$50 one-way, US$93 round-trip, 50 mins (no flight on Sun). **NB** For flights originating in Managua see page 75 and flights from Puerto Cabezas below. Managua offices of the airlines are in the domestic terminal at the airport. Bring passport, it is sometimes asked for in the departure lounge. There is a customs check on return to Managua.

Bluefields

To Pearl Lagoon & El Rama ▶

To El Bluff & Rama Cay ▶

To Four Brothers Disco

N
Not to scale

■ Sleeping
1 Bluefields Bay
2 Costa Sur
3 El Dorado
4 Hollywood
5 Hospedaje Pearl Lagoon

6 South Atlantic

● Eating
1 Bay View
2 Chez Marcel
3 Salmar
4 Tauro's

Land   Nearest overland access is via a horrible road that finishes in El Rama. From the port at *El Rama*, Bluefields is accessed by boat down the *Río Escondido*. See El Rama below.

Banks   There are surprisingly few banks to choose from in Bluefields and at the moment none of them will change travellers' cheques. If desperate try *Banco Caley Dagnall* in Barrio Central next to the Colegio Moravo, T822-2261. They have been reported as willing to change them in the past. As with Corn Island and the entire coast, cash is essential. For changing dollars and *córdobas* you can use *BANIC*, next to Radio Zinica, T822-0073 or *BanCentro*, Calle Cabezas, T822-0227. **Communications**   Internet: *Carlos and Betsy Biccsa*, across from *Correos de Nicaragua*, at US$4 per hour. **Post office:** *Correos de Nicaragua* is ½ c west of the *Lotería Nacional*, T822-1784. **Telephone:** *Enitel* is ½ c north and 2½ c west of the Moravian church, T822-2222. **Tourist office**   The local *INTUR* delegate is Miriam Santamaria, in the *Casa Lotería Nacional*, T822-1111 and T822-0221. **Useful numbers** Fire: T822-2298. **Hospital:** T822-2391, 822-2621. **Police:** T822-2448. **Red Cross:** T822-2582.

Directory

Excursions from Bluefields

This island in the Bay of Bluefields is home to the last tribe of Rama Indians, led by an elderly woman chief. The island lies only 20-30 minutes away by *panga* from Bluefields. The Ramas are pretty accustomed to visitors coming to check them out. They are very calm and friendly people who are famous among the rest of the Bluefields population for their kindness and generosity. Physically the Ramas are the most Asian in appearance of the ethnically indigenous groups of Nicaragua. They are one of three main indigenous groups of the Caribbean Coast, whose languages are all from the same linguistic root. A boat ride to the island will cost between US$15 and US$50, depending on whether you can find some other passengers to make the trip or not. Check at the southern dock next to the market to see if any boats are going, but if you hitch a ride, returning could be a problem.

Rama Cay
Colour map 4, grid B2
Population: 130

Boat trips to the beautiful and completely rural areas of the coast are the best excuse to visit Bluefields

El Bluff is a peninsula that separates the open sea from the Bay of Bluefields. It was was a busier port in happier days, now it is a bit depressed. It is the beach for the people of Bluefields and is dirty. There is a nice hike to the lighthouse where there's a fine view of the bay and the sea, and the locals are happy to see visitors. Boats leave from the southern dock next to the market. The boat waits until full and then leaves with a rate of about US$1.70.

El Bluff

Sleeping   **E** *El Bluff*, with bath, cheaper without, fan, limited water, friendly, restaurant, pleasant.

Pearl Lagoon/Laguna de Perlas

This oval-shaped coastal lagoon covers 518 sq km and is one of the most beautiful places on the coast. The lagoon is fed principally by the jungle-lined Río Kurinwás and also by the rivers Wawashán, Patch, Orinoco and Ñari. Pearl Lagoon is home to a great mix of cultures in its various villages. The **village of Pearl Lagoon** is the most developed, and is located in the far southwest of the estuary. Boats leave for Pearl Lagoon from the northern dock in Bluefields when full, usually twice a day, US$6.

A visit to **Tasbapauni** is worthwhile for it sits between the Pearl Lagoon and the Caribbean Sea. The beach is lovely, although it can be littered with debris;

Colour map 4, grid A3
Population: 7,437
Altitude: 3 m

Caribbean Coast and Islands

the locals are cleaning the one in front of the town. There are also Garífuna villages at **La Fe** and **Orinoco** and Miskito *pueblos* at **Raitipura** and **Kakabila**. In Raitipura there is a Danish housing project, run by Mogens Vibe who takes on volunteers (minimum 1 week). Recommended.

Sleeping   In **Pearl Lagoon village** **D** *Casa Blanca*, nice rooms with lots of wood, good beds, baths outside, screened window, loud on weekend nights, have boat and will do trips in the lagoon. Recommended. **E** *Williams Green Lodge*, 1 block south of the dock, T822-2355, simple, basic and friendly. **F** *Miss Ingrid's*, a very friendly stay, with entertaining family. In **Tasbapauni**   Lodging at **G** *Miss Margarita's*. The 2-floor pension has 8 rooms. Food is also available here and with a neighbouring family.

Río Kurinwás   Further afield, Río Kurinwás is a fascinating, largely uninhabited jungle area, where it is possible to see monkeys and much other wildlife. It might occasionally be possible to get a boat to the town of **Tortuguero** (also called Nuevo Amanecer) a *mestizo* (mixed-race) town which will really give you a taste of the frontier. Tortuguero is about a six-hour speedboat ride from Bluefields up Río Kurinwás; it takes several days by regular boat.

Río Grande   Río Grande is the next river north of Río Kurinwás, connected to the Pearl Lagoon by the Top-Lock Canal. At its mouth are five interesting villages: the four Miskito communities of Kara, Karawala, Sandy Bay Sirpi and Walpa, and the Creole village of La Barra. **Sandy Bay Sirpi** is situated on both the river and the Caribbean, and has a nice beach. Travelling upstream, Río Grande contrasts with jungly Río Kurinwás; it is much more settled, dotted with farms and grazing cattle. Some way upriver (also about a six-hour speedboat ride from Bluefields, several days by regular boat), you reach the *mestizo* town of **La Cruz de Río Grande**, which was founded about 1922 by Chinese traders to serve workers from a banana plantation (now defunct) further upstream. La Cruz has a very pretty church, and there are resident expatriate (US) priests of the Capuchin order in the town. The adventurous can walk between La Cruz and Tortuguero: each way takes about 10 hours in the dry season; 12 in the rainy.

Puerto Cabezas/Bilwi

Colour map 2, grid B5
Population: 50.941
Altitude: 10 m

Puerto Cabezas, or Bilwi as it is known locally, is the capital of the RAAN, the Northern Atlantic Coast Autonomous Region, and it has a distinctly different atmosphere from Bluefields. Principally a large Miskito village, Bilwi can offer an excellent introduction to the Miskito part of the country. You can arrange to visit and stay in small Miskito villages in the surrounding area. There are significant minorities of Hispanics and Creoles, many of whom came to 'Port' by way of Las Minas (see below). Spanish is a second language for the majority of people in Puerto Cabezas, although most speak it well; many speak at least some English, while for others, English is their native language.

History

The local name for Puerto Cabezas, Bilwi, is of Sumu Indian origin. The Sumus had traditionally occupied the Río Grande in Matagalpa and northward. They were forced east by the advances of Hispanic Nicaragua and this brought them into conflict with the Miskitos who used their alliance with the

British in the 17th and 18th centuries to dominate much of the Sumus' land and nearly all of the Rama Indians' territory. The proper name for the Sumus is actually **Mayagna**, but this is rarely used except in textbooks. Sumu basically means 'barbarian' in the Miskito language, much like the Nicaraguas Indians who named the tribes of the eastern shores of Lake Nicaragua and Managua, 'Chontales', which means 'barbarian' or 'outsider' in Náhuat. All three of the major tribes of Sumus, Ramas and Miskitos are believed to have migrated from South America, as all three of the languages are based on the Chibchas spoken from southern Honduras to Bogotá at the arrival of the Spanish. The northward migration is believed to have begun about 3000 BC, with the languages branching off to become distinct somewhere around the beginning of the Christian era. The **Sumus** and **Miskitos** share some 50% of words and both claim to have originated from the same spot, along the shores of the Río Patuka near its confluence with Río Wampú. It is likely that before the migrations from Central Mexico in and around AD 750 all of Nicaragua was occupied by these groups and their many fractions and variations.

The first European contact with the region was made by Christopher Columbus who arrived in the midst of a horrible storm and found refuge in the bay at the mouth of the Río Coco. He named it **Cabo Gracias a Dios** (Cape Thank God) for the protection it afforded his boats from the raging sea. In the early 1600s the British started trading with the coast and eventually made allies out of the Miskitos. Various shipwrecks, from pirates to slave ships, brought new influences to the area, but it is thought that Bilwi itself was not founded until the mid-19th century, when **Moravian missionaries** were also landing on the northern coast. More foreign interest arrived in the late 19th and early 20th century in the form of logging and banana-growing operations. After the Caribbean was incorporated into the rest of Nicaragua in the late 19th century the name Puerto Cabezas was given to the village. During the Contra War the village grew from 5,000 to more than 30,000 residents thanks to fighting in the region and the Sandinista administration's harshly implemented relocation programmes. The port was important during the same period for the unloading of Cuban and Soviet military aid.

The original name of Bilwi is now coming back into vogue for the town as a statement of indigenous recognition and frustration with the central government that is seen as selling off resources without any benefit for the local population.

Sights

The town itself will not win any beauty contests, but does have a far away, end-of-the-earth feel and a very long pier that stretches into the Caribbean Sea. The best reason for coming is to meet its friendly people and to visit nearby and not-so-nearby beauty spots. Bilwi has two main roads, the only paved streets, which run parallel to each other and to the sea. At the southern end of the town is the port area; the airport is at the northern end. The main market occupies the central part of town. There is a beach within the town limits, but it is dirty. A clean and lovely beach, **Poza Verde**, can be found several kilometres north of town; it has white sand, calm water and sandflies. Take the road out of town for about 15 minutes and turn right on the track marked *SW Tuapi* (*SW* stands for *switch*); follow it for a few kilometres to the sea. You can also walk 6 km along the beach from Puerto Cabezas, or take a taxi (US$30).

A walk along the pier at sunset is highly recommended

Caribbean Coast and Islands

Sleeping **C** *El Cortijo*, Barrio San Pedro, Calle Comercio, T282-2223, F282-2340. 7 rooms, private bath, a/c, cable TV, laundry service, parking. **D-E** *Ricardo Pérez*, Calle Central, T/F282-2362. Private bath, a/c or cheaper with fan, bar, fax, friendly, clean, all rooms have windows, meals available. **D** *Hotel El Pelícano*, in front of Catholic church, T282-2336, 2 blocks east of the plaza. Good, comfortable rooms with bath, clean, friendly, good view, breakfast by advance arrangement only. **D-G** *El Viajante*, Barrio Revolución, across from INSS, T282-2362. A/c with private bath, cheaper with fan and shared bath, clean, central, very friendly, basic wooden rooms, *comedor* serves good breakfast to its guests. **E** *Miss Judy's*, next to *Centro de Computación Ansell*, T282-2225. Private and shared baths, charming house decorated with eclectic furniture and owner's paintings. Recommended. **G** *Mar Azul*, at entrance to main market. Shared bath, basic, noisy, mosquitoes, better upstairs.

Eating *Atlántico*, Barrio Pancasán, Silais, 1 c west, T282-2274. Open 1200-0200, closed Tue, seafood soup, shrimp, chicken in wine sauce. Often recommended. *Dragón Chino*, Barrio Revolución, T282-2332. Open 1200-2300, closed Tue, Chinese food. *Jumbo*, across from *Dragón Chino*. Chinese food and the most popular place to dance at weekends, crowded. *Pizzería Mercedes*, near the harbour. Very good, expensive, with good selection of drinks, good service. Just south, near the pier, is a good seafood restaurant called *Malecón*. Popular, with TV, basic food and disappointing service is *El Zaire*. There are also numerous *comedores* as well as food in the *San Jerónimo Market*.

Transport **Driving** It is not possible to rent a vehicle or bicycle, but arrangements for a car and driver can be made with a taxi driver or others (ask at your *hospedaje*). Puerto is connected by road to Managua; however, this 559-km trip should only be attempted in the dry season, if at all, and in a 4WD vehicle with double spares. With luck, it will take only 2 days. The road, almost all of it unpaved, is not bad from Managua to Siuna, but becomes very difficult after that; do not drive at night anywhere in this region. **NB** Travel overland is not recommended for safety reasons night or day through the **Las Minas** areas (see page 257 the only way west by land). There is a famous armed gang operating

Puerto Cabezas

To Police Station (200m)

Cemetery

To Hospital (200m)

Moravian

To Market

Alcadía

Enitel

Banco Culey Dagnell

Catholic

Caribbean Sea

Dock

N

0 metres 200
0 yards 200

■ **Sleeping**
1 El Cortijo
2 El Pelicano
3 El Viajante
4 Mar Azul
5 Miss Judy's
6 Ricardo Pérez

● **Eating**
1 Malecón
2 Pizzería Mercedes

Barely afloat – the fourth and final voyage of Columbus

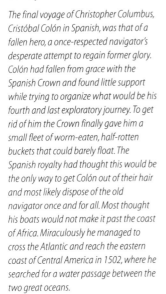

The final voyage of Christopher Columbus, Cristóbal Colón in Spanish, was that of a fallen hero, a once-respected navigator's desperate attempt to regain former glory. Colón had fallen from grace with the Spanish Crown and found little support while trying to organize what would be his fourth and last exploratory journey. To get rid of him the Crown finally gave him a small fleet of worm-eaten, half-rotten buckets that could barely float. The Spanish royalty had thought this would be the only way to get Colón out of their hair and most likely dispose of the old navigator once and for all. Most thought his boats would not make it past the coast of Africa. Miraculously he managed to cross the Atlantic and reach the eastern coast of Central America in 1502, where he searched for a water passage between the two great oceans.

Columbus ran the entire isthmus coast including the Caribbean seaboard of Nicaragua and the Corn Islands. Caught in a

violent storm, he found refuge at the mouth of the Río Coco and dubbed it Cabo Gracias a Dios (Cape Thank God). Somehow the great navigator managed to make it as far as Jamaica, where his disgruntled crew finally abandoned him and his tired ships drifted to the bottom of the sea.

On 7 July 1503, while trying to find a dugout canoe large enough to take him from Jamaica to Santo Domingo, Cristóbal Colón wrote to the Spanish Crown. The letter shows that he was barely literate, that he heard voices of saints and was unable to state with any clarity what had occurred on the voyage. According to a letter from Diego de Porras, a Columbus crew member and mutineer, most of the crew thought Columbus was an old nut-case and they had feared that he would kill them all with his deranged ideas.

Columbus was stranded on Jamaica for a year. He finally got back to Spain in 1504 and died two years later, mired in obscurity.

in the area (FUAC). They made some grisly attacks on locals in 2001 and although no assaults have been reported against foreigners, this gang is not to be taken lightly. Any claim to political objectives are unclear and the only apparent ones are intimidation and murder. Travel north of Puerto Cabezas is OK.

Buses Express **Managua-Puerto Cabezas**, Mon and Fri, 1800, 17+ hrs, US$15 from Mercado Mayoreo. **Express Puerto Cabezas-Managua**, Thu and Sat, 0800, US$15 from Enitel. There are also buses to **Rosita** and **Siuna** that connect to buses to Managua, neither of which can be recommended for safety reasons.

Air The airstrip is 3 km north of town. From the airport, it is possible to get a taxi that will charge US$1 to any point in Puerto Cabezas. *La Costeña* flies daily to Puerto Cabezas and there is 1 flight a day to **Bluefields** and back. *Atlantic Airlines* also flies to Puerto Cabezas; call office for details. See Managua transport for details of flights originating in the capital. **Puerto Cabezas-Bluefields**, daily, 1110, US$50 one-way, US$93 round-trip. **Puerto Cabezas-Managua**, daily 0820, 1220, 1610, US$56 one-way, US$94 round-trip.

NB Bring your passport: there are immigration checks by the police in Puerto Cabezas and sometimes in the waiting lounge in Managua; also all bags are X-rayed coming into the domestic terminal from any destination.

Boat You may be able to find a boat going to Bluefields, enquire at the dock. Boats can be hired for visits to outlying areas. It is recommended that you do not hire a boat with fewer than 2 people, and travel to the **Cayos Miskitos** is not recommended due to problems with drug runners from Colombia using the islands as a refuge.

Caribbean Coast and Islands

A nice boat trip would be to **Laguna Bismuna** on the northern coast, said to be one of the most beautiful lagoons in Nicaragua (though easiest access should be via Waspám).

Directory **Banks** Next to Enitel is Banco Caley Dagnall has been reported as cashing travellers' cheques in the past, but do not rely on travellers' cheques, as their standard policy is not to change them. Bring as much cash as necessary. If you can find Augusto Chow, "El Chino", in the market he reportedly will change travellers' cheques. **Communications** Post office and telephone: Just south of the park is Enitel that handles mail during the week and telephone service daily, T282-2237. **Useful numbers** Fire: T282-2255. **Hospital**: *Nuevo Amanecer*, T282-2259. **Police**: 282-2257. **Red Cross**: T282-2280.

Bosawás Biosphere Reserve

Area: 730,000 ha This, the largest forest reserve in Central America, is not only the most important area of rainforest on the isthmus, but also the most important cloud forest. All the diversity of species present in the Indio-Maíz reserve can also be found in Bosawás. In fact, there are even more species of flora and fauna here thanks to the changing altitudes in the Bosawás reserve. There are seven mountains with an altitude of above 1,200 m and the **Cerro Saslaya**, at 1,650 m, is the highest. The main rivers that cross the reserve all feed the Río Coco: **Río Bocay**, **Wina**, **Amaka**, **Río Lakus** and **Río Waspuk**. Exploring the reserve is still a challenge. The easiest and most organized way to visit is via Siuna (see below), but safety concerns mean that an even longer route is recommended to experience the beauty of the forest (see page 257).

Practical results from well-intentioned and planned ecotourism projects seem a long way off thanks to the remoteness of the reserve and the instability of the region. However, there is one exception: the **Proyecto Ecoturístico Rosa Grande**, supported by Nature Conservancy and the Peace Corps and based 25 km from Siuna, is near an area of virgin forest with a trail, waterfall on the river Labú and lots of wildlife including monkeys and large cats. One path leads to a lookout with a view over the Cerro Saslaya. Another, circular path to the northwest, goes to the **Rancho Alegre** falls. Guides can be hired for US$7 a day plus food. Excursions for two or more days cost only US$13 per person for guide, food and camping equipment. You may have to pay for a camp guard while hiking. Tourism is in its infancy here and you may find little things added on to your bill. Be certain you have enough supplies for your stay. For information contact Don Trinidad at the *comedor* on arrival in Santa Rosa. In Siuna you can contact the office of the Proyecto Bosawás, 200 m east of the airstrip; open Monday-Friday, 0800-1700. Groups of five or more must reserve in advance, contact the Amigos de Saslaya, c/o Proyecto Bosawás, Siuna, RAAN, by post or telegram. Large groups are not encouraged.

Sleeping **G** *BOSAWAS Field Station*, on the river Labú, very limited hammocks, clean but sim-
& eating ple, locally produced and cooked food about US$1.25. In **Rosa Grande** a meal at *Comedor Melania* costs about US$1.

Transport **Bus** Daily from Siuna market at 0500 and 0730, sometimes another at 1100, US$2.25.

Las Minas: the mining triangle

These three towns are known basically for their mines, but have recently **Siuna, Rosita**
become more famous in Nicaragua for the band of robbers that controls **& Bonanza**
them. This is the only place in the country where no Nicaraguan really wants
to visit. If you must go for mining or missionary business you will have deal
with the potential threat. Up to now the violence has been reserved for Nicaraguans and not the Canadian mining employees or the Evangelist missionaries
or Peace Corps, who make up the majority of the foreign population. Crimes
have included kidnapping and executions. You may read references to this
being the Wild West and other romantic allusions. However, any attempt to
laugh off the situation could be hazardous to your health. Unless you need to
visit this region for business, don't. It is possible to get to the Bosawás reserve
without travelling through the mining triangle (see below).

Siuna is the largest of the three towns, and while all are predominately *mestizo*, there is a Creole minority and the surrounding rural areas have a significant Sumu population as well as some Miskitos. There is a bank in Siuna.

Sleeping & eating   In Siuna: **E** *Chino*, the best and most expensive. **F** *Troysa*, clean.
F *Costeño*, 100 m east of airstrip. Basic. In Barrio La Luz there is a hotel above a billiard
hall. A recommended place to eat is either of the two *comedores* called **Desnuque**, 1 in
the market, and the other on a hill near the baseball stadium and airstrip; the latter has
good pizza as well as typical Nicaraguan food. **Comedor Siuna**, opposite *Hotel Costeño*,
has good *comida corriente*.

Transport   Air: *La Costeña* flies from the capital to Siuna direct daily, also Mon, Wed,
Fri, on the flight to **Bluefields** via **Siuna**, **Rosita**, **Bonanza** and **Puerto Cabezas**, reservations in Siuna, T263-2142.
   Road: There are 2 road links from Managua: one is through Matagalpa and Waslala
and the other goes through Boaco, Muy Muy, Matiguás and Río Blanco, a very scenic
330-km drive, about 7 hrs by 4WD vehicle in the dry season; this route is not in the
least bit safe at night and cannot be recommended during the day.

Wiwilí to Waspám, the river route

There is an alternative way to experience the wilderness of Bosawás without   *A jungle hammock*
exposing yourself to the risks of the Siuna area mining towns and their   *with built-in netting*
gun-toting band of un-merry robbers. With a great deal of time, patience   *(you zip yourself*
and a bit of luck you can see the great forest of Bosawás and explore a large   *inside) for insect*
part of the Río Coco in the process. The access is via Jinotega in central Nica-   *protection is a great*
ragua (see page 221). From Jinotega you can travel by bus either to Wiwilí on   *asset, as are all the*
the Río Coco or to San José de Bocay on the Río Bocay. Either land route   *survival goodies of*
from Managua will require at least 8-10 hours. You might sleep in Jinotega   *real exploration like a*
to arrive in time to start looking for a boat in one of the two locals. Then by   *first aid kit, water*
boat it is two days' travel into the reserve. Río Bocay converges with the Río   *purification tablets*
Coco and runs closer to the reserve, though the safer route is probably via   *and some kind of*
Wiwilí. The Río Coco skirts the northern border of Bosawás so you will have   *portable food*
to leave the river to go into the reserve. There are scattered settlements of
mostly Sumu Indians that can provide a place to string up a hammock. After
exploring the reserve with locally hired guides (a must) you can continue
down the river to finish in Waspám. From Waspám you can travel by bus to
Puerto Cabezas and fly back to Managua. Allow at least a week for this trip
and bring more money than you think you will need, in small notes. Check

with MARENA, T263-2617, in Managua, about the situation of any area you will visit in the Bosawás region.

Waspám and the Río Coco

Colour map 2, grid A5
Population: 38.701
Altitude: 14 m

The Spanish spelling
of the town is Waspán
The Río Coco is called
Wanki by the locals

This is the heart of Miskito country and though some Spanish is spoken in Waspám, only Miskito is spoken in the surrounding villages. This area was hard hit by Hurricane Mitch in 1998. At over 700 km Río Coco or Wanki is the longest river in Central America. The river's source is in the mountains near Somoto in northwestern Nicaragua and it passes Ocotal, Ciudad Antigua and Wiwilí before heading north to the border with Honduras. The rest of its length it acts as a border between the two countries, but for the Miskitos and Sumus this is all very hypothetical. Sadly, much of the river's banks are deforested and severely eroded. In 1998 Hurricane Mitch caused huge damage with the river over 10 m above normal in places. Thanks to its relative accessibility to Bilwi, Waspám is considered the capital of the Río Coco for the Miskitos. There is a good place to stay **F** *Las Cabañas*, wooden cabins with bath, mosquito netting, fan, water supply unreliable. During the dry season, the 130-km trip from Puerto Cabezas to Waspám should take about three hours by four-wheel drive vehicle (several hours longer by public bus, which leaves Puerto Cabezas 0700, Monday-Saturday and with luck returns from Waspám 1200). The bus can be boarded at several points in Puerto along the road leading out of town; cost is US$5. This trip will take you through the pine forests, red earth and plains north of Bilwi towards the Río Coco (also the border with Honduras), and you will pass through two Miskito villages, **Sisin** and **Santa Marta**. Hitching is possible if you cannot get all the way to Waspám; make sure you are left at Sisin, Santa Marta or La Tranquera. **NB** You can take lifts from the military but never travel at night.

Background

11

Background

History

Nicaragua was at the crossroads between northern and southern pre-Hispanic cultures for thousands of years. The original migration from Asia across the Bering Strait is believed to have occurred around 28,000 BC and the arrival of the southern migration of some of those peoples should have reached Nicaragua sometime before 18,000 BC. If migrations did occur from the Polynesian world to South America, as it is now starting to be believed, arrivals in South America from the South Pacific might have occurred around 8000 BC. In Managua, near the shores of the lake, there are some well-preserved human and animal footprints of what appears to be a family of 10 people leaving the area after a volcanic event in the year 4000 BC. Ceramic evidence of organized settlement in Nicaragua begins around 1000 BC and is prevalent in many areas of the Pacific. Nicaragua would receive migrations from both north and south until the first arrival of the Spanish explorers in 1522-23. The best understood culture is that of the **Nicaraguas**, whose final migration to Nicaragua from central Mexico to the shores of Lake Nicaragua occurred just 150-200 years before the arrival of the Spanish. They spoke Náhuat (a root version of the Azteca Náhuatl), which would become the lingua franca for the indigenous people after the conquest and may have already been widely used for trading in the region before the arrival of the first Europeans. The Nicaraguas shared the Pacific Basin of Nicaragua with the Chorotegas and Maribios. The **Chorotegas** also came from Mexico, though earlier, around AD 800 and were Mangue speakers. The two tribes seemed to have found some common commercial and perhaps religious ground and dominated most of the area west of the lakes. The **Maribios**, Hokano speakers, and believed to be originally from California and Baja California, in Mexico, populated the western slope of what is today the Maribios volcanic range, in northwestern Nicaragua. The Nicaraguas and Chorotegas were a very successful society that sat in the middle of a trade route that stretched from Mexico to Peru.

On the east side of the great lakes of Nicaragua the cultures were of South American origin. It is believed that the northern migrations of the people found in central and eastern Nicaragua at the time of the Conquest began around 3000 BC. The **Chontales** and **Matagalpas** may have been of the same language root (Chibcha) as the Caribbean Basin **Rama**, **Sumu** and **Miskito** cultures. In fact it could be that the Miskito are descendants of the original inhabitants of the Pacific that lost in wars to the invading tribes of Chorotegas in the ninth century. They would have been pushed to the east side of the lake and their name Chontales means 'barbarian' in Náhuat. The only indigenous languages still spoken in Nicaragua are of the Miskitos, Sumus and Ramas, with the Rama language now in threat of extinction. The Chontales appear to have been the most developed of the group, though little is known about their culture to date, despite ample and impressive archaeological evidence.

Christopher Columbus sailed the Caribbean shores of Nicaragua in 1502 on his fourth and final voyage and took refuge in the far northern part of today's Nicaragua before sailing to Jamaica. The Spanish explorer **Gil González Dávila** sailed from Panama to the Gulf of Nicoya and then travelled overland to the western shores of Lake Nicaragua to met the famous Nicaraguas tribe chief, Niqueragua, in April of 1523. After the conversion of 917 of the Nicaraguas élite to Christianity and a big take of gold, González Dávila travelled further north before being chased out of the area by a surprise attack of Chorotega warriors led by legendary chieftain, **Diriangén**. In 1524 a stronger army of 229 men was sent and the local populace was overcome. The captain of the expedition, **Francisco Hernández de Córdoba**, founded the cities of Granada and León on the shores of Lake Nicaragua and Lake

The Conquest of Nicaragua: a business trip

The meeting of the Spanish explorer Gil González and the philosophical Chief Niqueragua is a romantic story filled with fate, adventure and tragedy. But a brief glimpse at the cold numbers of the original expedition and the Conquest that followed paints a very different picture. According to local historian Patrick Werner (Los Reales de Minas de la Nicaragua Colonial y la Cuidad Perdida de Nueva Segovia, Instituto Nicaragüense de Cultura, 1996), Gil González received authorization for the expedition and make Europe's first business trip to the land of Nicaragua. A company was formed with four shareholders: the Spanish Crown 48%, Andrés Niño 29%, Cristóbal de Haro 15% and Gil González with 9% of the shares. The original investment totalled 8,000 gold pesos. They even took an accountant with them, Andrés de Cereceda who later reported the returns on the four-month business trip. The bottom line looked a lot better than your average start-up company: 112,524 gold pesos collected on an 8,000-peso investment.

Soon after it was the turn of Pedrarias Dávila to form a new company. The chief negotiator for this trip, Captain Francisco Hernández de Córdoba, with an army of 229 soldiers, produced spectacular returns on the investment, recovering 158,000 gold pesos while founding the cities of León and Granada. Within one year of the Conquest, the new franchises of León and Granada had collected a further 392,000 gold pesos. It was all the gold the Indians had ever owned; in less than three years, 700-800 years of accumulated gold had been taken.

The estimated indigenous population of the Pacific Basin upon the arrival of these two initial business ventures (1523 and 1524) was at least 500,000. Within 40 years the total population was no more than 50,000 people, and by 1610 the indigenous residents had been reduced to around 12,000. It wasn't until the 20th century that the population of Nicaragua returned to match pre-Conquest numbers.

Managua respectively. Little is known about the actual battles of the conquest, thanks to a lost letter from Córdoba to the country's first governor describing the events. Nueva Segovia was founded as third city in 1543 to try and capitalize on mineral resources in the northern mountains. **Pedrarias Dávila** was given the first governor's post in Nicaragua, one he would use as a personal empire. His rule set the stage for a tradition of *caudillos* (rulers of personality and favouritism, rather than of constitution and law) that would run and ruin Nicaragua, almost without exception, until the 21st century.

Colonial Era By the middle of the 16th century the Spanish had realized that Nicaragua was not going to produce the same kind of mineral riches they were taking out of Mexico and Peru. Gold reserves of the indigenous population had been robbed blind in the first three years of occupation and mines in the north did not seem to be as productive as was hoped. What Nicaragua did have was a solid population base and this was exploited to its maximum. There are no accurate figures for slave trade in early to mid-16th century Nicaragua, as it was not an approved activity and was made officially illegal by the Spanish Crown in 1542. It is estimated that 200,000 to 500,000 Nicaraguans were either exported as slaves to work in Panama and Peru or in the gold mines near Nueva Segovia, Nicaragua.

The **Consejo de Indias** (Indian Council) and the **Casa de Contratación** (Legal Office) in Seville managed affairs in Spain for Nicaragua. These administrative bodies controlled immigration to the Americas, acted as a court for disputes, and provided nominees for local rulers to the Spanish Crown. On a local level the province of Nicaragua belonged to the **Reino de Guatemala** (Kingdom of Guatemala) and was administered by a Spanish governor in León. While the conquistadores were busy pillaging the New World, there were serious discussions in Spain as to the legality of Spanish action in the Americas. Thanks in part to some tough lobbying by the famous humanist priest, Fray Bartolomé de Las Casas, laws were passed in 1542 to protect the rights of the Indians, outlawing slavery and granting them (in theory) equal rights. Sadly, implementation of these laws was nearly impossible due to communication obstacles and the sheer distance of the colony from Spain. Due to exhaustion of the Indian population and mineral resources, many of the Spanish left Nicaragua, looking for greener pastures. The ones that stayed on became involved in agriculture. Cattle were introduced and they took over cacao production, which was already very big upon their arrival. Indigo was the other principal crop, along with some trade in wood. The beef, leather and indigo were imported to Guatemala, the cacao to El Salvador. The exports were traded for other goods, such as food and clothing, and the local population lived primarily off locally grown corn and beans. There was also a busy commercial route between Granada and the Caribbean colonial states via the Río San Juan and trade between Nicaragua and Peru. Granada became much wealthier thanks to its advantageous position along the international trade routes, but administrative and church authority remained in León, creating a rivalry that would explode after Independence from Spain. By 1585, the majority of the local population had been converted to Christianity. During the 17th century Nicaragua was victim of multiple attacks from Dutch, French and British pirates as well as more officially sanctioned aggression by the British in the 18th century.

After 297 years as a colony of Spain, Nicaragua achieved Independence. It was not a romantic revolution, more an Independence on paper, though it was one that would release built-up tensions and rivalries into an open and bloody playing field. What followed was the least stable period in the history of the country: a general anarchy that only an outside invader would stop, by uniting Nicaraguans in a common cause, against a common enemy.

Independence from Spain

In 1808 Spain was invaded by French troops and Fernando VII King of Spain was held in captivity. Since the American colonies of Spain recognized Fernando as the legitimate ruler of Spain and its colonies (a ruler with zero effective power), the foundation was laid for the collapse of the world's greatest empire. The greatest impulse for the demise of Spanish rule came from a new social class created during the colonial period. Known locally as *criollos*, they were descendants of Spaniards born in the Americas. At the beginning of the 19th century they still only represented 5% of the population, but they were the owners of great agricultural empires, wealthy and increasingly powerful, indeed a class only the Spanish Crown could rival. The *criollos* did not openly oppose the colonial system, but rather chipped away at its control, in search of the power that they knew would be theirs without colonial rule. They continued to organize and institutionalize power until 5 November 1811 when El Salvador moved to replace all the Spaniards in its local government with *criollos*. One week later, in León, Nicaragua, the local population rebelled. The people of León took to the streets demanding the creation of a new government, new judges, abolition of the government monopoly to produce liquor, lower prices for tobacco and an end to taxes on beef, paper and general sales. All the demands were granted. There were also demonstrations in Masaya, Rivas and Granada. In September 1821 Mexico declared Independence from Spain. A meeting was called on 15 September 1821 in Guatemala City. At the meeting were the representatives of the central government in Spain, Spanish representatives from every country in Central America, the heads of the Catholic Church from each province, the archbishop of Guatemala and the local senators of the provinces. Independence from Spain was declared; yet in Nicaragua the wars had just begun.

León vs Granada   In October 1821 the authorities in León declared that Nicaragua would become part of the Mexican Empire, while the Guatemalan office of Central America created a local Central American government office in Granada, increasing sentiments of separatism in Granada. Regardless, Nicaragua remained more or less part of the federation of Mexico and Central America until 1823 when the **United Provinces of Central America** met and declared themselves free of Mexican domain and any other foreign power. The five members were a federation free to administer their own countries and in November of 1824 a new constitution for the **Central America Federation** was decreed. Nicaraguans, however, were already fighting amongst themselves. In April 1824 León and Granada both proclaimed themselves capital of the country. Other cities chose sides with one or the other, while Managua created a third 'government', proclaiming Managua as the new capital. The in-fighting continued until, in 1827, civil war erupted. It was not until Guatemala sent another general that peace was achieved and a new chief of state named in 1834. The civilian head of state was **Dr José Núñez**, but the military chiefs were not pleased and he was soon thrown out. In 1835 **José Zepeda** was named head of state but still more violence followed. In 1836 Zepeda was thrown in prison, put against a wall and shot. The state of anarchy in Nicaragua was common across Central America, as the power vacuum of 300 years of colonial rule wreaked havoc upon the isthmus. The federal government in Guatemala was increasingly helpless and impotent. On 30 April 1838 the legislative assembly of Nicaragua, in a rare moment of relevance, declared Nicaragua independent of any other power and Nicaragua was completely independent. The Central American Federation collapsed, with the other states also declaring the Federation to be history. A new constitution was written for Nicaragua, one that would have little effect on the constant power struggle. In 1853 Granada General Fruto Chamorro took over the post of Director of State, with hope of establishing something that resembled peace. Informed of an armed uprising being planned in León, he ordered the capture of the principal perpetrators, but most escaped to Honduras. In 1854 yet another new constitution was written. This one changed the post of Director of State to 'President' which meant that Conservative **General Fruto Chamorro** was technically no longer in power. However the assembly, going against the constitution they had just approved, named him as president anyway. The Liberal León generals in Honduras had seen enough and decided to attack. **Máximo Jerez** (later a hero in the war against William Walker and who has a statue above the fountain in León's Parque Central) led the attack. In 1854 the country was at war once again with Fruto and Granada fighting against Máximo and León. The León contingent hired US mercenary **Byron Cole** to give them a hand against Granada. He signed a contract and returned to the US where he gave the job to the man every single Nicaraguan (but not a single North American) schoolchild has heard of, William Walker.

William Walker & the Guerra Nacional   On 13 June 1855, North American William Walker and his 55 hired guns set sail for Nicaragua. The group was armed with the latest in firepower and a very well-planned scheme to create a new slave state in Nicaragua. His idea was for a new colony to be settled by North American Anglos (to own the lands and slaves) and blacks (to do all the work). William Walker not only planned to conquer and colonize Nicaragua, but also all of Central America, isolating what remained of Mexico, which had just lost one-third of its territory to the US in the Mexican-American War. Key to the success would be the ready-made inter-oceanic transportation of Cornelius Vanderbilt's steamship service from San Francisco to New York via San Juan del Sur, La Virgen, the Río San Juan and San Juan del Norte. In September of the same year, Walker and his little battalion landed in San Juan del Sur, confronted Granada's Conservative Party army in La Virgen and won easily. On 13 October 1855 he travelled north, attacked and took Granada with the local generals escaping to Masaya and later signing a peace pact. As per prior agreement, **Patricio Rivas** of León's Liberal Party was named president of the republic and Walker as the head of the military. Rivas, following Walker's wishes, confiscated the steamship line of Vanderbilt, which Walker then used to ship in more arms, ammunitions and mercenary soldiers from the US. Soon he had the best-equipped and most modern fighting force in Central America.. On 6 June,1856, Walker appeared in León, demanding that he be allowed to confiscate the properties of Granada's Conservative Party. President Patricio Rivas and his ministers refused. After numerous meetings and no agreements William Walker left León for Granada, but the people with power in León had finally understood what they were up against and contacted generals in El Salvador and Guatemala for help. Soon all of Central America would be united against the army of William Walker. From 22-24 June 1856 farcical elections were held and William Walker was named President of the Republic. On 12 July, Walker officially took office with a pompous parade through Granada, while flying his new flag for the country. A series of decrees were proclaimed during that month, including the legalization of slavery, the immediate confiscation of all properties of all 'enemies of the state' and English was made the official language of business (to see that North American colonists would receive all the land confiscated). The government of Walker was recognized by the pre-civil war US government as legitimate. What would follow is known to Nicaraguans as the *Guerra Nacional* (National War) and its victory is celebrated today with decidedly more vigour than the anniversary of Nicaragua's Independence from Spain. The turning point in William Walker's troops' apparent invincibility came at the little ranch north of Tipitapa called San Jacinto. It is a museum today and a mandatory visit for all Nicaraguan primary schoolchildren.

Walker had never been able to control Matagalpa and a division of the rebel Nicaraguan army was sent south from Matagalpa to try and stop the confiscation of cattle ranches in the area of San Jacinto. The two forces met. The Nicaraguan division used the little house in San Jacinto, with its thick adobe walls, as their fort and it provided great protection. A battle on 5 September was a slight victory for the Nicaraguans, but both sent for reinforcements and on 14 September (the national holiday celebrated annually), 200 of Walker's troops lost a bloody and difficult battle to 160 Nicaraguan troops. The Nicaraguan battalion included a contingent of Matagalpa Indians. The tide had turned and battles in Masaya, Rivas and Granada would prove victorious for the combined Central American forces. William Walker escaped to a steamship where he watched the final grisly actions of his troops in Granada, who, completely drunk, proceeded to rape and kill the fleeing natives of Granada and then burned the city to the ground. As they mounted the steamship in Lake Nicaragua they planted a makeshift sign saying, "Here was Granada". Walker would later return to Nicaragua, before just escaping with his life. He then tried his luck in Honduras where he was taken prisoner by Captain Salmon of the British Navy and handed over to the Honduran authorities. He was tried, put against a wall and shot by the Honduran armed forces on 12 September 1860.

For the next 30-plus years , the wealthy families of Granada would control the government, thanks partly to a law stating that, to have the right to vote, you must possess 100 pesos, and in order to be a presidential candidate you must have over 4,000 pesos. Mark Twain noted on his visit in 1866 that only 'land owners' had the right to vote. But, in 1893, the Conservative president was overthrown by a movement led by Liberal Party General José Santos Zelaya. Zelaya did much to modernize Nicaragua. A new constitution was written in 1893 and put into effect the following year. The separation of church and state was instituted, with ideas of equality and liberty for all, respect for private property, civil marriage, divorce, the death penalty abolished and debtors' prison banned and freedom of expression guaranteed. Construction

General José Santos Zelaya

Background

was rampant, with new roads, docks, postal offices, shipping routes and electricity installed in Managua and Chinandega. A whole raft of new laws to facilitate business, proper police and military codes were passed and a Supreme Court was created. The Caribbean Coast was finally officially incorporated into the country in 1894. Despite all of this, Zelaya did not endear himself to the US. With the canal project close at hand in either Panama or Nicaragua, Zelaya insisted that no single country would be permitted to finance a canal project in Nicaragua and, what's more, only Nicaragua could have sovereignty over a canal inside its country. The project went to Panama. In 1909 Zelaya was pushed out of power with the help of the US Marines.

US Marines –
Augusto
Sandino
In 1909 there was an uprising in Bluefields against Zelaya led by General Juan Estrada, with the support of the Granada Conservative Party. Estrada took control of the east coast. In May of 1910 the US Marines arrived in Bluefields to establish what they termed a 'neutral zone'. General Estrada marched into Managua to install himself as the new president of Nicaragua. Stuck with debts from European creditors, Juan Estrada was forced to borrow from the North American banks to pay debts. He then gave the US control over collection of duties, as a guarantee for those loans. The Nicaraguan National Bank and a new monetary unit called the *córdoba* were established in 1912. The Granada aristocrats were not happy with General Estrada and a new round of fighting between León Liberals and Granada Conservatives erupted. On 4 August the US Marines entered Managua to secure order and establish their choice, Adolfo Díaz, as president of the country. Two years later, under occupation of the Marines, Nicaragua signed the Chamorro-Bryan Treaty, with Nicaragua conceding perpetual rights of any Nicaraguan canal project to the US, in exchange for US$3 mn, which went to pay US banks for outstanding debts. There was no intention to build a canal in Nicaragua, rather to keep someone else from building a competing one. In 1917 Emiliano Chamorro took control of the presidency and more problems followed. Díaz, still fighting to regain the presidency, called for more Marines to be sent from the US; over 2,000 troops arrived, Díaz made it back into the presidency, but nothing could be done to bring together the various factions. In May 1927, the US State Department agreed a plan with the Nicaraguan authorities to organize a non-political army, disarm both the Liberal and Conservative armies and hold new elections. The new army would be called the *Guardia Nacional* (National Guard). Most parties agreed to the solution, with the exception of General Augusto Sandino, who had been fighting under the command of Liberal General José María Moncada. Sandino returned to the northern mountains determined to fight against the government of Adolfo Díaz, whom he panned as a US puppet president. In 1928, José María Moncada, under supervision of the US government, won the elections. General Sandino, with his former commander in power, took the fight directly to the US Marines. Fighting side by side with the Marines, to exterminate Augusto Sandino and his rebel army, was the newly created Guardia Nacional. The Marines thought they would defeat General Sandino's rebel forces quickly, in particular with the air power that they had brought with them. In Nicaragua's northern mountains they were to experiment with air bomb attacks for the first time while trying to take out Sandino and his men. The charismatic general had widespread support in the north and was not defeated. Sandino relentlessly attacked US Marine positions with the (some say first) use of modern guerrilla warfare. Finally with elections approaching in 1933 and with the National Guard under the command of Anastasio Somoza García, US envoy Harry Stimson announced that the Marines would pull out when the new president took power. Juan Bautista Sacasa was elected, and the day he took power, 1 January 1933, the last regiment of Marines left Nicaragua by boat from Corinto. Twenty-four years of intervention had ended.

With the US Marines gone, General Augusto Sandino went directly to the presidential palace (today the Parque Loma de Tiscapa) and signed a peace and disarmament treaty with President Sacasa that same day. It stipulated that the rebel army would gradually turn over their weapons and receive amnesty, with ample job opportunities for ex-rebel fighters. One year later, on 21 February 1934, when Sandino returned to the presidential palace for dinner with President Sacasa, the commander of the Guardia Nacional, Anastasio Somoza García, demanded the last of Sandino's weapons. Sandino claimed that the Constitution allowed him to retain some weapons and, after Sandino left the dinner party, Somoza García had him abducted and executed. Rumours have it that Sandino's head was sent to Washington DC as physical proof of his elimination. With the death of Sandino the Liberal Party was divided into two camps, one that supported Somoza and the other President Sacasa. Somoza attacked the fort above León in May 1936 and the Guardia Nacional demanded Sacasa's resignation. A month later Sacasa resigned and new elections were won by Somoza García. Yet again a leader of Nicaragua's military took state office. The history of the 19th and early 20th century was to be repeated, only now the opposition was no longer able to mount challenges, thanks to the unity and sweeping efficiency of the Guardia Nacional. Various 'presidents' were elected from 1937-79, but there was never any doubt who was running the show. Anastasio Somoza García and later his son Anastasio Somoza Debayle maintained effective power and the country enjoyed a period of relative stability and economic growth. The relationship between the US and Nicaragua had never been better, with close co-operation, including the use of Nicaragua as a training and launching ground for the Bay of Pigs invasion in Cuba. Somoza used the Guardia Nacional to keep the populace at bay and the technique of *pactos* (political pacts) to keep political opponents in on some of the Somoza family's ever-increasing riches and power. During the Second World War, Nicaragua entered on the side of the US and Somoza García used the war to confiscate as much property from German nationals as possible (including what is today Montelimar Beach Resort). This formed a basis for building a business empire that used state money to grow. (By the time his son, Somoza Debayle, was kicked out in 1979, the family owned more than 50% of all arable land and controlled an estimated 65% of the GDP.) After accepting the Liberal Party nomination for the election of 1956, Somoza García was shot and killed by a young León poet named Rigoberto López Pérez. Despite his death, the family dynasty continued with Somoza García's sons, Luis and Anastasio. Together they lasted 42 years in power, one of the longest and bloodiest dictatorships in Latin American history.

In 1954, 1958 and 1959 armed attempts at dethroning the Somozas failed, and in 1961 the **Frente Sandinista de Liberación Nacional** (FSLN) was founded. Anti-government demonstrations in Managua in 1967 were fiercely repressed by the Guardia Nacional who attacked the demonstrators, killing some and injuring many. In 1972, after the great earthquake of Managua, millions of dollars of aid and reconstruction money were lost in the hands of Somoza's companies and bank accounts. The last straw came in January 1978, when Pedro Joaquín Chamorro, editor of the country's oldest newspaper and a respected member of the upper class, was shot to death. Chamorro had been part of the failed 1959 overthrow attempt and founder of an opposition group to Somoza Debayle, so most people assumed his death was the work of the Guardia Nacional. The 'Revolution' or 'war against Somoza' was in full swing with support from all social classes.

The two-year Revolution was the culmination of a 20-year struggle led for 15 years by Carlos Fonseca Amador (who died in combat in 1976). At the huge cost of more than 50,000 Nicaraguan lives, Somoza Debayle and the Guardia National were finally chased out of Nicaragua. The Revolution brought major damage to cities like

The Somoza family

1978-79 Revolution

The Contra War

US President Ronald Reagan baptized the Contras the 'Freedom Fighters', and on one occasion even sported a T-shirt that read, 'I'm a Contra too'. His administration lobbied to maintain and increase military aid to the Nicaraguan Contras fighting the Sandinista Revolution during the 1980s. The first bands of Contras were organized shortly after the Sandinistas took power in 1979. They were mainly ex-officials and soldiers loyal to the overthrown general Anastasio Somoza Debayle. Thanks to the United States, the Contras grew quickly and became the largest guerrilla army in Latin America. When they demobilized in May 1990, they had 15,000 troops.

The Contras divided Nicaragua in two: war zones and zones that were not at war. They also divided United States public opinion between those who supported President Reagan's policy and those who opposed it. The US House of Representatives and the Senate were likewise divided. The Contras are also associated with one of the biggest political scandals in the US after Watergate.

The so-called 'Iran-Contra Affair' broke at the end of 1986, when a C-123 supply plane with a US flight crew was shot down over Nicaraguan territory. The scandal that followed caused some US government officials to resign, including Lieutenant Colonel Oliver North. The intellectual authors of the affair remained unscathed.

The most famous Contra leader was former Guardia Nacional Colonel Enrique Bermúdez, known in the war as 'Commander 3-80'. In February 1991, Bermúdez was shot dead in the parking lot of Managua's Intercontinental Hotel. The 'strange circumstances' surrounding his death were never clarified, and the killers were never apprehended.

After agreeing to disarm in 1990, the majority of the Contra troops returned to a normal civilian life. However, most of them never received the land, credit, work implements, etc. they had been promised. They formed a political party called the Resistencia Nicaragüense (Nicaraguan Resistance) that has been ineffective due to internal disputes and divisions.

Masaya, Managua, León and Estelí, and to Nicaragua's economy in general. Somoza finally fled on 17 July 1979, after a prolonged and horrifying series of battles that saw the Guardia Nacional bombing Nicaraguan neighbourhoods from the air. The war was won by a broad coalition of labour unions, private enterprise, the Catholic Church, various political parties and the most visible of all, the FSLN or Sandinistas. Somoza escaped to Miami and later to Paraguay, where he was taken out by a left-wing Argentinian hit squad a year later.

Sandinista Government and the Contra War A committee assumed power of Nicaragua on 19 July 1979 made up of five members: **Daniel Ortega**, **Sergio Ramírez**, **Moisés Hassan**, **Violeta Barrios de Chamorro** and **Alfonso Robelo**. The first act of the committee was to abolish the old Constitution and confiscate all property belonging to Somoza and his 'allies'. A new legislative body was organized to write yet another Constitution. Several key bodies were created by the Sandinistas that helped them to consolidate power quickly, like the Comités de Defensa Sandinista (CDS) that was organized in the barrios of Managua and the countryside to be the 'eyes and ears of the Revolution'. The unions were put under Sandinista control with the creation of the Central Sandinista de Trabajadores (CST) and FETSALUD for the health workers. The police force and military were both put under party control, with the military being renamed the Ejército Popular Sandinista (EPS). The EPS and Policía Sandinista were both put under control of key party members. Any idea of shared power amongst other groups led by Violeta Barrios de Chamorro or the non-communist forces of Edén Pastora were quickly dashed. Many who fought had believed that the Revolution was about getting rid of Somoza and establishing a democratic system, while the Sandinistas aim was to change society as a whole by installing a Marxist system. Peace was short lived, as rebel groups began to form in the northern mountains and in Honduras, and in 1982 the **Resistencia Nicaragüense** better known as the Contras (short for counter-revolutionary in Spanish), began attacks. The Sandinistas are credited with important socio-political achievements including the Literacy Crusade, the Agrarian Reform, a new sense of nationalism, and the Co-operative Movement. Yet the Contra movement would spell its doom.

Elections were held on 4 November 1984 for an augmented National Constituent Assembly with 96 seats: the Sandinista Liberation Front won 61 seats, and **Daniel Ortega**, who had headed the committee, was elected president. The Democratic Conservatives won 14 seats, the Independent Liberals nine seats, the Popular Social Christians six and the Socialists, Communists and Marxists/Leninists won two seats each. The failure of the Sandinista Government to meet the demands of the Democratic Co-ordinating Board (CDN) led to this coalition boycotting the elections and to the US administration failing to recognize the elected government. Meanwhile ex-Guardia members found US support to turn the Contra conflict into something much bigger and better financed. Ex-revolutionary Edén Pastora created a southern front to fight the new Nicaraguan government from Costa Rica, and the US poured money into Honduras for the northern front forces. The Contras were heavily outmanned, but well trained, and since the majority of the Contra fighters were *campesinos,* they were well equipped to weather the difficult conditions of the Nicaraguan wilderness. By introducing mandatory military service, the Sandinista army swelled to over 200,000 to fight the combined Contra forces of an estimated 20-30,000 soldiers. The national monetary reserves were increasingly taxed with more than half the national budget going on military spending, and a US economic embargo sending inflation spinning out of control, annihilating the already beleaguered economy. Massive immigration to avoid the war changed the face of Nicaragua, with exiles choosing departmental capitals, Managua or Costa Rica, while those who could afford it fled to Miami.

Progress in education and culture was impressive during the Sandinista years, especially considering the circumstances, but the cost was too high for the majority of the Nicaraguan people. Personal freedoms were the same or worse (especially in regards to freedom of speech and press) as they had been in the time of Somoza's rule, and fatigue from the death and poverty caused by the Contra War was extreme. A peace agreement was reached in Sapoá, Rivas and elections were held in 1990. Daniel Ortega (40.8%) lost to Violeta Chamorro (55.2%). After losing the elections the Sandinistas bravely handed over power to Doña Violeta. Then they proceeded frantically to divide and distribute state-held assets (which included thousands of confiscated properties) amongst leading party members, in what has since been known simply as the *piñata.*

Modern Nicaragua

After an entire century (and in many ways 450 years) of limited personal freedoms and military backed governments, most Nicaraguans consider the election of Doña Violeta as the beginning of democracy in Nicaragua. Violeta Barrios de Chamorro had her sons on both sides of the fence in the 1980s: the elder, Pedro Joaquín junior, was with the Contras, while the younger, Carlos Fernando, was with the Sandinistas. As she brought together her family, she brought together the country. Doña Violeta was forced to compromise on many issues and at times the country looked set to collapse back into war, but Nicaragua's first woman president spent the next five years mending the

Violeta Barrios de Chamorro

Cuba and Nicaragua – love hurts

Over the years, Cuba and Nicaragua have had a love-hate relationship. The Bay of Pigs invasion to overthrow the government of Fidel Castro embarked from Puerto Cabezas on the North Atlantic of Nicaragua. As they left Nicaragua, Anastasio Somoza Debayle requested that they bring him "a piece of hair from Castro's beard". That adventure ended in a humiliating defeat for the anti-Castro invaders. Later, ironically, Castro's Cuba was one of the first countries to send humanitarian aid to Nicaragua after the violent earthquake that destroyed most of Managua in December 1972. Somoza Debayle had no choice but to accept the aid and to accept Cuban doctors. Cuba also played a very important role in the Sandinista victory of July 1979. The Caribbean nation became Nicaragua's main ally, especially in the areas of military assistance, health care and education. By the mid-1980s around 9,000 Cuban advisers were in Nicaragua, 3,000 of whom were working with the country's security

forces. At the same time, thousands of Nicaraguans, especially those from poor families, went to Cuba to finish secondary school or to study in the vocational schools and universities. Likewise, thousands went to Cuba for free medical attention they couldn't receive in Nicaragua due to a lack of specialists, hospitals and modern equipment. While many Nicaraguans were grateful to the Cubans for their assistance, others didn't want them in the country. In the South Atlantic Region, the population publicly demanded that the Cubans leave the area at the beginning of the 1980s.

Today, official relations between Cuba and Nicaragua have 'chilled'. Both countries have low-level diplomats in their respective capitals and there is almost no commercial interchange between them. Nonetheless, hundreds of Nicaraguan students are currently attending medical school in Havana with scholarships granted by the Cuban government after Hurricane Mitch struck Central America in October 1998.

country into one whole piece. The Nicaraguan military was de-politicized, put under civilian rule and reduced from over 200,000 to less than 30,000. Uprisings were common with small groups taking up arms or demonstrations meant to destabilize the government. Despite claims that her son-in-law, Antonio Lacayo, was actually running the country and that some of her administration was financially corrupt, by the time Doña Violeta handed over the presidency in 1997, Nicaragua was fully at peace and economically crawling back to form.

Arnoldo Alemán On 8 November 1996 Liberal Party candidate Arnoldo Alemán won 51% of the vote against the 37.7% garnered by his opponent Daniel Ortega, with the rest divided among an incredible 21 different presidential candidates. The Sandinistas maintained pressure on the Alemán government with strikes, protests and intermittent negotiations. Another in the historical parade of closed-door pacts between seemingly opposed political parties, this time between the Liberals and the Sandinistas, created compromised and politicized government institutions and much controversy. Sandinista objectors to the pact were tossed out of the party. Alemán made great strides in increasing economic growth and foreign investment in Nicaragua and improveming education and road infrastructure. He also managed to buy up huge tracts of land and build expensive highways that led to his multiplying properties. Accusations of enrichment and corruption have drowned out many of his achievements and he leaves office with an approval rating of less than 30%. The 1998 hurricane disaster encouraged foreign countries to consider external debt pardon, a possible saviour to the world's most indebted country in proportion to its GDP.

Background

As this book goes to print, the Nicaraguan people have just cast their vote in the first presidential elections of the 21st century. Despite the fact that the Sandinista Party candidate, former President **Daniel Ortega**, had been ahead in all the polls, the electorate once again voted for the safer option, the Liberals, and Ortega was pipped at the post by the Liberal Party candidate **Enrique Bolaños**. Daniel Ortega came under heavy pressure from the US Embassy, in a very transparent power play by Washington to show the Nicaraguan public that they did not approve of Ortega or the Sandinista Party. Threats included cancellation of all aid programmes, which are the largest of any foreign donor to Nicaragua. The last-minute swing of allegiance in fact means that Ortega has lost by more than 10%. The result is being considered a vote against Ortega rather than a vindication of Bolaños or his policies. The Conservative Party ticket, **Alberto Saborío**, came in a very distant third.

Elections of 2001

Government

A new Constitution, approved by the 92-member National Constituent Assembly in 1986, came into effect on 9 January 1987, and has since been amended regularly. Legislative power is vested in a unicameral, directly elected National Assembly of 92 representatives, each with an alternate representative, with a six-year term. In addition, unelected presidential and vice-presidential candidates become representatives and alternates respectively if they receive a certain percentage of the votes. Executive power is vested in the President, assisted by a Vice-President and an appointed Cabinet. The presidential term is five years. Presidential elections are taking place in November 2001 with the new President of Nicaragua taking office in January of 2002.

Economy

The World Bank classes Nicaragua among the world's poorest countries and its per capita income is the lowest in Latin America. The economy is based on agriculture, which contributes more than 35% of the GDP. The principal export items and their value for the year 2000 (all figures in millions of US dollars): coffee $169.5, shrimp $56, lobster $54.1, beef $50.9, gold $29.5, sugar $28.7, and bananas $10.6 mn dollars. The Government has encouraged diversification, and exports such as tobacco and manufactured products have gained in importance. After being hampered in the early 1990s by social unrest and lack of credit, the agricultural sector has been slow to recover because of adverse weather conditions, low prices and mounting debts owed by farmers to state development banks. In 1997 a rural debt-relief programme was announced, whereby farmers could either pay off their debts immediately and escape interest and penalty charges, or have the debt cut by half and repay it over 10 years with interest. Hurricane Mitch inflicted further blows on agriculture in 1998 with widespread destruction of peanut, rice, sugar, banana, shrimp and coffee crops. In 2001 a worldwide drop in coffee prices forced many small farmers into bankruptcy, creating protest against banks in the northern coffee growing areas and sending unemployed coffee workers into Matagalpa looking for food. Nicaraguan banks themselves saw problems in 2000 and 2001 with several big establishments going under thanks to poor management and uncollected loans.

Background

In 1992 inflation was brought down to only 3.9%. The trend was reversed in 1993 owing to deep austerity and political instability; the GDP fell and inflation rose to 28.3%. In 1994, GDP growth returned, but per capita GDP continued to decline. In the five years to 1994 it had fallen by 48. Some sectors, for example energy, tourism and gold mining, benefited from foreign investment in the mid-1990s and the seafood

Recent trends

industry showed marked improvement. Overall, though, progress was hampered by the farming crisis, the large trade deficit, a lack of reserves and the demands on resources arising from foreign debt repayment. President Alemán promised to continue the structural adjustment programme of the Chamorro government and to create 100,000 jobs a year by reactivating agriculture, tourism and attracting foreign investment. The reduction of poverty and the promotion of growth were to be given high priority, while further debt relief was being sought. Nicaragua is a candidate for debt relief under the new Highly Indebted Poor Country (HIPC) initiative, provided it has an International Monetary Fund (IMF) agreement in place. External debt totalled around US$6 bn in 1998, three times the size of GDP. Nicaragua's entire economic outlook was radically altered, however, by Hurricane Mitch (October 1998). With reconstruction forced to the top of the agenda and a new focus given to the issue of debt relief, there were signs that financial resources were being targeted at areas of greatest need, and that a political unity not seen for many years was emerging. In 1999 Nicaragua's ranking among world markets for its level of free-market openness moved from 68th to 34th on the list of 130+ countries. Annual inflation dropped from just over 11% to 9% between 1999 and 2000. Export earnings have risen slowly since 1990 with a total of US$625.3 mn in 2000 compared to the 1990 earnings total of US$330.5 mn.

Land and environment

Geography

Nicaragua is located between the tropic of Cancer and the equator ranging from 11°-15° north and between 83°-88° longitude. It is often depicted as a big triangle, including on its national flag. The 530-km northern border of Nicaragua runs from the Golfo de Fonseca to Cabo Gracias a Dios, much of it marked by the Río Coco. The Caribbean Coast from Gracias a Dios to just south of the mouth of the Río San Juan is 509 km. From the Caribbean outlet of the RíoSan Juan to the Bay of Salinas is the 313-km border with Costa Rica. The Pacific Coast is 325 km from Salinas to the Golfo de Fonseca. The total surface area of the country is 131,812 sq km; 10,384 sq km of this is covered by lakes and coastal lagoons. Despite losing more than 40,000 sq km of territory over the last two centuries to Honduras in the north, to Costa Rica in the south and to Colombia in the Caribbean, Nicaragua is still the biggest of the Central American republics.

The land is can be divided into three principal divisions. The first is the **Caribbean lowlands**, which include pine savannahs in the north and, further south, the largest remaining expanse of rainforest on the Central American isthmus. The Caribbean region is crossed by numerous rivers that drain the central mountain range to the emerald sea. The second principal section is the **central and northern mountains and plains**, which are geologically the oldest in the country, with many long-extinct volcanoes. The mountains are low, with an elevation ranging from 500 m in the far south of the zone rising to 2,000 m as they reach the border with Honduras in the north. This is a mineral-rich area that has been prospected for centuries. The ecosystem diversity is immense with rainforest giving way to tropical dry forest in the south and cloud forest to pines in the north. The third division is the **Pacific Basin**, which is marked by numerous crater lakes, the two great lakes of Managua and Nicaragua and the lumpy spine of volcanoes, the **Cordillera Los Maribios**, that run from the extreme northwest at Volcán Cosiguina to the dual volcano island of Ometepe in Lake Nicaragua. The area is a mixture of tropical dry forest and savannah with two cloud forests on Volcán Mombacho and Volcán Maderas, and a pine forest on the Volcán Casita.

On the Pacific Basin plain are 15 crater lakes and the two largest sheets of water in Central America . The capital, Managua, on the shores of **Lake Managua** (also known by one of its indigenous labels, Xolotlán) is 52 km long, 15-25 km wide, and sits 39 m above sea level. Its maximum depth is only 30 m and it has a surface area of 1,025 sq km. The Peninsula of Chiltepe juts out into Lake Managua and holds two crater lakes, Xiloá and Apoyeque. Managua also houses four small crater lakes. Lake Managua drains to Lake Nicaragua via the Río Tipitapa just east of the capital. The mighty **Lake Nicaragua**, often called by one of its pre-Conquest names, Cocibolca, is 160 km long, 65 km at its widest, and 32 m above the level of the sea. This massive sheet of water averages 20 m in depth with a maximum depth of 60 m. Lake Nicaragua covers a total of 8,264 sq km. Just 18 km separates the big lake from the Pacific Ocean on the southern part of its western shores. But Lake Nicaragua drains 190 km to the Caribbean Sea via the **Río San Juan**, the second longest river in Central America behind the 680 km **Río Coco** in Nicaragua's north. There are 96 principal rivers in all in the country, most lying east of the great lakes.

Lakes & rivers

Nicaragua is one of the most geologically active countries in the world. It lies at the intersection of the Coco and Caribe continental plates. Subduction of the Coco plate underneath the Caribe plate is at a rate of 8-9 cm per year, the fastest rate of plate collision in the hemisphere. The newest of the countries in the Americas in geological terms (8-9 million years old), its constant subterranean movement results in some 300+ low level tremors per day in the region, with the majority occurring on the Pacific shelf. Another result of the land in upheaval is a line of more than 40 beautiful volcanoes, six of which have been active within the last 100 years. The volcanoes run 300 km from north to south along a fault line that is full of magma 10 km below the topsoil. The northernmost is **Volcán Cosigüina**, overlooking the Golfo de Fonseca, at 800 m with a lake in its crater. Its final eruption was in 1835 in what is believed to have been the most violent in recorded history in the Americas with ash being thrown as far as Mexico and the ground shaking as far south as Colombia. Just to the southeast continues the Maribios volcanic chain, with the now extinct **Volcán Chonco** (1,105 m) and the country's highest, the cone of **Volcán San Cristóbal** (1,745 m). San Cristóbal recommenced erupting in 1971 after a long period of inactivity that occurred after the highly explosive years of 1684-1885. Since 1999 it has been throwing up a lot of ash and its last activity was in July 2001. Just south rises the extinct cone of **Volcán Casita**, which is notable for its pine forest, the southernmost of its kind in the American continent's northern hemisphere. One side of Casita collapsed during the torrential rains of Hurricane Mitch in 1998, burying numerous villages in the municipality of Posoltega and killing more than 2,000 people. Further south, just before León, is the very active **Volcán Telica** (1,061 m) with eruptions occurring often in the 1990s and early 21st century. It was recorded erupting in 1529, 1685 and between 1965-68 with more activity in 1971. It seems to erupt in unison with San Cristóbal and had its last major activity in 1999. Next to the bald, eroding summit of Telica are the dormant cones of little **Volcán Santa Clara** (or Volcán San Jacinto) and **Volcán Rota** (or Volcán Orata at 836 m), which is believed to be the oldest in the chain. Just south of León is one of the youngest volcanoes on the planet, Cerro Negro; born in 1850 it has risen from just above sea level to 450 m in this short period. Major eruptions occurred in 1867, 1914, 1923, 1947, 1950, 1952, 1954, 1968, 1971, 1992, 1995 and 1999. This is the most dangerous of the volcanoes with violent eruptions and lava flows, and the eruption in August 1999 opened new craters at its southern base. **Volcán Pilas** is formed of various craters, the highest of which rises 1,001 m and contains one active crater known as **El Hoyo**, which last erupted from 1952-55, though it is still smoking. Other extinct cones lie between Pilas and the majestic **Volcán Momotombo** (1,300 m), which overlooks the shores of Lake

Volcanoes

Background

Managua. Momotombo eruptions in the late 1500s convinced the residents of León Viejo to leave. It erupted with force in 1764, from 1858 to 1866 was in regular eruptions and had its most recent significant eruption in 1905 with a large lava flow to its east side. Today a geothermal plant on the base of its west side utilizes its considerable fumarolic energy on a daily basis. The chain ends with little extinct **Volcán Momotombito**, which forms an island in Lake Managua. Managua's volcanoes are all extinct and six contain crater lakes.

The Dirianes volcanic chain begins just north of Masaya with the complex of **Volcán Masaya**, including the smoking, lava-filled Santiago crater as well as four extinct craters and a lagoon. Masaya is the only volcano on the American continent, and one of four in the world, with a constant pool of lava. Amongst its very active recent history have been noteworthy eruptions in 1670, 1772, 1858-59, 1902-05, 1924, 1946, 1965, 1970-72. It fell dormant for two decades before coming alive again with up to 400 tons per day of sulphur output from 1995 until today. It had a small, but nasty little eruption on 23 April 2001, with more expected. South between Masaya and Granada is the extinct Apoyo, which died very violently 20,000 years ago, leaving the deep blue **Laguna de Apoyo**, 6 km in diameter. Along the shores of Lake Nicaragua and shadowing Granada is dormant and mildly fumarolic **Volcán Mombacho** (1,345 m), wrapped in cloud forest. Mombacho had a major structural collapse in 1570 that wiped out a Chorotega village at its base. Fall-out and lava flows from a prehistoric eruption (estimated at 6000 BC) of the Mombacho cone created Las Isletas in Lake Nicaragua.

The volcanoes of Lake Nicaragua include the extinct and heavily eroded cone that makes the **Isla de Zapatera** (600 m), a national park and a very important pre-Columbian site. The last two volcanoes in the Nicaraguan chain of fire make up the stunning Isla de Ometepe: the symmetrical and active cone of **Volcán Concepción** (1,610 m), which became very active between 1883-87, 1908-10, 1921, 1948, the last major lava flow in 1957 and continued ash emissions until 1999. The cloud forest covered **Volcán Maderas** (1,394 m) is believed to be extinct and it holds a lake in its misty summit. In reality there are many, many more volcanoes, some are so heavily eroded that they no longer warrant admiration, but Nicaragua, in essence, is one relief of volcanoes from west to east varying in age from eight million to 160 years.

Climate

Located between the tropic of Cancer and the equator (between 11°-15° north) dictates a well defined annual wet and dry season, which the Nicaraguans refer to as winter and summer respectively. This despite the fact that the rainy season is in the northern hemisphere's summer. Bands of high pressure areas arrive from the South Pacific and collide with Caribbean low pressure areas in the rainy season from May to November in most of the country. During the dry season Pacific low pressure heads south pushed by bands of high pressure from the northeast, creating rains in the southern hemisphere tropics and dry winds in Nicaragua.

Rain or sun   The trade winds from the Caribbean modify the pattern, creating a longer rainy season directly proportional to the proximity to the Caribbean Sea.

The rain-soaked **Caribbean Coast** receives up to 5,000 mm of rain annually at San Juan del Norte with inland jungle and northern Caribbean coastal areas soaking in 4,000 to 2,500 mm annually. The dry season is between two and three months long depending on position, with San Juan del Norte receiving a break from the rains only from mid-March to the end of April. The **central and northern highlands** between 500 and 1,500 m have their own weather profile, with rainfall averaging between 1,500 to 2,500 mm annually. The rainy season is shorter than it is on the Caribbean Coast and jungles, but still longer than the Pacific lowlands with seven to eight months of rain and a January to April dry season. The **Pacific Basin** is classic dry tropical with 700 to 1,500 mm of rain annually, coming almost exclusively during the six-month wet season from mid-May to mid-November followed by a very dry six-month period.

Temperatures are directly related to altitude in Nicaragua. In essence, every 140 m of altitude above sea level translates into a 1°C lower temperature. This means that it can be 32°C in Managua and in the mid-20s in the mountain regions. The forest also has a cooling effect with trapped moisture after rains keeping the mercury from shooting back up. World weather irregularities due to global warming have also been felt in Nicaragua with rain in the dry season, dry during the rainy season and hurricanes of record force. Even the usually infallible weather rhythms of the tropics have been fouled.

Monthly profile

In a typical year, **January and February** are dry windy months, night time temperatures are cool, dropping down to 18-20°C. The landscape is beginning to turn brown though many tropical trees are beginning to flower on the savannahs. **March and April** means much higher temperature, the landscape now very dry and dusty with the added smoke of farmers burning brush and sugar cane refuse. Jungle trees come into full bloom during this period. **May and June** starts the rainy season, humidity can be very high, above 85%, during these months as the weather changes. Rains are in the afternoon and at night, though some storms will bring two or three days of rain. The landscape transforms into a spectacular green after the third good rain, a green that builds all the way to November. **July and August** are rainy with a two-week break in the rain known locally as *veranillo* (little summer). The forest is now in full swing and green is the dominant colour. **September and October** are very rainy months with high hurricane risk and tropical depressions bringing two or three blocks of rainy days. The landscape is lush and the temperature is moderate. **November and December** are transitional months with rain tapering off and warm, clear days.

Flora and fauna

Like all neotropical countries, Nicaragua is blessed with rich bio-diversity and, thanks to its relatively low population, economic underdevelopment and many nature reserves, much of the country's native flora and fauna have been preserved. Some species endangered in neighbouring countries are prevalent here, like the howler monkey, which enjoys many habitats and a population of thousands. Nonetheless, Nicaragua has not been immune to the world plague of deforestation, most of which has occurred to clear land for farming, along with limited logging. Forest coverage has been reduced from 7,000,000 ha in 1950 to less than 4,000,000 ha in the late 20th century. Compounding the problem is the dominant use of wood for energy, with kindling wood (*leña*) still the main fuel for cooking. *Leña* represents 57% of the national consumption of energy, while petroleum is only at 30%. The development of responsible tourism to Nicaragua's outstanding natural areas provides hope for economic viability and nature conservation.

Background

The Pacific Basin is dominated by **savannah and tropical dry forest**. There are several significant **mangrove** forests and major areas of **wetlands** in diverse parts of the country. The biggest expanse of **cloud forest** in Central America is present on Pacific volcanoes and northern mountain ranges, especially within the Bosawás reserve.

Principal ecosystems

Pine forests run along the northern territories all the way to the Caribbean with the central-northern mountains home to extensive, but dwindling numbers. Transitional **tropical wet forests** are present on the east side of the great lakes and Lake Nicaragua's southern coast. The most extensive growth of primary **rainforest** on the isthmus dominants the Río San Juan's Indio-Maíz reserve and much of the northeastern and Caribbean lowlands.

Plant species are of course diverse with 350 species of tree, which are part of 12,000 total species of flora that have been classified so far with at least another 5,000 yet to be documented. Those classified include more than 600 species of orchid alone. **Animal species** are equally impressive, most of all the insect life with an estimated 250,000 species, though only about 10,000 of those have been documented to date. Mammals include some 251 species along with 234 different variations of reptile and amphibian. **Bird diversity** is particularly impressive with the ever-growing list of species now at 688 from 59 familie; there are 19 'speciality' bird species (those found only in Central America), more than in any other country.

National parks & reserves The *Ministro de Medio Ambiente y Recursos Naturales* (Ministry of Environment and Natural Resources) better known as MARENA is responsible for the administration of Nicaragua's 73 protected areas that cover 17% of its land. The organization is gravely underfunded and understaffed, but tries hard to overcome these shortcomings to preserve Nicaragua's spectacular natural resources. The ministry is open to tourism, but has yet to fathom how to utilize visitors as a means of financing preservation. The exceptions are the well-organized parks where the non-profit Cocibolca Foundation has joined forces with MARENA to offer a viable ecological experience for foreign and national visitors. If you have some grasp of Spanish you will find the *guardabosques* (park guards) to be very friendly and helpful in any natural reserve. It is important to realize that the MARENA park guards are very well intentioned, earnest and serious about their responsibility, despite being dramatically underpaid. They will ask for proof of permission for entrance into some areas and should be treated with respect and appreciation for the critical role they play in preservation of reserves and parks. Check with MARENA before setting out to visit one of the lesser known reserves. Parks and reserves that charge admission (see individual destinations) are prepared and welcome visitors, but many areas, like the remote reaches of the Indio-Maíz Biological Reserve, cannot be entered without prior consent from MARENA. This process will require some fluency in Spanish or the aid of a tour operator or translator. If you are coming to Nicaragua to do environmental research you can also try to enlist the help of the Cocibolca Foundation (though the small staff of scientists there do not have time to supply information for other visitors). MARENA, Km 12½ Carretera Norte, Managua, Nicaragua, T233-1278, F233-2618. Fundación Cocibolca, *Hotel Colón* 1 c arriba, 1 c al sur, ½ c al lago, No 26, Managua, Nicaragua, T277-1681, F270-0578, fcocibolca@sdnnic.org.ni

Volcanic parks & reserves Along with the flagship **Parque Nacional Volcán Masaya**, many of Nicaragua's volcanoes have forest set aside as reserve. Ancient volcanoes in the central and eastern all have forest reserves on them, critical for the local climate and water tables:part of the country are often covered in rain and cloud forest and there are more than 28 such reserves set aside as protected areas. The following Pacific Basin volcanoes **Momotombo**, **Pilas**, **San Cristóbal**, **Casita**, **Telica**, **Rota**, **Concepción**, **Maderas**, **Cosigüina** and **Mombacho**.

Volcanic crater lakes and their forests are also set aside as protected areas, such as Laguna de Apoyo, Laguna de Asososca, Laguna de Nejapa, Laguna de Tiscapa and the two crater lakes of Península de Chiltepe, Laguna Apoyeque and Laguna Xiloá.

Perhaps some of the most rewarding of all parks to visit are the wildlife refuges set aside for the massive arrival of egg-laying sea turtles. Along the central Pacific Coast is **Chacocente** and its tropical dry forest reserve. More accessible is the beach at **La Flor**, south of San Juan del Sur. **Isla Juan Venado** is also a place to see turtles, not in the quantity of the other reserves, but with the added attraction of accessible mangroves and their fauna.

Turtle nesting sites & mangroves

Granted the current inaccessibility of the great, protected cloud forests of the **Bosawás Reserve**, the best place to enjoy the flora of the cloud forest is on the **Volcán Mombacho**, just outside Granada and **Volcán Maderas** on Ometepe Island. In Matagalpa the **Selva Negra Reserve** is also easy to access as well as the **Arenal Reserve** (by permission only) on the border of Jinotega and Matagalpa. A very good option is the **Miraflor Reserve** in Estelí.

Cloud forest reserves

With the two biggest rainforest reserves in Central America, Nicaragua is the place to be for the rainforest enthusiast who does not need luxury lodging. The best, for its access and reliable lodging, is Indio-Maíz. Bosawás is the biggest area of forest on the isthmus although travel safety is an issue in the region (see page 257 for details). If you are planning to visit Bosawás, check with MARENA to see which entrance to the park is most advisable.

Rainforest reserves

Nothing can match the natural splendour of the wetlands in **Los Guatuzos**, what one US environmental writer called "one of the most beautiful places on earth". This wildlife refuge has basic and rustic lodging, but is well worth the effort to see its fauna.

Wetland reserves

Archipiélago Solentiname is great for culture lovers as well as birders. Solentiname's 36 islands are teeming with bird life and are home to a very interesting community of rural artists. The fortress at **El Castillo** is an important historic landmark set on a beautiful hill above the majestic Río San Juan.

National monument parks

Culture

Music

Nicaraguan music is richly diverse. Rock, popular, folkloric, regionalist, romantic and protest music are all part of the national offering. Music is an integral part of Nicaraguan life with everything from traditional festivals to political rallies using music as its driving backbone.

Classical music was the music of *criollos* in Nicaragua and the original European-influenced music of the country. The classical symphony music of the Nicaraguan artists of the 19th century was played by orchestras in León. Key names like Juan Bautista Prado, Manuel Ibarra, Alfonso Zelaya, Salvador Martínez, Santos Cermeño, Alfonso Solórzano and Lizandro Ramírez dominated the classical music scene of Nicaragua that survives today, though original compositions have diminished greatly since the end of the 1800s. The greatest of all Nicaraguan classical composers was the León artist José de la Cruz Mena, who received international recognition before dying of leprosy (see page 189). The poet Salomón Ibarra Mayorga authored the Nicaraguan national anthem. The short piece was written on 16 December 1910 and was performed by the greatest musicians of the time, the masters Abraham Delgadillo Rivas and Carlos Alberto Ramírez Velásquez.

Marimba is the most traditional among these varieties of rhythms. It is known as Nicaragua's 'national piano' and though its origin has never been well defined, most believe it has its roots in Africa. In musical terms it is a complex instrument. Shaped in the form of a triangle and composed of 22 wood keys, it can be made of either of mahogany or cedar. The marimba player uses two sticks with rubber heads called *bolillos*. The instrument has very clear and sonorous tonalities. In the past the marimba was used to play folkloric pieces and typical music of the countryside, but today it has been diversified, with the *marimberos* performing any rhythm from salsa or merengue to cumbia. The country's best *marimberos* are from Monimbó, the Indian Barrio of Masaya, where there is a generations-long tradition of marimba playing.

Folk Music also has its routes in Masaya, with many artists known as *orejeros* (those who learn to play by ear). Nicaraguan rhythms such as *Mamá Ramona* come from the city. The *orejeros* are famous as being deft guitar players. One of the most important creators of Nicaraguan song is Víctor M Leiva (born 1916) who authored the song *El Caballo Cimarrón* (The Untamed Horse) in 1948, the first Nicaraguan song recorded in the country. During more than 50 years of performing and composing Leiva painted portraits of the Nicaraguan's daily life, landscape and labour. Some of his most famous compositions include *Santo Domingo de Guzmán*, *Tata Chombo*, *Coffee Season*, *El Toro Huaco* and *La Chapandonga*. Victor M Leiva received a Gold Palm award in United States, as the second greatest folkloric composer in Latin America.

Another important folk singer songwriter is Camilo Zapata, the 'Master of Regionalism'. Born in 1917 and still composing and performing today, he wrote his first song *Caballito Chontaleno* (Little Horse from Chontales) at the age of 14. In 1948 Zapata sprang to national fame with songs like *El Nandaimeno*, *El Ganado Colorado*, *El Solar de Monimbó*, *Flor de Mi Colina* , *Minga Rosa Pineda*, *El Arriero* and other romantic compositions such as *Facing the sun*, *Cariño*.

Misa Campesina With marimbas, guitars, atabales (Indian drums), violins and mazurcas and Nicaraguan rhythm, a new style in popular religious music was born with La Misa Campesina or the 'Peasant Mass'. The songs were composed by folk singer **Carlos Mejía Godoy** and were recorded in the 1980s, by the 'Popular Sound Workshop'. This populist mass was composed 26 years ago in Solentiname, where priest Ernesto Cardenal was preaching, and later it was extended to all the 'people's churches' and even to Spain. It is Carlos Mejía's dearest body of work in spite of the fact it was prohibited by the Catholic Church in Nicaragua on orders directly from Pope John Paul II at the Vatican. But the lack of acceptance by the church did little to diminish the world-wide acceptance of the music. La Misa Campesina has been translated into numerous languages and is even sung by Anglicans, Mormons, Baptists, and Mennonites in the United States. The mass is composed of 10 songs, among the most loved are the Welcome Song, The Creed, The Meditation Song, Kirye, Saint and Communion.

Chicheros are an integral part of any festival or traditional party. The Chichero Band consists of six to eight amateur musicians who play snare drums, bass drum, cymbal, trumpet, flute, clarinet and trombone. Their music ranges from hyped up dance tunes to tragic funeral marches.

Protest music had its glory days during the years leading up to the Revolution. This music of pop and folkloric rhythms brought to fame such bands as Engel Ortega, Norma Elena Gadea and Eduardo Araica, the Pancasan Band, Duo Guardabarranco formed by Katia and Salvador Cardenal, Keyla Rodríguez and Luis Enrique Mejía Godoy.

Palo de Mayo is a collection of native music from the Caribbean Coast of Nicaragua. The music is characterized by its vibrant rhythm. The songs that are a joy hymn for the Afro-Caribbean Nicaraguans include *Tululu Pass Under*, *Oh Nancy*, *Oh, Simón Canta Simón* and *Mayaya Oh*. To perform the Caribbean rhythms local musicians incorporate numerous unusual instruments such as cow and donkey jawbones, combs and pots, as well as more common instruments such as drums and guitars.

Rock and pop from North America and England began to influence local Nicaraguan music in the 1960s and 1970s with the boom of the pop and rock music by the Beatles, Santana, Elvis Presley and the songs of Paul Anka, all of which were played in Nicaraguan cafés and bars. From this time, national rock bands such as Los Rockets, Wuana, Zona Púrpura, Río Sangre and Soul Power emerged.

Dance

During the early years of Spanish Colonization, dance, as a discipline, did not have a defined style. Indian dances were considered heretical due to the ceremonial nature of some of them (though many were danced for pure pleasure) and therefore discourage or banned. The dances considered folkloric or traditional in Nicaragua today are a mixture of African, Indian and European dances and cultures. In the colonial period, celebrations of religious festivities for the upper class included Spanish and other European dances that were in fashion in Europe.

The term *son* is used to define the dances that first appeared in the 1700s, such as the *jarabe*, *jaranas* and **huapangos**. These dances are the local adaptations of the *Fandango* and Spanish tap dance. In Nicaragua the dances or *sones Jarabe Chichón* and *Jarabe Repicado* are still performed today in the festivals of Masaya and its pueblos. Masaya is at the heart of folkloric dance traditions and nearly every traditional dance is performed there at some time during the year. Many have a love message; a good example is the flirtatious *Baile de las Inditas* (**Dance of the Indian Girls**) or the hilarious physical satire on relationships known as the *Baile del Viejo y la Vieja* (**Dance of the Old Man and Lady**). In the latter, the *viejo* and *vieja* are both performed by men: the woman is played by a tall dancer sporting a very heavily stuffed rear-end while the man is played by a very short dancer, supported by a walking cane, and dressed to appear 20 to 30 years older than the woman. The old woman flirts to excite the old man over and over again; each time rejecting his increasingly desperate advances, to the point of his immanent cardiac arrest, only to revive him with her sexiness to tease him yet more. Audience members are pulled out to dance by the old woman, to make the old man jealous. However, as soon as the old man does the same with a female audience member the old woman tosses aside her new partner, and jealously sets about keeping the old man from dancing with anyone but her.

Other well-known dances are the *Danza de las Negritas* (**Dance of the Black Girls**), one of many dances performed only by men in drag, and a spectacular and colourful traditional dance called *Los Diablitos* (**The Little Demons**). This is a mock-up of an Iberian masquerade ball, danced in the streets with performers' costumes representing every possible character from Death to a Tiger, a giant Parrot or the Devil himself. One of the most traditional dances from Masaya is **El Torovenado**, a street performance-protest against social injustice and government corruption, where the dancers follow the rhythm of marimbas and *chicheros*. The participants are all male and dress in costumes representing both male and female politicians and members of the upper class. Their handmade masks and costumes satirize important events happening in the country or the behaviour of the moneyed class. This tradition was brought to national attention recently, when a native of Masaya appeared at a Managua Sandinista rally for the 2001 elections, dressed as

Nicaragua's Cardinal Miguel Obando y Bravo, holding a chalice. Another of the many traditional Nicaraguan dances is the *Danza de la Húngaras* (**Dance of the Hungarians**), which originated from the early 20th-century immigration of eastern European gypsies to Nicaragua.

Dances & regions

Masaya is far from unique in its local dances, for the richness of Nicaragua in regional dances is impressive and across the board. The most famous of all is El Güegüence (see page 99) is disputed as to whether it is from the highland village of Diriamba or Masaya. The small, but historic village of Nindirí is home to many dances such as *Los Chinegros, El Ensartado* and *Las Canas*. León is the origin of the spectacular joke on the early colonizers called *El Baile de La Gigantona y el Enano Cabezón,* in which a 3-m tall blonde woman spins and dances circles around an old dwarf with a big bald head. León is also home to *Los Mantudos* and *El Baile del Toro*. Managua has *La Danza de la Vaca,* and Boaco has *Los Moros y Cristianos* Moors and the Christians). Very special in Nicaragua is a dance only performed on the Island of Ometepe in the village of Altagracia (see page 142) called the *El Baile de Los Zompopos* (**Dance of the Leaf-Cutter Ants**).

In the northern cities of Matagalpa and Jinotega the coffee immigrants who came from Germany and other parts of northern Europe in the late 19th century have violin and guitar-driven polkas, *jamaquellos* and mazurkas.

The Caribbean Coast is home to some little-known Garífuna dances that are now being performed in Managua, and some Miskito Indian dances that have also been recognized and performed by dance troupes on the Pacific side. The favourite of both coasts for its raw energy may be the **Palo de Mayo** (Maypole) dance, which is a hybrid of English Maypole traditions and Afro-Caribbean rain and fertility dances.

Apart from the tradition of dancing in festivals, the folkloric dances of Nicaragua have been brought to the stage and are performed regularly in Managua and Masaya with less frequent performances in other parts of Nicaragua. Masaya often has dance groups performing on Thursday nights at the craft market and, in the capital, the Centro Cultural Managua and Teatro Rubén Darío also have regular shows.

Festivals

With Catholicism remaining the predominant religion, Nicaragua's religious festivals are alive and well, though being chipped away at by a mix of international pop culture and US evangelist churches (the latter claiming the festivals to be sacrilegious). Some 70% of the population are still Catholic, down from 90% just a few decades ago. Despite the obvious Catholic theme and origin of the festivals, many are laced with indigenous traditions, subtle indicators cultural resistance during the colonial period.

Every village in Nicaragua has a patron saint, whose image is in the local church and who is required to help the local population to overcome illnesses and serious family problems. Believers make promises to the saint, whose celebration takes place annually on a set date. A promise can be paid in the form of feeding the entire village on the day of the procession, walking for kilometres during a procession or dancing in one of the numerous processions for the saint. In some cases risking life and limb can be part of a promise in the often violent ritual games like bullfights and hand-to-hand combat. Fruits can be brought to the saint or some believers simply follow during the procession and pray with increased intensity.

The following are some of the most important festivals:

During the celebrations for **San Lázaro**, believers dress their dogs in elaborate, home-made costumes and take them to the church of Magdalena in Masaya. The dogs and the master share the duty to distribute *chicha* (a corn drink) and food for the participants of the procession. This celebration takes place on the eve of Holy

Week and is a promise made by pet owners to San Lázaro, for good canine health. Masaya is best known for its festivities in honour of **San Jerónimo**, the patron saint of the city. This is Nicaragua's longest festival starting officially on 30 September (but with events two weeks before, and continuing until the last Sunday in November). Saint Jerome is known as the doctor who cures. His devotees come from all over the country asking for his blessing and help with illness. Even the local politicians ask for San Jerónimo's blessing, an act often rejected by the population.

Pilgrimages are also common. Such is the case of the one in honour of **Jesús del Rescate** in Popoyuapa, Rivas. This gruelling four-day pilgrimage takes families in brightly decorated oxcarts from Masaya, Granada and Los Pueblos all the way south to a small town next to Rivas. The families in the oxcarts have all made a promise to Jesús del Rescate and the journey is the fulfilment of their end of the deal. When they arrive, normally in more than 100 oxcarts,there is a massive celebration in Popoyuapa. One of the most popular festivities is the **Encuentro de los Santos**, which is held near San Marcos, Carazo. The image of San Marcos, the Virgen de Monserrat, San Sebastián and Santiago get together. The encounter happens in the place known as Las Pilas in San Marcos. The first to arrive are the Virgen de Monserrat and San Marcos, with much fanfare, then the images of San Sebastián and Santiago arrive accompanied by even more musicians, folkloric dances and *promesantes*. Since each saint represents a local village the meeting of the four is a raucous party for all the believers of each town. The **Virgen del Carmen** is celebrated in Estelí, El Carmen, Río Blanco and San Juan del Sur. Since the virgin of El Carmen is the patron saint of the fishermen and sailors, in San Juan del Sur the virgin is taken out for a little boat ride in the ocean. From 1-10 August, Managua celebrates the festivities of its patron saint **Santo Domingo de Guzmán**. The country's capital is paralyzed on 1 and 10 August. On 1 August Santo Domingo leaves his altar in Las Sierritas de Managua (the hills on the south side of the city) and is brought in a raucous procession with heavy police protection to the Church of Santo Domingo in the north side of the city. He stays for 10 days in Managua until his return to his church in the hills on 10 August. Thousands escort the tiny image of the saint, which is protected under a glass cover. The procession takes several hours and during the entire route devotees and *promesantes* dance La Vaquita around the image, while others cover themselves with black oil and soot or dress in indigenous costumes. Others pay their promise to the saint by walking on their knees from the entry of the temple to the altar of the saint.

As in most of Latin America, the biggest celebration of the year is **Semana Santa** or Holy Week, to celebrate the rebirth of Jesus Christ. In general terms it is also the biggest vacation week of the year, when some Nicaraguans go to church, or take part in processions or meditatation, while many others take advantage of the free time to go to the beaches. The most famous Holy Week tradition is performed in Subtiava, the indigenous neighbourhood in León. Beautiful carpets are created out of coloured sawdust, recreating different moments of the Passion of Christ (see page 195).

La Purísima

December is not only the month in which the birth of Christ is celebrated, but it also has the defining celebration of Nicaragua's religious culture. The Immaculate Conception of the Virgin Mary, which culminates every 7 December, is celebrated as La Purísima or **La Gritería**. This festival is without any doubt the biggest religious expression that Nicaragua can call its very own. This ceremony, one of many demonstrations of Nicaragua's devotion to Santa María, was one of the main reasons why Pope Juan Pablo II proclaimed the Nicaraguans as among the world's most devout Marian worshippers. The tradition to pray *la novena* (a nine-day prayer) to the Virgin arrived with the Franciscans around 1550. The ingenious creativity of the Nicaraguan people is reborn every December with the decoration of home-made altars in honour of the Virgin. The house altars are adorned with *madroño* branches, palm leaves, flowers, basil candles and sardines. Groups of believers (most of them children and women) travel from altar to altar singing and praying. When each group arrives, the host shouts "Who is the cause of so much happiness?" The group answers back "The Conception of Mary!" Traditional songs to the Virgin are sung and the host gives sweets and small gifts to the group. At night fireworks are let off and special sweets and drinks are consumed: *gofios*, which are candies made of corn, cacao, milk, anisette and sugar; *rapadura de dulce*, a sugar cane candy; and *rompopo*, which is an egg nog made of milk, sugar, eggs and rum. Fruits are also a big part of the celebration, and limes, sweet lemons, oranges and bananas are handed round. Soft drinks have worked their way into the picture, but many traditional drinks remain including a liquor made of corn and *coyolito* (a bitter palm fruit), as well as pineapple or cacao drinks. The celebration has been taken abroad with Nicaraguan immigrants who keep the La Purísima alive in Costa Rica and Miami.

Painting and sculpture

Without a doubt Nicaragua is the land of literature and poetry; nonetheless there have been some artists of note in the country's recent history. The oldest paintings in Nicaragua are the **petroglyphs**, which were made by the indigenous inhabitants of Nicaragua by carving scenes out of rocks. The quantity and diversity of these petroglyphs is staggering and may be unparalleled in the Americas. There is literally no part of the country that does not have dozens of depictions of ancient beliefs, family histories, calendars and many other scenes in relief that remain almost a total mystery to today's art lovers and archaeologists alike. With the arrival of the Spanish in the 16th century this art form was lost.

The first of the notable Nicaraguan (as opposed to Spanish) artist appear in the 19th century, with the work of **Toribio Jerez**, who painted the collection of portraits, Bishops of Nicaragua. At the beginning of the 20th century the most popular work was that of **Antonio Sarria**, whose portraits of Bolívar, Roosevelt and Napoleon were well known. **Alonso Rochi** also gained fame for his paintings of urban scenes and flowers. The search for Nicaraguan masters leads to León artist **Rodrigo Peñalba** (1908-79) who spent years studying and painting in Rome and gained local fame in the 1940s. The central gallery at the Museo Nacional bears his name and you can see his expressionist paintings in León at the gallery across from the Iglesia San Francisco and at the museum in Volcán Masaya. Another key figure emerged in the 1950s under the tutelage of Peñalba. **Armando Morales** (born 1927), perhaps the best-known Nicaraguan painter, is noted for the chromatic versatility of his works, the control of shadow and highlights. The artists whose works are still revered today are **Omar D'León**, **César Caracas**, **Guillermo Rivas Navas**, **Arnoldo Guillén** and **Leoncio Sáenz**.

Primitivism At the beginning of the 1950s the work of **Asilia Guillén** (1887-1964) brought primitivism (naïve) painting to the forefront of Nicaraguan art. Also pioneering the style in Nicaragua were **Salvadora Henríquez de Noguera**, **Adela Vargas** and **Manuel García**. Primitivism is perhaps the most famous school of painting in Nicaragua, thanks largely to the left-wing priest **Ernesto Cardenal**, its most enthusiastic promoter. It was Cardenal who took the style to the naturally talented *campesinos* of the **Archipiélago Solentiname** in Lake Nicaragua in the mid-1960s. The islanders paint their love for the vibrant natural beauty of their islands, as well as demonstrate their faith in God and the Bible with numerous biblical scenes and key legends like the *Viejo del Monte* (Old Man from the Wilderness). Most of the scenes are set on the islands and in the wildlife refuge of **Los Guatuzos**, though the style has been used to depict Pacific Basin cultural traditions and rural village life. The naïve painting of Solentiname has taken the island artists to far off places like Finland and Japan, and their work can be found in galleries around the world.

These revolutionary artists proclaimed a new style of painting that was at once an attack on the traditional concepts introduced by Rodrigo Peñalba, and an ideological statement against the power and corruption of the Somoza regime. In the 1970s, Grupo Praxis favoured art that was both monochromatic and abstract with the main theme being the ever-changing volcanic landscape of the Pacific Coast of Nicaragua. Leading artists of the group include **Alejandro Aróstegui** (born 1935) and **César Izquierdo** (born 1937) and, using bright colours towards the end of the movement, **Leonel Vanegas** (born 1942).

Grupo Praxis

This Nicaraguan Postmodernist movement included the artists **Leonel Cerrato**, **Bayardo Gámez**, **Donaldo Altamirano**, **Rolando Castellón** and **Carlos Montenegro**. The school was first active in 1963 and is said to have rescued the collective memory of Nicaraguans, by using trademark iconography like the figure of *El Güegüence* (see page 99). Another persistent current inside the postmodernist world is art inspired by ancient works like petroglyphs and paintings found on pre-Hispanic indigenous ceramics. **Leoncio Saenz** is the principal exponent of this style. Known for his depictions of colonial houses and villages, **Alfonso Ximenes** takes everyday Nicaraguan scenes and bathes them in vibrant colours with subtle plays of light. The women artists of the 1960s included **Ilse Ortíz de Manzanarez**, **Rosario Ortiz de Chamorro**, **María Gallo**, and the naïve painter, **June Beer**, who incorporated the characteristics and emotions of the inhabitants of the Caribbean Coast of Nicaragua.

Post-modernists

With the advent of the Revolution, the 1980s saw an outburst of mural painting that now, sadly, is vanishing. The subject manner was normally didactic, but the colour they added to the cities and towns of Nicaragua is sorely missed once they are painted over. Most of the murals used the Revolution as their theme, along with women's issues, literacy goals, Ronald Reagan, Somoza, Uncle Sam, etc. One of the most famous of the Nicaraguan artists who participated in the painting of murals was **Alejandro Canales**. In the Iglesia de Los Angeles, in the barrio of El Riguero in Managua, you can still see an impressive mural representing 'liberation theology' that can be summed up by its famous slogan 'Without Christians the Revolution does not exist'. A very dynamic mural inside the Palacio Cultural, which was created with the help of Mexican muralists, depicts the history of Managua from pre-Columbian times of peace to the disastrous earthquake of 1972 and beyond, towards hope of future peace and prosperity.

Murals

In the 1990s, the group *Artifact*, integrated by the young painters **Raúl Quintanilla Armijo**, **David Ocón**, **Patricia Belli** and **Teresa Codina**, broke away from the constraints imposed in the 1980s. The 90s also marked the reappearance of hyperrealism and figurative painting; among its major proponents are **Leónidas Correa**, **Zenelia Roiz** and the young **Alicia Zamora**.

Plurality

Nicaraguan sculpture begins with one of the founders of the National School of Fine Arts, **Genaro Amador Lira** (1910-83) who was a sculptor and teacher and was responsible for inspiring numerous artists. Among his students was **Fernando Saravia**. Saravia learned with Lira to create classical models of Greek and Latin sculpture, to clay cast, mould and carve stone and wood. Saravia became famous for his original sculptures and in turn he went on to help train the best known of modern Nicaraguan

Sculpture

Background

sculptors: **Ernesto Cardenal**, **Noel Flores**, **Orlando Sobalvarro**, **Arnoldo Guillén**, and **Erasmo Moya**. Many of their themes dealt with fertility and maternity. In the 1980s, with Ernesto Cardenal as the Minister of Culture, a programme was created in San Juan de Limay, a small village north of Estelí. There had long been a tradition of soapstone (*marmolina*) carving there. The stone is very colourful and is found in abundance in San Juan at Tipiscayán. The goal of the project was to increase the quality of San Juan de Limay's artisan sculpting. During this period sculptors such as **Luis Morales Alonso** and **Aparicio Artola** came to fame with some superb works in soapstone. The work of the artists of San Juan de Limay can now be found across Central America with fine pieces to be seen in the galleries of Managua and the market in Masaya. Perhaps the most talented and complete modern Nicaraguan sculptor is **Miguel Angel Abarca**, the son of coffin carvers. There is no material that he has not mastered, from marble and granite to wood. Abarca never stops experimenting with styles and materials, and it is his mastery of both that makes him truly unique in the Nicaraguan art scene.

Literature

Early Nicaraguan poetry and narrative, influenced from the beginning by the chronicles of the West Indies, uses a straightforward descriptive style to depict the life of the indigenous people and the Spanish conquest through colourful narratives. This type of native literature was the most prevalent during the pre-Hispanic era. One of the original works was *Canto al sol de los Nicaraguas,* dedicated to the principal cultures to inhabit this remote region, the Nicaraguas and Chorotega tribes. The writing of the indigenous peoples, generally pictographs, called books by Fernández de Oviedo for their manuscript form, is largely anonymous. While the native languages would later become mixed with Spanish, a series of primitive dialects were conserved, so that later it was possible to recover and compile different works, including Sumu poetry, Miskito songs, Subtiavan poems, Carib music and native myths from different regions of Nicaragua. These were songs related to the Spanish conquest or religion – a product of the colonization process – sayings, riddles, ballads and children's games that would later reappear in different narratives and poetic forms.

The first book attributed to a Nicaraguan-born writer was the little-known *Relaciones verdaderas de la deducción de los indios infieles, de la provincia de Teguzgalpa* (True Stories about the Pagan Indians from the Province of Teguzgalpa) by Francisco Fernandez Espino, which appeared in 1674. Two centuries later, in 1876 (according to literary critic Ricardo Llopesa), the first literary group *La Montaña,* was founded in Granada; and two years after that, the first literary anthology, entitled *Lira Nicaragüense,* was published.

The father of modernism **Rubén Darío** (1867-1916) overshadowed his contemporaries with his proposals for innovation in the Spanish language. The Modernist school, founded by Darío, advocated aestheticism, the search for sensory and even sensual values, and the artistic effects of colour, sound, voice and synthesis. His first verses were published in 1879. In 1881 he edited his first complete work, *Poesías y artículos en prosa,* which was published after his death and *Epístolas y poemas* in 1888. That same year *Azul,* one of the fundamental works for understanding Modernism, was published. In 1896, Darío published *Los raros y Prosas profanas,* in Buenos Aires (with a second edition in 1901). In Valparaíso, Chile, he published *Abrojos* (1887) and his novel *Emelina.* Other Darío narratives include *El fardo, Invernal, El rey burgués,* and *La ninfa.* In 1916, after many years of absence, Darío returned to the city of León, Nicaragua where he died on 6 February (see page 192).

Sergio Ramírez – revolutionary novelist

Former Vice-President (1984-1990) Sergio Ramírez Mercado, tired of political setbacks, has now returned to his literary roots. His last incursion into politics was made in 1996 as the presidential candidate for the Sandinista breakaway party Movimiento Renovador Sandinista (MRS), but he received a very low percentage of votes, barely enough for one party seat in the 92-member legislature.

Putting the adverse results behind him, Ramírez wrote Margarita está linda la mar, *a novel that won a prestigious award for fiction from the Alfaguara Spanish publishing house. That same year another one of his novels,* Baile de máscaras, *won a French award.*

Ramírez is back to writing full-time. He calls it "the best job in the world". Besides novels, he writes articles for important international newspapers such as the Madrid daily El País, *and does stints as a guest professor at several universities in the US, Germany and Latin America.*

Sergio Ramírez, who was born in 1942, graduated with a degree in law and had his first book published in Managua in 1963 under the title Cuentos. *He was living in Costa Rica when he was asked to participate in the struggle against Somoza and in 1977 he became totally involved. Following the 1979 victory of the Sandinista Revolution, Ramírez became a member of the first Junta de Gobierno de Reconstrucción Nacional (JGRN), made up of five prominent Nicaraguans. Later, in November 1984, he was elected vice-president as part of the ticket headed by Daniel Ortega. They both sought re-election in 1990, but were defeated by Violeta Barrios de Chamorro.*

In 1999, twenty years after the violent overthrow of the Somoza dictatorship, Ramírez Mercado published Adiós Muchachos, *his personal memoirs of the Sandinista Revolution.*

The Vanguard

Founded by **Luis Alberto Cabrales** (1901-74) and **José Coronel Urtecho** (1906-94) this Vanguard movement exerted an important renovating influence on Nicaraguan literature. Coronel Utrecho's work *Oda a Rubén Darío* (1927) contains the essence of the new style and marks the transition from the Darío school of Modernism to the Vanguard movement. **Pablo Antonio Cuadra** (born 1912), the movement's principal author, wrote a declaration reaffirming the national identity, which was later incorporated into his first book *Poemas nicaragüenses* (1934). Together with Coronel Urtecho, Luis Cabrales and **Joaquín Pasos** (1914-47), Cuadra released the movement's *Anti-Academia de la lengua* declaration.

Generation of the 1940s & Expressionist poetry

The main themes of the generation of the 1940s were love and freedom, reflected in the poetry of Francisco Pérez Estrada (1917-82), Enrique Fernández Morales, and Julio Ycaza Tigerino (1919-2001). However the 40s is especially known for the emergence of three great poets: **Ernesto Mejía Sánchez** (1923-85), **Carlos Martínez Rivas** (1924-99), and **Ernesto Cardenal** (born 1923).

Ernesto Cardenal: Expressionist poetry to Exteriorism

Cardenal, whose poetry uses simple expressions and reflects everyday spoken language, is the founder of the Expressionist movement, which opposed the subjectivity of lyrical poetry. Through his poetry he attacked the Somoza family dictatorship for over four decades. Also a priest, he founded the Christian community of Solentiname on a group of islands in Lago de Nicaragua. His extensive work has been translated into several languages. *La ciudad deshabitada* (1946), *Hora 0* (1960), *Oración por Marylin Monroe y otras poemas* (1966), are poems reflecting religious, historical and Christian themes as well as that of social commitment.

In the 1980s, when Cardenal was the Sandinista Government's Minister of Culture, he founded a new literary phenomenon called Exteriorism, which advocated political and

Background

'objective' poetry. Poetry workshops were established where members of the army, the recently literate farming population and the other sectors of the country were encouraged to write. This promotion of a unified style for the workshops was later criticized, and with the end of the Sandinista government the poetry workshops disappeared.

Current trends In the 1990s a more intimate style of poetry emerged. The traditional literary topics are prevalent: death, existentialism and love, along with new themes such as homosexuality, women's rights and the environment, among others. In this decade new writers have emerged: poets such as **Blanca Castellón**, **Erick Aguirre**, **Pedro Xavier Solís**, **Juan Sobalvarro**, **Isolda Hurtado**, **Marta Leonor González** and **Ariel Montoya**.

People

Ethnicity As in the rest of the Americas, the origins of the Nicaraguan population are diverse. The pre-Conquest cultures of the central and western sections of the countries have been mixed with small waves of European immigration, beginning in the 16th century and continuing today. The eastern section of Nicaragua remained in relative isolation for the first few centuries and fairly well-defined ethnic cultures are still present in the communities of **Miskito**, **Rama** and **Sumu** indigenous cultures as well as **Afro-Caribbeans** from Jamaica (Creole) and San Vincent (Garífuna) Islands. The Hispanic **mestizo** (mixed race) culture of the western two-thirds of the country dominates the ethnic profile of Nicaragua. Recent surveys suggest the country is 96% mestizo, 3% indigenous and 1% Afro-Caribbean. Amongst the peoples classified as mestizo, however, are many with almost pure indigenous roots who have lost their distinguishing language, but have retained many of their pre-Columbian traits. There is also a very small, nearly pure **European** sector that has traditionally controlled the country's economic and land assets. Massive movements of population during the troubled years of the 1980s has blurred these once well-defined lines, though some definite ethnic tendencies still exist in each of the country's departments.

Population density Total population for the country was estimated at 5,126,860 according to the year 2000 census. Population density varies widely from department to department with the obvious concentration of people in the Managua vicinity and the traditionally (since pre-Conquest times) populous cities of the Pacific Basin where 83% of Nicaragua's population lives. Nicaragua is the least densely populated country in Central America with just 42 people per square kilometre.

Religion Just over 70% of the population is Roman Catholic. There are also many Protestant sects. Religion and spirituality in general are very important parts of Nicaraguan life. The combined forces of the **Evangelist** churches have their own political party in *Camino Christiano* who won the third largest tally of votes in the 1996 campaign and who joined in alliance with the Liberal Party for the elections in 2001. The **Catholic Church** has no official political wing, but plays an important role in the political scene with Cardinal Miguel Obando y Bravo being one of the most influential figures in the country in the past 30 years.(You can hear the cardinal's allegorical sermons at the 1100 Mass on Sundays in Managua's New Cathedral.)

Footnotes

12

Footnotes

Basic Spanish

Whether you have been taught the 'Castillian' pronounciation (all *z's*, and *c's* followed by *i* or *e*, are pronunounced as the *th* in *think*) or the 'American' pronounciation (they are pronounced as *s*) you will encounter little difficulty in understanding either: Spanish pronunciation varies geographically much less than English.

Using basic Spanish
For a few tips on Nicaraguan slang, see page 16

Pronouns   In the Americas, the plural, familiar pronoun *vosotros* (with the verb endings – *áis*, – *éis*), though much used in Spain, is never heard: two or more people, whoever they are, are always addressed as *Ustedes (Uds)*. The singular, familiar prounoun *tú* is replaced in many areas by the pronoun *vos*; when it is, the accent on the verb tends to move toward the end: instead of *tú quieres*, one hears *vos querés* (though both will be understood).

Expressions of time   Many misunderstandings about engagements stem from terminology rather than tardiness. *Ahora* is often a synonym for *hoy*, 'today', not the 'now' in the dictionary; 'now' or 'soon' are *ahorita*; 'right now' is *ahora mismo* or *enseguida*.

While *en la tarde* could conceivably mean at 1230 or 1300 in the afternoon, it is more likely to mean 1500 or 1600, even 1730 or 1800. A polite way of pinning down a vague commitment is to ask '*¿A qué hora más o menos?*'

Terms of address   Almost anyone qualified to a title uses it. A physician, dentist, or vet is always addressed as *Doctor(a)*, as is any holder of a doctoral degree. Primary school teachers are always *Maestro(a)*, as are some skilled crafts people, builders, etc. Secondary school and all university teachers are always addressed as *Profesor(a)*, or, informally by their students, as *Profe*. Lawyers and university graduates in any of the arts or social sciences are addressed as *Licenciado(a)*, abbreviated *Lic*; graduate engineers, and holders of any degree in a technical field, use *Ingeniero(a)*, abbreviated *Ing*. Architects use *Arquitecto(a)*, abbreviated *Arq*. Protestant clergy are always *Reverendo(a)*, never just *Sr(a)*.

Address male strangers over the age of 20 or so as Señor, or, if substantially older than you, as *Don*. Younger men may be addressed as *Joven*. Address female strangers over the age of 20 or so, or younger women if they are obvious004ly accompanied by (their own) children or a husband, as *Señora*. Younger women can safely be addressed as *Señorita*. Address middle-aged or older women as *Doña*.Note that the terms *Señorita* and *Señora* can have implications of virginity as well as marital status. An elderly woman who has no children and has never married may well correct you if addressed as Señora. *Don* and *Doña* also enable you to use a person's first name without sounding disrespectful, as in Don Juan or Doña Josefina.

Bs and Vs   Travellers whose names include the letters '*b*' or '*v*' (pronounced the same in Spanish) should learn to distinguish between them when spelling aloud as *be larga* or *be grande* and *ve corta*, *ve chica* or *uve*. (Children often say *ve de vaca* and *be de burro* to distinguish between the two letters.)

Greetings & courtesies	Spanish		
Hello/	*Hola/*	Yes/no	*(muchas)*
Good morning	*Buenos días*	Excuse me/	*Sí/no*
Good afternoon/	*Buenas tardes/*	I'm sorry	*Con permiso*
evening/night	*noches*	I don't understand	*Lo siento/disculpe*
Goodbye	*Adiós/chao*	I don't want it	*No entiendo*
See you later	*Hasta luego*	Please speak slowly	*No lo quiero*
How are you?	*¿Cómo está/*		*Hable despacio,*
	estás?	What's your name?	*por favor*
I'm fine	*Muy bien gracias*	I'm called_	*¿Cómo se llama?*
Pleased to	*Mucho gusto/*	Go away!	*Me llamo_*
meet you	*encantado/a*	Leave me alone	*¡Váyase!*
Please	*Por favor*	I'm off/leaving	*¡No me moleste!*
Thank you	*(Muchas) gracias*		*Me voy*

Questions			
Where is_?	*¿Dónde está_?*	How do I get to_?	*¿Cómo llego a_?*
I should like	*Me gustaría/quisiera*	Do you have_?	*¿Tiene_?*
How much does	*¿Cuánto vale?/¿cuánto*	Are there any rooms	*¿Hay cuartos para esta*
it cost?	*cuesta?*	tonight	*noche?*
When?	*¿Cuándo?/¿ a qué hora?*	Bring me the bill, please	*La cuenta por favor*
When does the bus	*¿A qué hora sale/llega*	Can I have my change,	*Deme el cambio, por*
leave/arrive?	*el autobus?*	please	*favor*
Why?	*¿Por qué?*	Can I make a phone call?	*¿Puedo llamar por*
			teléfono?

Basics			
police (policeman)	*la policía (el policía)/*	bank	*el banco*
	el carabinero	exchange house	*la casa de cambio*
hotel	*el hotel (la pensión,*	exchange rate	*la tasa de cambio*
	el residehcial,	travellers' cheques	*los travelers/*
	el hospedaje)		*los cheques de*
room	*el cuarto/*		*viajero*
	la habitación	cash	*el efectivo*
single/double	*sencilla/doble*	breakfast	*el desayuno*
with two beds	*con dos camas*	lunch	*el almuerzo/la*
bathroom/toilet	*el baño*		*comida*
hot/cold water	*el agua caliente/fría*	dinner/supper	*la cena*
toilet paper	*el papel higiénico*	meal	*la comida*
restaurant	*el restaurant*	drink	*la bebida*
post office/	*el correo/el*	mineral water	*el agua mineral*
telephone office	*centro de llamadas*	beer	*la cerveza*
supermarket	*el supermercado*	with/without sugar	*con/sin azúcar*
market	*el mercado*		

Getting around			
on the left/right	*a la izquierda/*	train/(train) station	*el tren/la estación*
	derecha		*(de tren)*
straight on	*derecho*	airport	*el aeropuerto*
bus station	*la terminal*	aeroplane	*el avión*
	(terrestre)	ticket	*el boleto*
bus stop	*la parada/el*	ticket office	*la taquilla*
	paradero	luggage	*el equipaje*
interurban bus	*el bus/el*	rucksack	*la mochila*
	camión	bag	*la bolsa*
urban bus	*el micro*		

Time

What time is it?	*¿Qué hora es?*
At half past two	*A las dos y media*
Ten minutes	*Diez minutos*
Five hours	*Cinco horas*
It's one o'clock	*Es la una*
It's seven o'clock	*Son las siete*
It's ten to seven	*Son las siete menos diez*
It's 6.20	*Son las seis y veinte*

Medical terms

It hurts here	*Me duele aquí*
I have a headache /stomach ache	*Tengo dolor de cabeza/de estómago*
I don't feel well	*No me siento bien*
I need a doctor	*Necesito asistencia médica*

Numbers

Numbers	Spanish				
1	*uno/una*	11	*once*	21	*veintiuno*
2	*dos*	12	*doce*	30	*treinta*
3	*tres*	13	*trece*	40	*cuarenta*
4	*cuatro*	14	*catorce*	50	*cincuenta*
5	*cinco*	15	*quince*	60	*sesenta*
6	*seis*	16	*dieciséis*	70	*setenta*
7	*siete*	17	*diecisiete*	80	*ochenta*
8	*ocho*	18	*dieciocho*	90	*noventa*
9	*nueve*	19	*diecinueve*	100	*cien*
10	*diez*	20	*veinte*	1000	*mil*

Days/months

Monday	*lunes*		March	*marzo*
Tuesday	*martes*		April	*abril*
Wednesday	*miércoles*		May	*mayo*
Thursday	*jueves*		June	*junio*
Friday	*viernes*		July	*julio*
Saturday	*sábado*		August	*agosto*
Sunday	*domingo*		September	*septiembre*
			October	*octubre*
January	*enero*		November	*noviembre*
February	*febrero*		December	*diciembre*

Key verbs

To go	*Ir*
I go	*voy*
you go	*vas*
s/he/it goes	*va*
you (formal) go	*va*
we go	*vamos*
they/you (plural) go	*van*

To be (in a permanent state)	*Ser*
I am	*soy*
you are	*eres*
s/he/it is	*es*
you (formal) are	*es*
we are	*somos*
they/you (plural) are	*son*

To have	*Tener*
I have	*tengo*
you have	*tienes*
s/he/it has	*tiene*
you (formal) have	*tiene*
we have	*tenemos*
they/you (plural) have	*tienen*

To be (positional or temporary state)	*Estar*
I am	*estoy*
you are	*estás*
s/he/it is	*está*
you (formal) are	*está*
we are	*estamos*
they/you (plural) are	*están*

Index

Shorts

Footnotes

Maps

Advertisers

Updates

We try as hard as we can to make each Footprint Handbook as up-to-date and accurate as possible but, of course, things always change. Many people email or write to us – with corrections, new information, or simply comments. If you want to let us know about your experiences and adventures – be they good, bad or ugly – then don't delay; we're dying to hear from you. And please try to include all the relevant details and juicy bits. Your help will be greatly appreciated, especially by other travellers. In return we will send you details about our special guidebook offer. Why not contact us via our **website**:

www.footprintbooks.com
A new place to visit

Alternatively email Footprint at:
nic1_online@footprintbooks.com
or write to:
Elizabeth Taylor, Footprint Handbooks,
6 Riverside Court, Lower Bristol Road, Bath BA2 3DZ UK